HELLBOY ™

DARKNESS CALLS

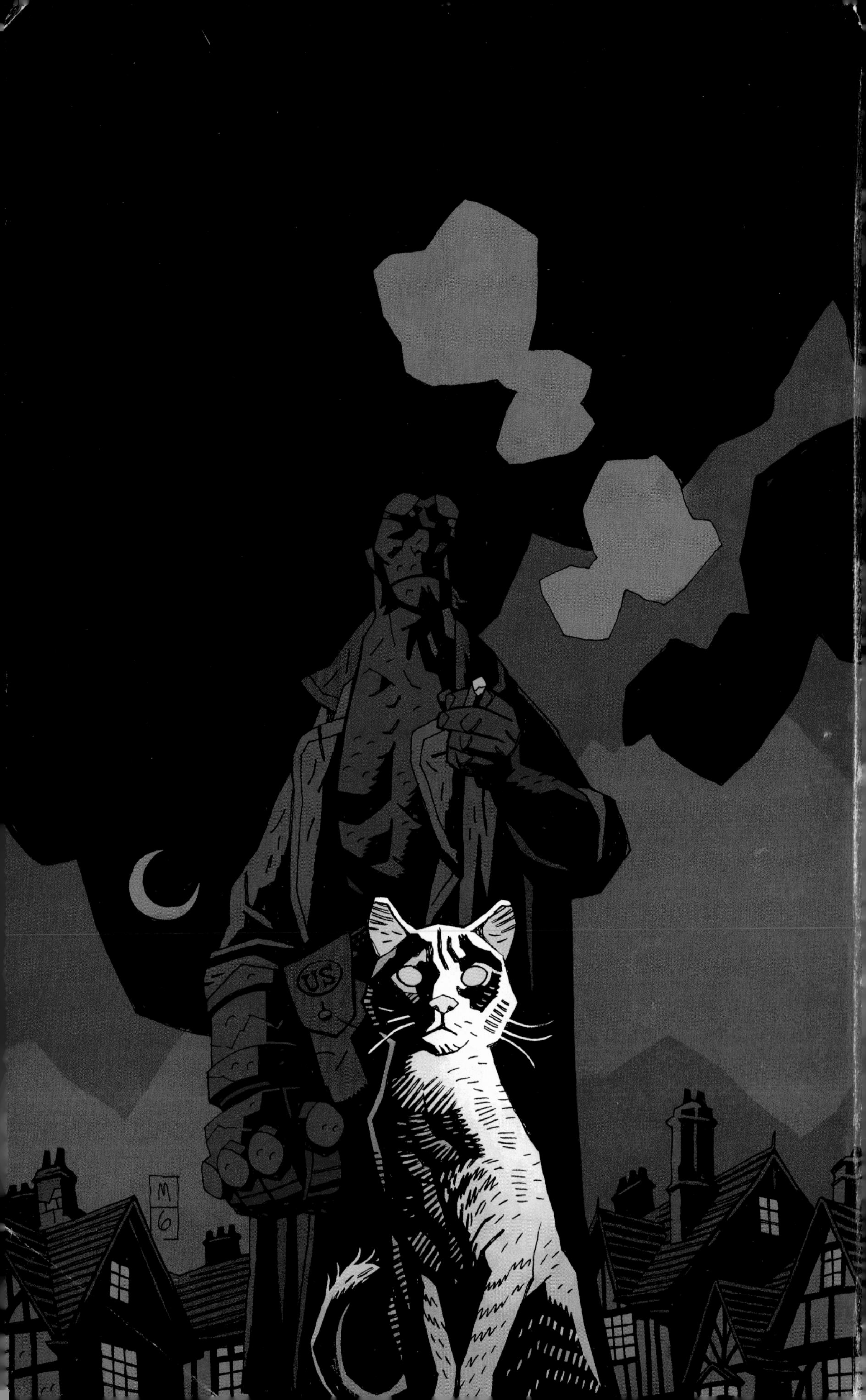
US

DARKNESS CALLS

Story by
MIKE MIGNOLA

Art by
DUNCAN FEGREDO

Colored by
DAVE STEWART

Lettered by
CLEM ROBINS

✠

Introduction by
JANE YOLEN

Edited by
SCOTT ALLIE

Hellboy logo designed by
KEVIN NOWLAN

Collection designed by
MIKE MIGNOLA & CARY GRAZZINI

Publisher
MIKE RICHARDSON

DARK HORSE BOOKS®

Published by
Dark Horse Books
A division of Dark Horse Comics, Inc.
10956 SE Main St.
Milwaukie, OR 97222

First Edition
May 2008
ISBN 978-1-59307-896-6

This volume collects *Hellboy: Darkness Calls* #1–6, published by Dark Horse Comics.

1 3 5 7 9 10 8 6 4 2

PRINTED IN CANADA

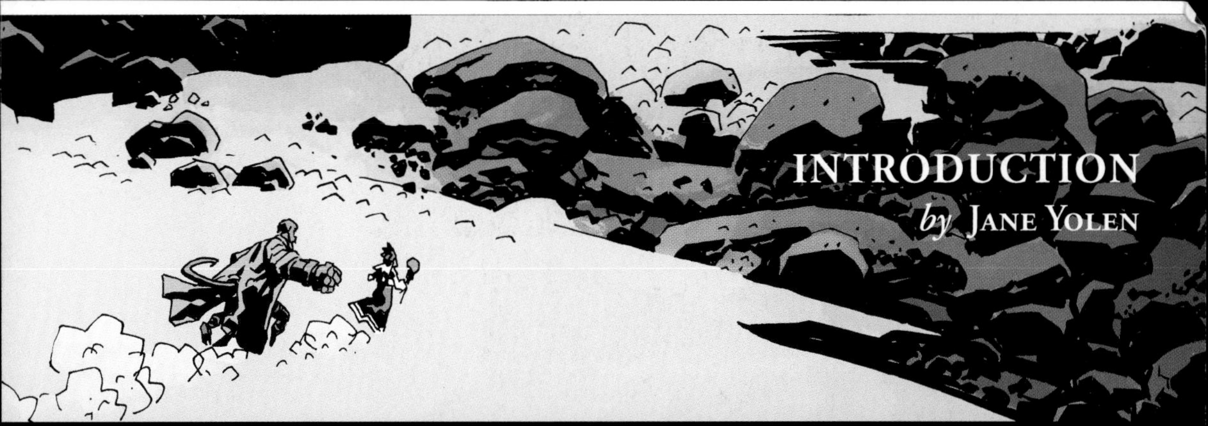

INTRODUCTION

by Jane Yolen

Mike Mignola and I are twins separated at birth. Would I lie?

Okay, I am twenty-plus years older, have more hair, and I have always lived on the East Coast (Well, except for a couple of childhood years in Califunny, and that fact may be important).

Mignola is twenty years younger, is going bald, and has mostly lived on the West Coast. (Okay, so he did live in New York for a while. But that doesn't count. Everybody in the arts has to live there some time. Otherwise they write/paint/make movies about why they never got to the Big Apple.)

Mike likes the dark side of things and I prefer the light. Well, except that I have written about the Holocaust and his Hellboy loves to interrupt the bad guys' pompous posturing with outbursts such as: "Big talk for a guy with no pants," and, "Hey! That you making all that noise?" and, "You girls look like crap." But still I insist we are twins. Separated at birth.

Look at the facts: Who else do you know writes about Baba Yaga and Kostchai and Vasilisa, about Nazis and Hecate, about vampires and Rasputin? (I may be mistaken about Rasputin, but I can sing the old disco song along with my son's old band, "Boiled in Lead.") Who else has written about harpies and mermen and mermaids and selchies? (Oops, I don't remember selchies in *Hellboy*, but there's always the next installment.) And while he has a steampunk look and mine is more fairy punk, while his work is more for adults (if you call thirteen-year-old boys adults) and mine for children (except a good portion of my fans are grown-up librarians), it becomes instantly clear that we are twins separated at birth.

Would I lie?

Of course I would. Story is the best kind of lie-telling. It exaggerates the real, replaces it with something larger and more imaginative in order to illuminate our somewhat smaller lives. And Mike Mignola can lie with illustrations as well as words, those dark, bulky pictures where the dark defines the space. Where your eye is sometimes directed away from the action and at other times lands you with a BLAM right in the middle of it.

Okay, so he's the most talented twin of the two of us. A double whammy. Words and pictures. Even when he lets someone else—like Duncan Fegredo in this series—do the pictures, they are still mightily informed by Mignola's *Hellboy* work before.

Mike uses history, mythology, horror tropes, and good old-fashioned storytelling to pull the reader along at a hellacious pace. But go back a second and a third time to see the mastery of the interplay between words and pictures, between what is said, what is implied, what must be inferred, and what must be teased out. He is a very sophisticated teller and his pacing is impeccable. Make your eyes into slits and you can see the movie of these panels as they rush along with an incredible *whoosh*. And yet they will suddenly slow, even stop at the very moment you need to linger.

Also, Mignola's Hellboy—unlike the usual super-guy or gal of the comics world—is more akin to the hero of dark fantasy literature: strong, suffering, self-aware, ready for what Tolkien has called "the eucatastrophe," where self is willingly sacrificed for the good of all humankind. Interestingly, what Mignola does is smart writing that often poses as an anti-intellectual screed. Yet the story—moving backwards and forwards in time, weaving threads of historical reality shot through with references to books, folklore, theology, Celtic miasma, Ragnarok, or Russian demonology, rooted in mythology and the cosmic End of the World scenarios from many cultures—is not a cold thing. It is not telling-above-the-fray. It is a deeply human story for all its monsters. Think Beowulf, Frankenstein, Jekyll and Hyde. Think Captain Ahab battling Moby Dick. Think the Golem, think Dracula pursued relentlessly by Van Helsing. Think the boy galumphing back with the Jabberwocky's head. Okay—that last is a bit of a stretch. But he does bring it back to his waiting father. "Come to my arms, my beamish boy."

Here in Hellboy, we have the unwanted child who overcompensates, the unlovable boy who keeps searching for love, the friend who helps his friends by constantly putting his own life in danger, the man who values the world more than himself. The existential hero. Though Hellboy might read all this and respond: "Guess there's no point trying to reason with you, Furball, huh?"

Guess not, Mignola … er … Hellboy. Maybe someday we can actually meet and trade … well, trade stories. And you will realize that whoever our mothers and fathers were, whatever coast we landed on, however different our ages may be, we really are twins.

For Duncan Fegredo, for taking over some of the
heavy lifting—and not a second too soon.
M. M.

CHAPTER ONE

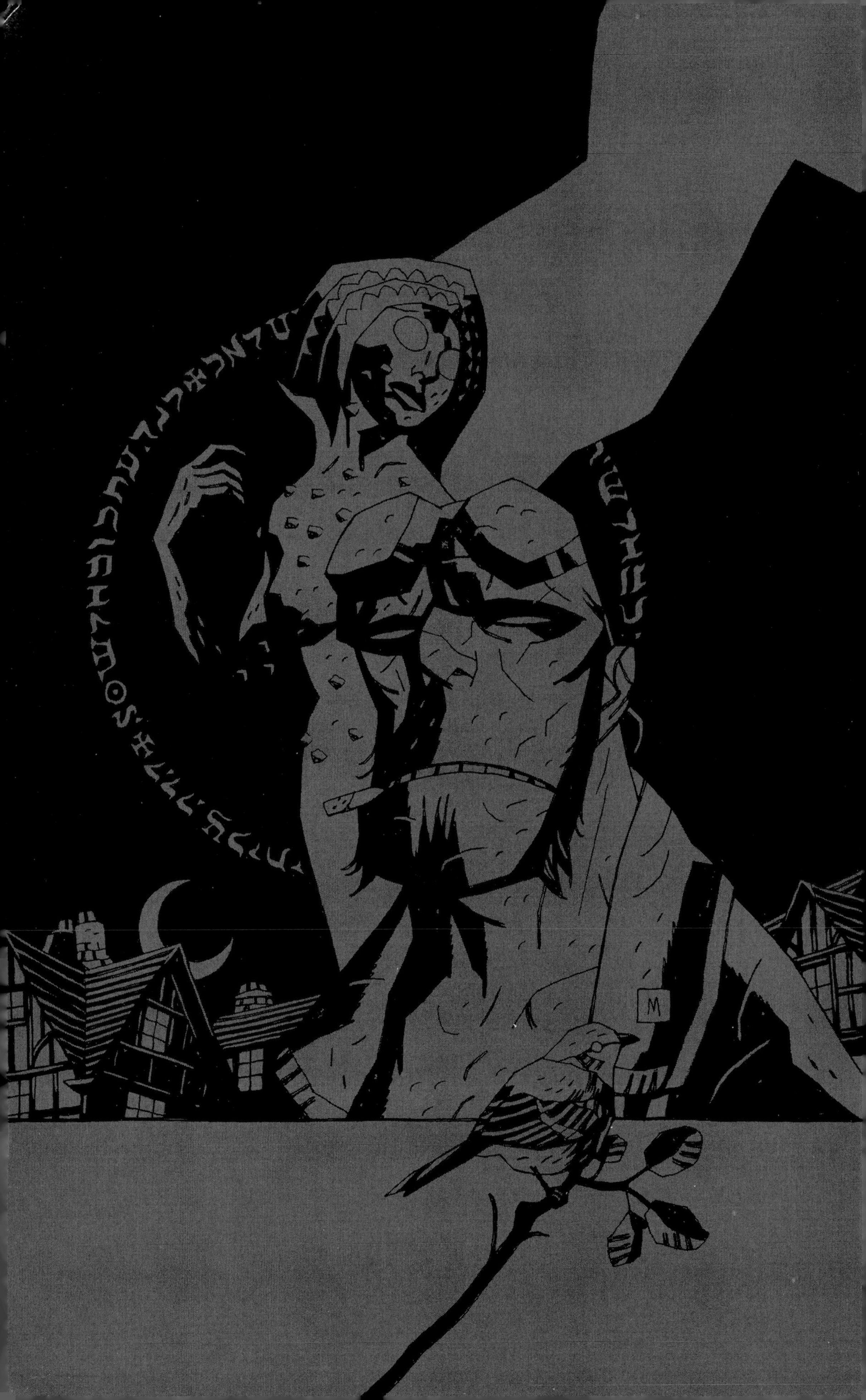

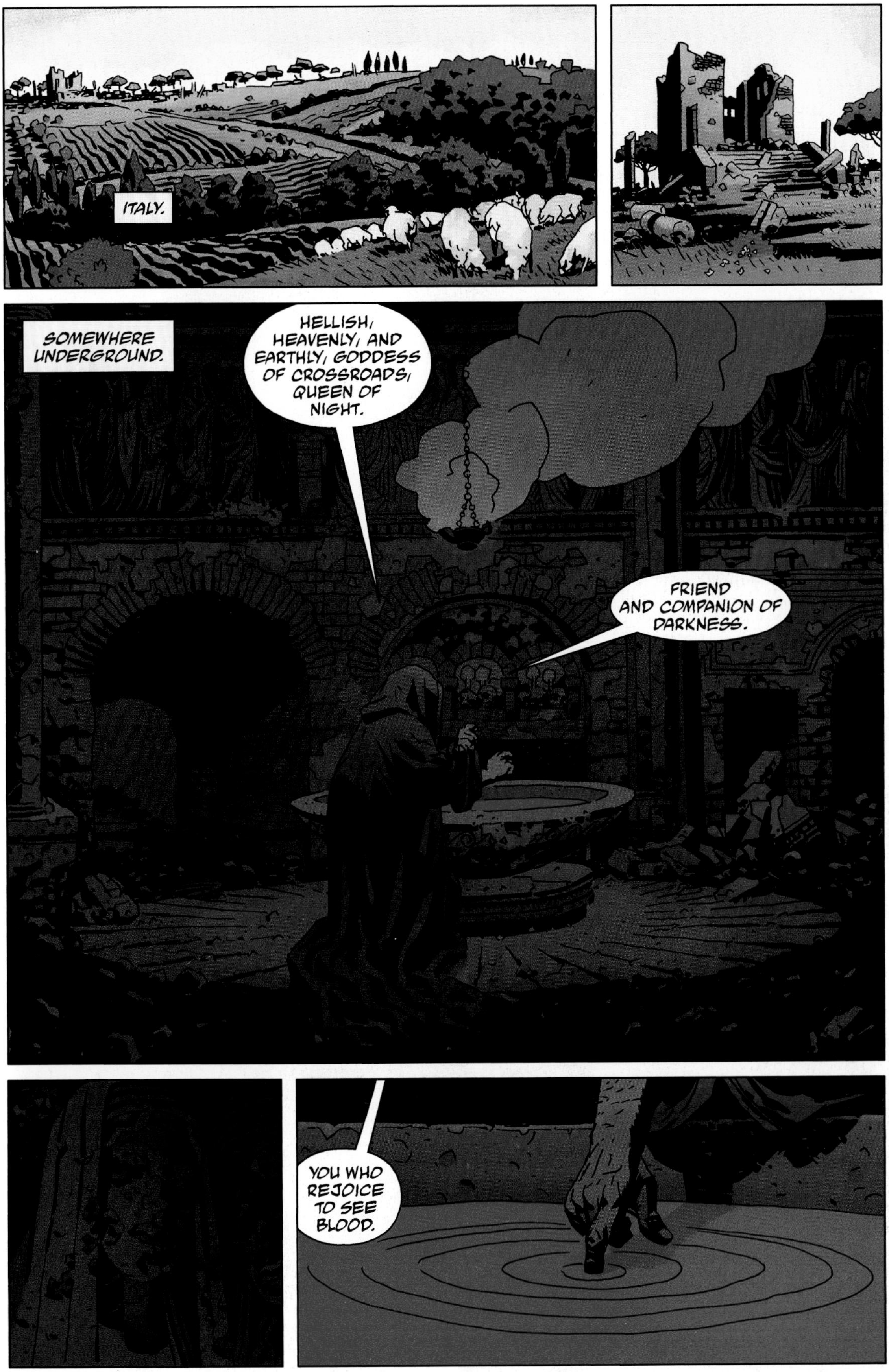
ITALY.
SOMEWHERE UNDERGROUND.
HELLISH, HEAVENLY, AND EARTHLY, GODDESS OF CROSSROADS, QUEEN OF NIGHT.
FRIEND AND COMPANION OF DARKNESS.
YOU WHO REJOICE TO SEE BLOOD.

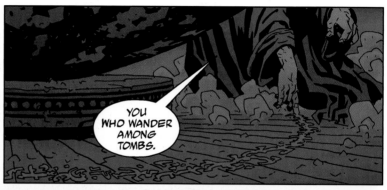

YOU WHO WANDER AMONG TOMBS.

YOU WHO THIRST FOR BLOOD AND THE TERROR OF MORTAL MEN.

GORGO, MORMO, MOON OF A THOUSAND FORMS...

HECATE.

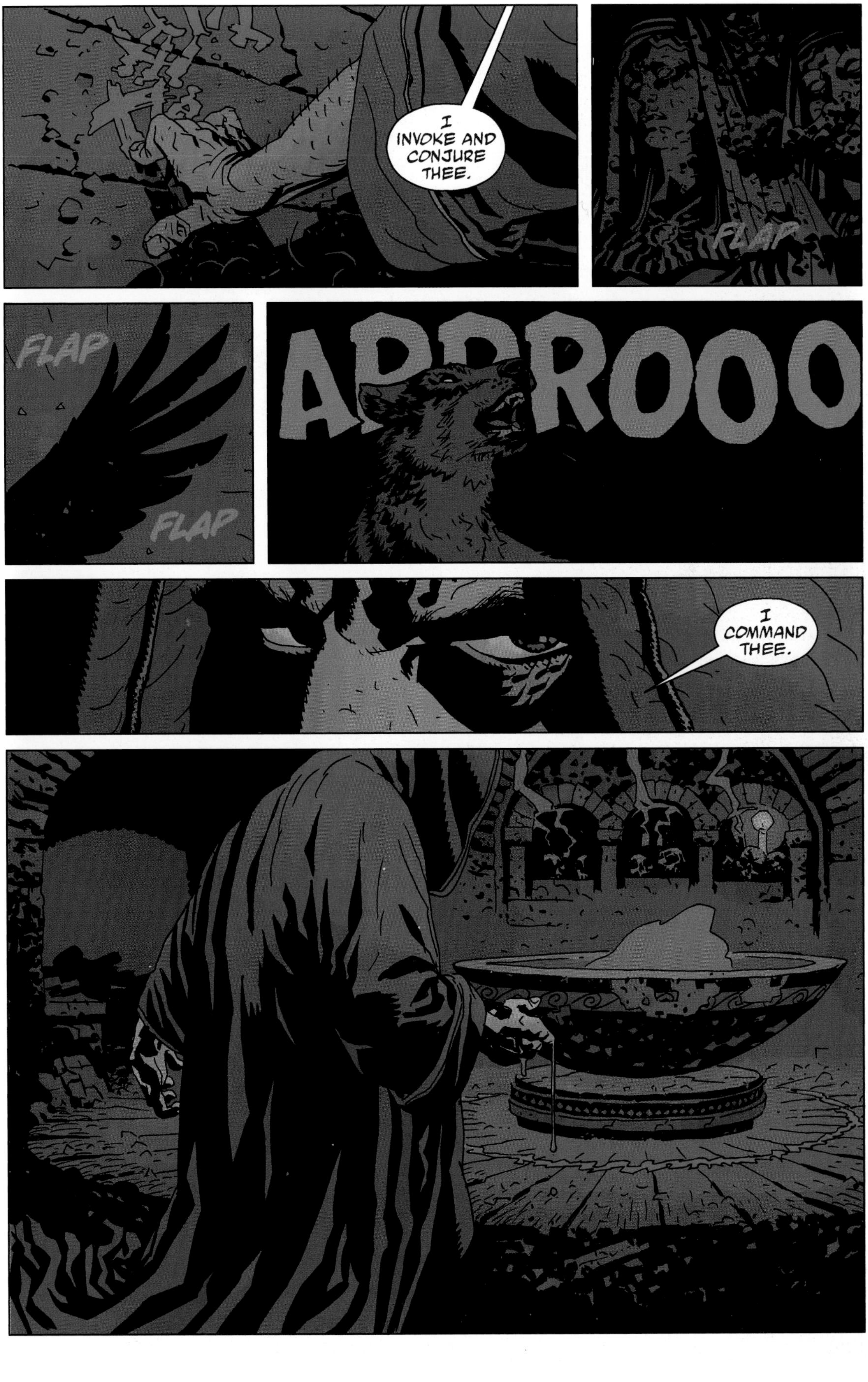
I INVOKE AND CONJURE THEE.
FLAP
FLAP
FLAP
ARRROOO
I COMMAND THEE.

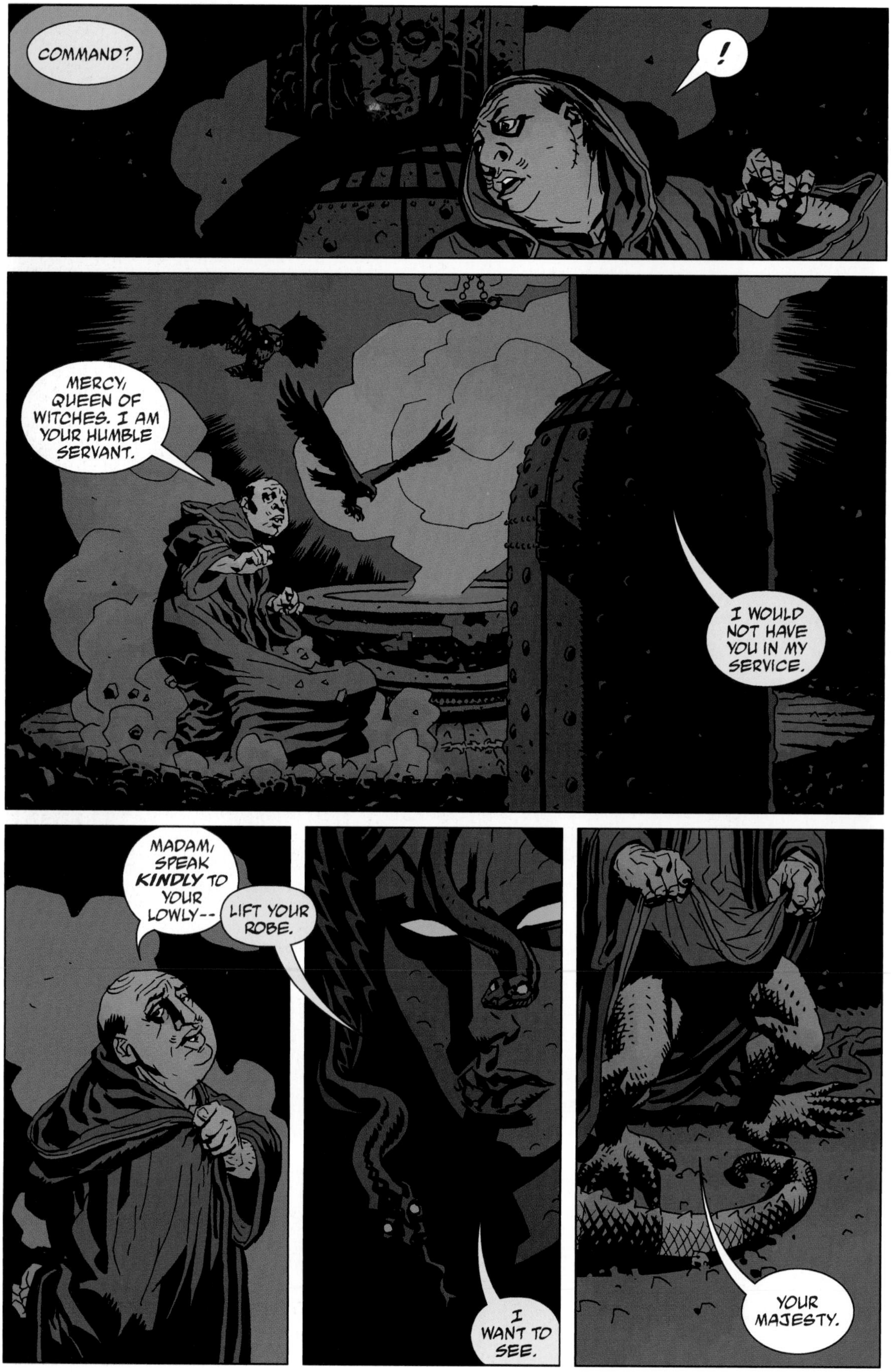
COMMAND?
!
MERCY, QUEEN OF WITCHES. I AM YOUR HUMBLE SERVANT.
I WOULD NOT HAVE YOU IN MY SERVICE.
MADAM, SPEAK KINDLY TO YOUR LOWLY--
LIFT YOUR ROBE.
I WANT TO SEE.
YOUR MAJESTY.

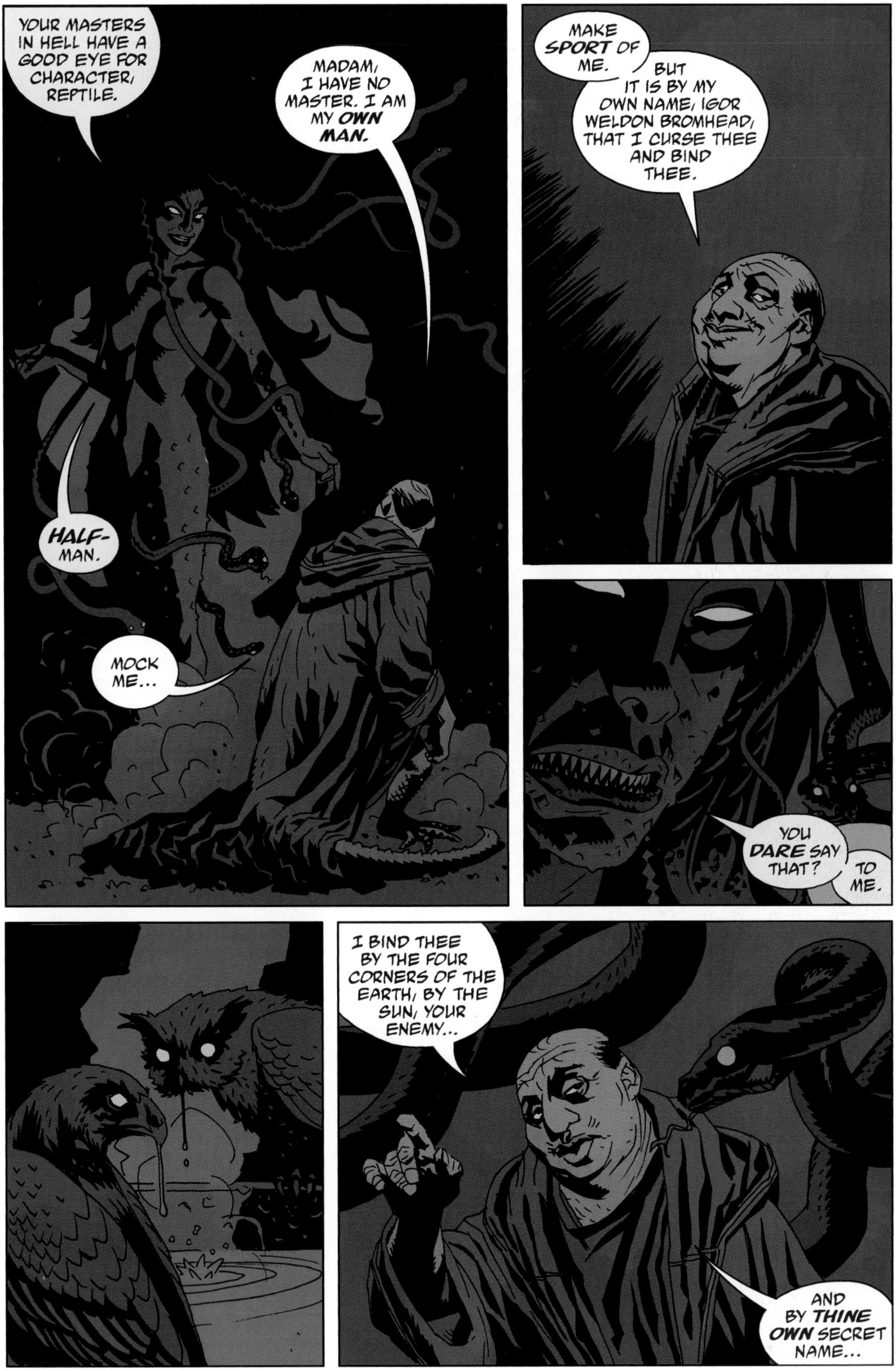
YOUR MASTERS IN HELL HAVE A GOOD EYE FOR CHARACTER, REPTILE.
MADAM, I HAVE NO MASTER. I AM MY OWN MAN.
HALF-MAN.
MOCK ME...
MAKE SPORT OF ME.
BUT IT IS BY MY OWN NAME, IGOR WELDON BROMHEAD, THAT I CURSE THEE AND BIND THEE.
YOU DARE SAY THAT?
TO ME.
I BIND THEE BY THE FOUR CORNERS OF THE EARTH, BY THE SUN, YOUR ENEMY...
AND BY THINE OWN SECRET NAME...

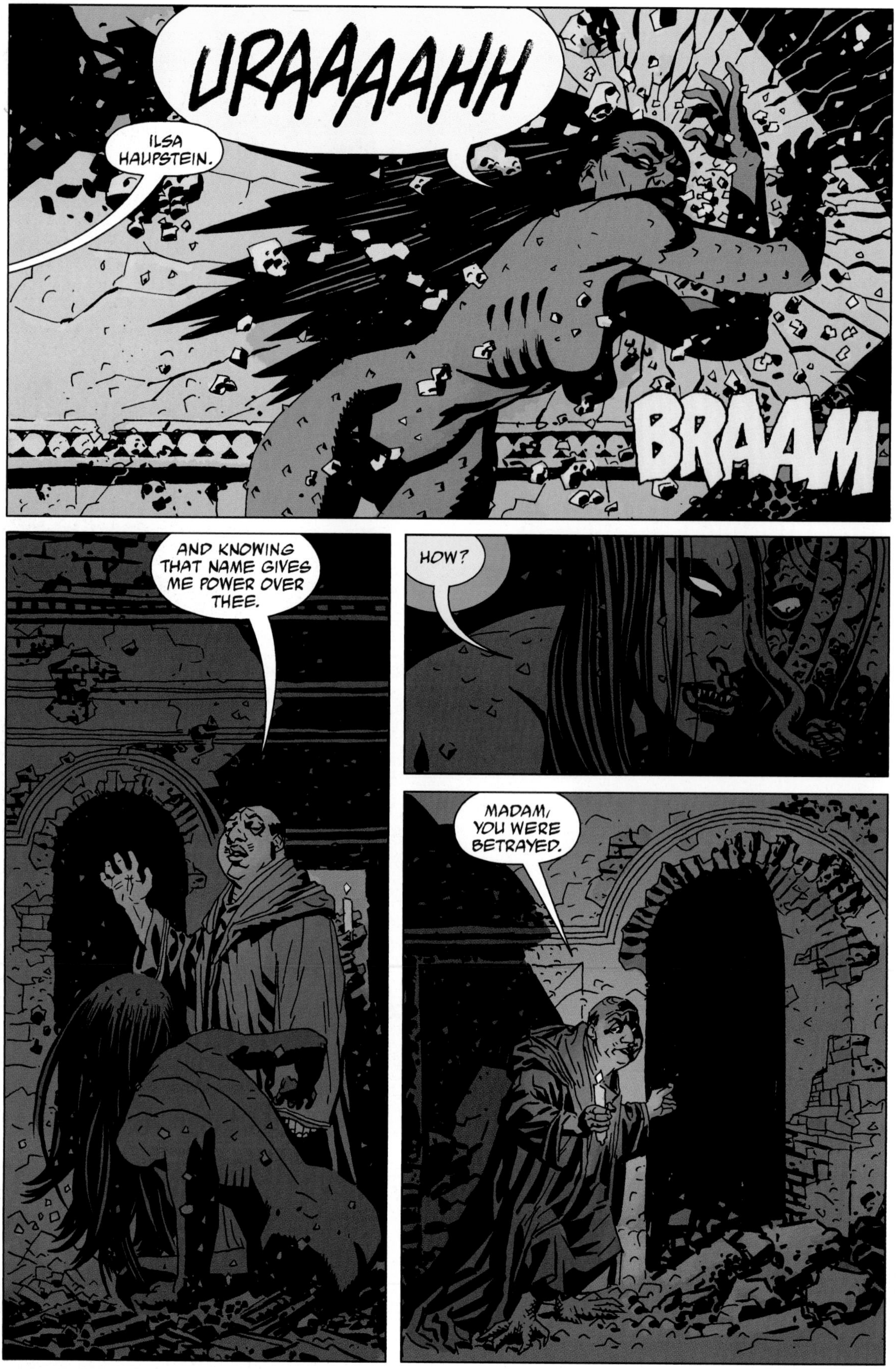
URAAAAAHH
ILSA HAUPSTEIN.
BRAAM
AND KNOWING THAT NAME GIVES ME POWER OVER THEE.
HOW?
MADAM, YOU WERE BETRAYED.

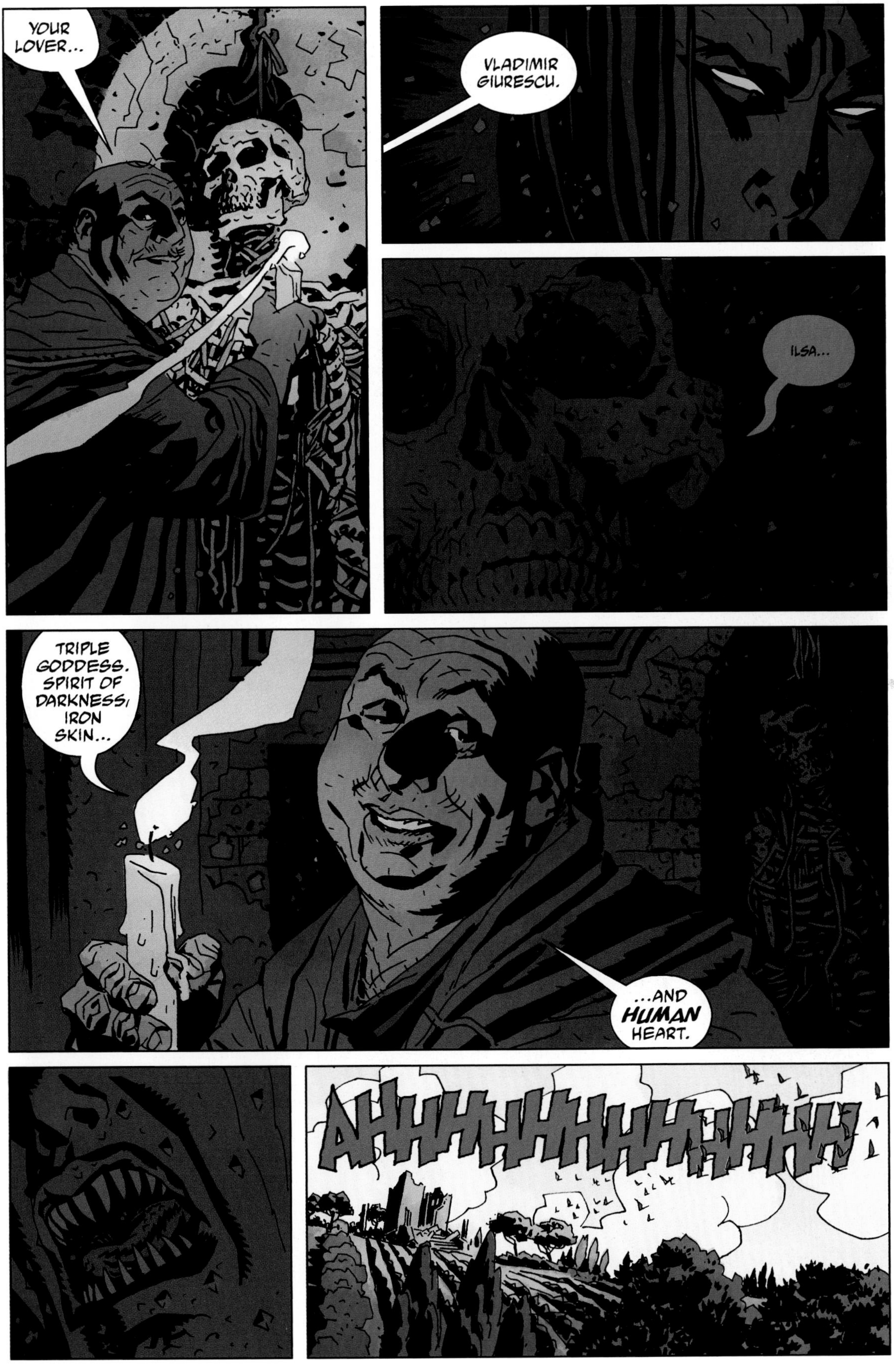
YOUR LOVER...
VLADIMIR GIURESCU.
ILSA...
TRIPLE GODDESS. SPIRIT OF DARKNESS, IRON SKIN...
...AND HUMAN HEART.
AHHHHHHHHHHHHH

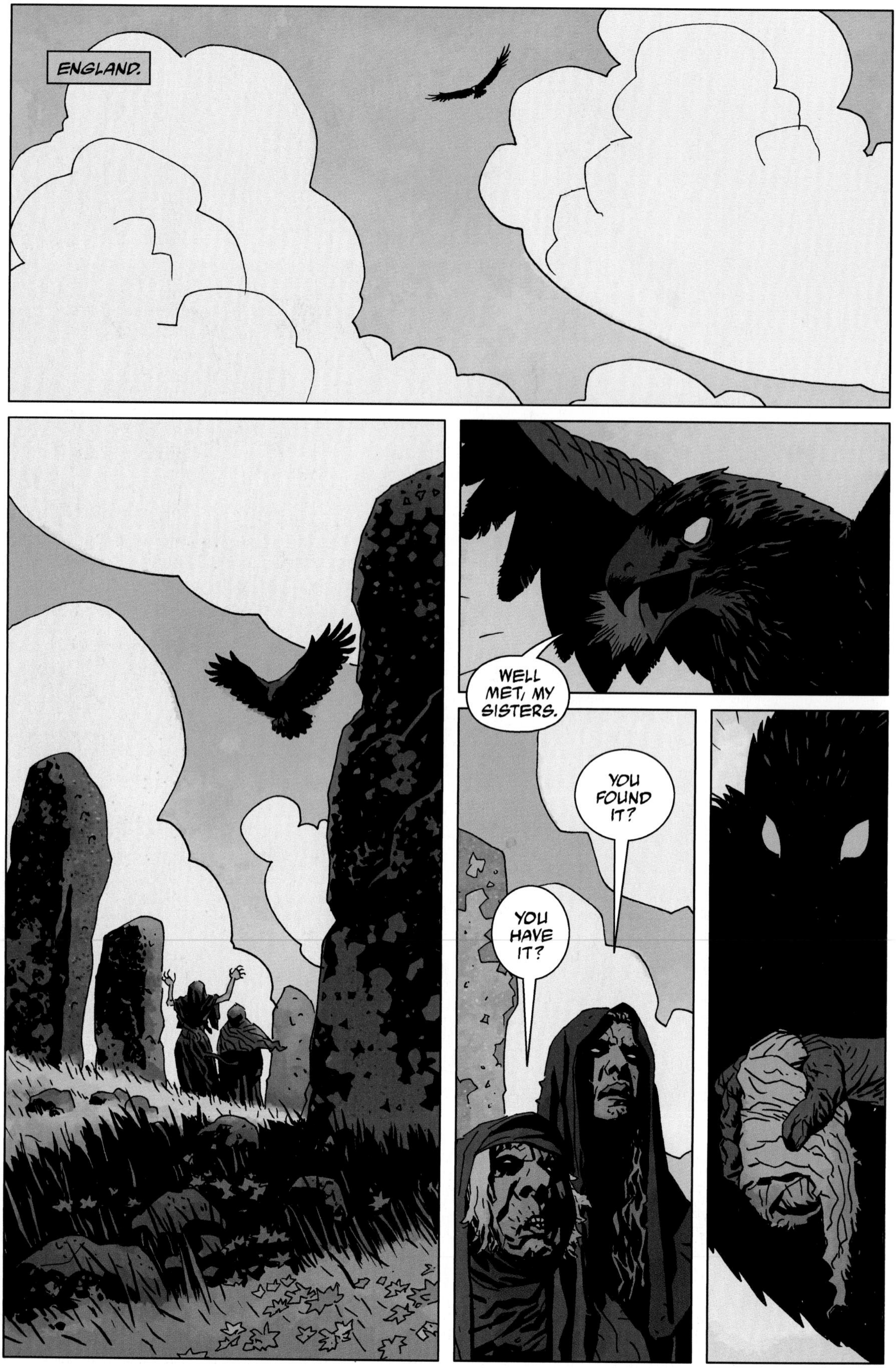
ENGLAND.
WELL MET, MY SISTERS.
YOU FOUND IT?
YOU HAVE IT?

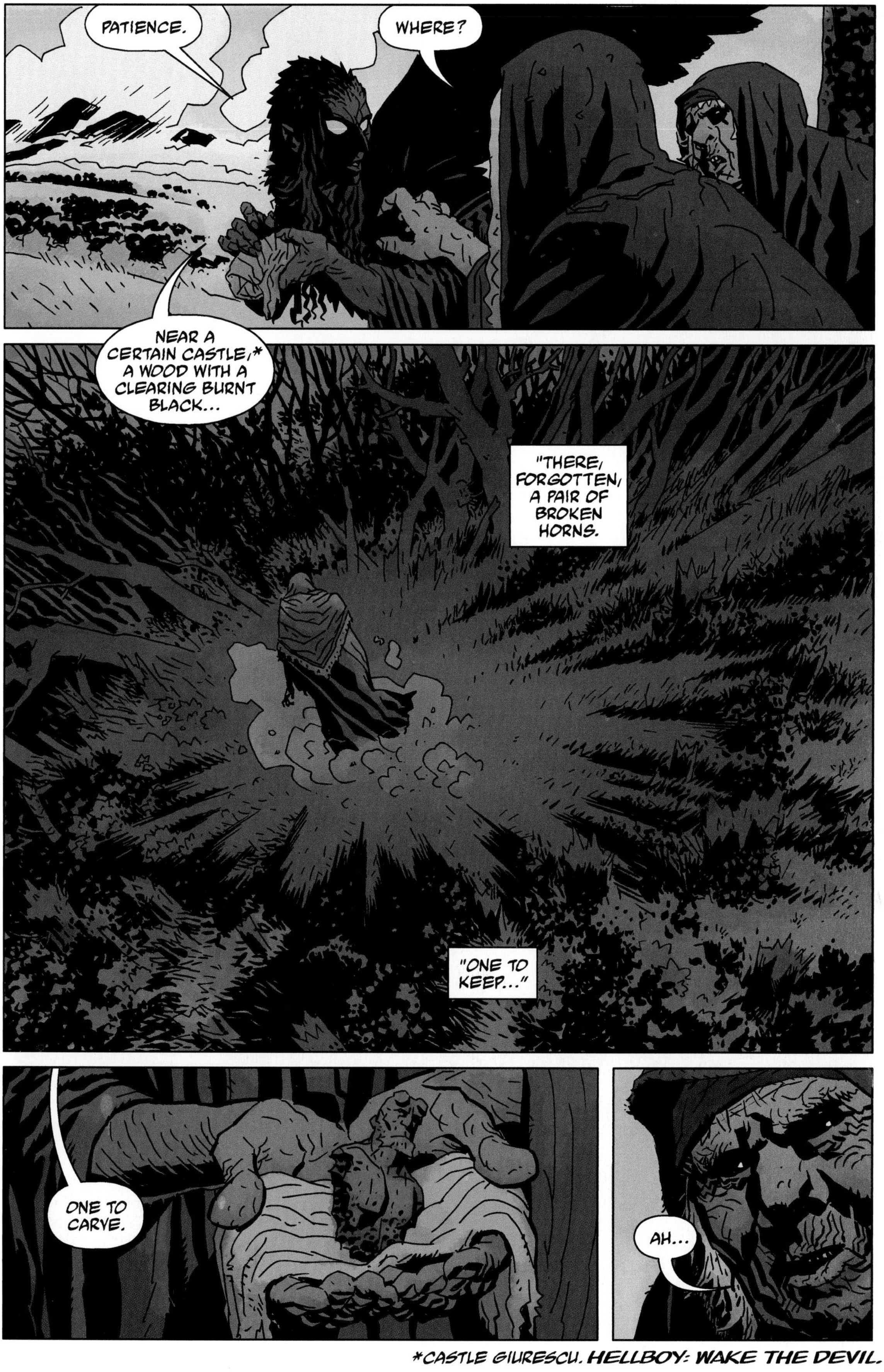
PATIENCE.
WHERE?
NEAR A CERTAIN CASTLE,* A WOOD WITH A CLEARING BURNT BLACK...
"THERE, FORGOTTEN, A PAIR OF BROKEN HORNS.
"ONE TO KEEP..."
ONE TO CARVE.
AH...

*CASTLE GIURESCU. ***HELLBOY: WAKE THE DEVIL.***

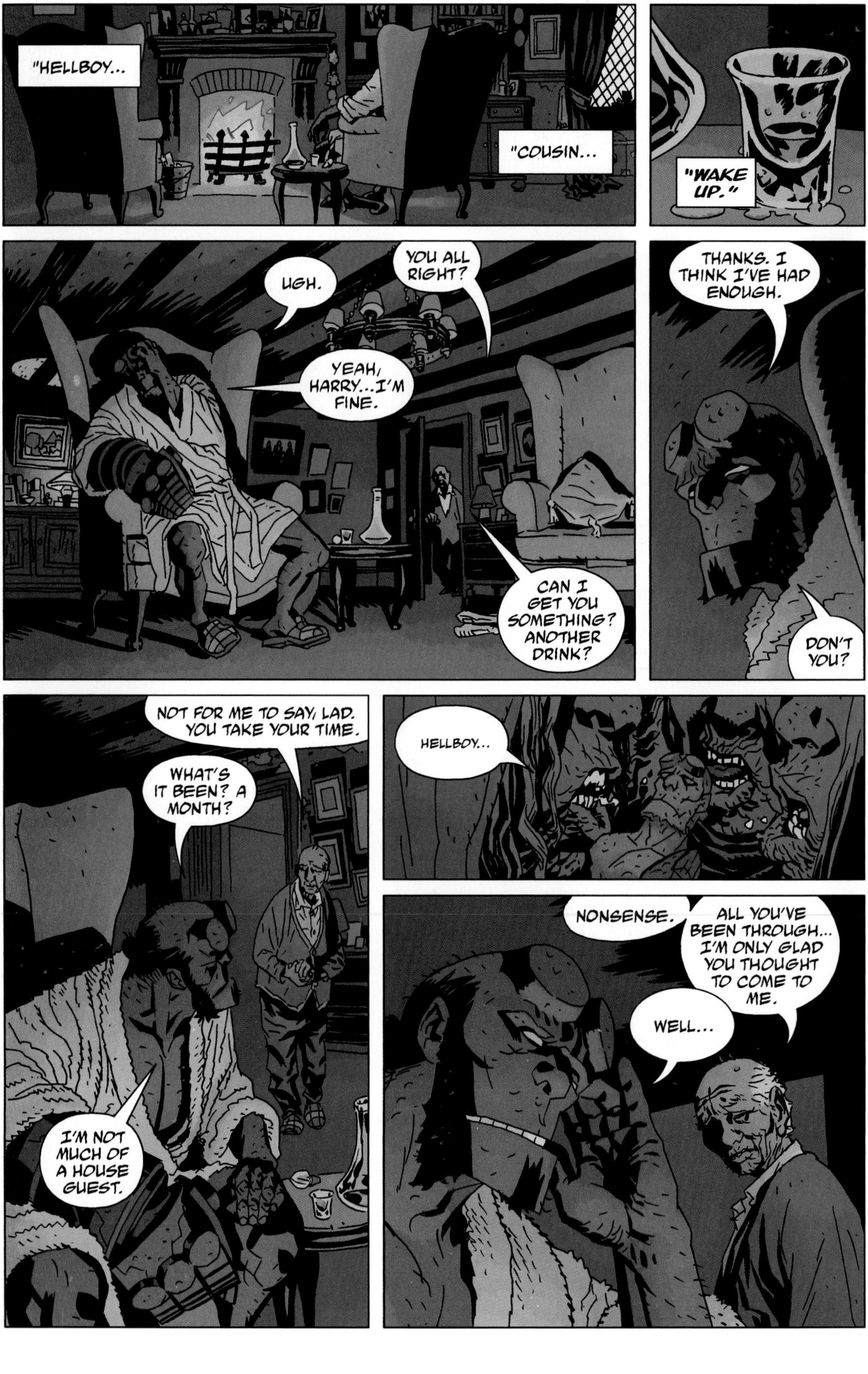
"HELLBOY...
"COUSIN...
"WAKE UP."
UGH.
YOU ALL RIGHT?
YEAH, HARRY...I'M FINE.
CAN I GET YOU SOMETHING? ANOTHER DRINK?
THANKS. I THINK I'VE HAD ENOUGH.
DON'T YOU?
NOT FOR ME TO SAY, LAD. YOU TAKE YOUR TIME.
WHAT'S IT BEEN? A MONTH?
I'M NOT MUCH OF A HOUSE GUEST.
HELLBOY...
NONSENSE.
ALL YOU'VE BEEN THROUGH... I'M ONLY GLAD YOU THOUGHT TO COME TO ME.
WELL...

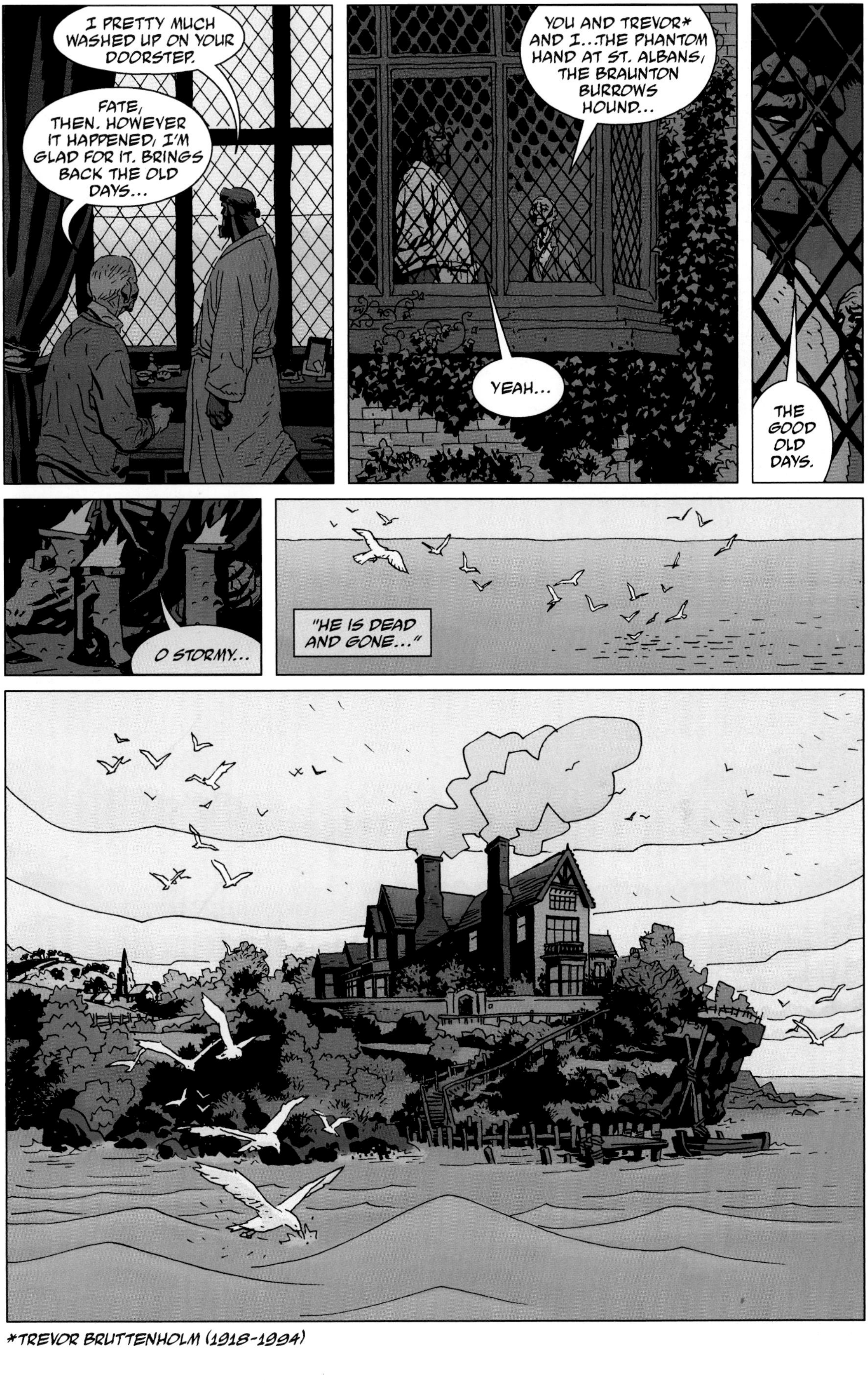
I PRETTY MUCH WASHED UP ON YOUR DOORSTEP.
FATE, THEN. HOWEVER IT HAPPENED, I'M GLAD FOR IT. BRINGS BACK THE OLD DAYS...
YOU AND TREVOR* AND I...THE PHANTOM HAND AT ST. ALBANS, THE BRAUNTON BURROWS HOUND...
YEAH...
THE GOOD OLD DAYS.
O STORMY...
"HE IS DEAD AND GONE..."

*TREVOR BRUTTENHOLM (1918-1994)

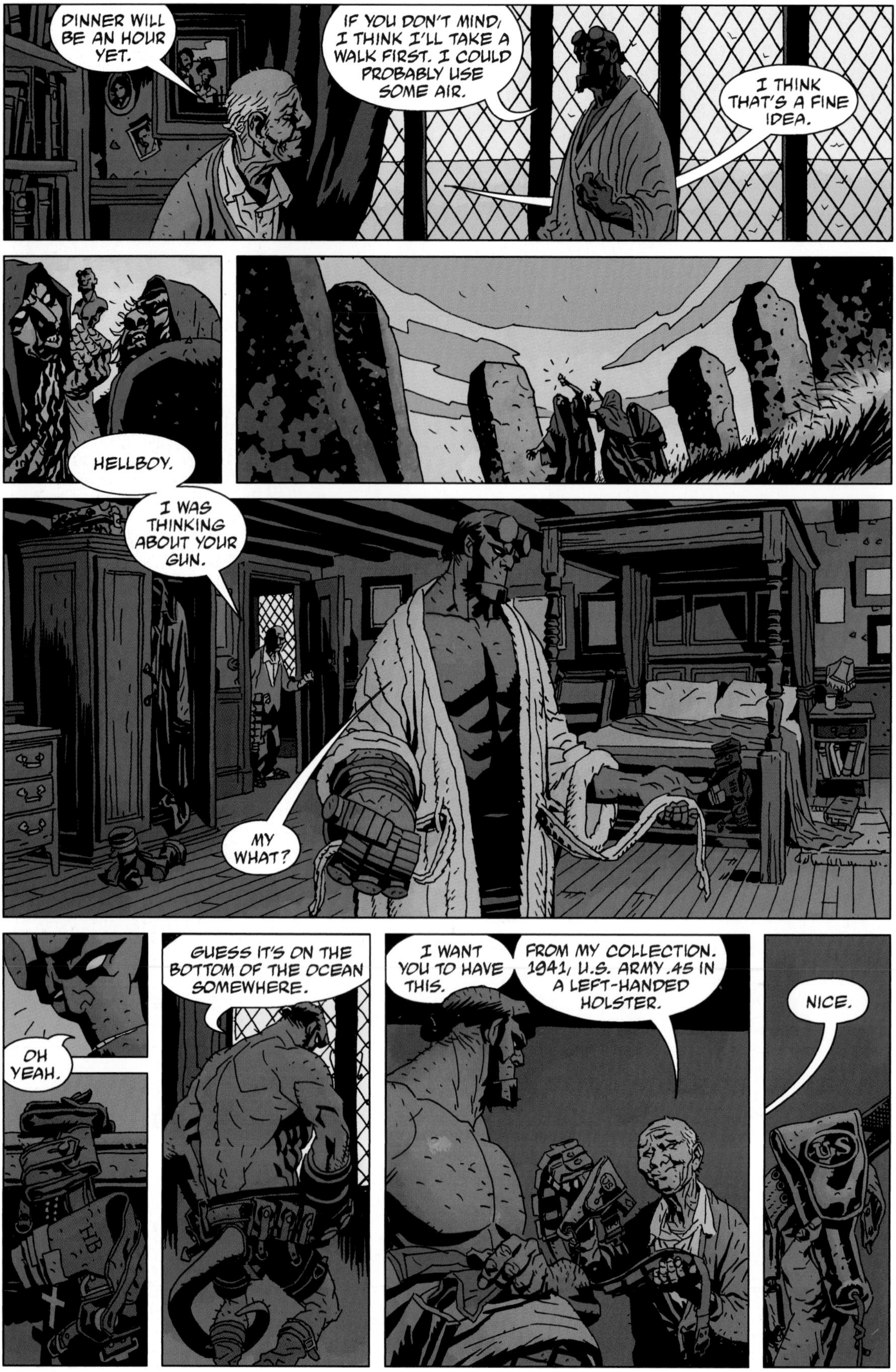

DINNER WILL BE AN HOUR YET.
IF YOU DON'T MIND, I THINK I'LL TAKE A WALK FIRST. I COULD PROBABLY USE SOME AIR.
I THINK THAT'S A FINE IDEA.
HELLBOY.
I WAS THINKING ABOUT YOUR GUN.
MY WHAT?
OH YEAH.
GUESS IT'S ON THE BOTTOM OF THE OCEAN SOMEWHERE.
I WANT YOU TO HAVE THIS.
FROM MY COLLECTION. 1941, U.S. ARMY .45 IN A LEFT-HANDED HOLSTER.
NICE.

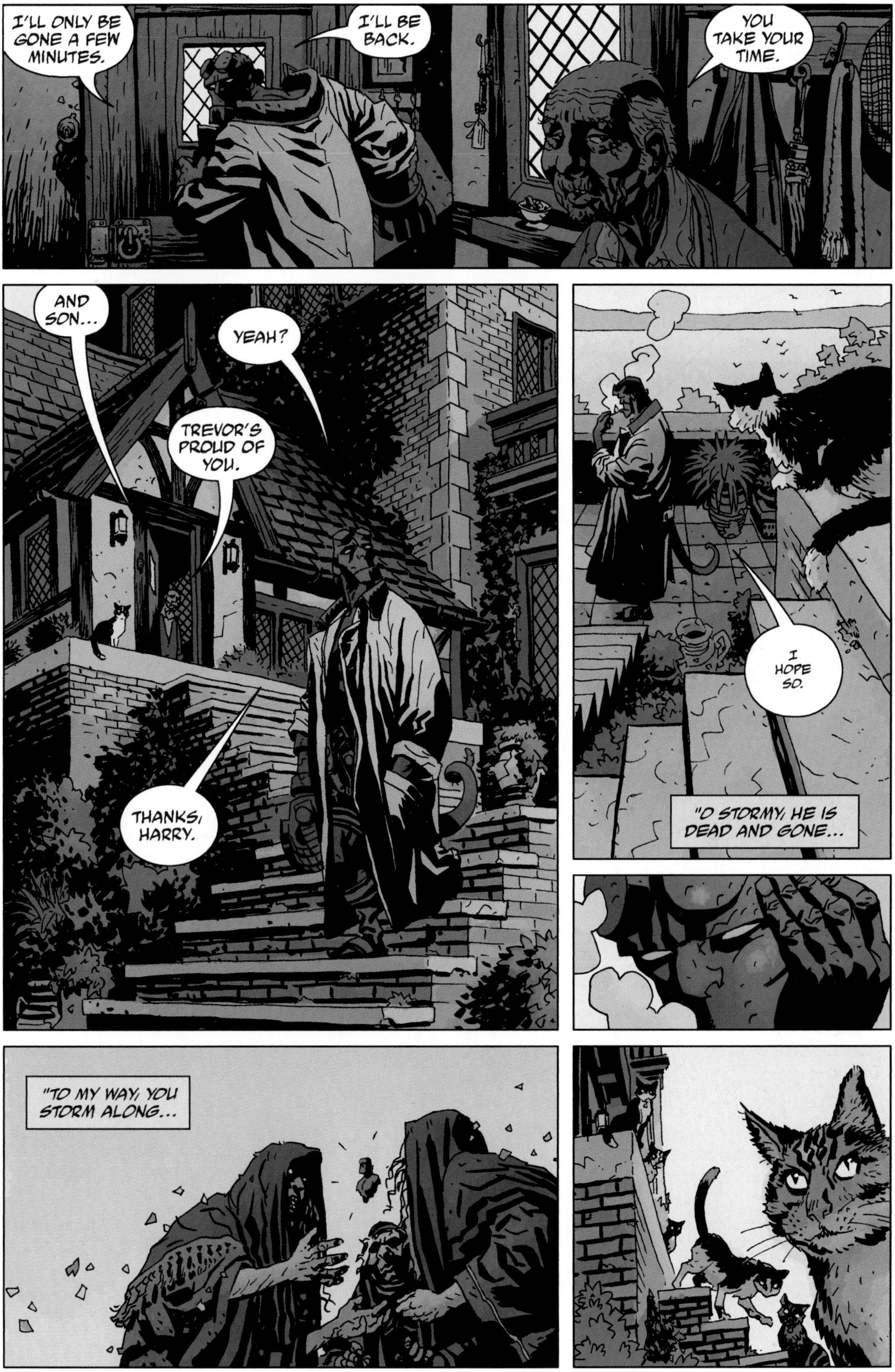
I'LL ONLY BE GONE A FEW MINUTES.
I'LL BE BACK.
YOU TAKE YOUR TIME.
AND SON...
YEAH?
TREVOR'S PROUD OF YOU.
THANKS, HARRY.
I HOPE SO.
"O STORMY, HE IS DEAD AND GONE...
"TO MY WAY, YOU STORM ALONG...

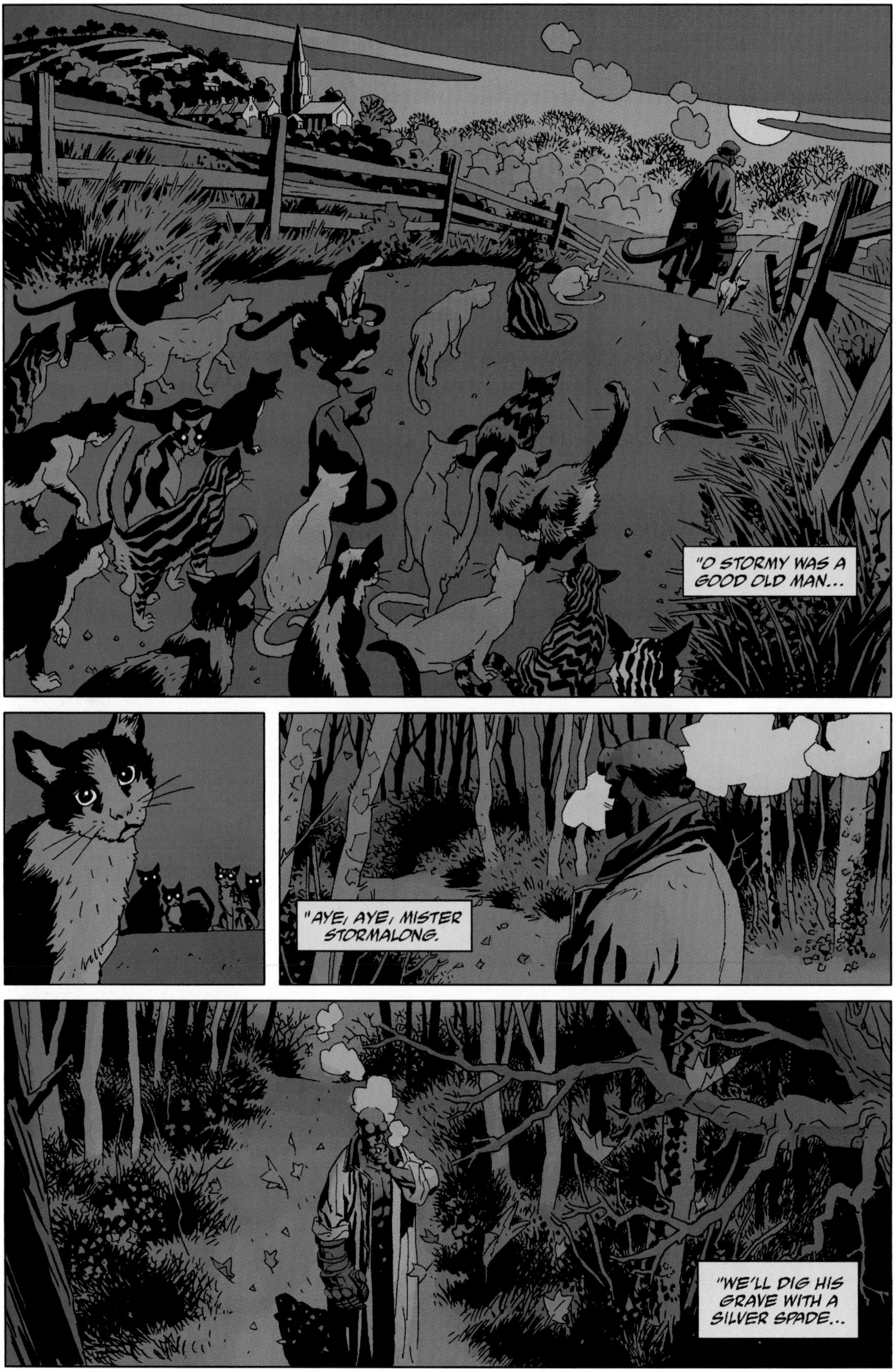
"O STORMY WAS A GOOD OLD MAN...
"AYE, AYE, MISTER STORMALONG.
"WE'LL DIG HIS GRAVE WITH A SILVER SPADE...

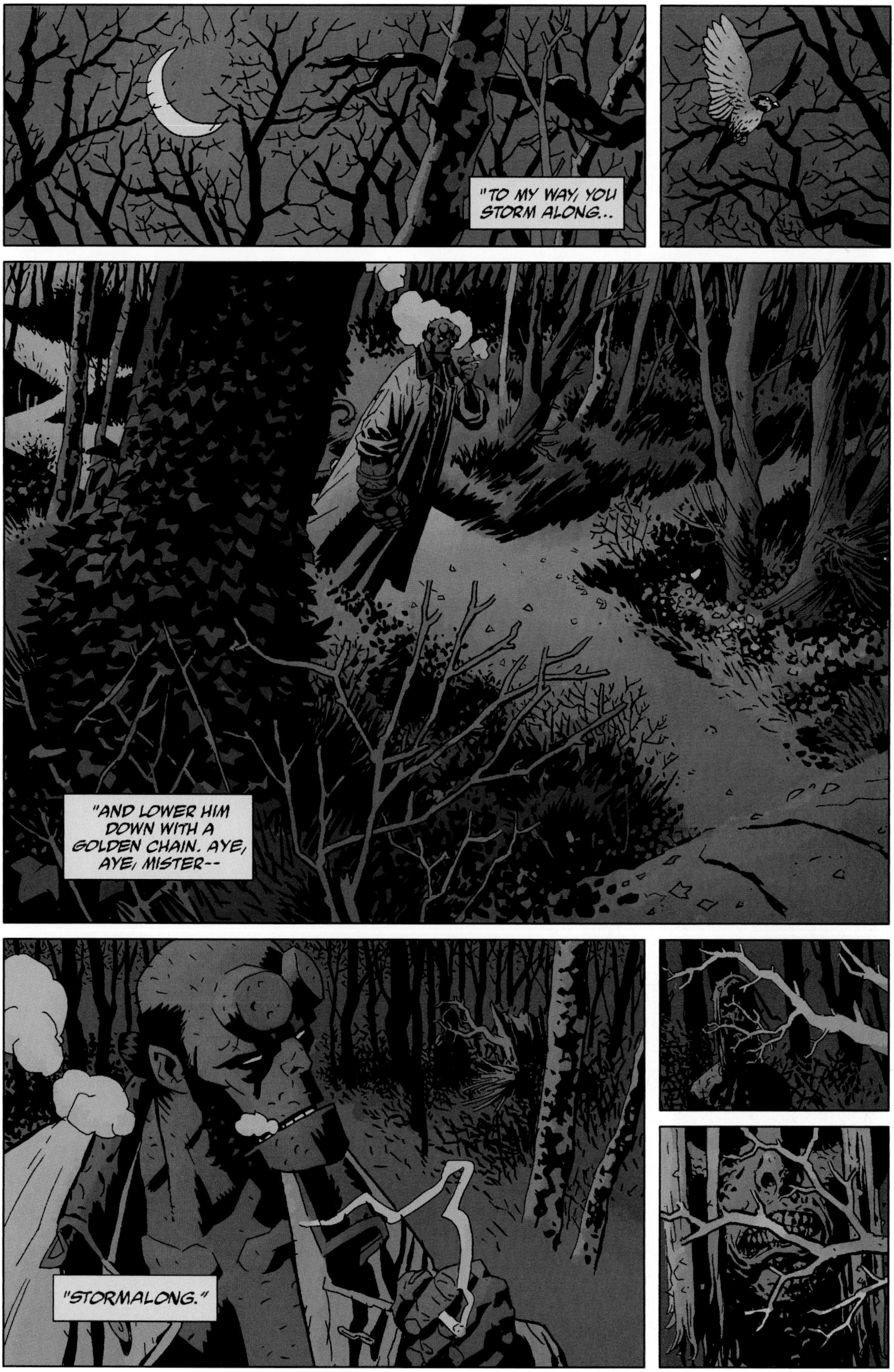
"TO MY WAY, YOU STORM ALONG...
"AND LOWER HIM DOWN WITH A GOLDEN CHAIN. AYE, AYE, MISTER--
"STORMALONG."

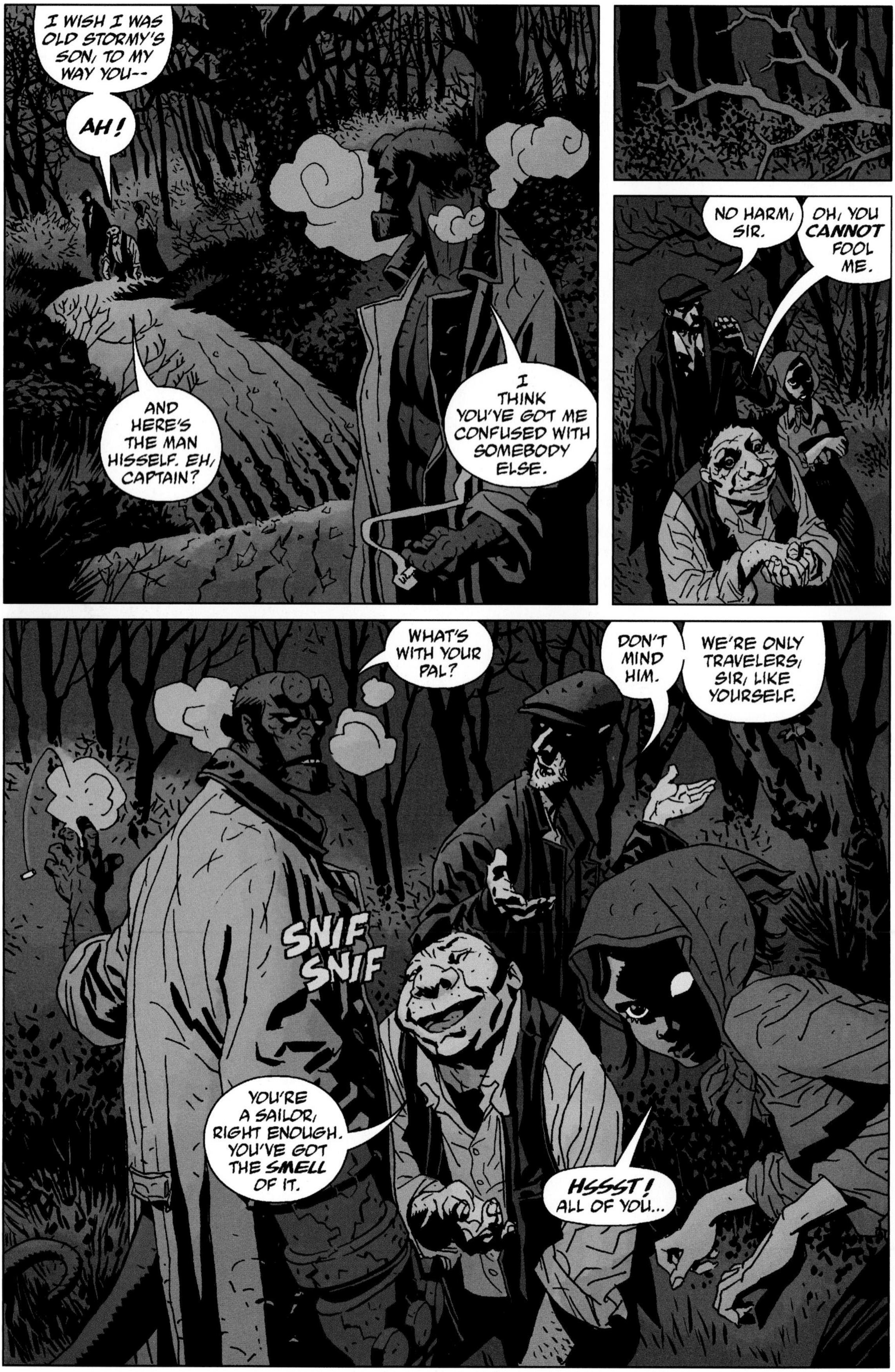
I WISH I WAS OLD STORMY'S SON, TO MY WAY YOU--
AH!
AND HERE'S THE MAN HISSELF. EH, CAPTAIN?
I THINK YOU'VE GOT ME CONFUSED WITH SOMEBODY ELSE.
NO HARM, SIR.
OH, YOU CANNOT FOOL ME.
WHAT'S WITH YOUR PAL?
DON'T MIND HIM.
WE'RE ONLY TRAVELERS, SIR, LIKE YOURSELF.
SNIF SNIF
YOU'RE A SAILOR, RIGHT ENOUGH. YOU'VE GOT THE SMELL OF IT.
HSSST! ALL OF YOU...

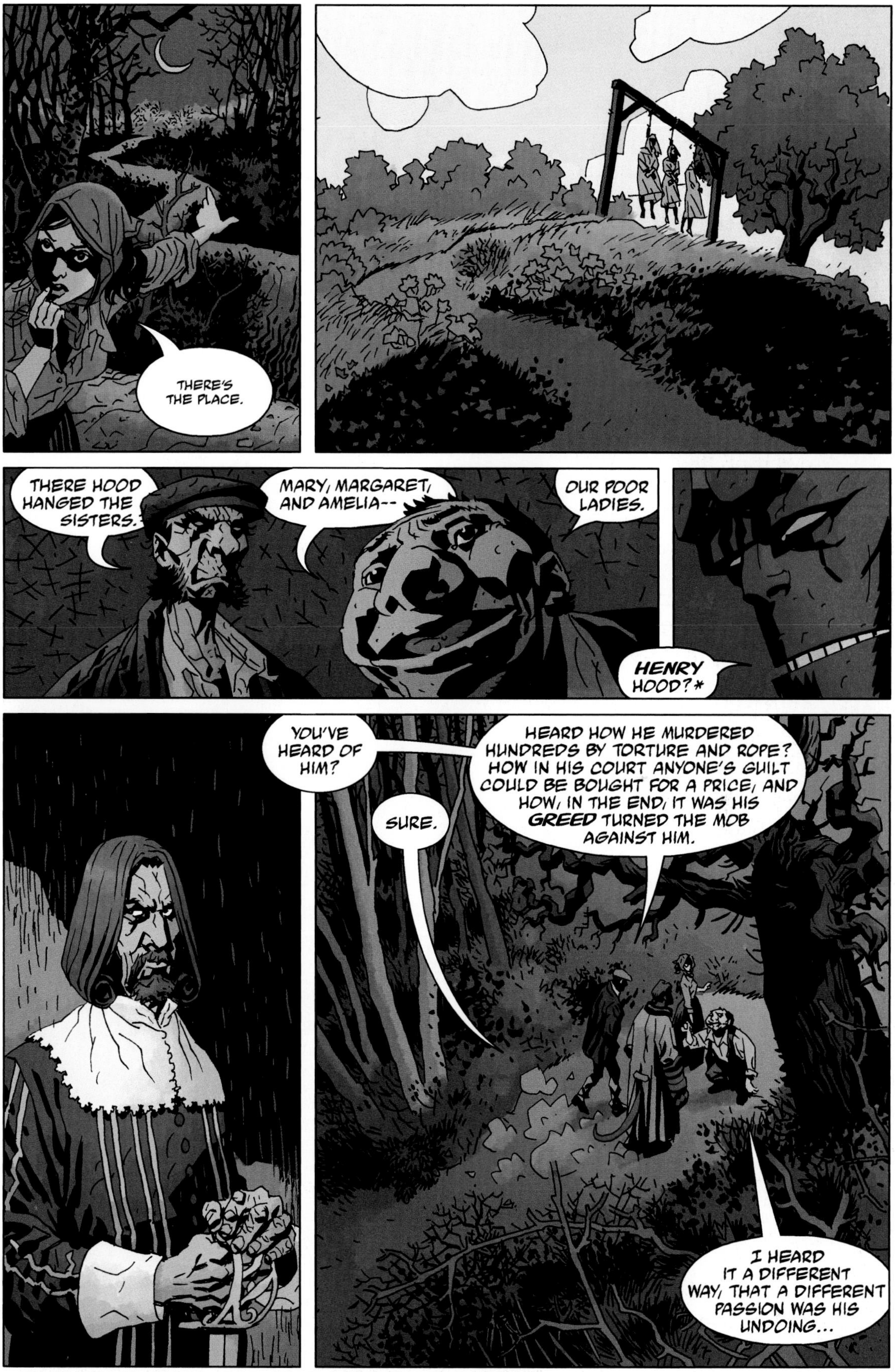
THERE'S THE PLACE.
THERE HOOD HANGED THE SISTERS.
MARY, MARGARET, AND AMELIA--
OUR POOR LADIES.
HENRY HOOD?*
YOU'VE HEARD OF HIM?
SURE.
HEARD HOW HE MURDERED HUNDREDS BY TORTURE AND ROPE? HOW IN HIS COURT ANYONE'S GUILT COULD BE BOUGHT FOR A PRICE, AND HOW, IN THE END, IT WAS HIS GREED TURNED THE MOB AGAINST HIM.
I HEARD IT A DIFFERENT WAY, THAT A DIFFERENT PASSION WAS HIS UNDOING...

*WITCHFINDER HENRY HOOD. RESPONSIBLE FOR THE HANGING OF OVER 260 WOMEN BETWEEN APRIL 1645 AND OCTOBER 1646.

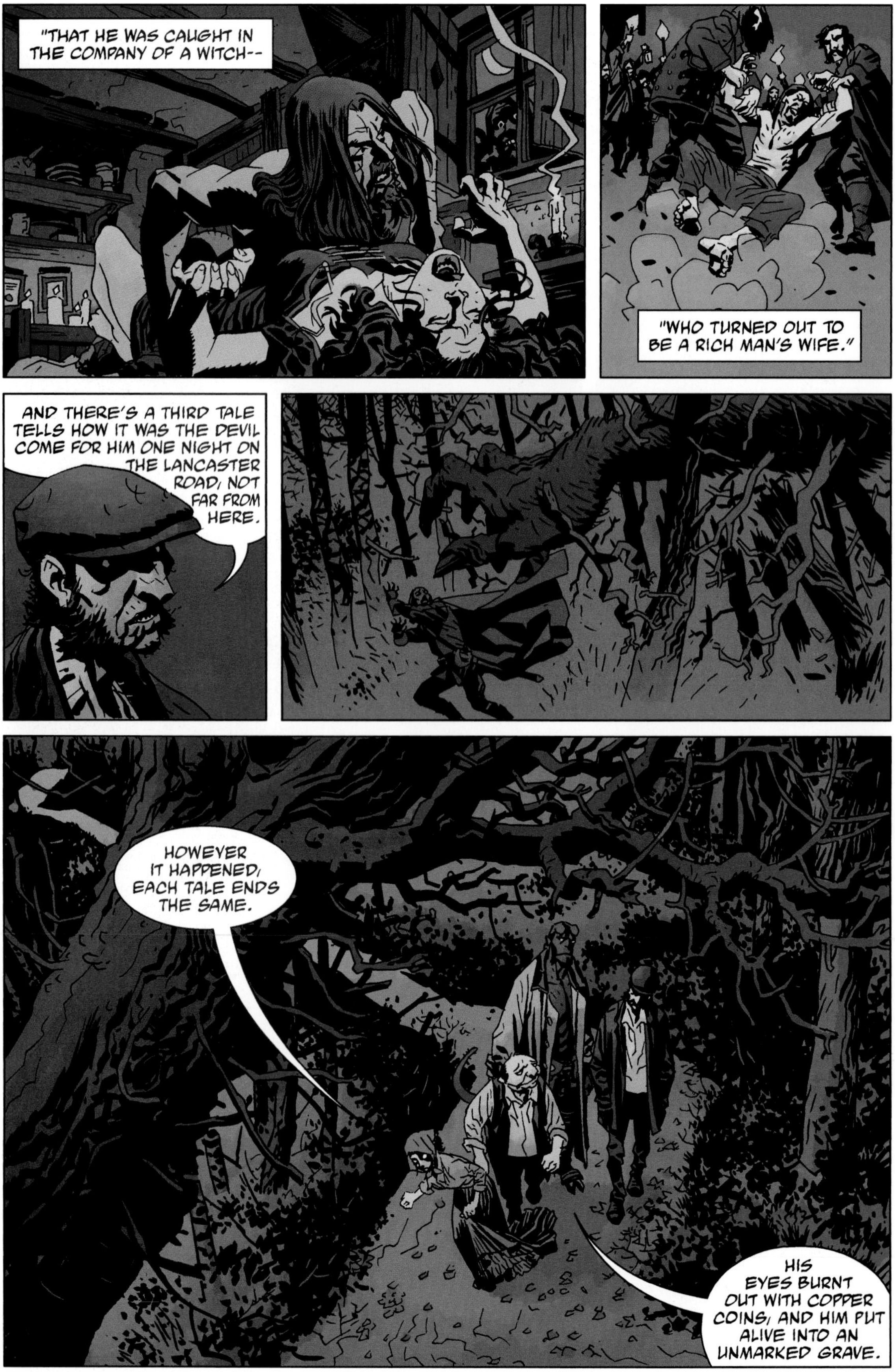
"THAT HE WAS CAUGHT IN THE COMPANY OF A WITCH--
"WHO TURNED OUT TO BE A RICH MAN'S WIFE."
AND THERE'S A THIRD TALE TELLS HOW IT WAS THE DEVIL COME FOR HIM ONE NIGHT ON THE LANCASTER ROAD, NOT FAR FROM HERE.
HOWEVER IT HAPPENED, EACH TALE ENDS THE SAME.
HIS EYES BURNT OUT WITH COPPER COINS, AND HIM PUT ALIVE INTO AN UNMARKED GRAVE.

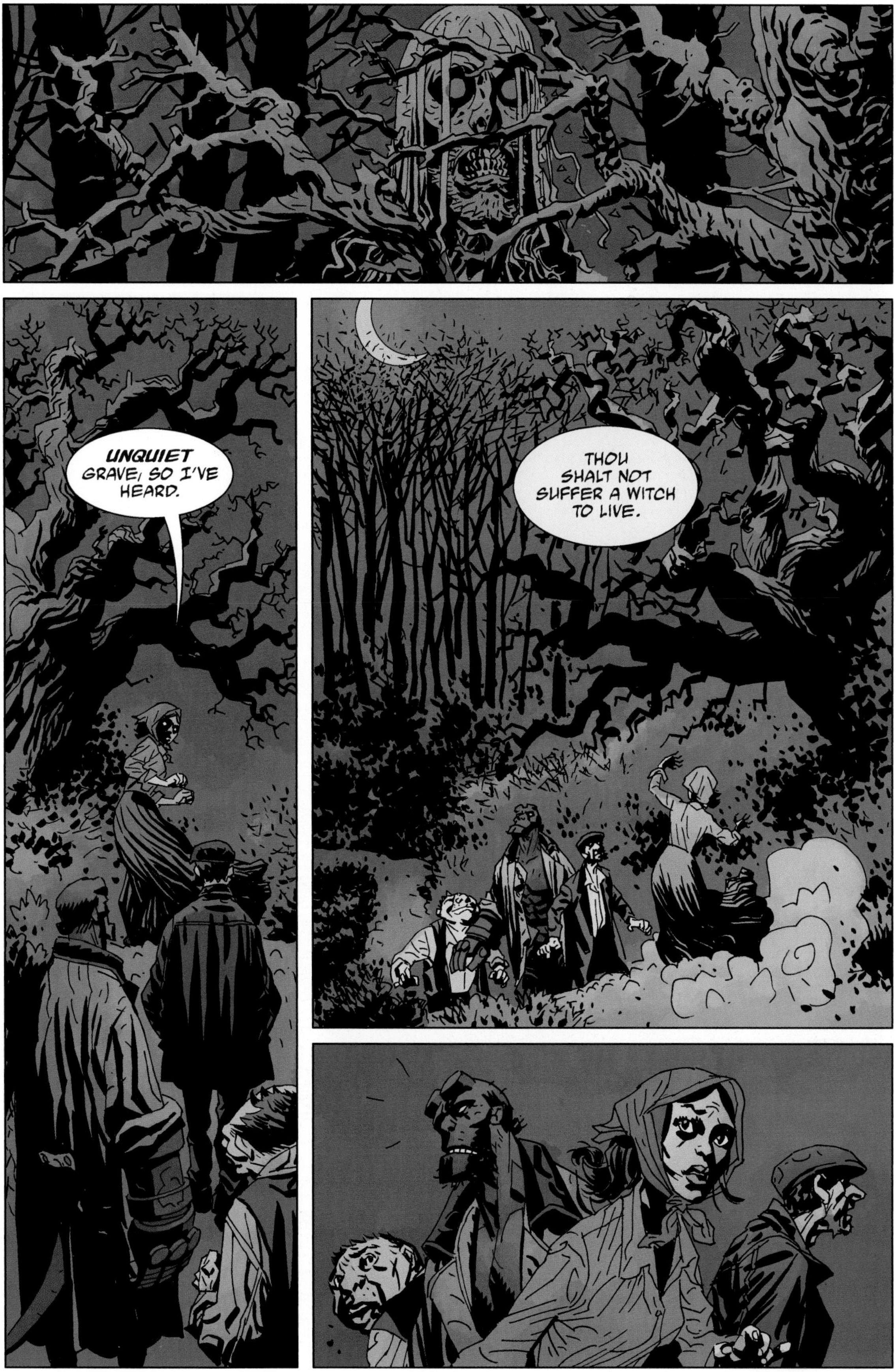
UNQUIET GRAVE, SO I'VE HEARD.
THOU SHALT NOT SUFFER A WITCH TO LIVE.

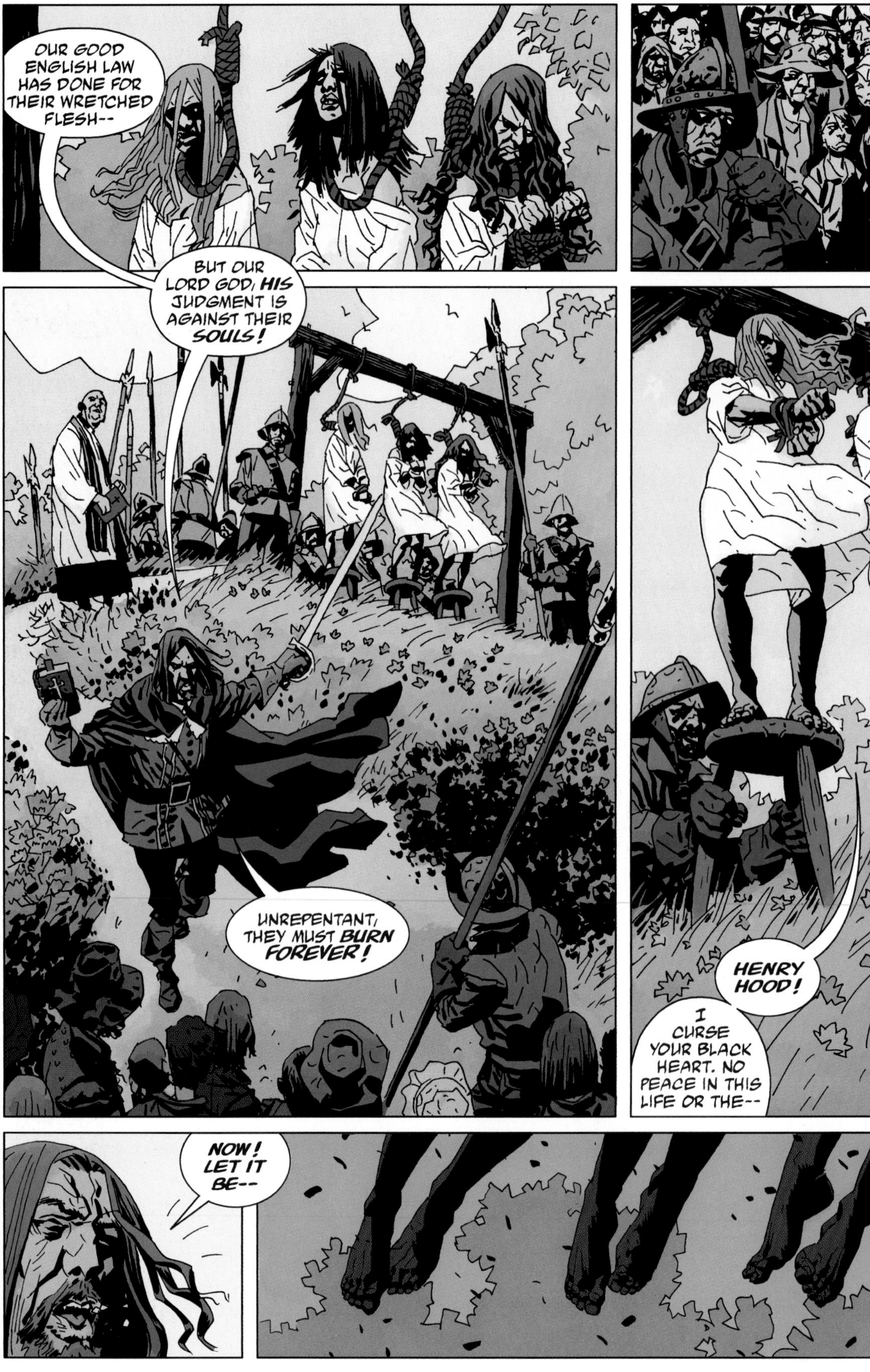
OUR GOOD ENGLISH LAW HAS DONE FOR THEIR WRETCHED FLESH--
BUT OUR LORD GOD, HIS JUDGMENT IS AGAINST THEIR SOULS!
UNREPENTANT, THEY MUST BURN FOREVER!
HENRY HOOD!
I CURSE YOUR BLACK HEART. NO PEACE IN THIS LIFE OR THE--
NOW! LET IT BE--

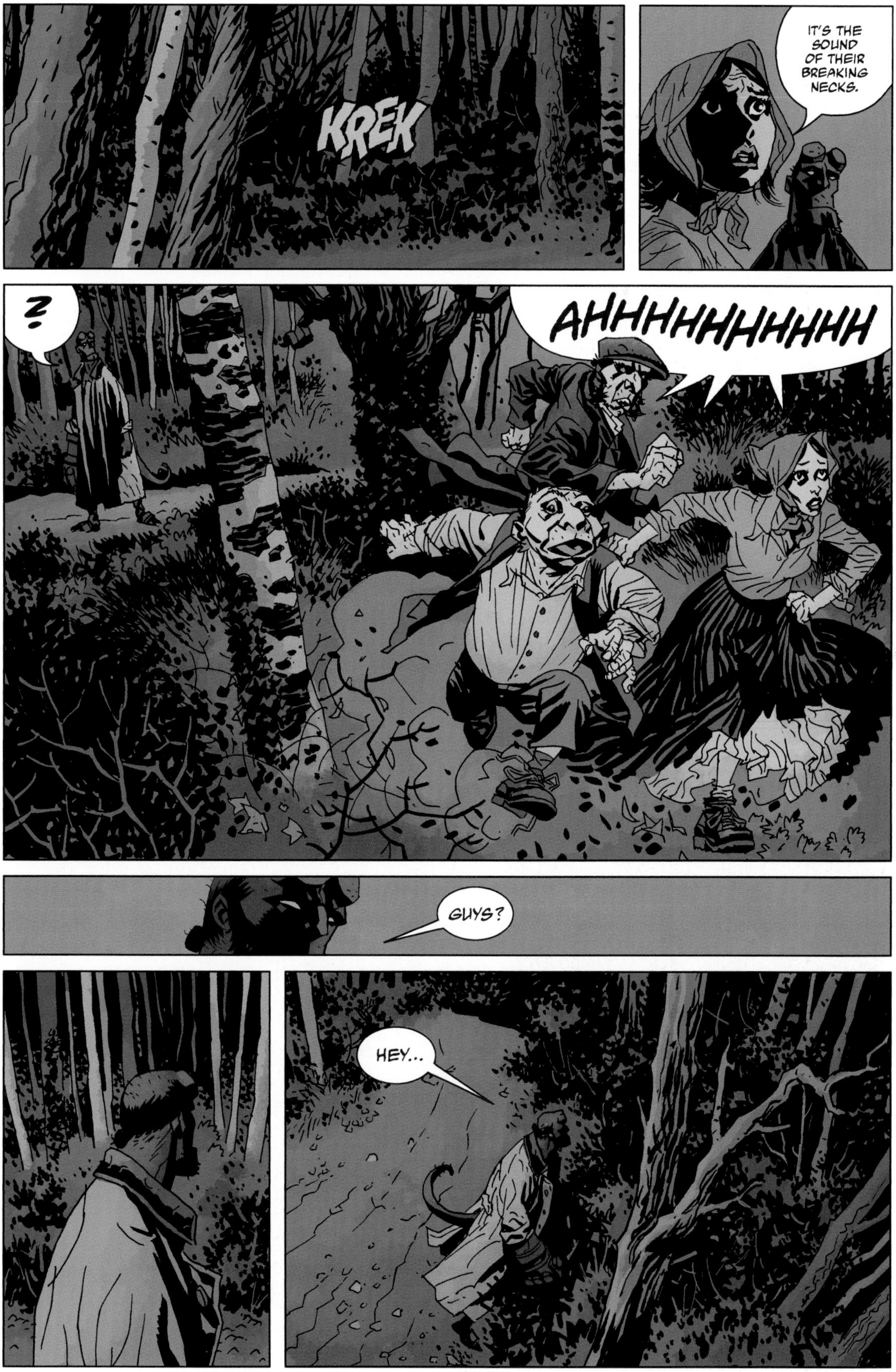
KREK
IT'S THE SOUND OF THEIR BREAKING NECKS.
?
AHHHHHHHHHH
GUYS?
HEY...

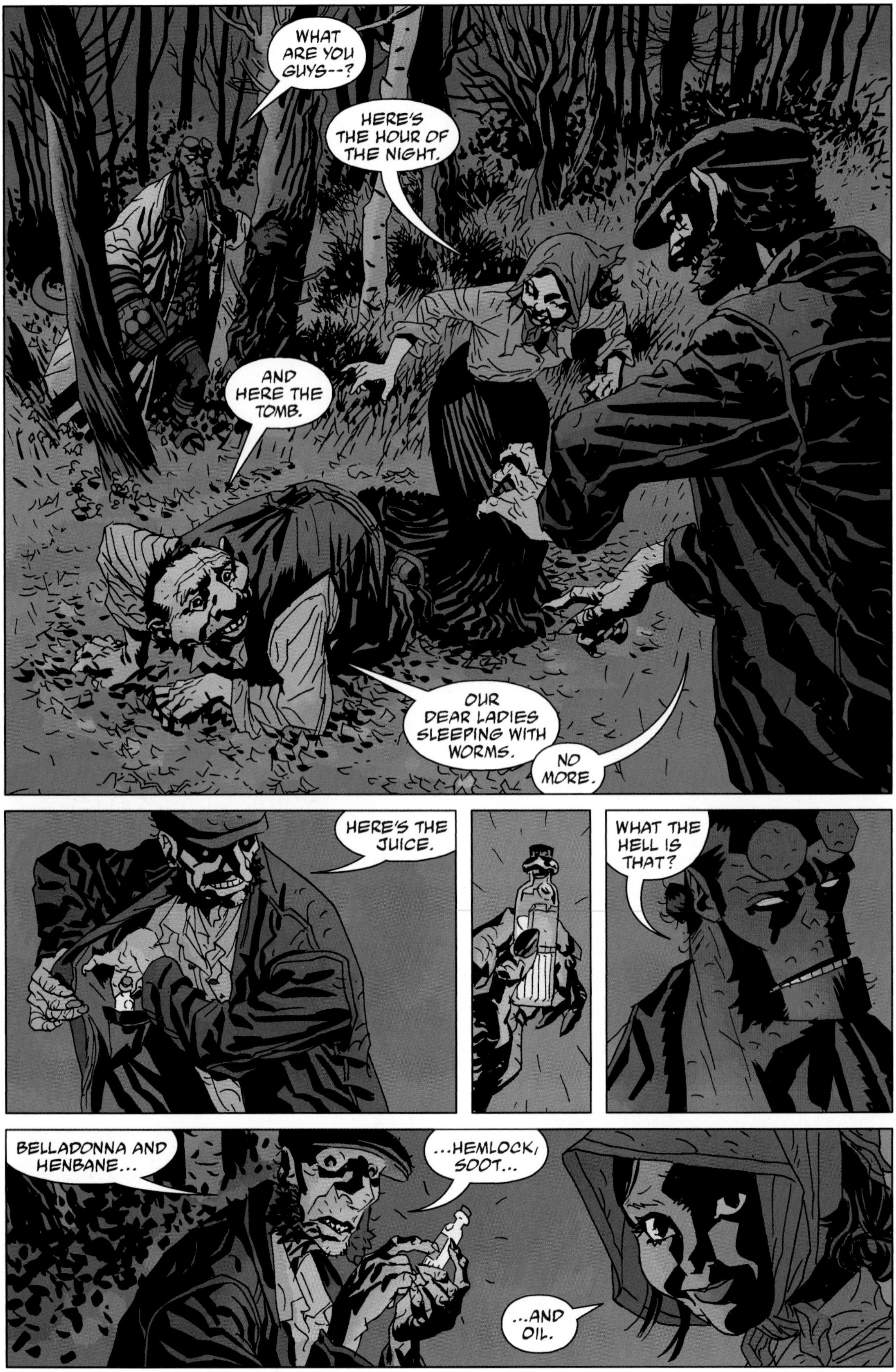
WHAT ARE YOU GUYS--?
HERE'S THE HOUR OF THE NIGHT.
AND HERE THE TOMB.
OUR DEAR LADIES SLEEPING WITH WORMS.
NO MORE.
HERE'S THE JUICE.
WHAT THE HELL IS THAT?
BELLADONNA AND HENBANE...
...HEMLOCK, SOOT...
...AND OIL.

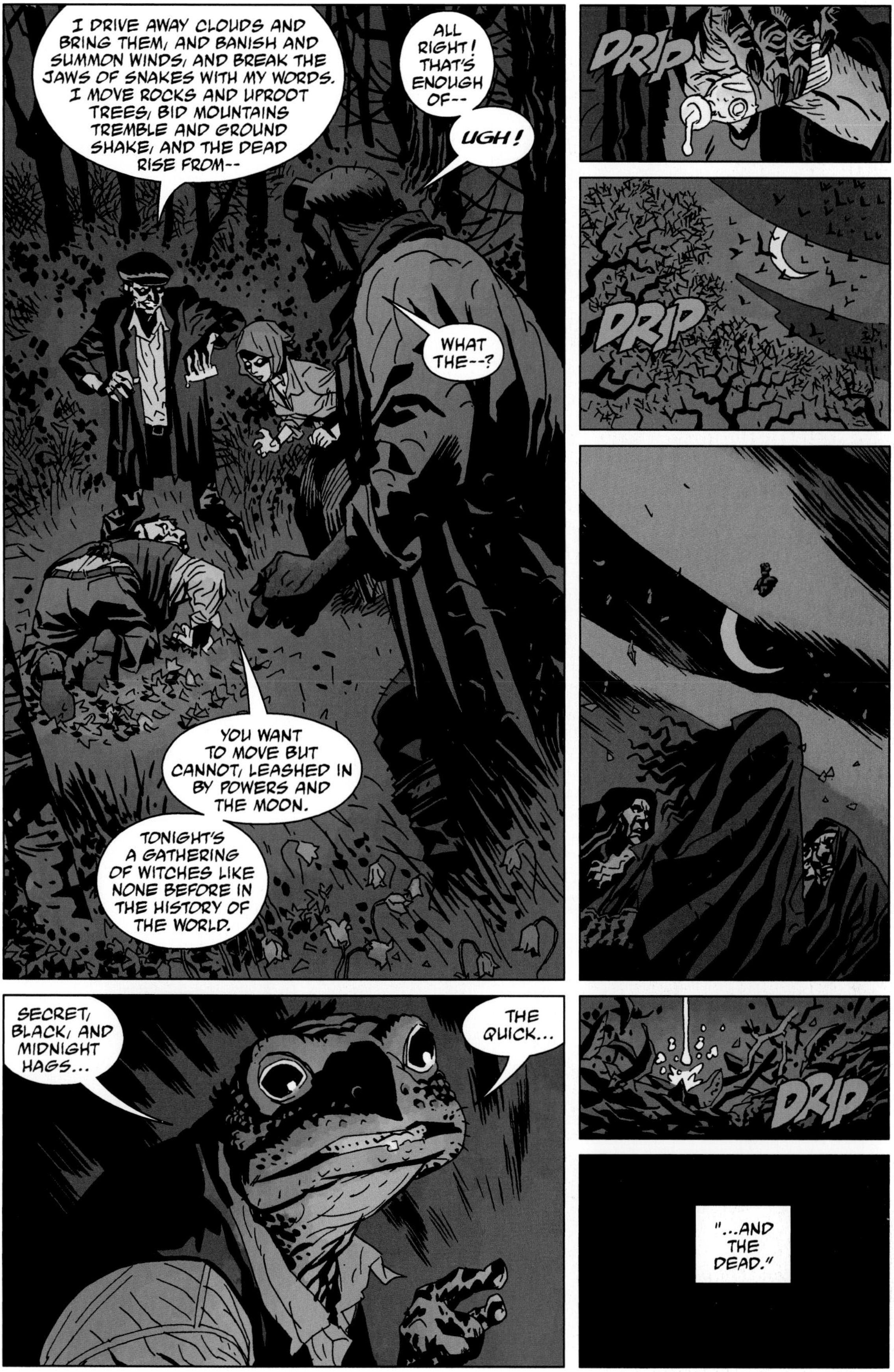
I DRIVE AWAY CLOUDS AND BRING THEM, AND BANISH AND SUMMON WINDS, AND BREAK THE JAWS OF SNAKES WITH MY WORDS. I MOVE ROCKS AND UPROOT TREES, BID MOUNTAINS TREMBLE AND GROUND SHAKE, AND THE DEAD RISE FROM--
ALL RIGHT! THAT'S ENOUGH OF--
UGH!
WHAT THE--?
YOU WANT TO MOVE BUT CANNOT, LEASHED IN BY POWERS AND THE MOON.
TONIGHT'S A GATHERING OF WITCHES LIKE NONE BEFORE IN THE HISTORY OF THE WORLD.
DRIP
DRIP
SECRET, BLACK, AND MIDNIGHT HAGS...
THE QUICK...
DRIP
"...AND THE DEAD."

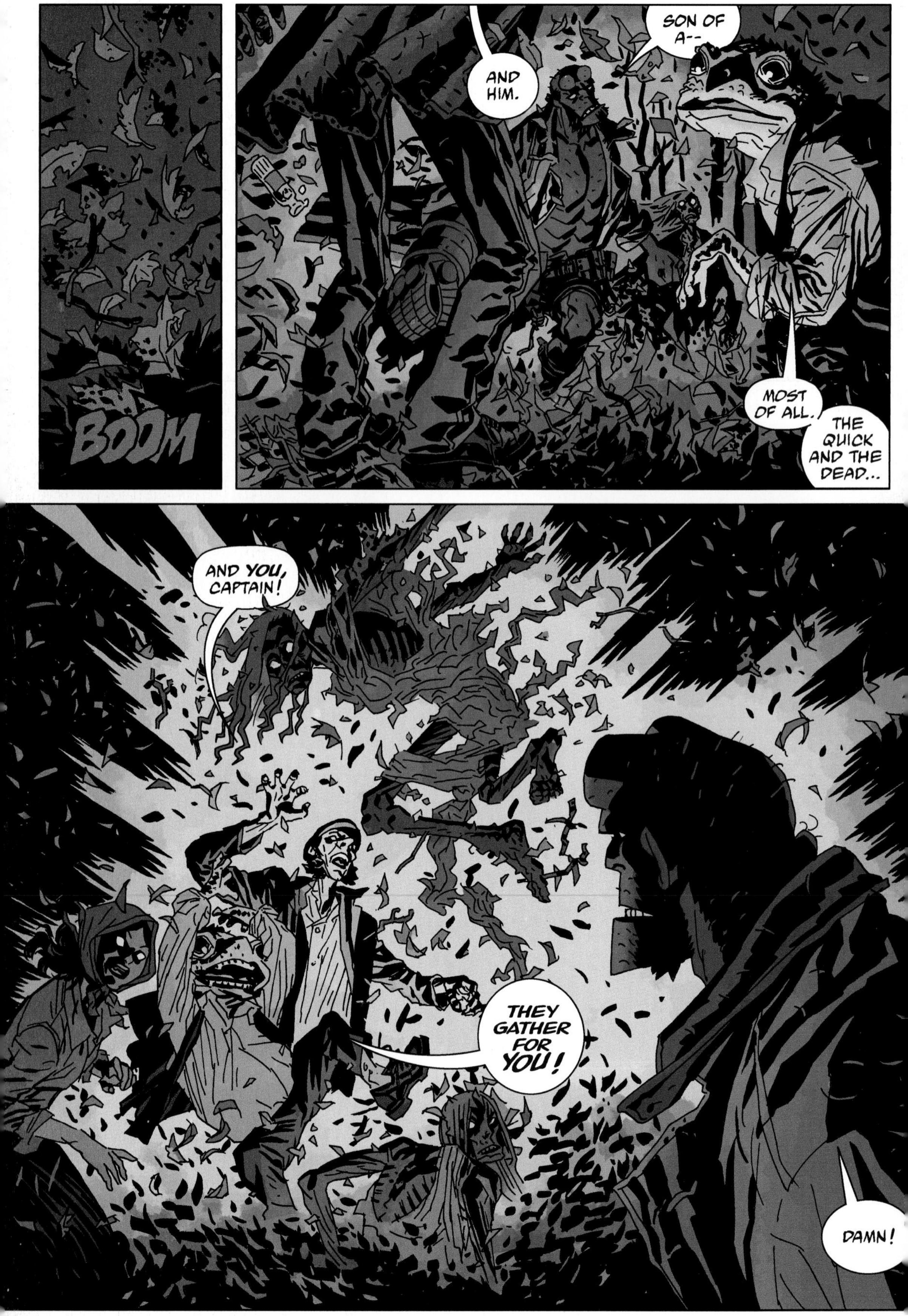
BOOM
AND HIM.
SON OF A--
MOST OF ALL.
THE QUICK AND THE DEAD...
AND YOU, CAPTAIN!
THEY GATHER FOR YOU!
DAMN!

CHAPTER TWO

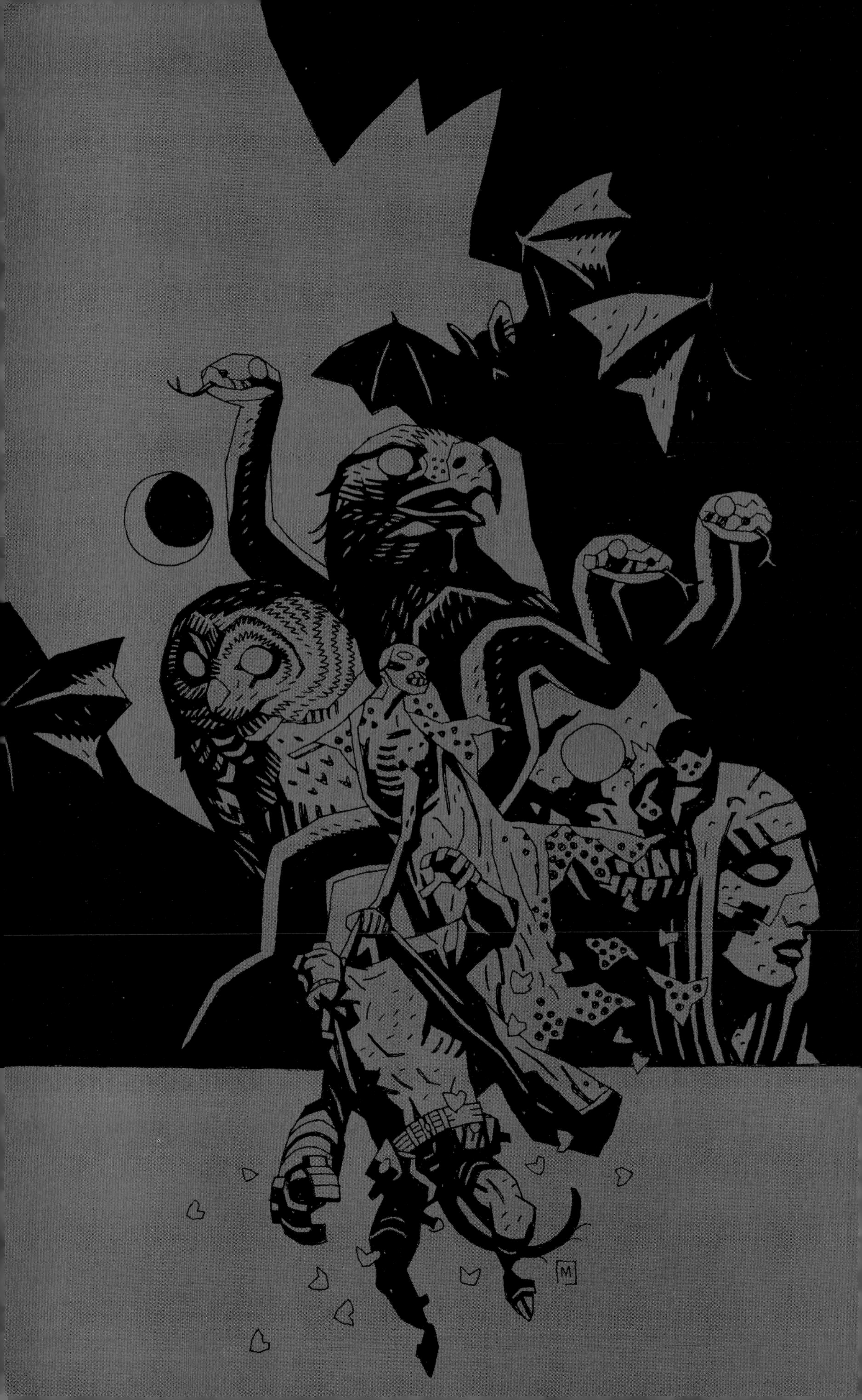

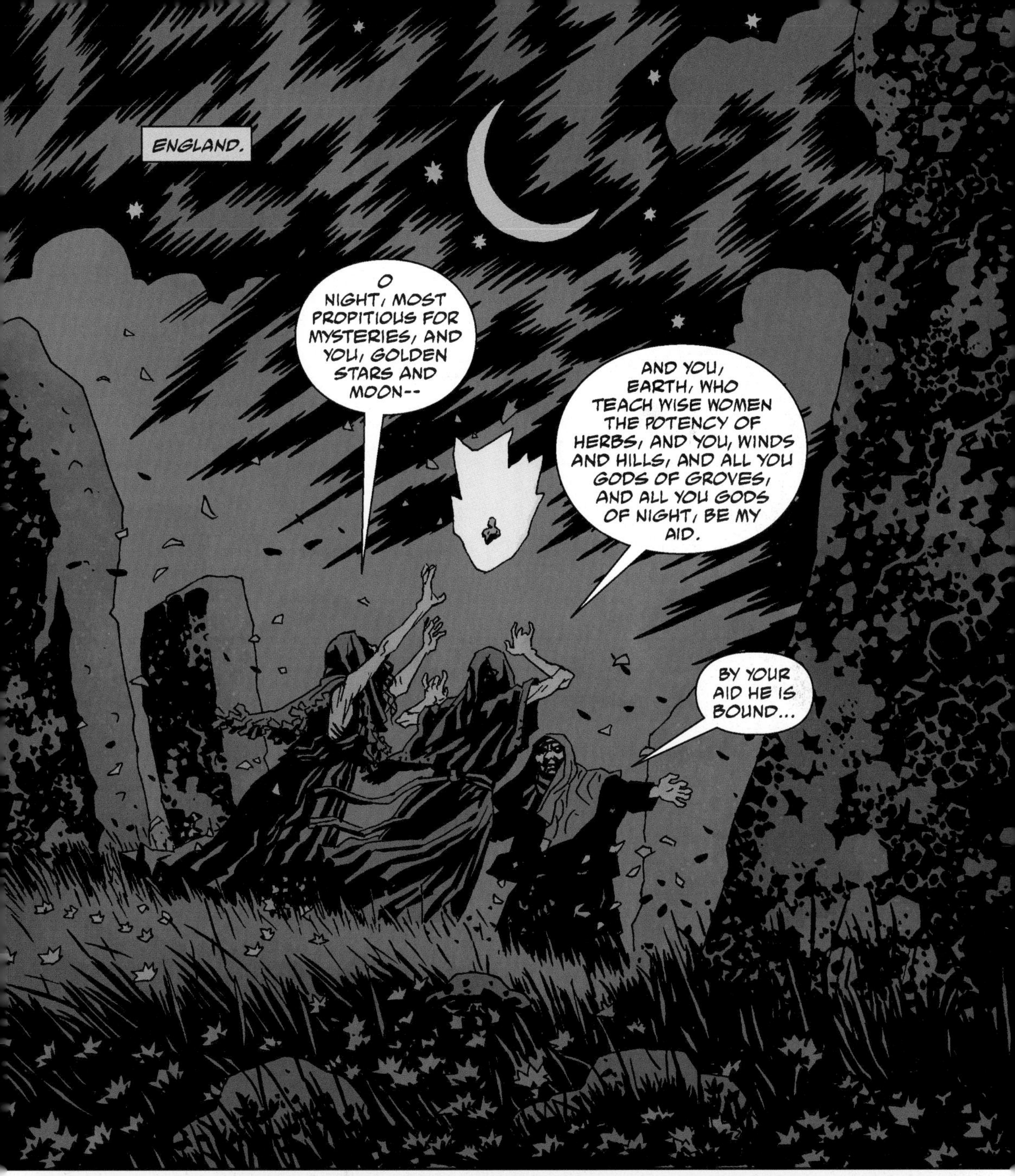
ENGLAND.
O NIGHT, MOST PROPITIOUS FOR MYSTERIES, AND YOU, GOLDEN STARS AND MOON--
AND YOU, EARTH, WHO TEACH WISE WOMEN THE POTENCY OF HERBS, AND YOU, WINDS AND HILLS, AND ALL YOU GODS OF GROVES, AND ALL YOU GODS OF NIGHT, BE MY AID.
BY YOUR AID HE IS BOUND...

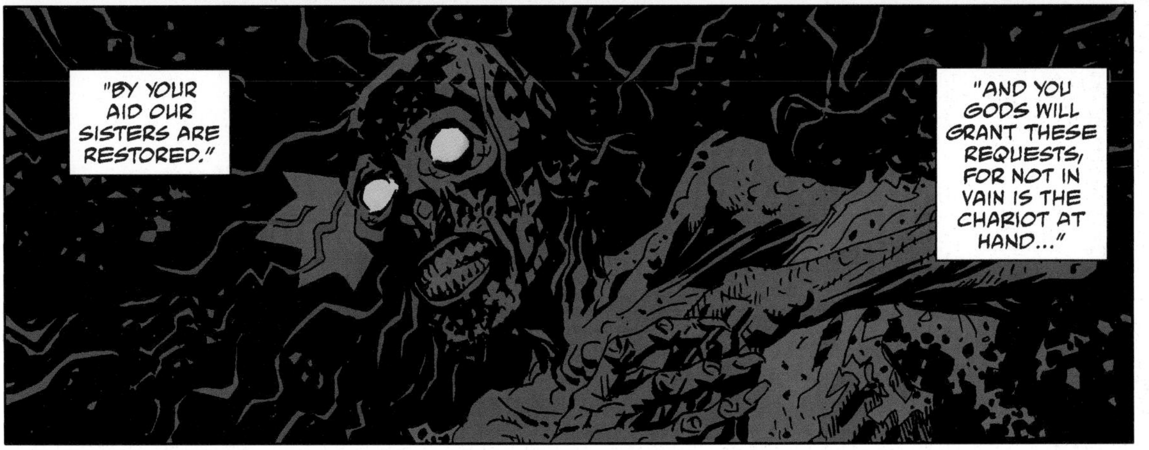
"BY YOUR AID OUR SISTERS ARE RESTORED."
"AND YOU GODS WILL GRANT THESE REQUESTS, FOR NOT IN VAIN IS THE CHARIOT AT HAND..."

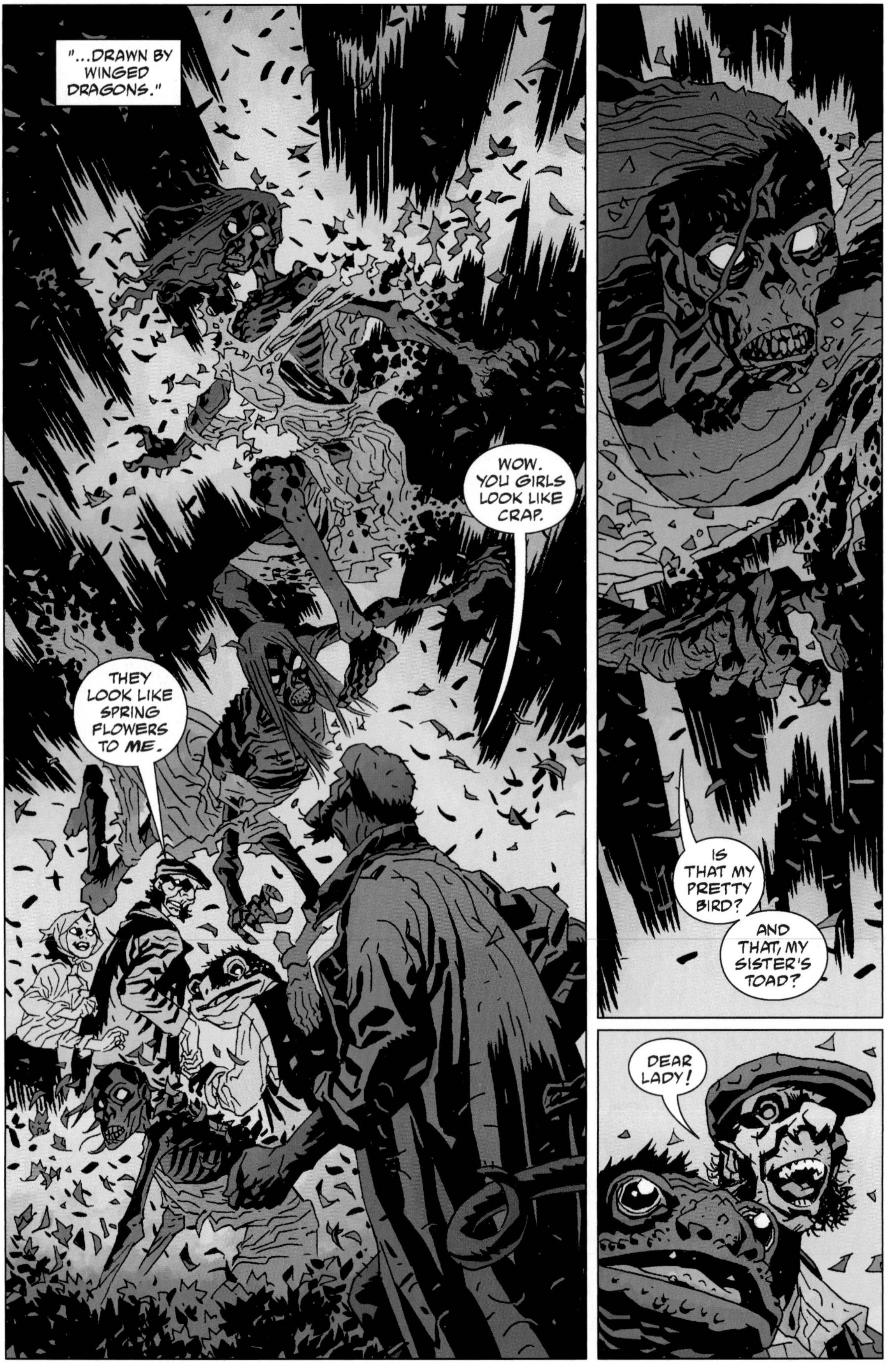
"...DRAWN BY WINGED DRAGONS."
WOW. YOU GIRLS LOOK LIKE CRAP.
THEY LOOK LIKE SPRING FLOWERS TO ME.
IS THAT MY PRETTY BIRD?
AND THAT, MY SISTER'S TOAD?
DEAR LADY!

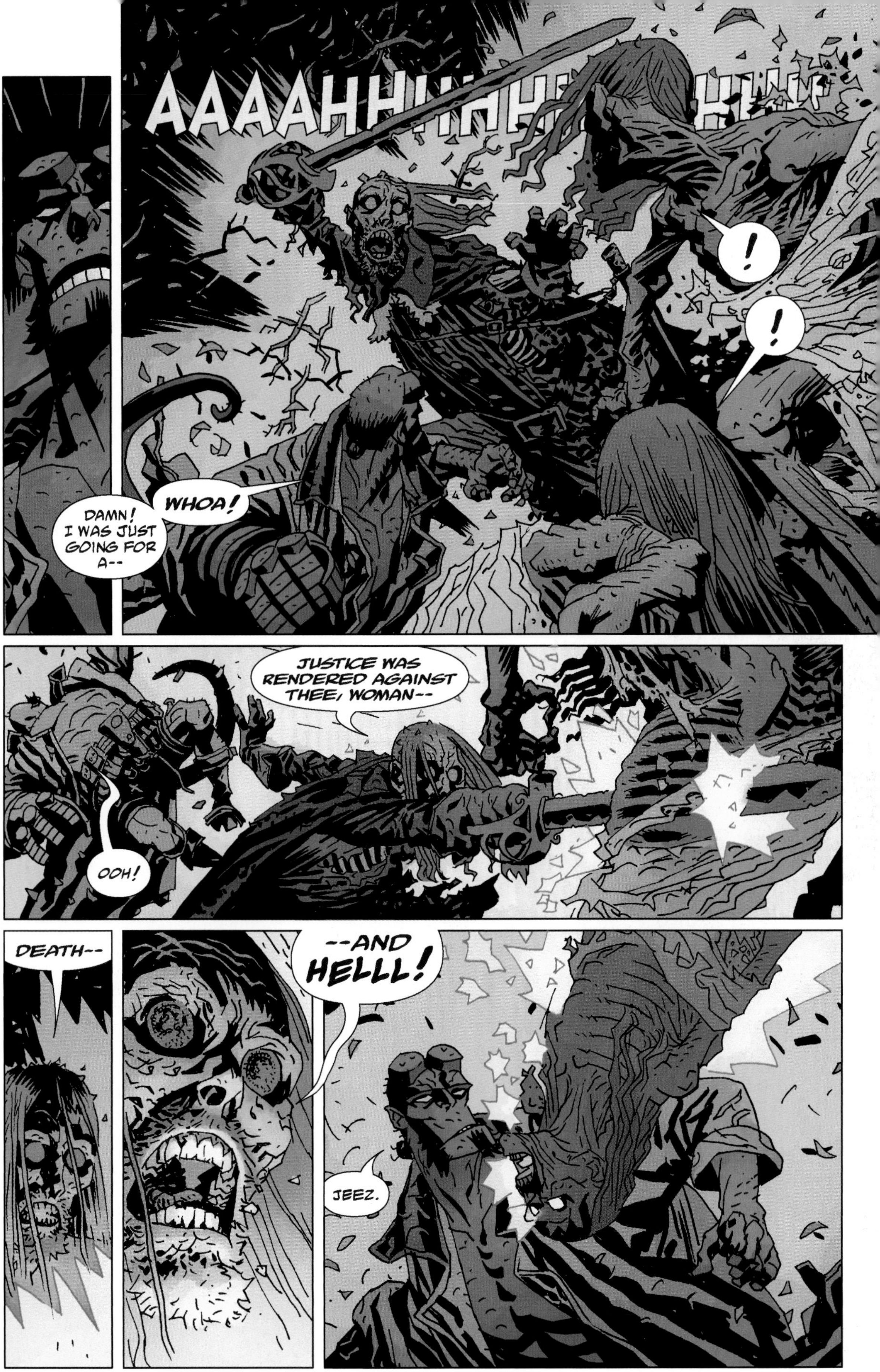
AAAAHHHHHHHHHHH
!
!
WHOA!
DAMN! I WAS JUST GOING FOR A--
JUSTICE WAS RENDERED AGAINST THEE, WOMAN--
OOH!
DEATH--
--AND HELLL!
JEEZ.

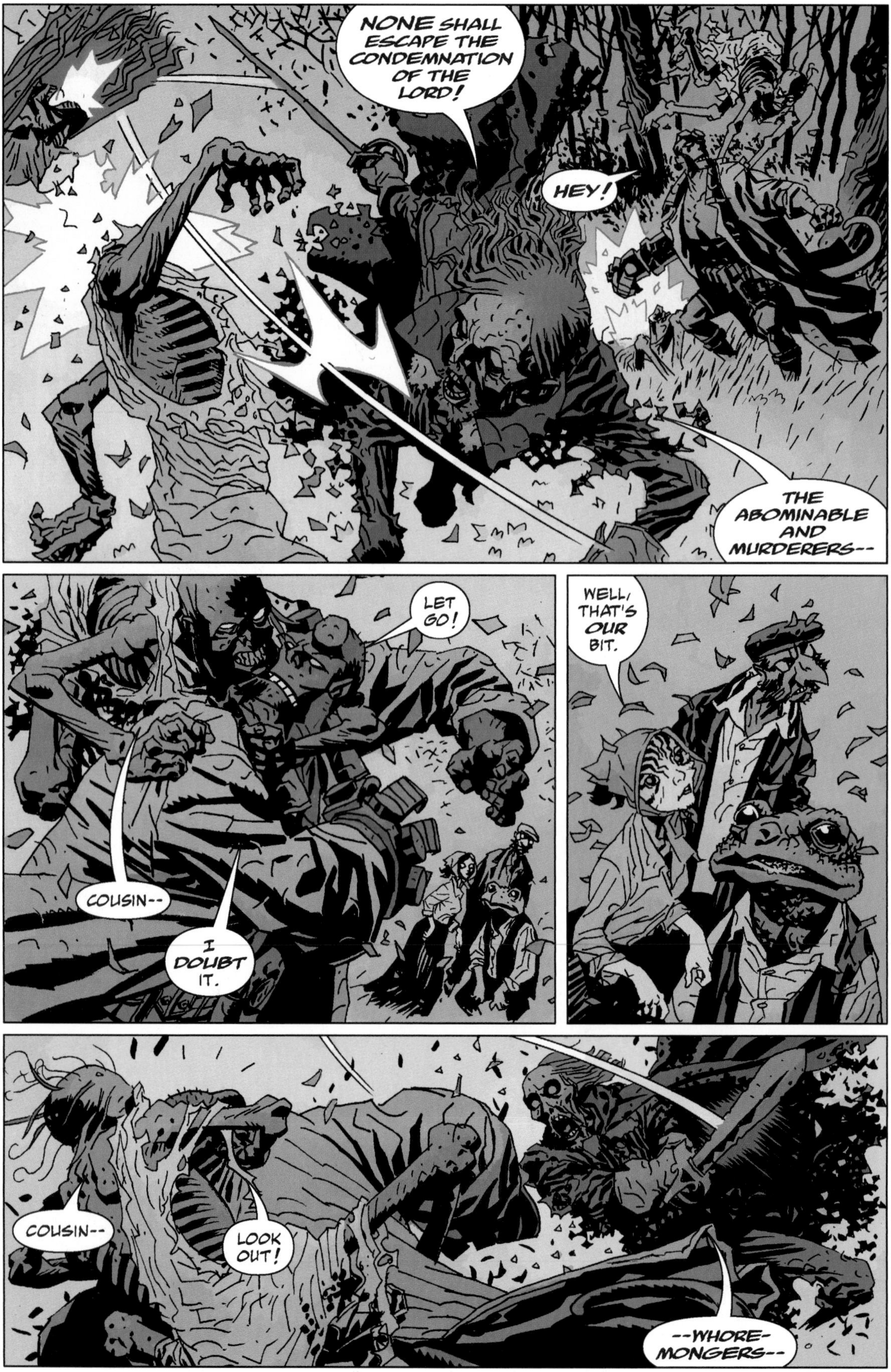
NONE SHALL ESCAPE THE CONDEMNATION OF THE LORD!
HEY!
THE ABOMINABLE AND MURDERERS--
LET GO!
COUSIN--
I DOUBT IT.
WELL, THAT'S OUR BIT.
COUSIN--
LOOK OUT!
--WHORE-MONGERS--

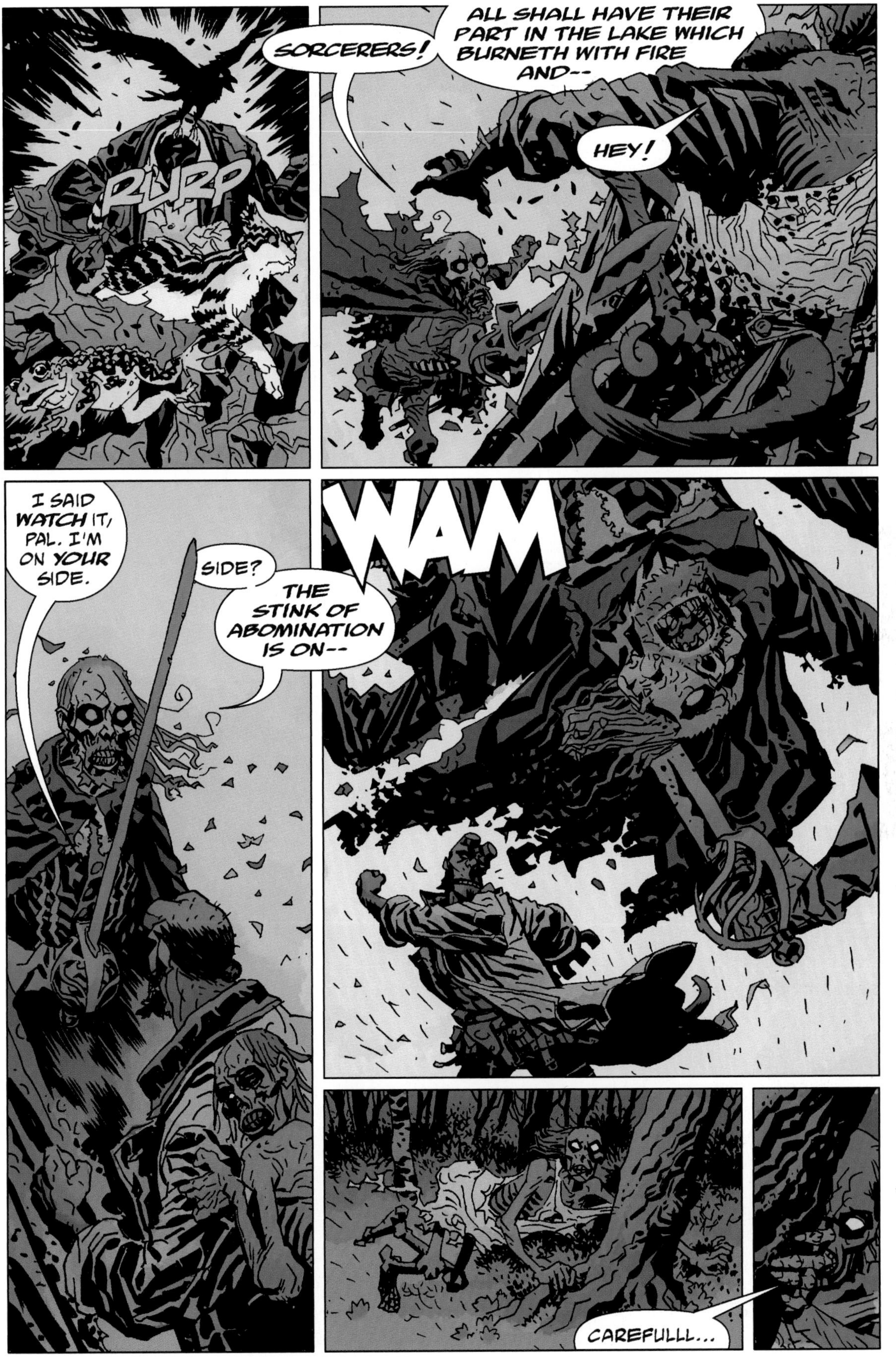
RURP
SORCERERS!
ALL SHALL HAVE THEIR PART IN THE LAKE WHICH BURNETH WITH FIRE AND--
HEY!
I SAID WATCH IT, PAL. I'M ON YOUR SIDE.
SIDE?
THE STINK OF ABOMINATION IS ON--
WAM
CAREFULLL...

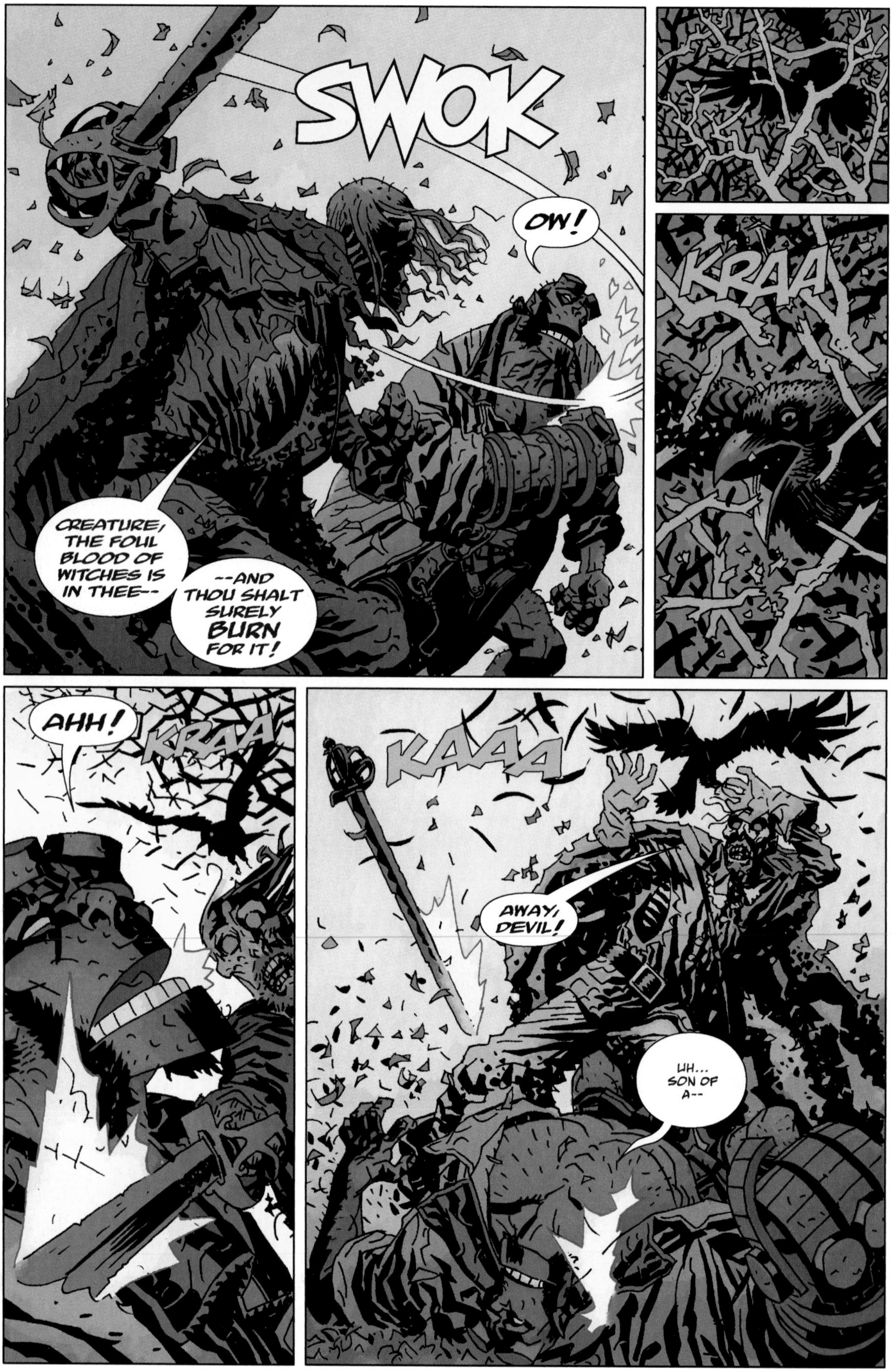

SWOK
OW!
CREATURE, THE FOUL BLOOD OF WITCHES IS IN THEE--
--AND THOU SHALT SURELY BURN FOR IT!
KRAA
AHH!
KRAA
KAAA
AWAY, DEVIL!
UH... SON OF A--

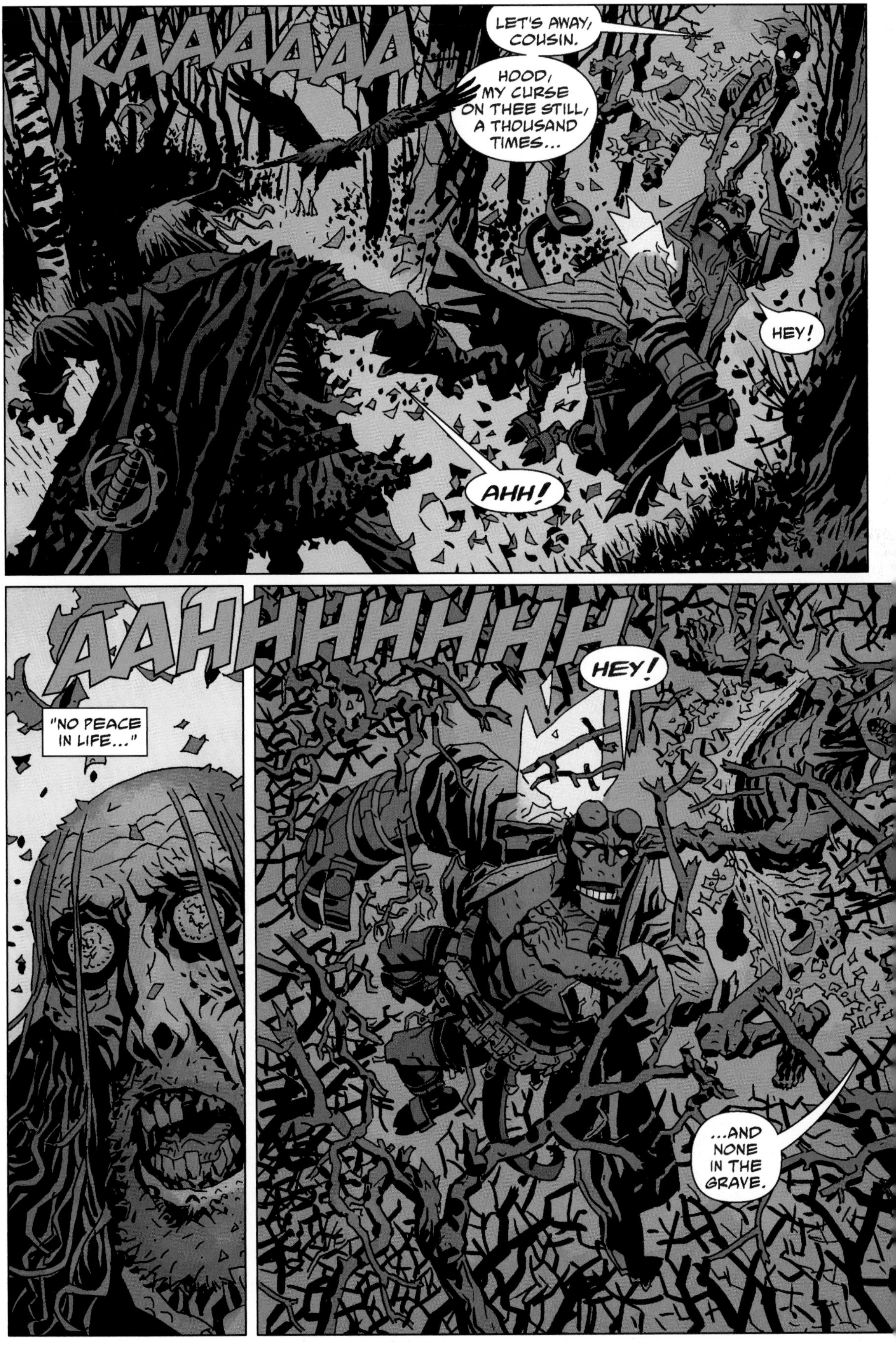
KAAAAAA
LET'S AWAY, COUSIN.
HOOD, MY CURSE ON THEE STILL, A THOUSAND TIMES...
HEY!
AHH!
AAHHHHHHH
"NO PEACE IN LIFE..."
HEY!
...AND NONE IN THE GRAVE.

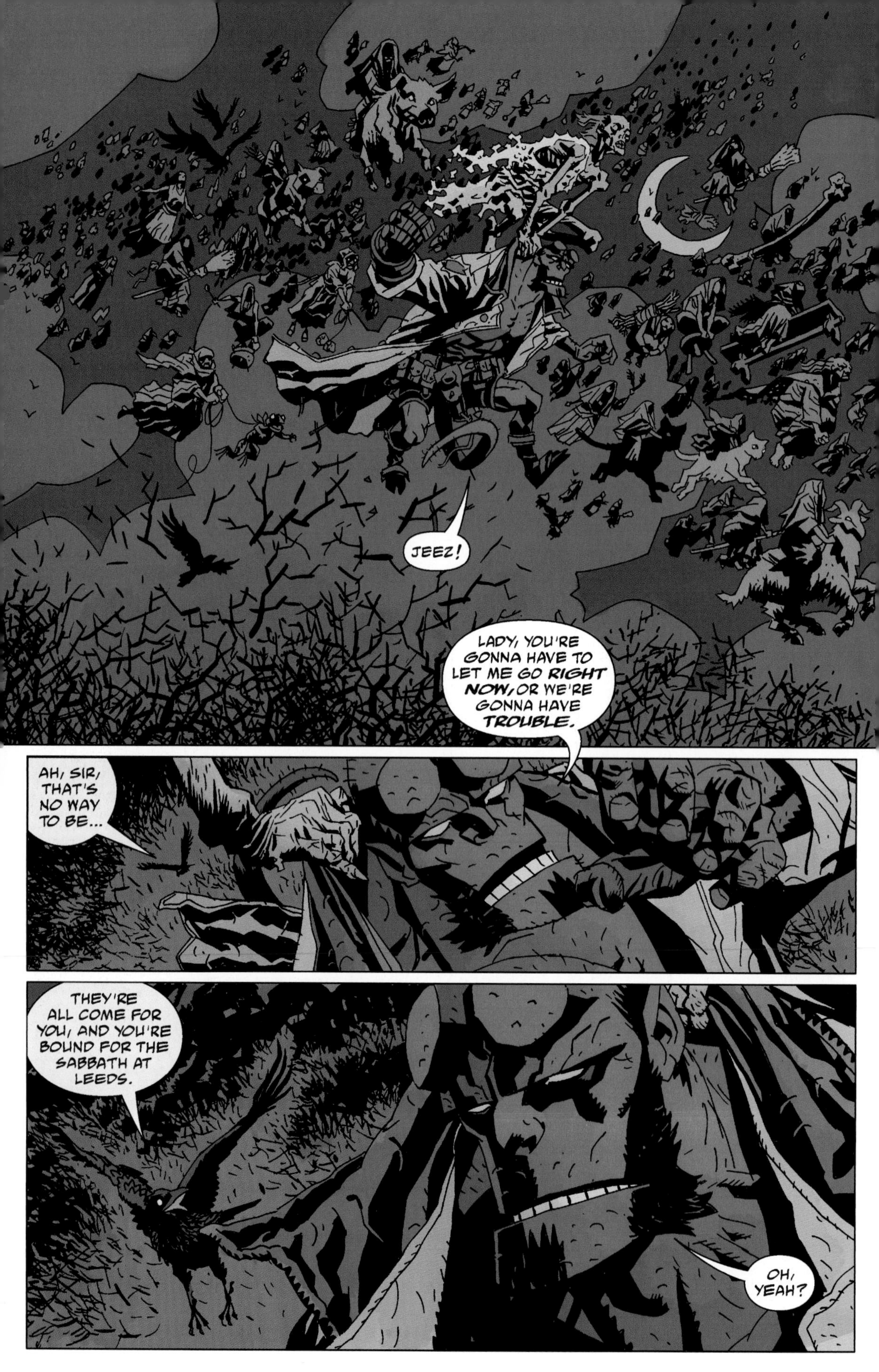
JEEZ!
LADY, YOU'RE GONNA HAVE TO LET ME GO RIGHT NOW, OR WE'RE GONNA HAVE TROUBLE.
AH, SIR, THAT'S NO WAY TO BE...
THEY'RE ALL COME FOR YOU, AND YOU'RE BOUND FOR THE SABBATH AT LEEDS.
OH, YEAH?

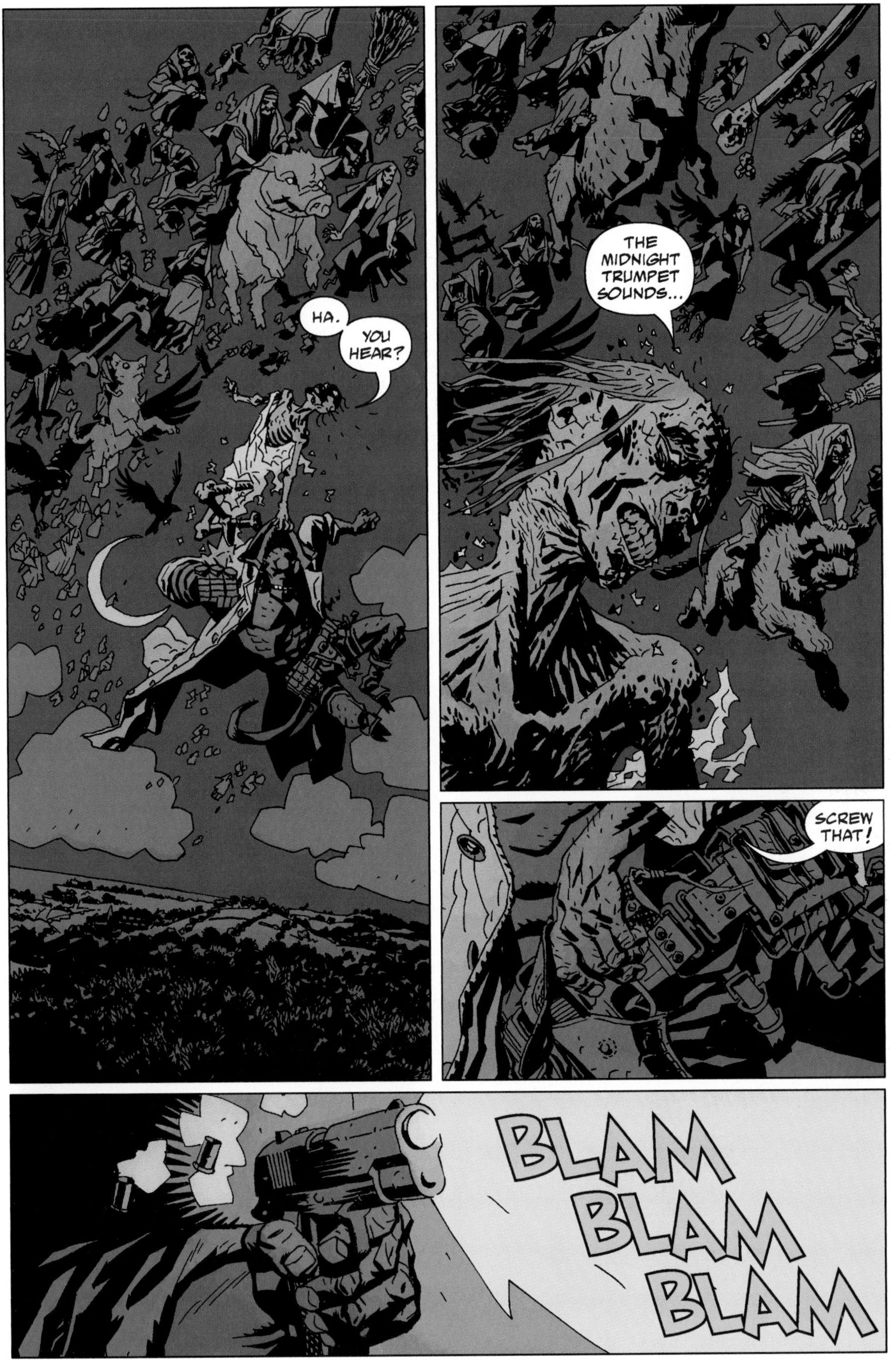
HA.
YOU HEAR?
THE MIDNIGHT TRUMPET SOUNDS...
SCREW THAT!
BLAM
BLAM
BLAM

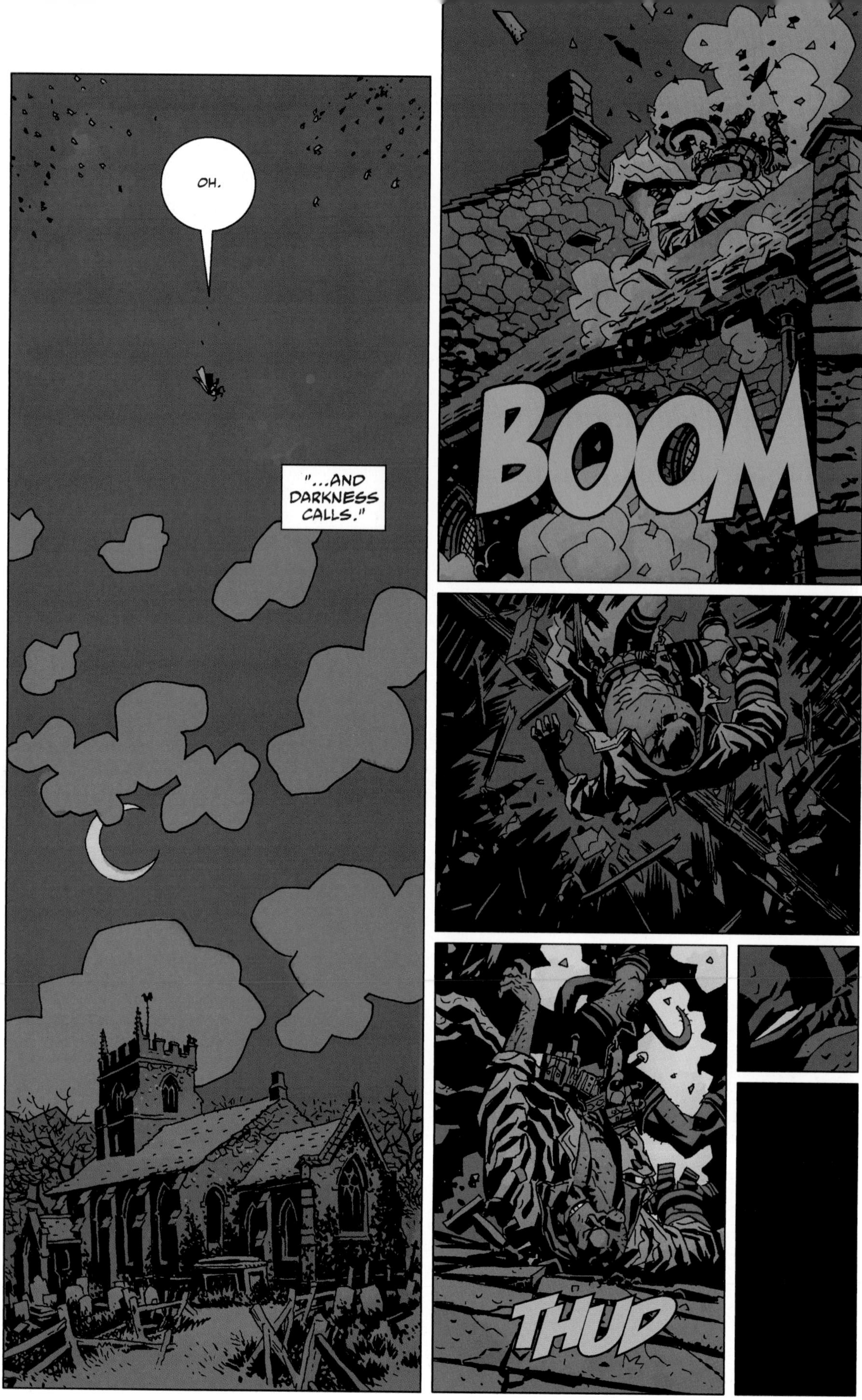
OH.
"...AND DARKNESS CALLS."
BOOM
THUD

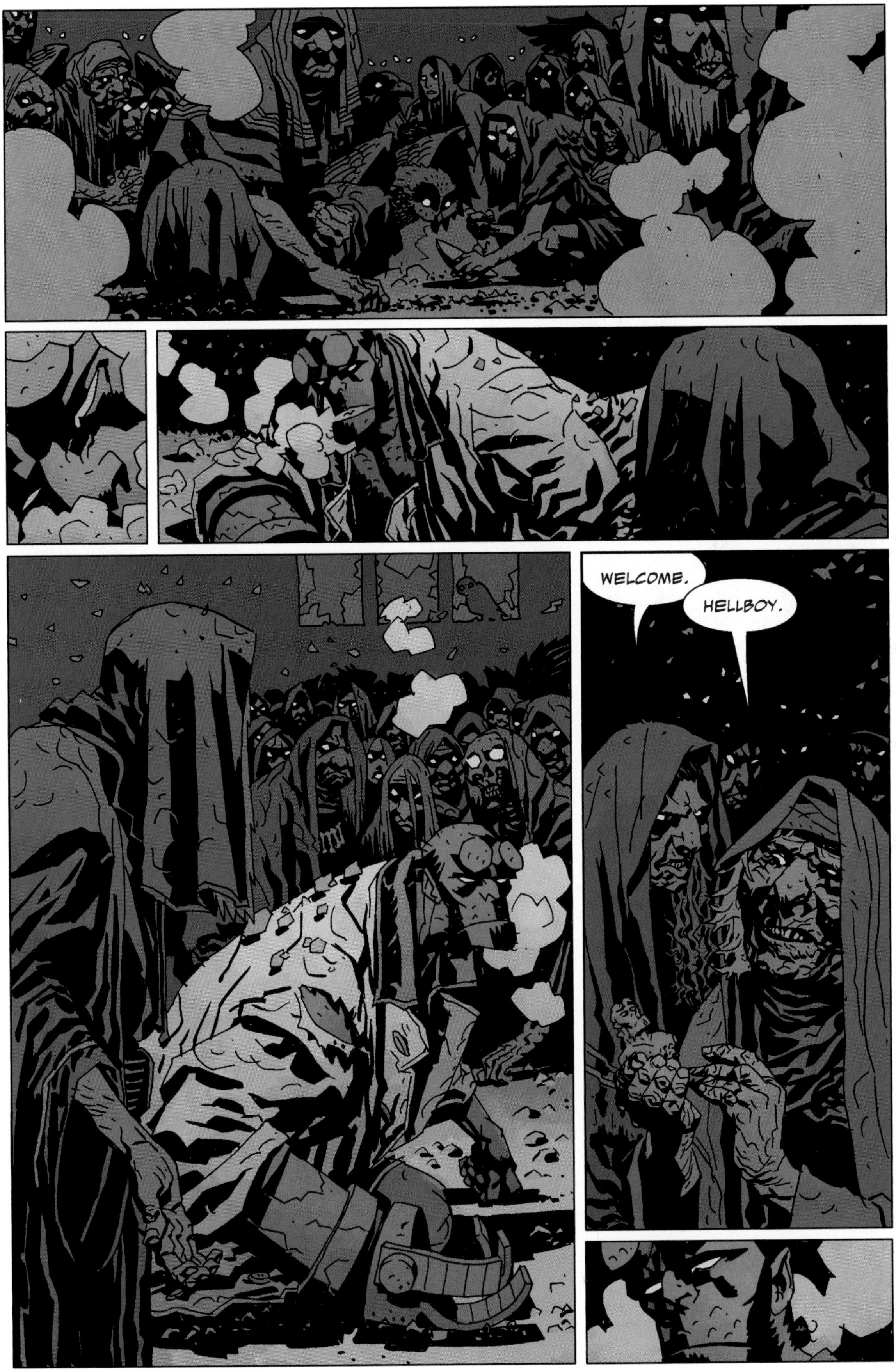
WELCOME.
HELLBOY.

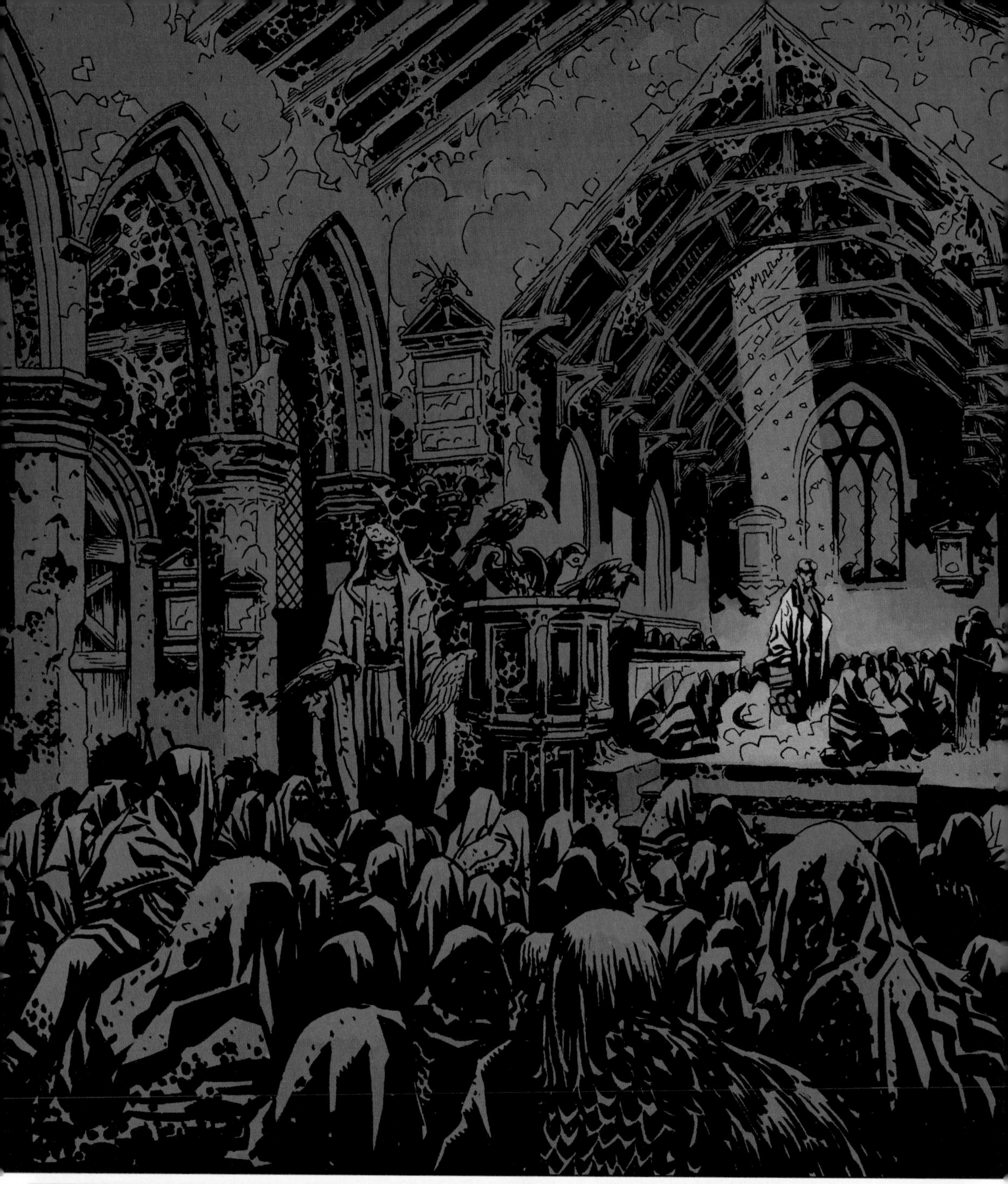

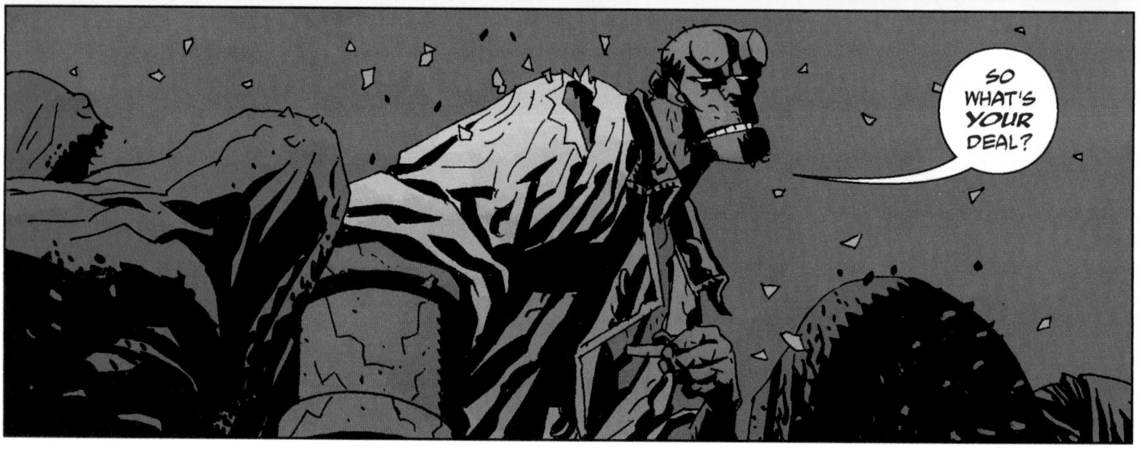
SO WHAT'S YOUR DEAL?

IGOR BROMHEAD.

LITTLE GUY. ROUND HEAD. WEIRD MUSTACHE.

HE ESCAPED FROM YOU.*

SO?

AND HE HAS BEEN HIDING IN A TOMB NEAR LUCCA.

"SO?"

"WITH THE BONES OF VLADIMIR GIURESCU."

YOU REMEMBER GIURESCU.

BROMHEAD'S WRUNG FROM THOSE BONES, BY NECROMANTIC ART, ALL THAT TRANSPIRED AT CASTLE GIURESCU...

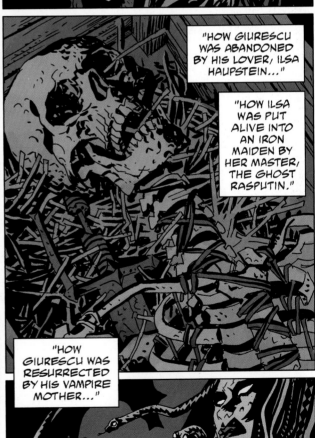

"HOW GIURESCU WAS ABANDONED BY HIS LOVER, ILSA HAUPSTEIN..."

"HOW ILSA WAS PUT ALIVE INTO AN IRON MAIDEN BY HER MASTER, THE GHOST RASPUTIN."

"HOW GIURESCU WAS RESURRECTED BY HIS VAMPIRE MOTHER..."

*HELLBOY: BOX FULL OF EVIL.

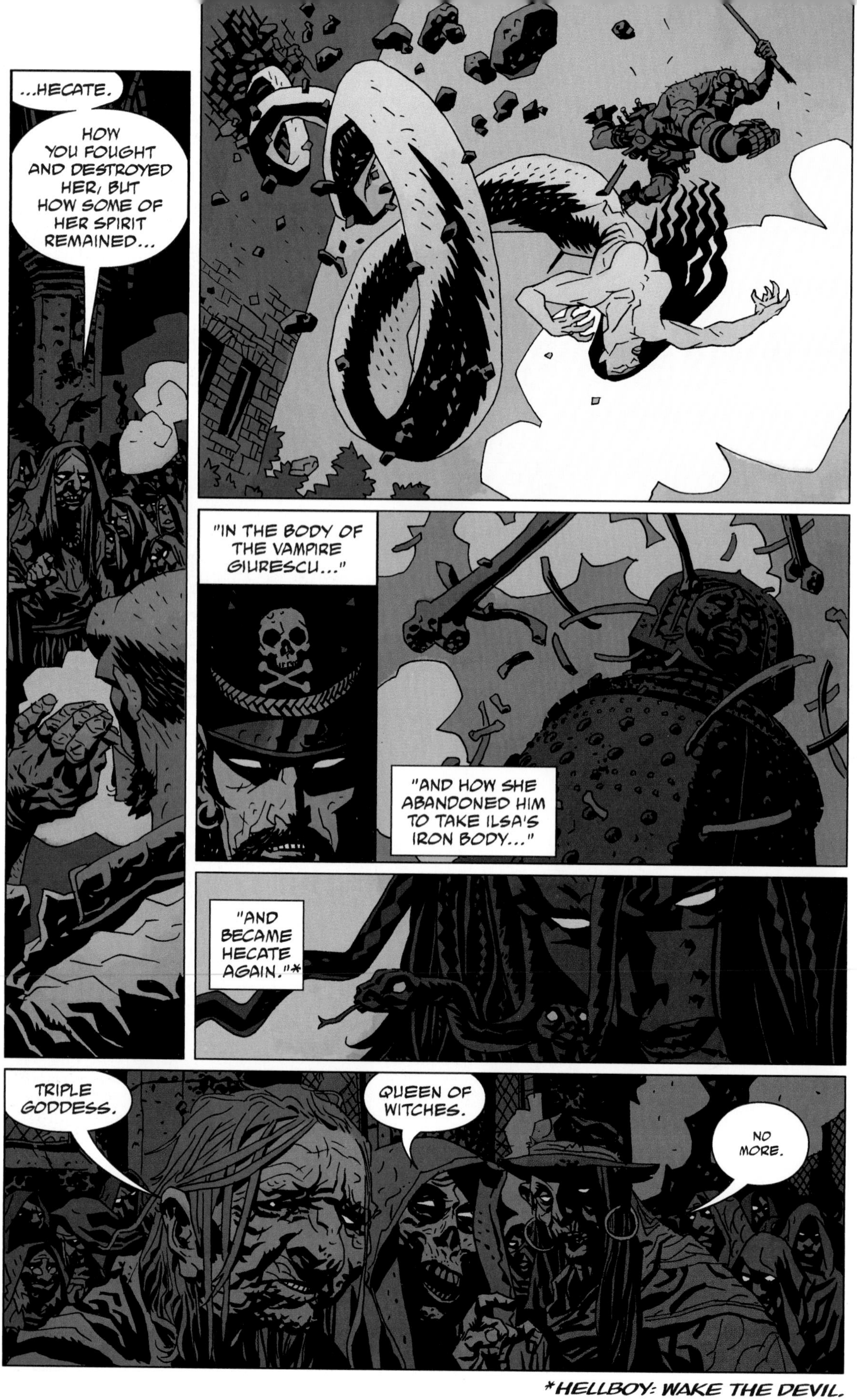
...HECATE.
HOW YOU FOUGHT AND DESTROYED HER, BUT HOW SOME OF HER SPIRIT REMAINED...
"IN THE BODY OF THE VAMPIRE GIURESCU..."
"AND HOW SHE ABANDONED HIM TO TAKE ILSA'S IRON BODY..."
"AND BECAME HECATE AGAIN."*
TRIPLE GODDESS.
QUEEN OF WITCHES.
NO MORE.

*HELLBOY: WAKE THE DEVIL.

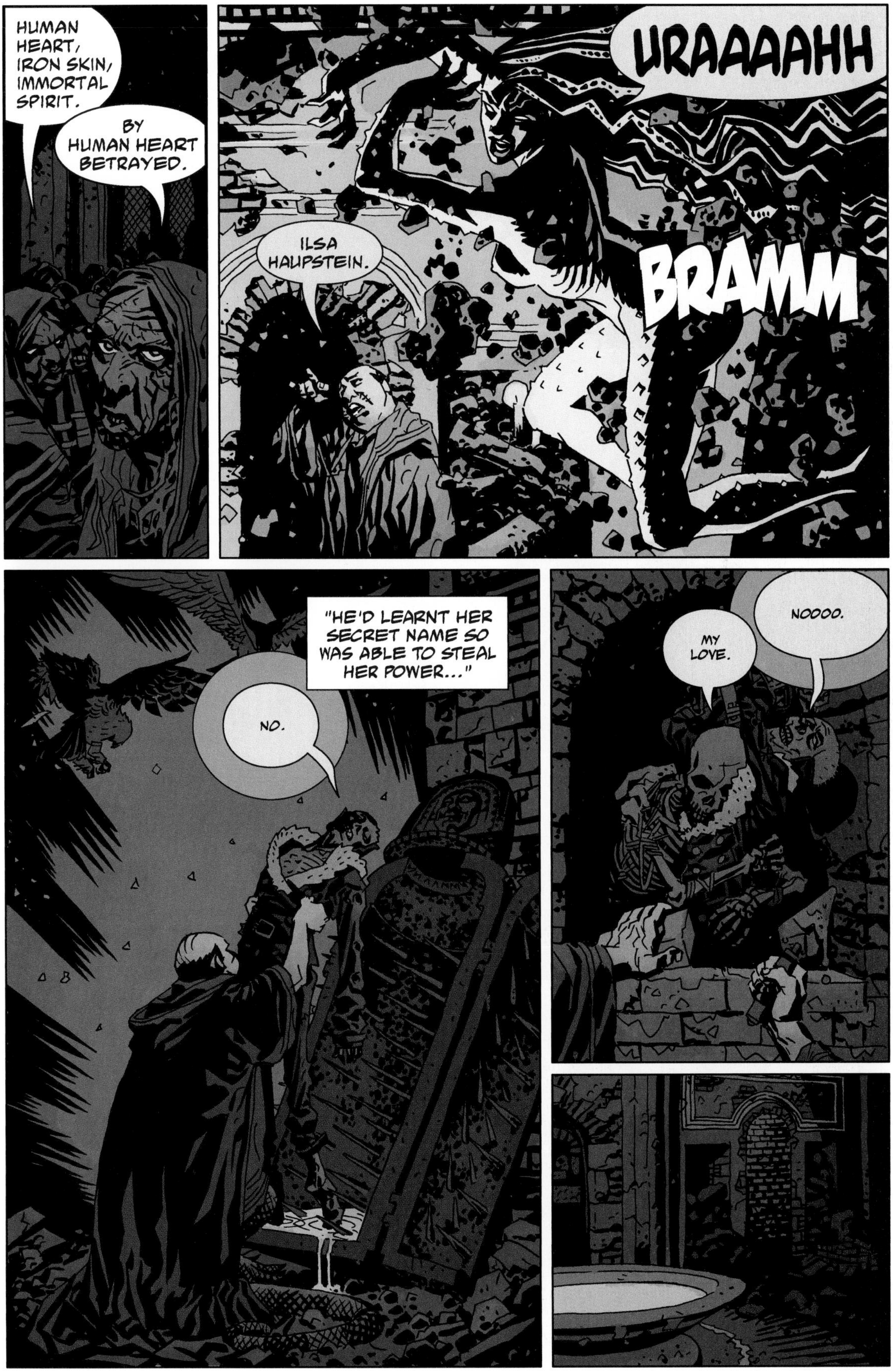
HUMAN HEART, IRON SKIN, IMMORTAL SPIRIT.
BY HUMAN HEART BETRAYED.
URAAAAHH
ILSA HAUPSTEIN.
BRAMM
"HE'D LEARNT HER SECRET NAME SO WAS ABLE TO STEAL HER POWER..."
NO.
MY LOVE.
NOOOO.

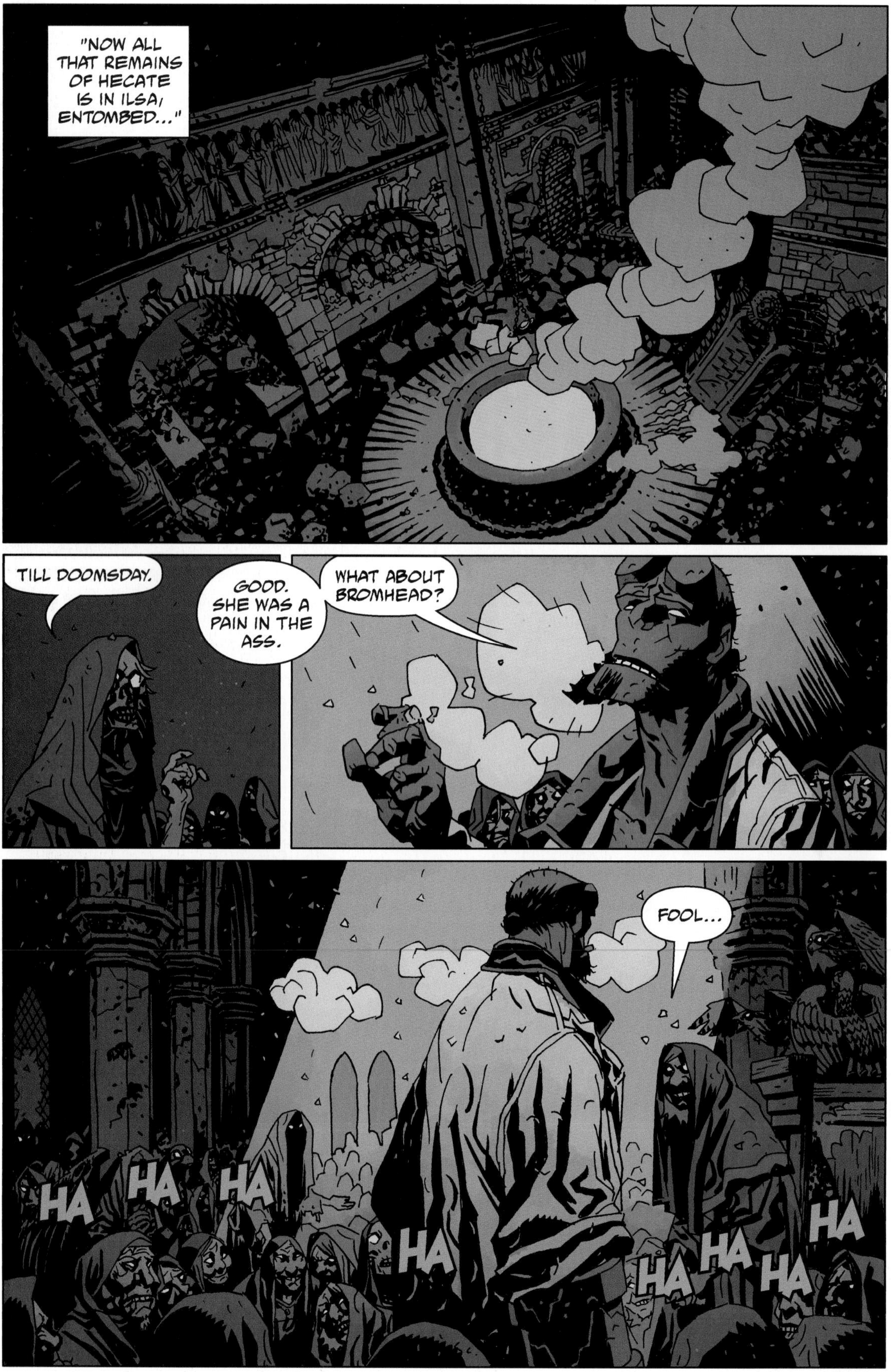
"NOW ALL THAT REMAINS OF HECATE IS IN ILSA, ENTOMBED..."
TILL DOOMSDAY.
GOOD. SHE WAS A PAIN IN THE ASS.
WHAT ABOUT BROMHEAD?
FOOL...
HA HA HA
HA
HA HA HA HA

ECCO AMMUNI HAMMA!

"HE TRIED TO MAKE HIMSELF KING."

NOTHING. I CALL, BUT THE WITCHES DON'T ANSWER.

DO NOT GIVE UP.

THE MOON! YOUR STRENGTH IS IN THE MOON!

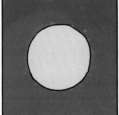

YES! YES!

CALL DOWN THE MOON!

ECCO AMMUN--

AHHHH

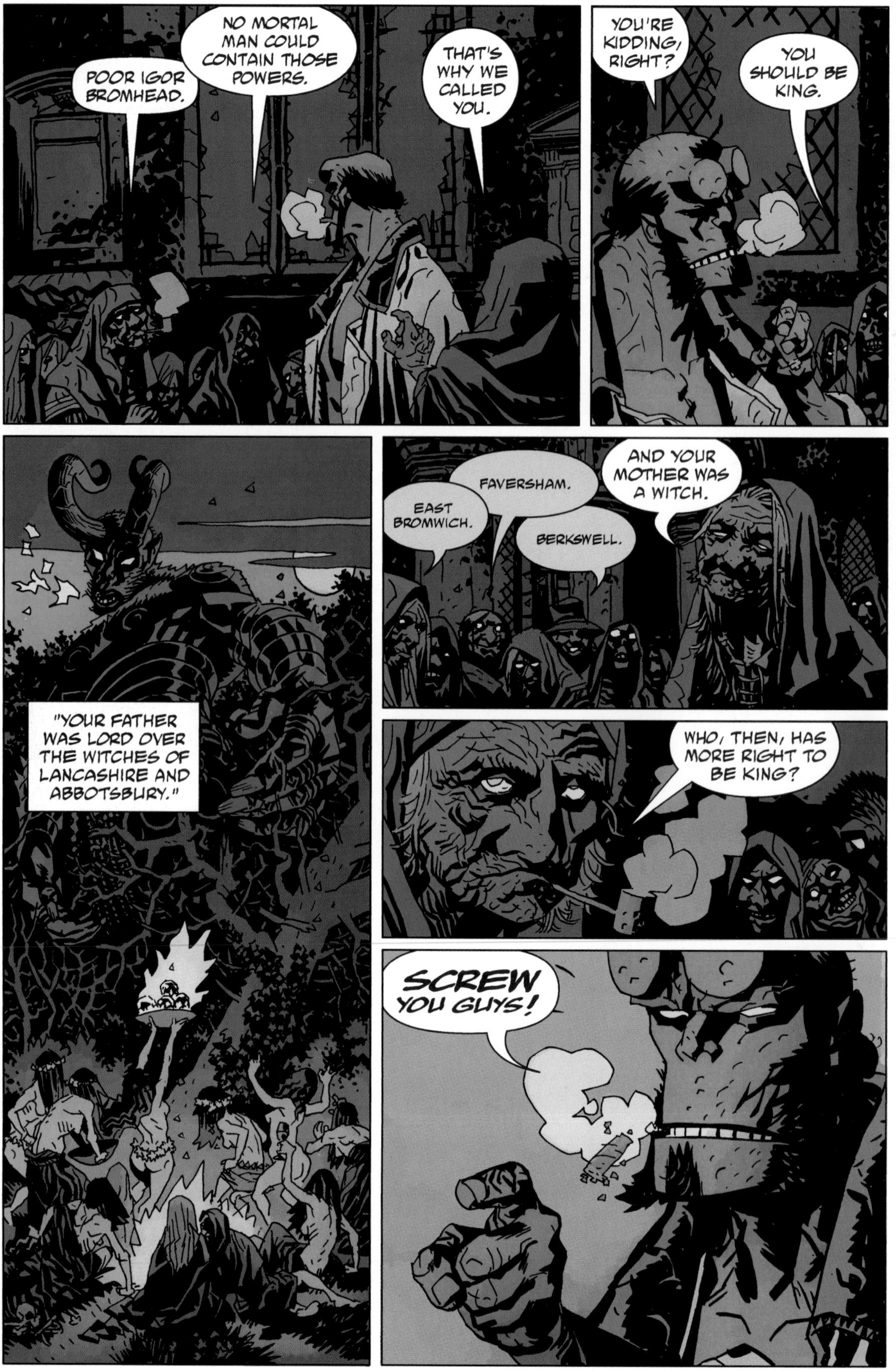
POOR IGOR BROMHEAD.
NO MORTAL MAN COULD CONTAIN THOSE POWERS.
THAT'S WHY WE CALLED YOU.
YOU'RE KIDDING, RIGHT?
YOU SHOULD BE KING.
"YOUR FATHER WAS LORD OVER THE WITCHES OF LANCASHIRE AND ABBOTSBURY."
EAST BROMWICH.
FAVERSHAM.
BERKSWELL.
AND YOUR MOTHER WAS A WITCH.
WHO, THEN, HAS MORE RIGHT TO BE KING?
SCREW YOU GUYS!

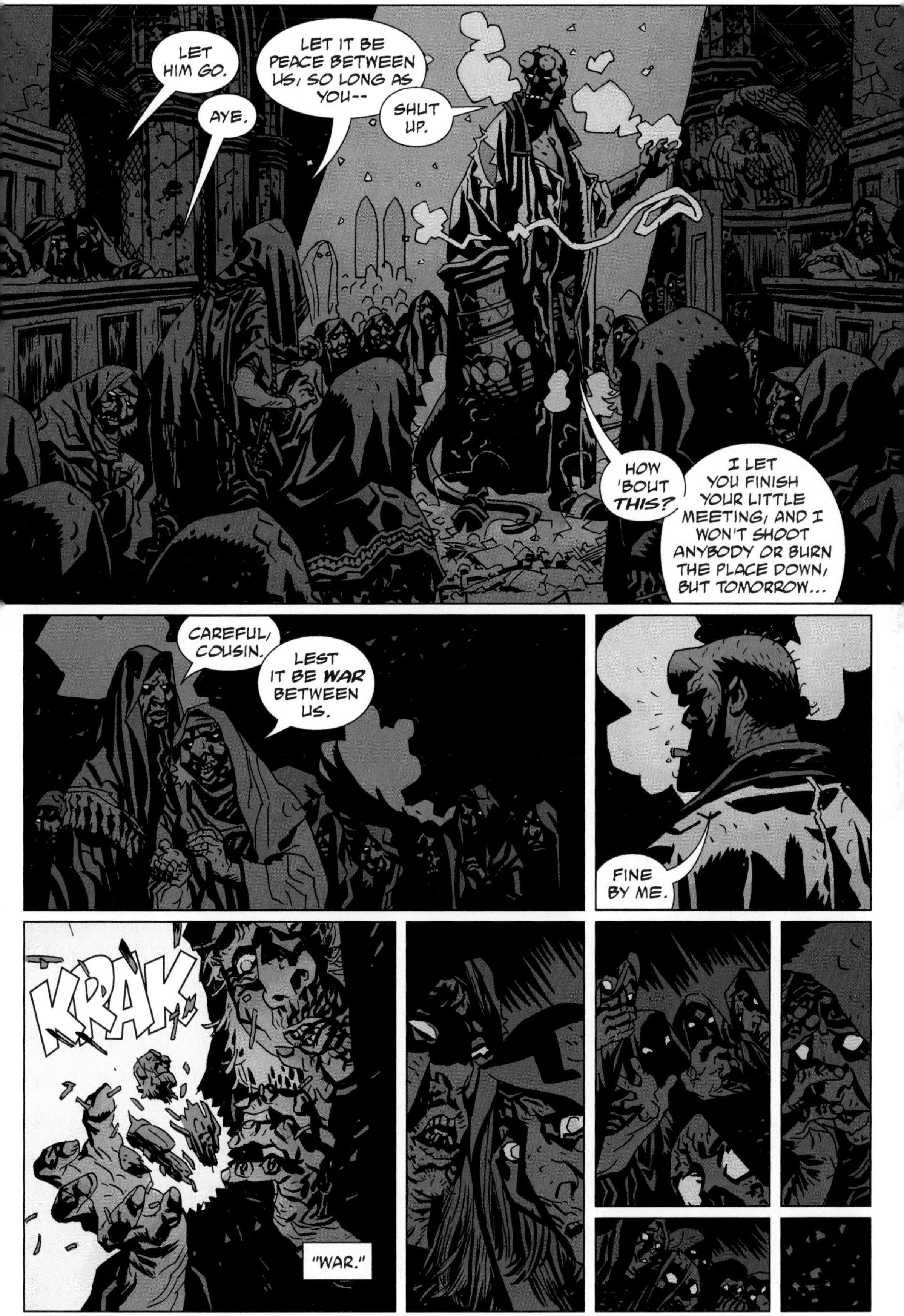
LET HIM GO.
AYE.
LET IT BE PEACE BETWEEN US, SO LONG AS YOU--
SHUT UP.
HOW 'BOUT THIS?
I LET YOU FINISH YOUR LITTLE MEETING, AND I WON'T SHOOT ANYBODY OR BURN THE PLACE DOWN, BUT TOMORROW...
CAREFUL, COUSIN.
LEST IT BE WAR BETWEEN US.
FINE BY ME.
KRAK
"WAR."

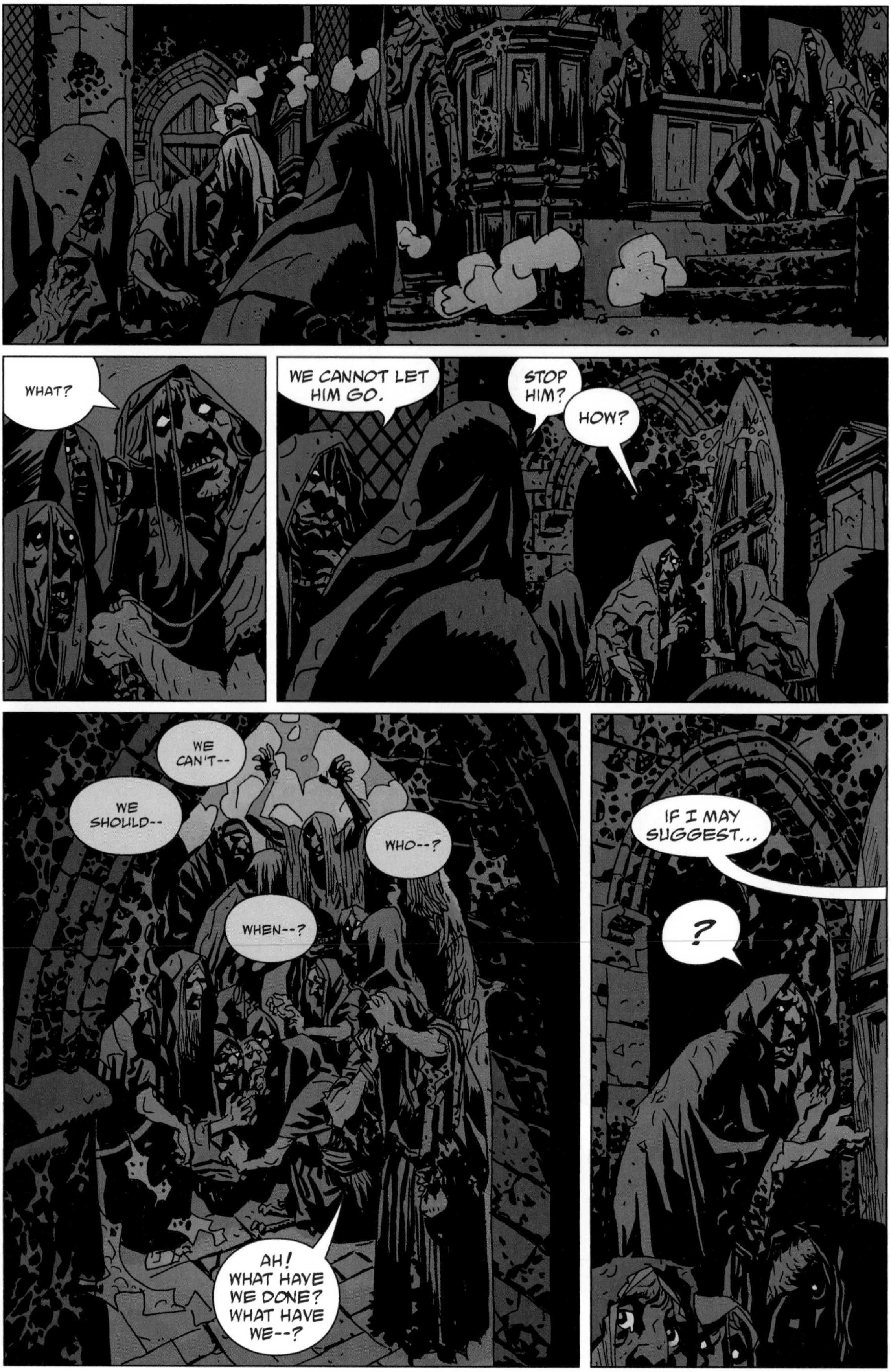
WHAT?
WE CANNOT LET HIM GO.
STOP HIM?
HOW?
WE CAN'T--
WE SHOULD--
WHO--?
WHEN--?
AH! WHAT HAVE WE DONE? WHAT HAVE WE--?
IF I MAY SUGGEST...
?

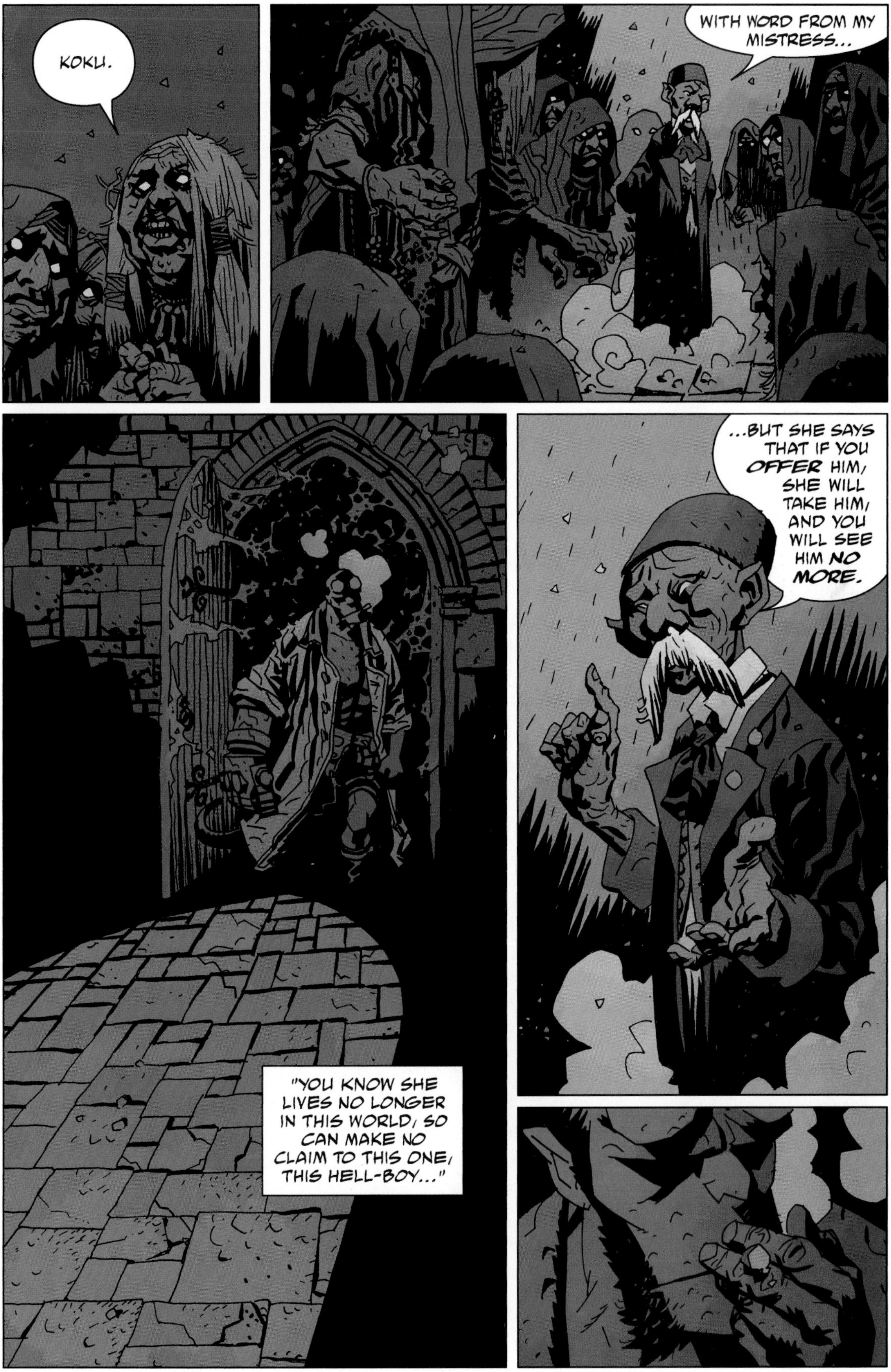
KOKU.
WITH WORD FROM MY MISTRESS...
...BUT SHE SAYS THAT IF YOU OFFER HIM, SHE WILL TAKE HIM, AND YOU WILL SEE HIM NO MORE.
"YOU KNOW SHE LIVES NO LONGER IN THIS WORLD, SO CAN MAKE NO CLAIM TO THIS ONE, THIS HELL-BOY..."

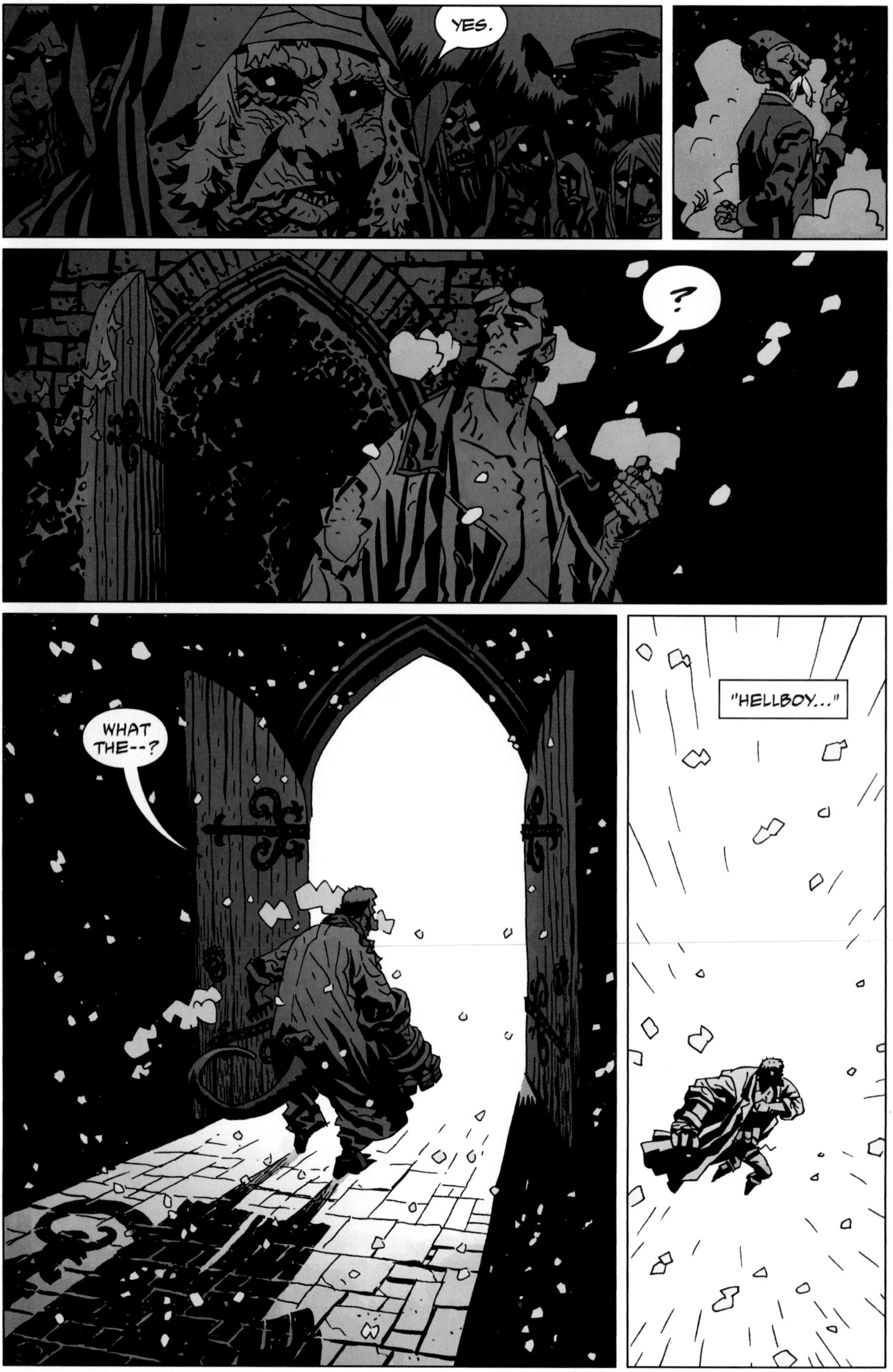
YES.
?
WHAT THE--?
"HELLBOY..."

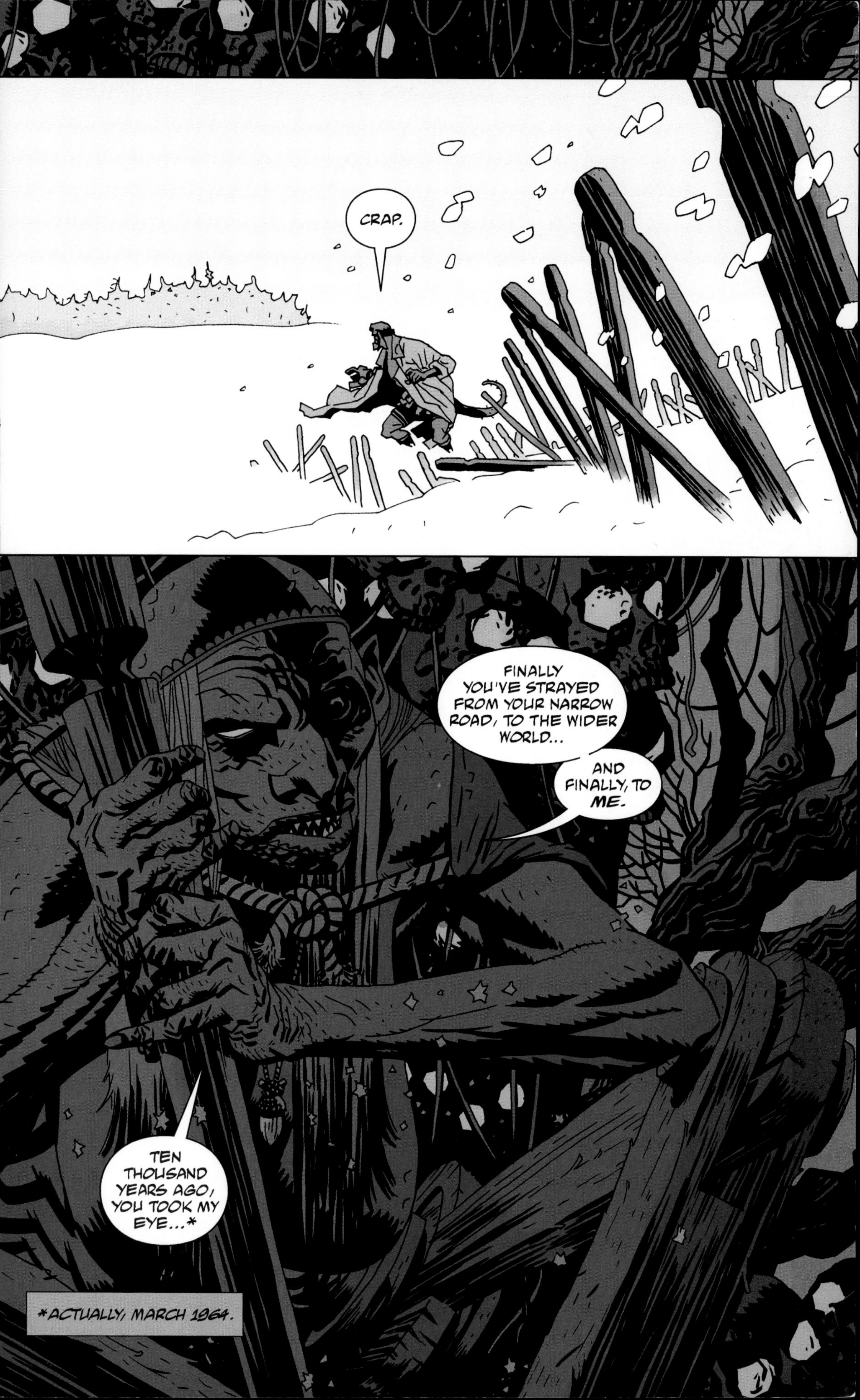

CRAP.
FINALLY YOU'VE STRAYED FROM YOUR NARROW ROAD, TO THE WIDER WORLD...
AND FINALLY, TO ME.
TEN THOUSAND YEARS AGO, YOU TOOK MY EYE...*
*ACTUALLY, MARCH 1964.

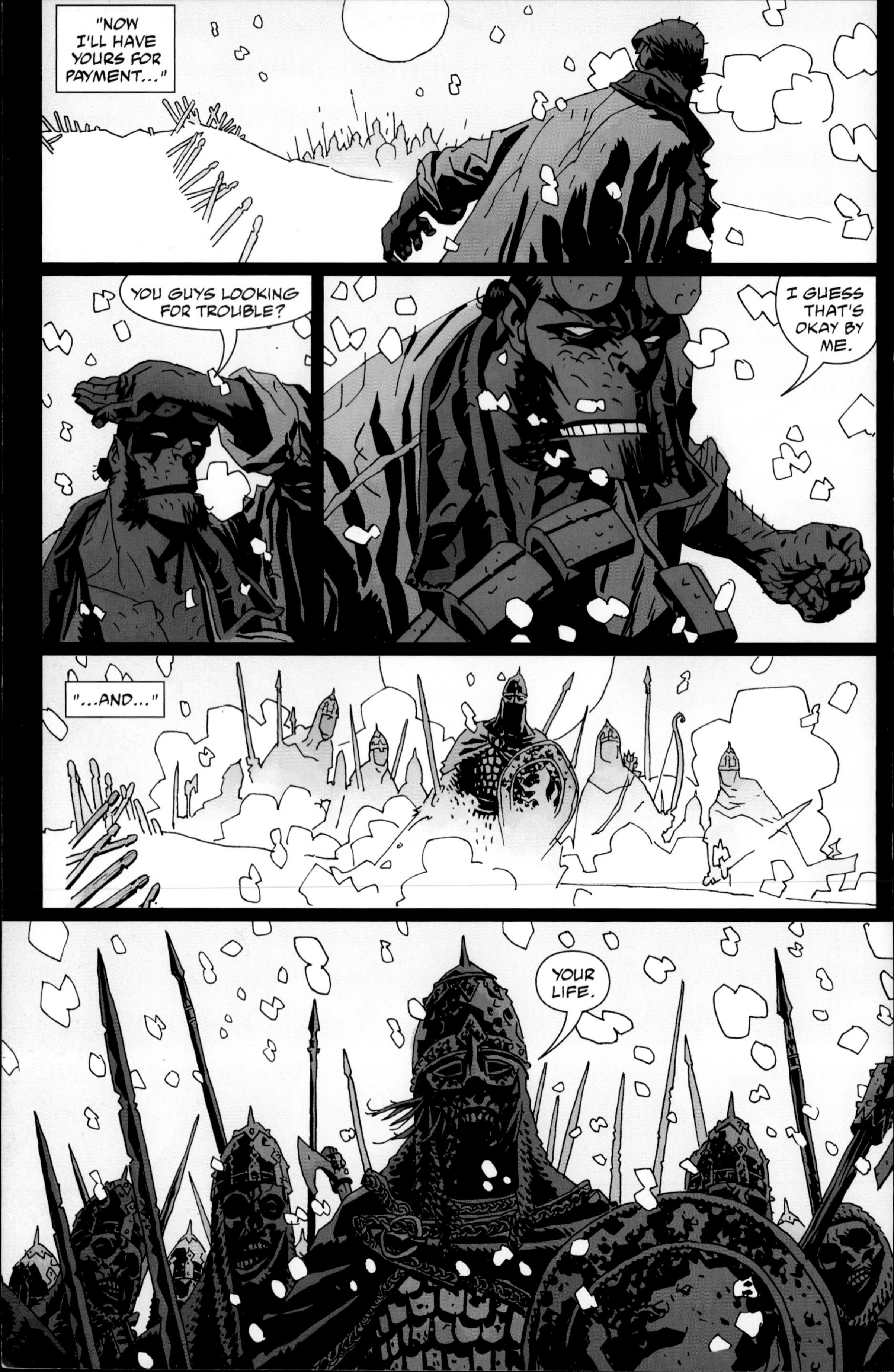
"NOW I'LL HAVE YOURS FOR PAYMENT..."
YOU GUYS LOOKING FOR TROUBLE?
I GUESS THAT'S OKAY BY ME.
"...AND..."
YOUR LIFE.

CHAPTER THREE

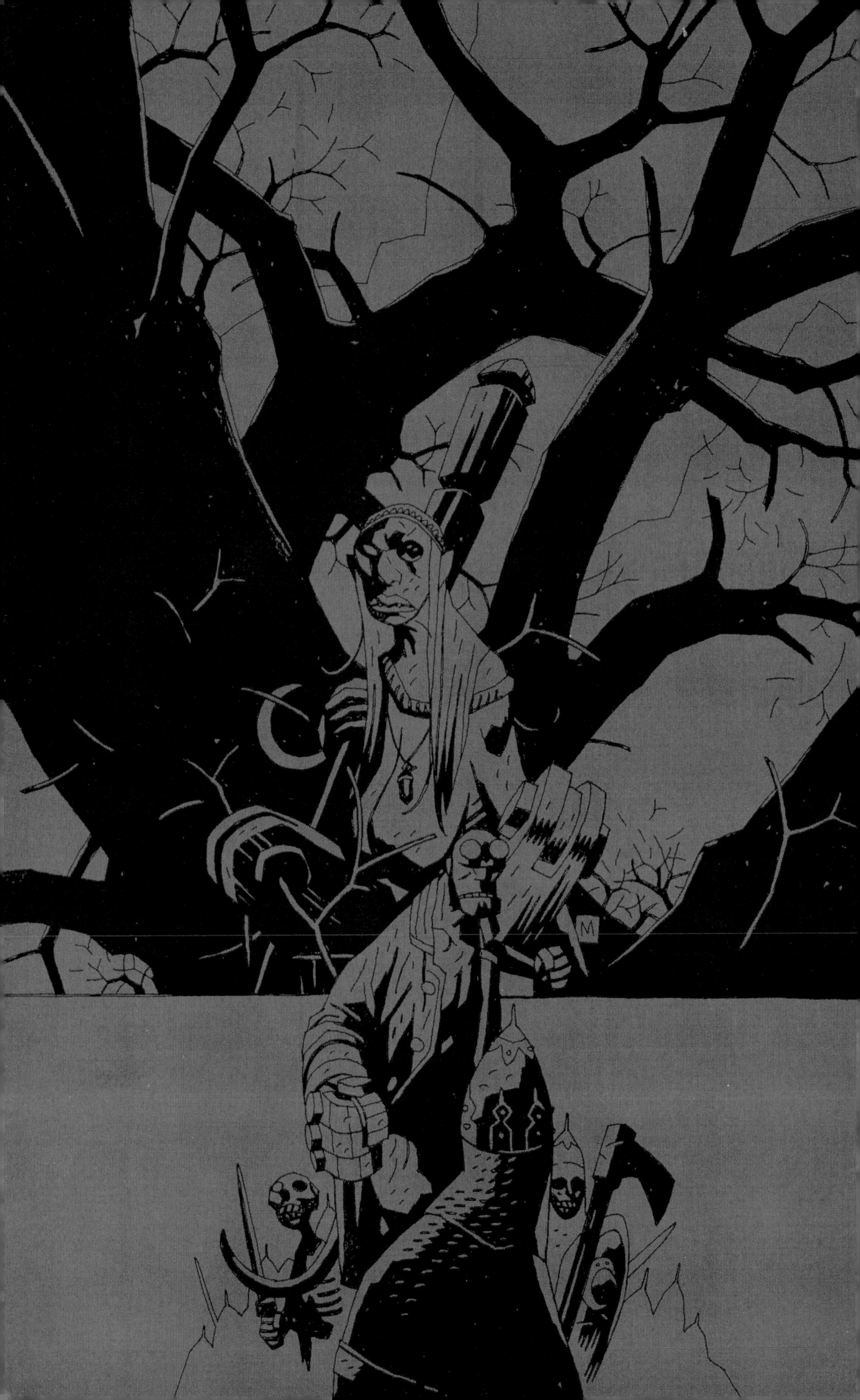

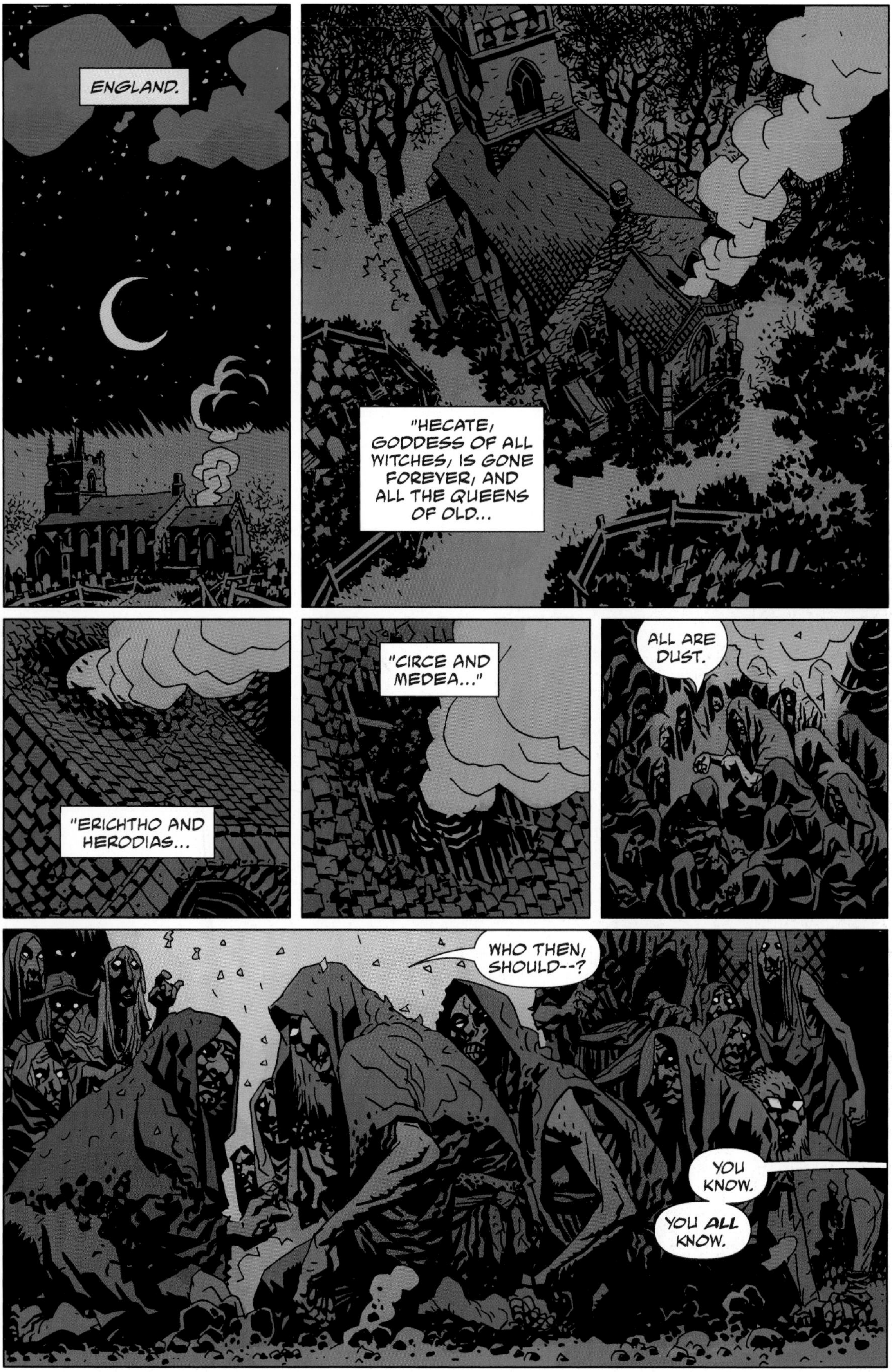
ENGLAND.
"HECATE, GODDESS OF ALL WITCHES, IS GONE FOREVER, AND ALL THE QUEENS OF OLD...
"ERICHTHO AND HERODIAS...
"CIRCE AND MEDEA..."
ALL ARE DUST.
WHO THEN, SHOULD--?
YOU KNOW.
YOU ALL KNOW.

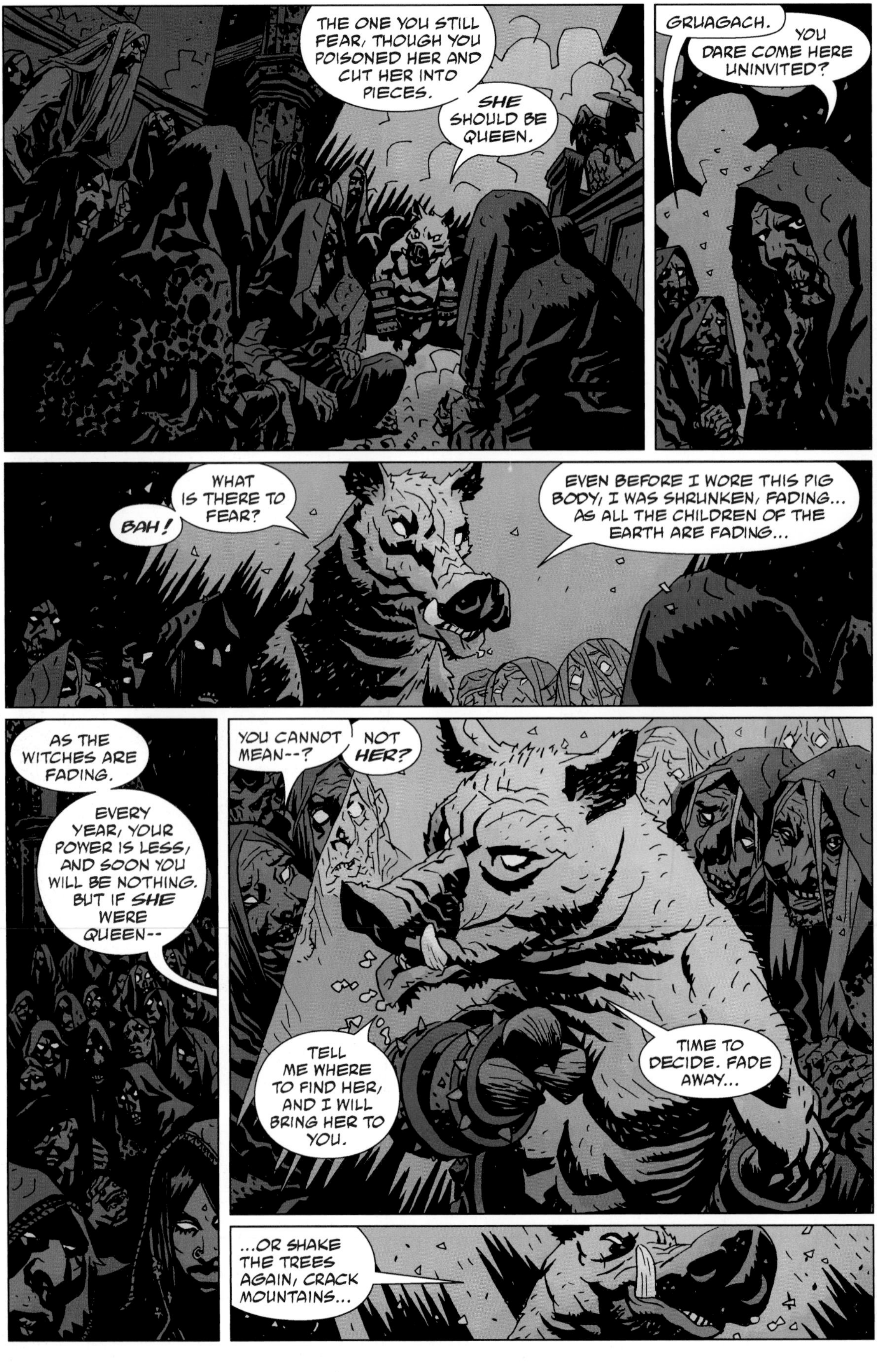
THE ONE YOU STILL FEAR, THOUGH YOU POISONED HER AND CUT HER INTO PIECES.
SHE SHOULD BE QUEEN.
GRUAGACH.
YOU DARE COME HERE UNINVITED?
BAH!
WHAT IS THERE TO FEAR?
EVEN BEFORE I WORE THIS PIG BODY, I WAS SHRUNKEN, FADING... AS ALL THE CHILDREN OF THE EARTH ARE FADING...
AS THE WITCHES ARE FADING.
EVERY YEAR, YOUR POWER IS LESS, AND SOON YOU WILL BE NOTHING. BUT IF SHE WERE QUEEN--
YOU CANNOT MEAN--?
NOT HER?
TELL ME WHERE TO FIND HER, AND I WILL BRING HER TO YOU.
TIME TO DECIDE. FADE AWAY...
...OR SHAKE THE TREES AGAIN, CRACK MOUNTAINS...

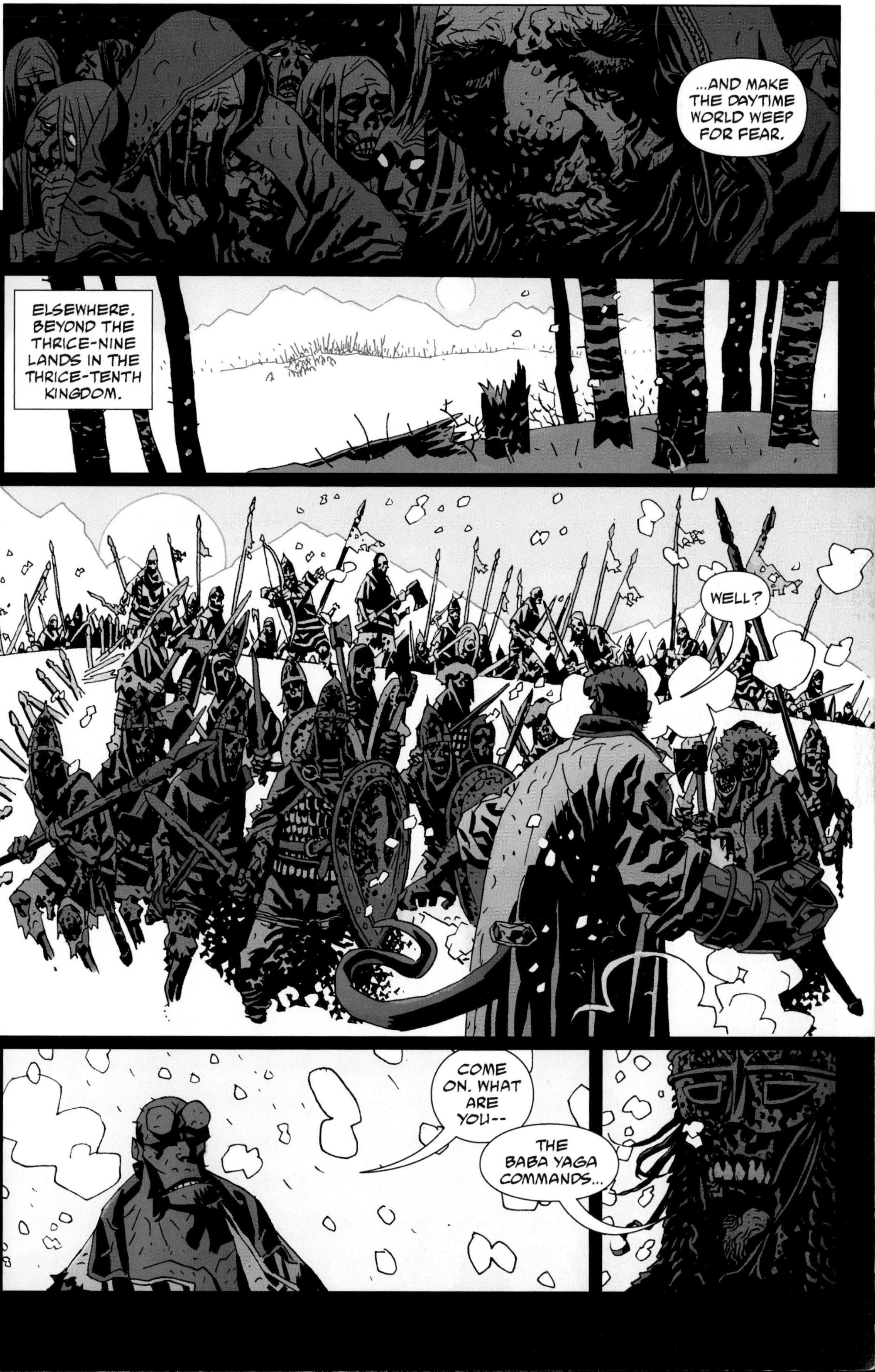
...AND MAKE THE DAYTIME WORLD WEEP FOR FEAR.
ELSEWHERE. BEYOND THE THRICE-NINE LANDS IN THE THRICE-TENTH KINGDOM.
WELL?
COME ON. WHAT ARE YOU--
THE BABA YAGA COMMANDS...

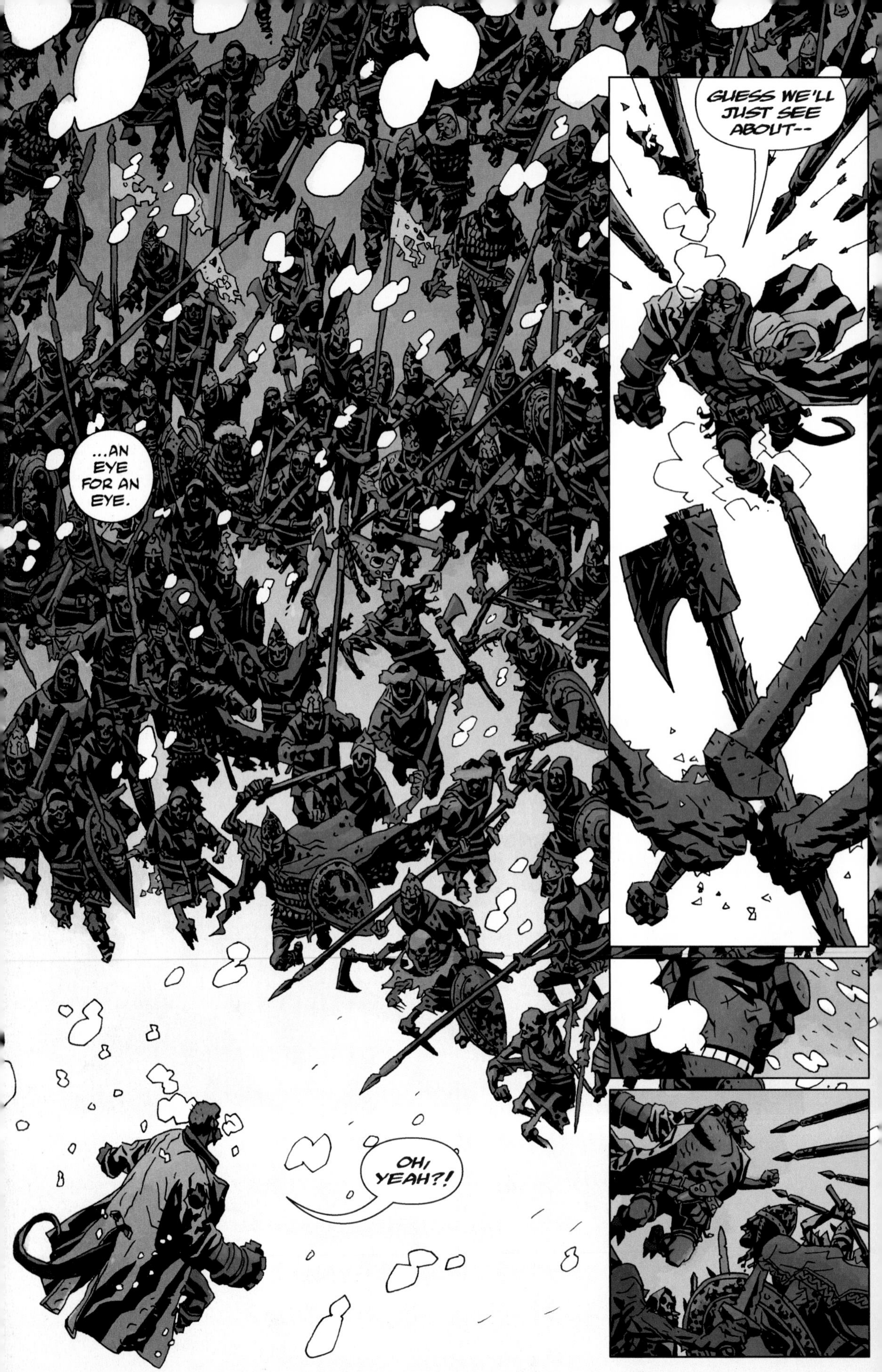
...AN EYE FOR AN EYE.
GUESS WE'LL JUST SEE ABOUT--
OH, YEAH?!

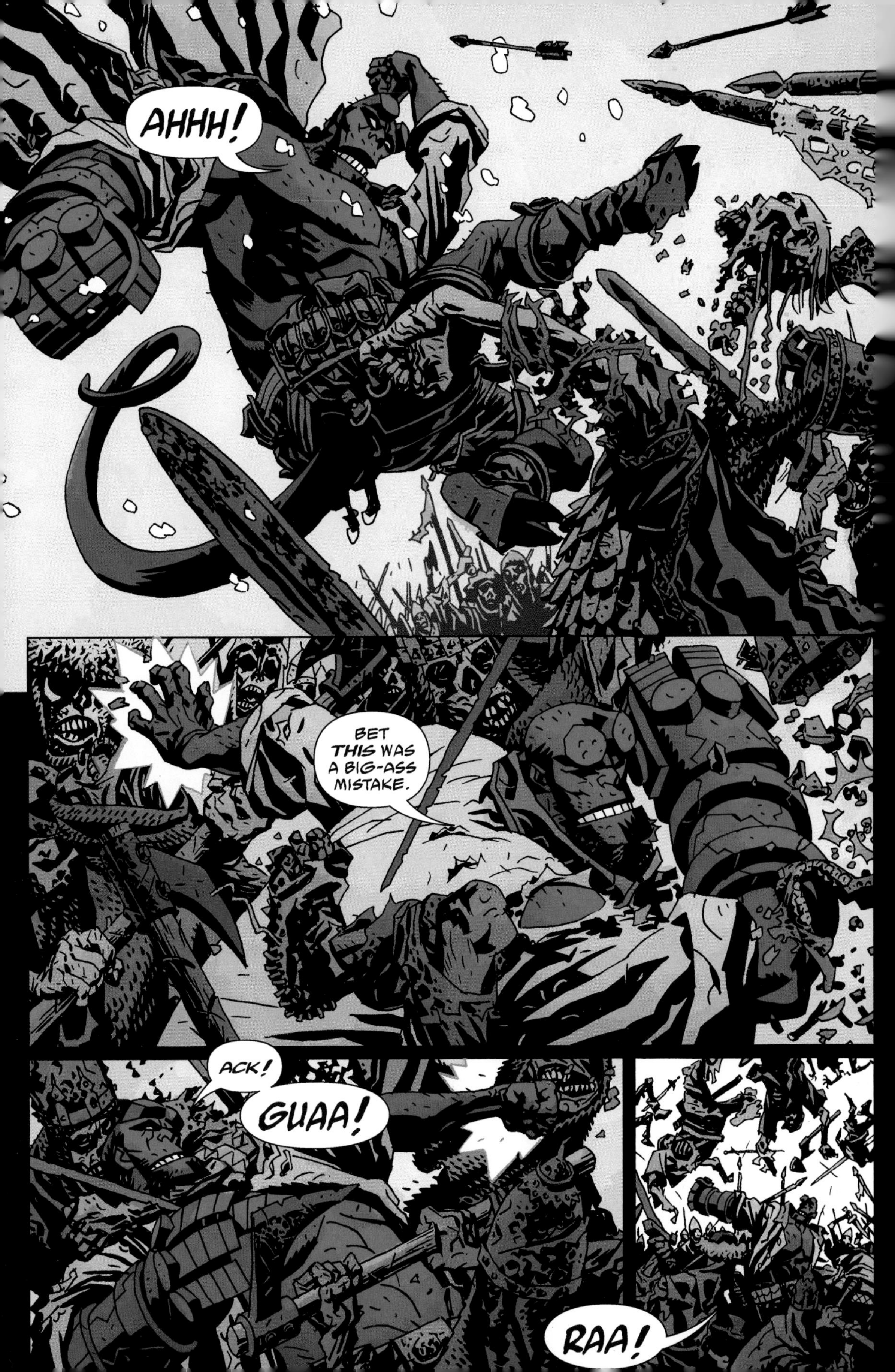
AHHH!
BET THIS WAS A BIG-ASS MISTAKE.
ACK!
GUAA!
RAA!

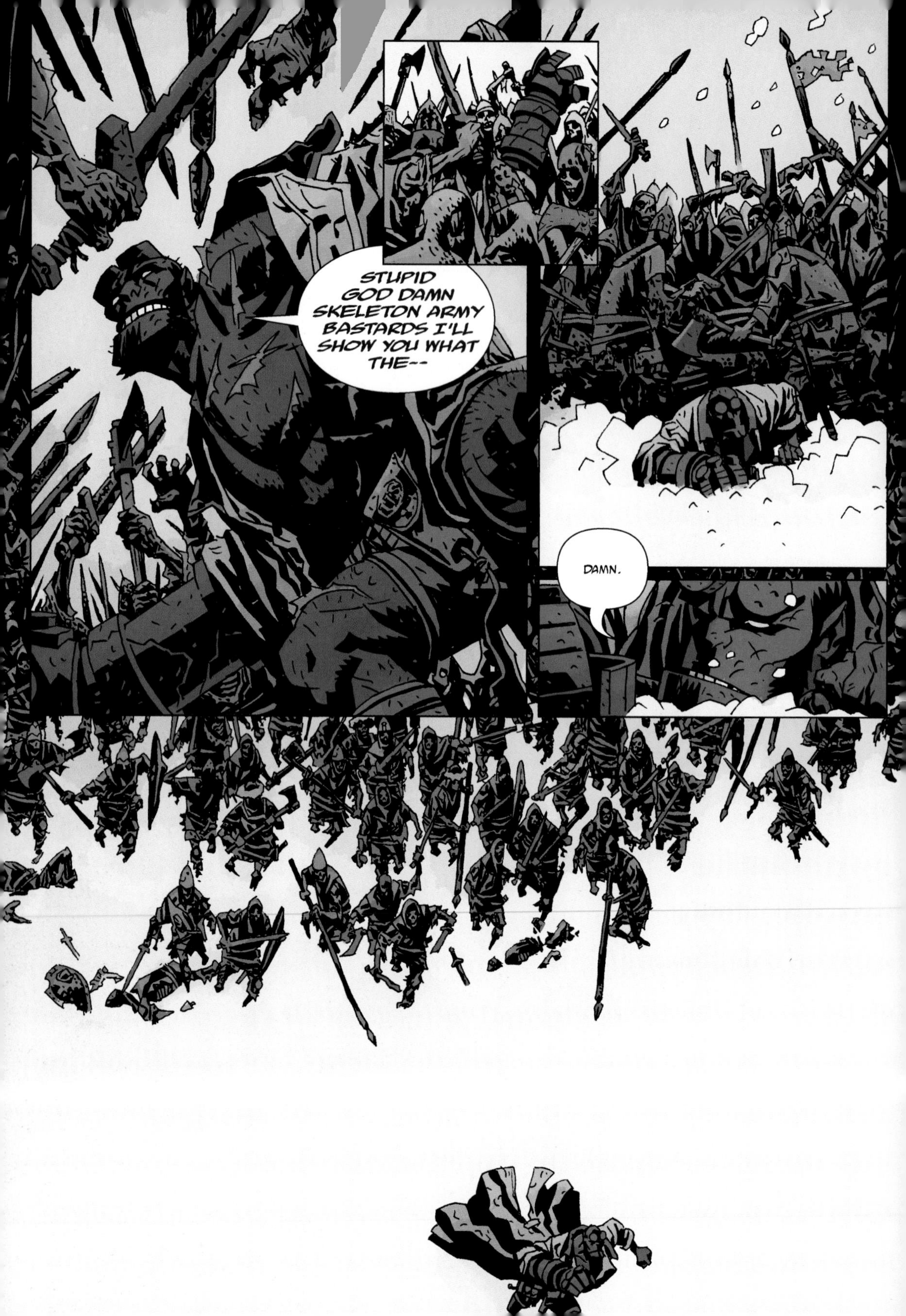
STUPID GOD DAMN SKELETON ARMY BASTARDS I'LL SHOW YOU WHAT THE--
DAMN.

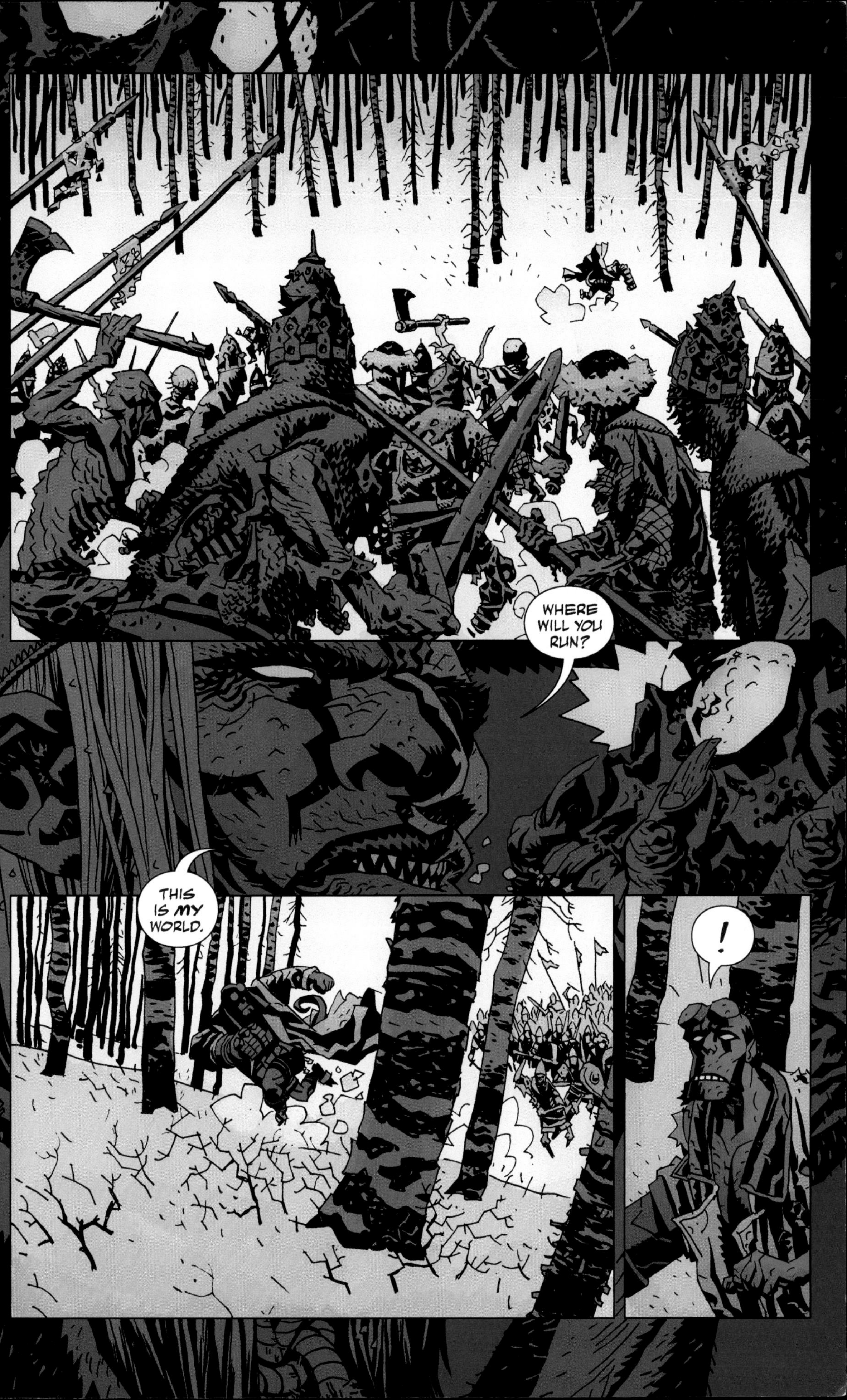
WHERE WILL YOU RUN?
THIS IS MY WORLD.
!

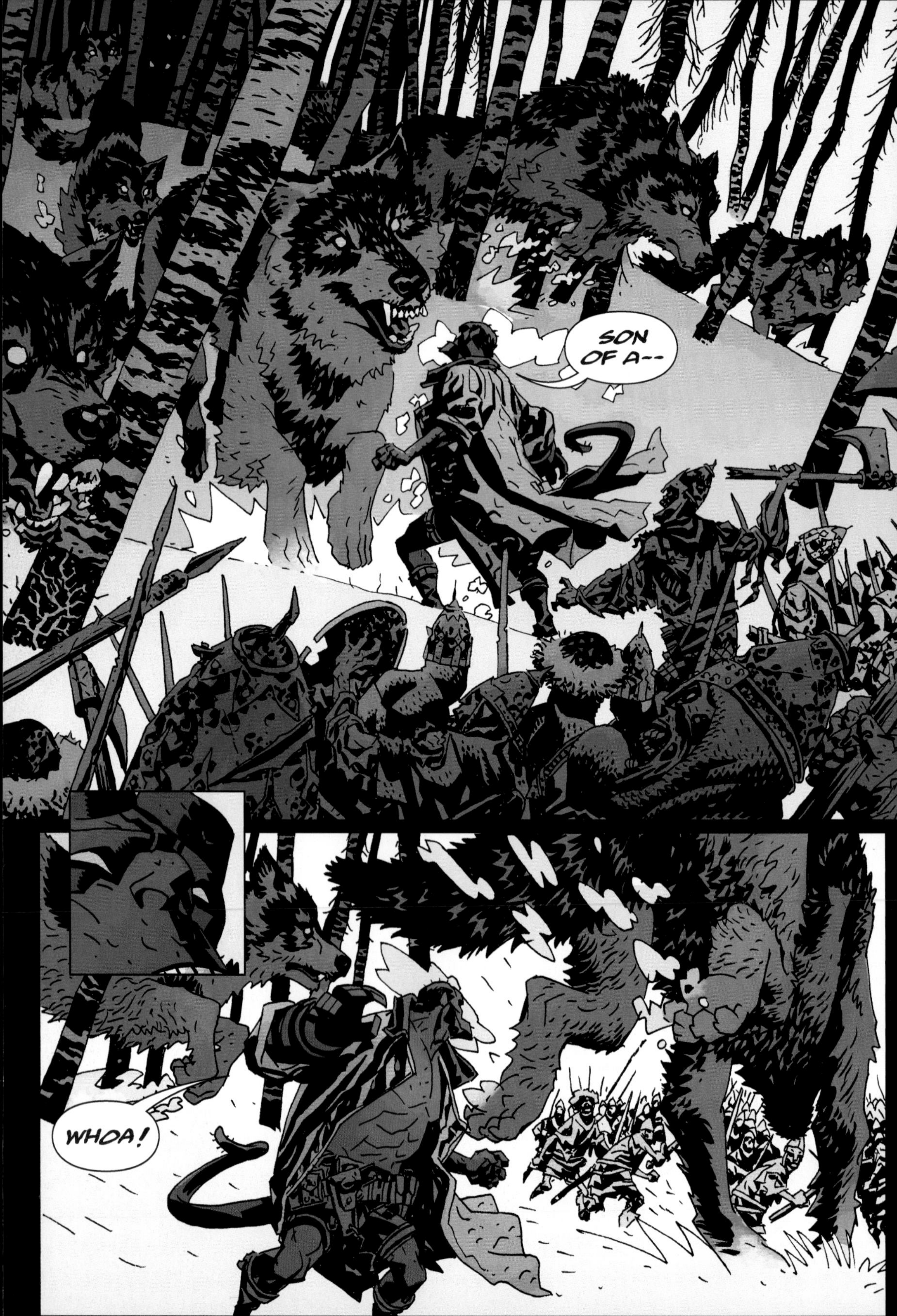
SON OF A--
WHOA!

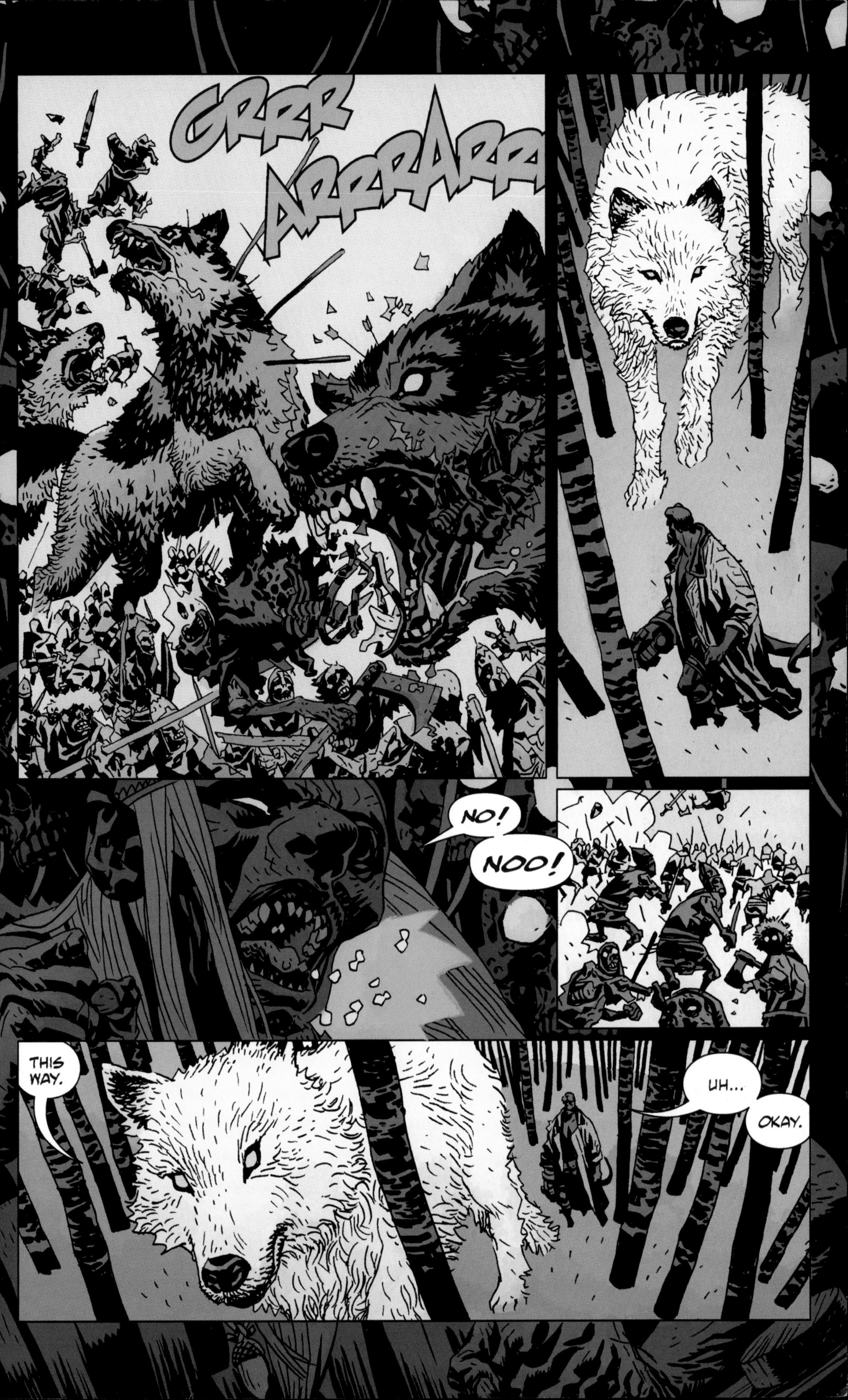
GRRR
ARRRARR
NO!
NOO!
THIS WAY.
UH...
OKAY.

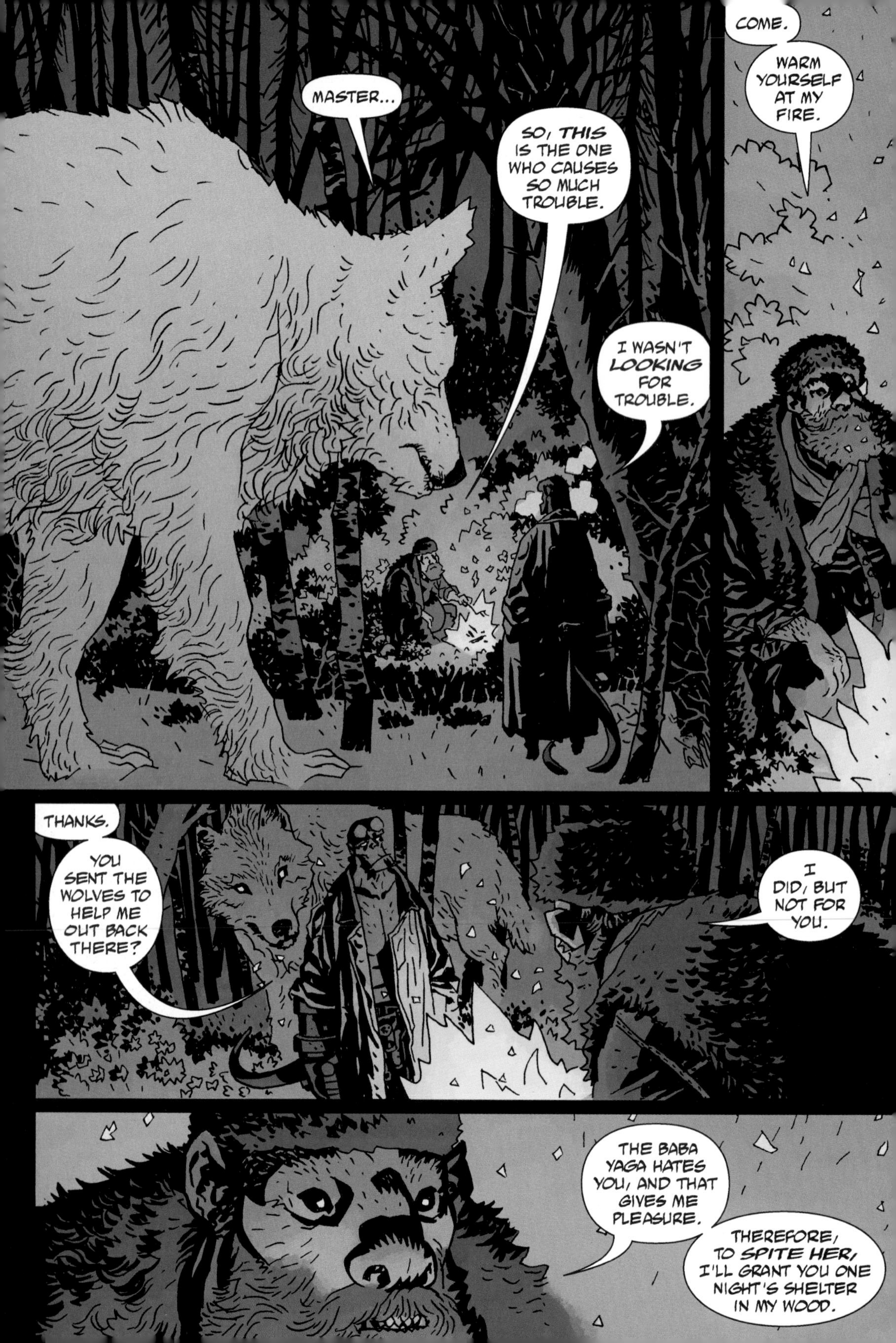
MASTER...
SO, THIS IS THE ONE WHO CAUSES SO MUCH TROUBLE.
I WASN'T LOOKING FOR TROUBLE.
COME.
WARM YOURSELF AT MY FIRE.
THANKS.
YOU SENT THE WOLVES TO HELP ME OUT BACK THERE?
I DID, BUT NOT FOR YOU.
THE BABA YAGA HATES YOU, AND THAT GIVES ME PLEASURE.
THEREFORE, TO SPITE HER, I'LL GRANT YOU ONE NIGHT'S SHELTER IN MY WOOD.

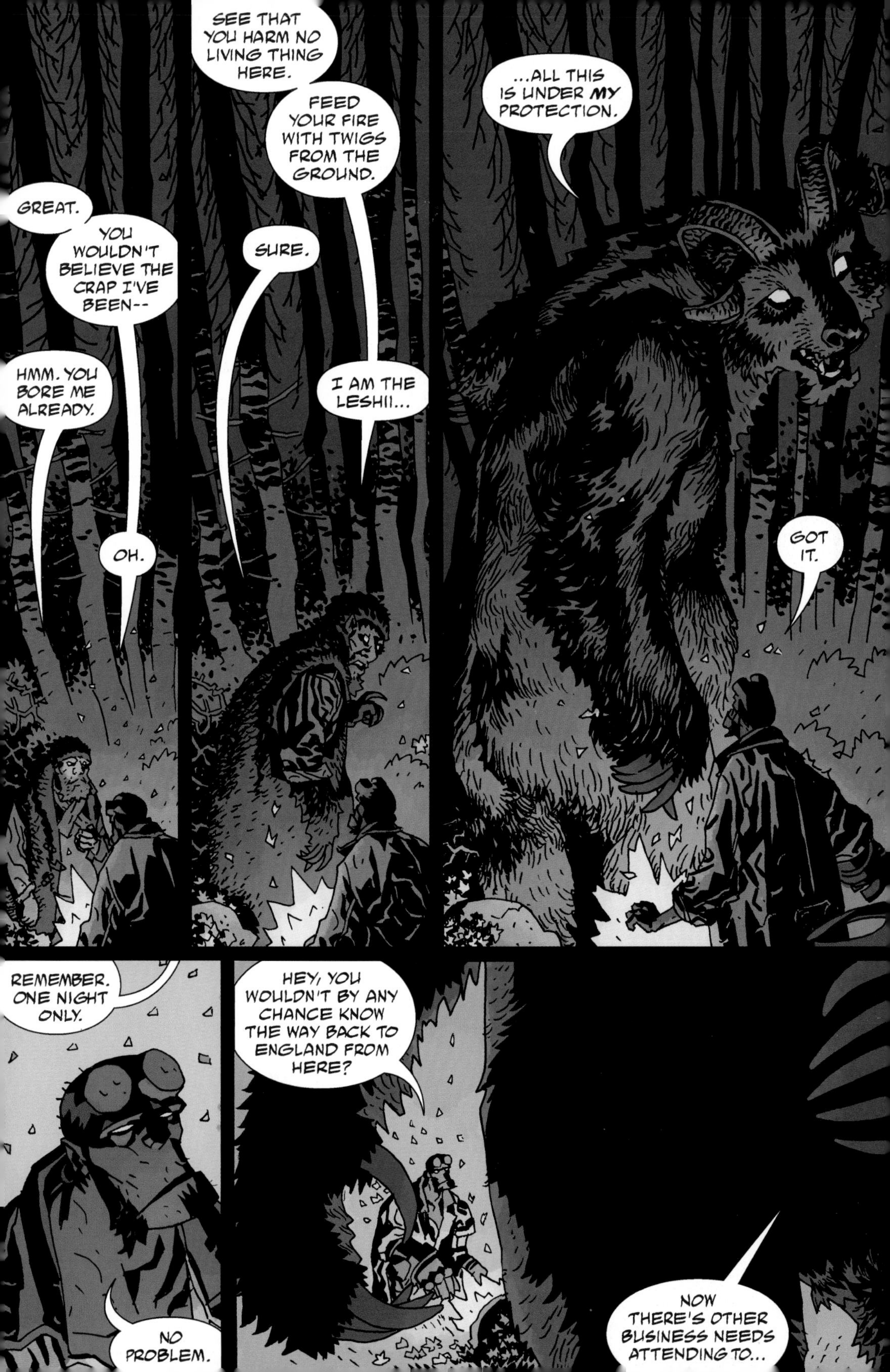
GREAT.
YOU WOULDN'T BELIEVE THE CRAP I'VE BEEN--
HMM. YOU BORE ME ALREADY.
OH.
SEE THAT YOU HARM NO LIVING THING HERE.
SURE.
FEED YOUR FIRE WITH TWIGS FROM THE GROUND.
I AM THE LESHII...
...ALL THIS IS UNDER MY PROTECTION.
GOT IT.
REMEMBER. ONE NIGHT ONLY.
NO PROBLEM.
HEY, YOU WOULDN'T BY ANY CHANCE KNOW THE WAY BACK TO ENGLAND FROM HERE?
NOW THERE'S OTHER BUSINESS NEEDS ATTENDING TO...

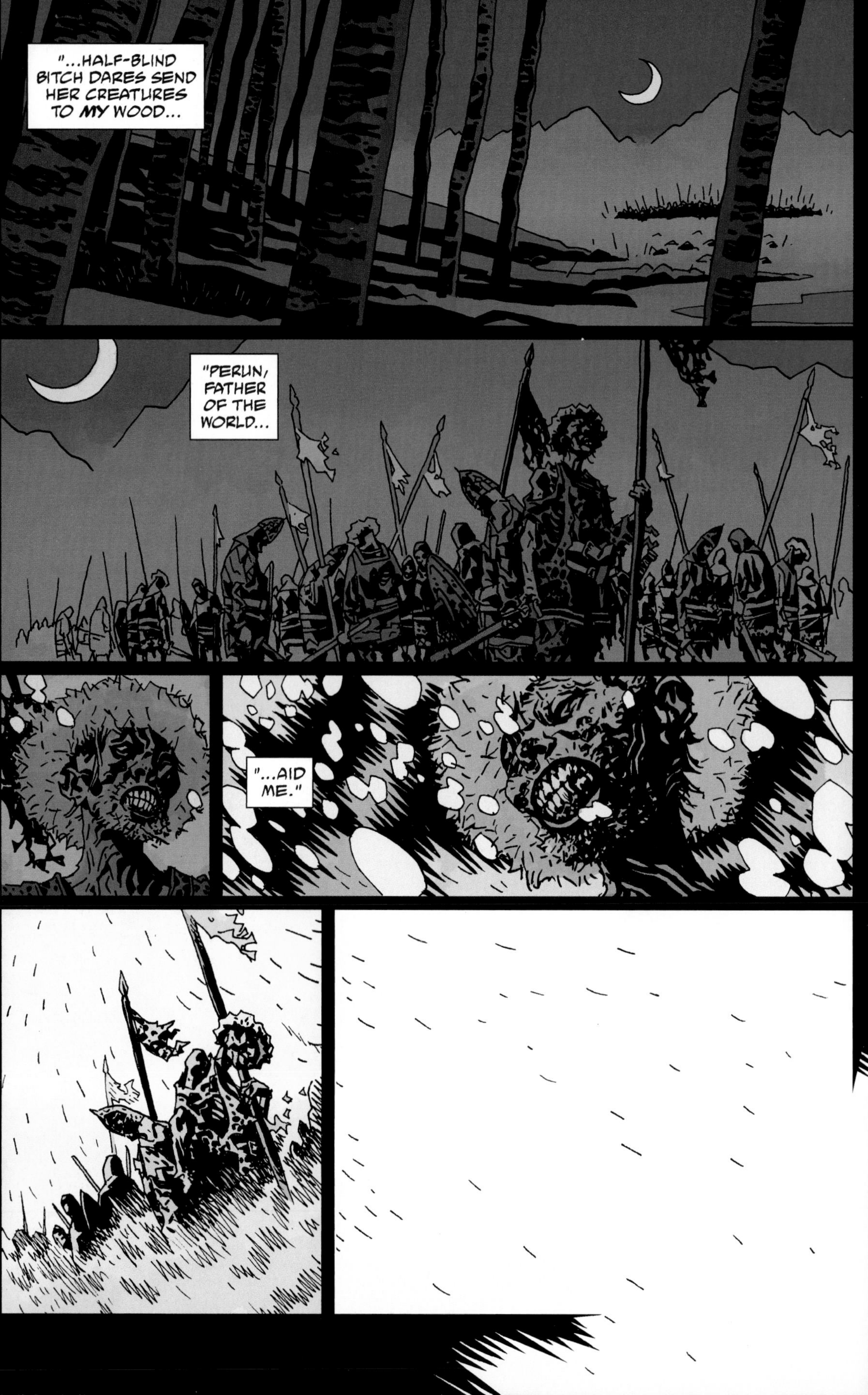
"...HALF-BLIND BITCH DARES SEND HER CREATURES TO MY WOOD...
"PERUN, FATHER OF THE WORLD...
"...AID ME."

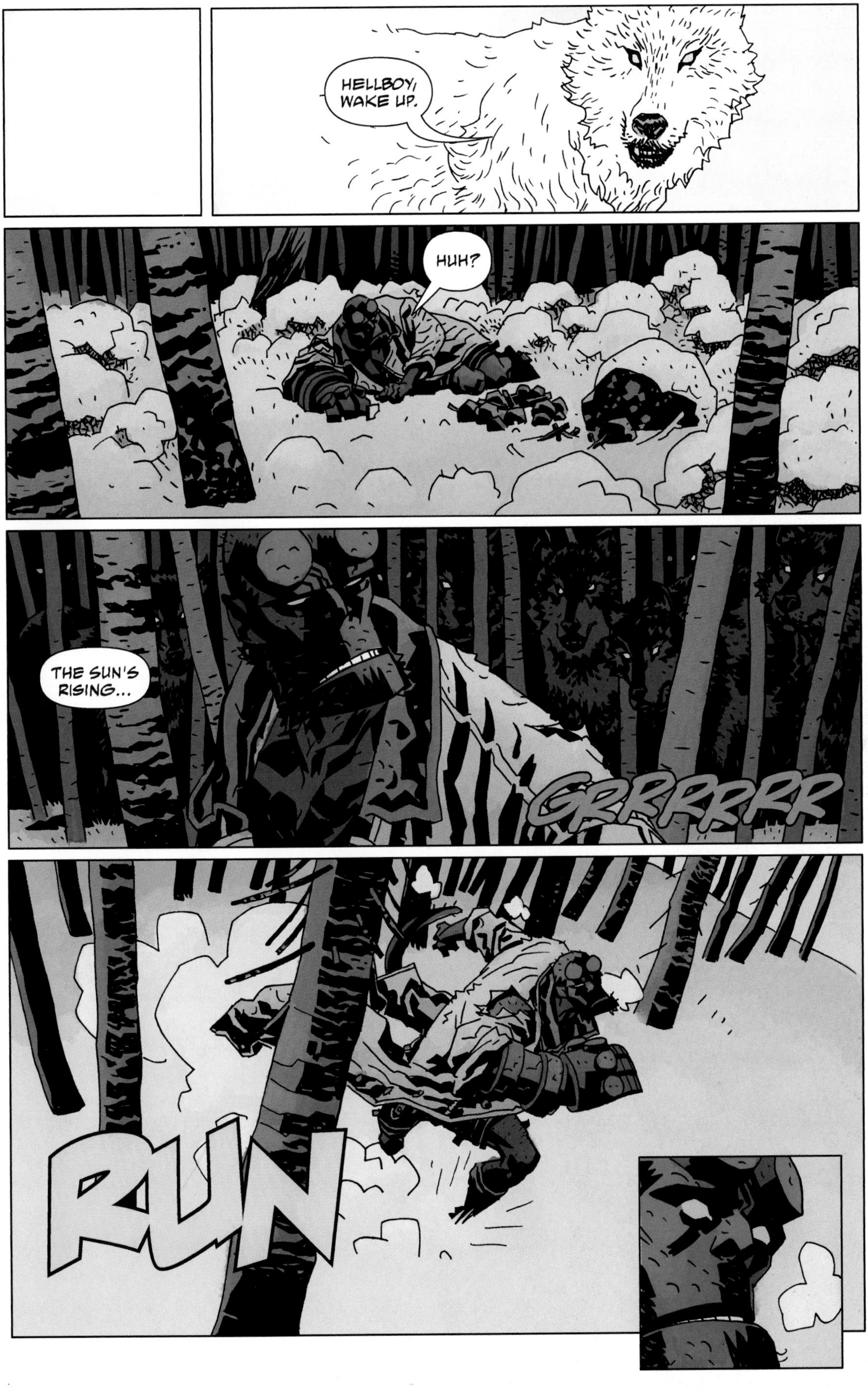
HELLBOY, WAKE UP.
HUH?
THE SUN'S RISING...
GRRRRRR
RUN

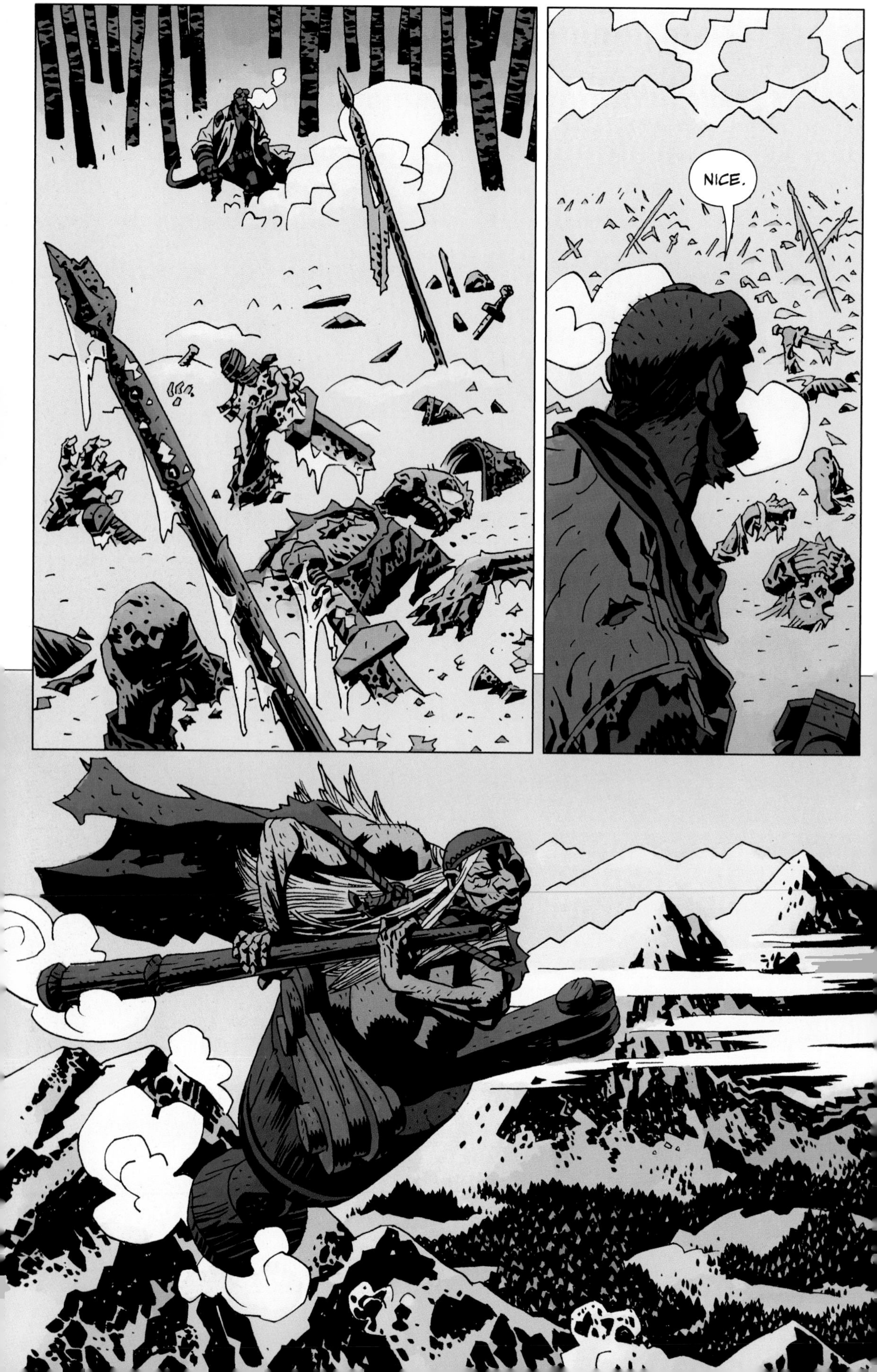
NICE.

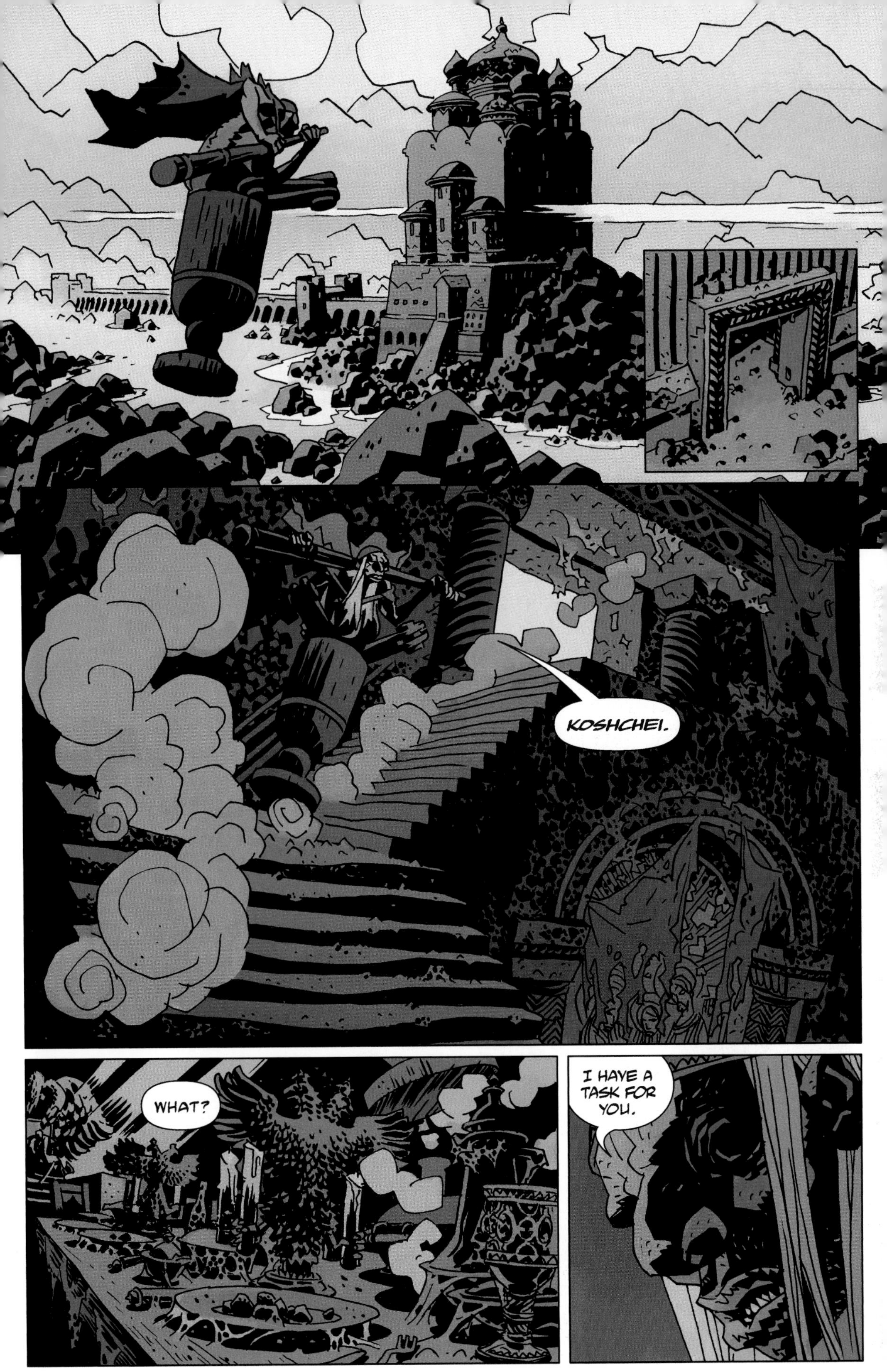
KOSHCHEI.
WHAT?
I HAVE A TASK FOR YOU.

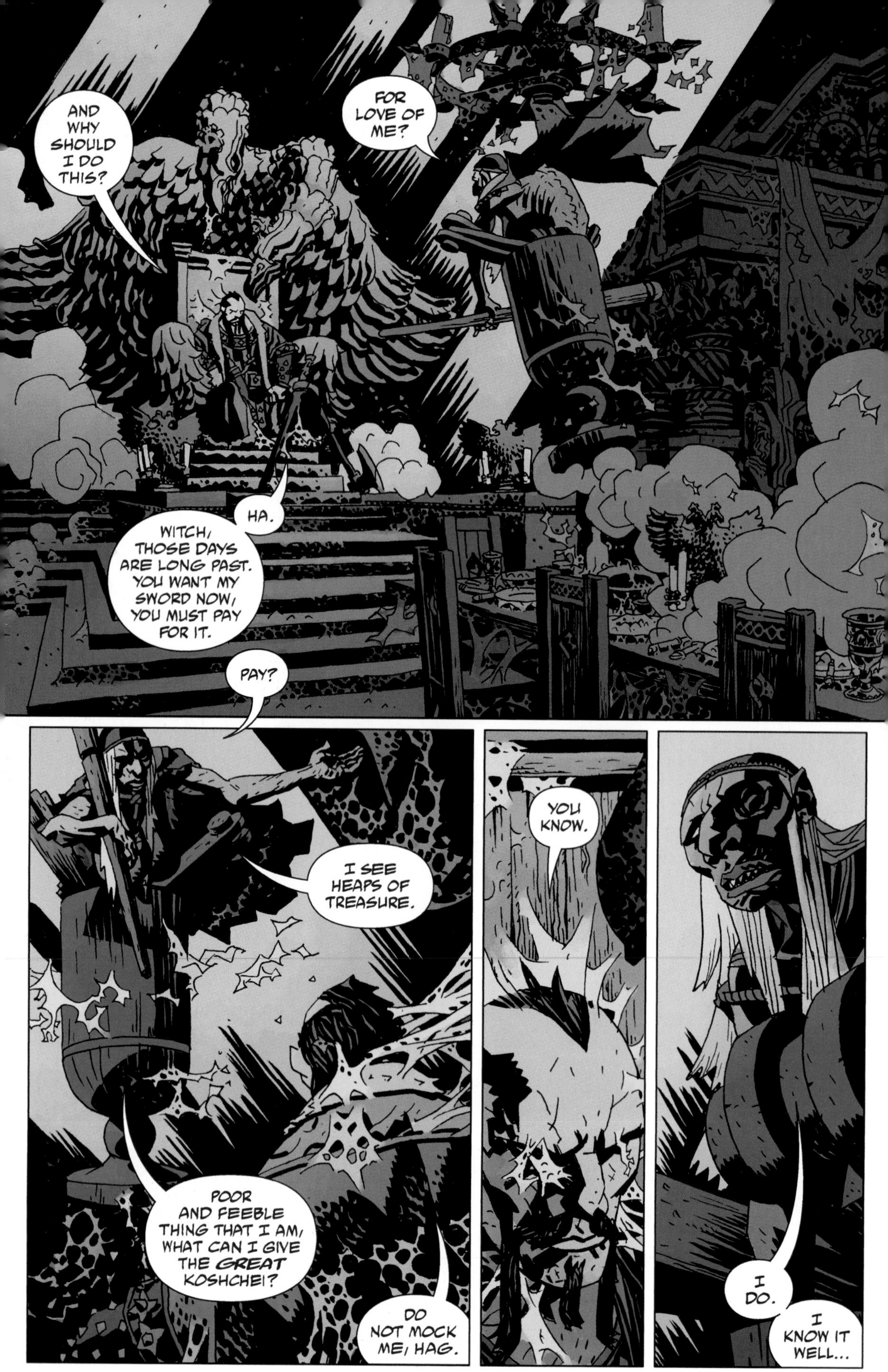
AND WHY SHOULD I DO THIS?
FOR LOVE OF ME?
HA.
WITCH, THOSE DAYS ARE LONG PAST. YOU WANT MY SWORD NOW, YOU MUST PAY FOR IT.
PAY?
I SEE HEAPS OF TREASURE.
POOR AND FEEBLE THING THAT I AM, WHAT CAN I GIVE THE *GREAT* KOSHCHEI?
DO NOT MOCK ME, HAG.
YOU KNOW.
I DO.
I KNOW IT WELL...

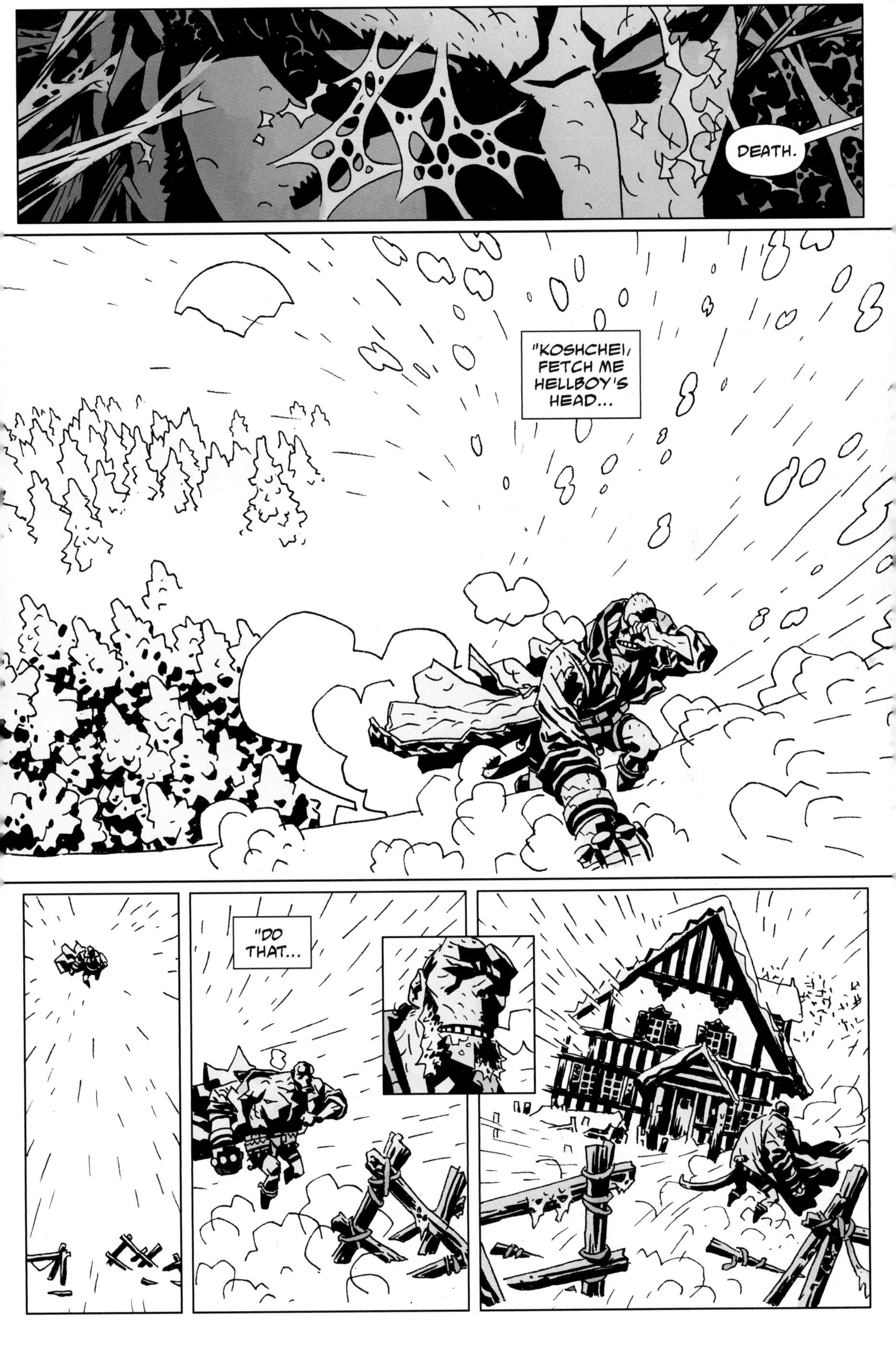
DEATH.
"KOSHCHEI, FETCH ME HELLBOY'S HEAD...
"DO THAT...

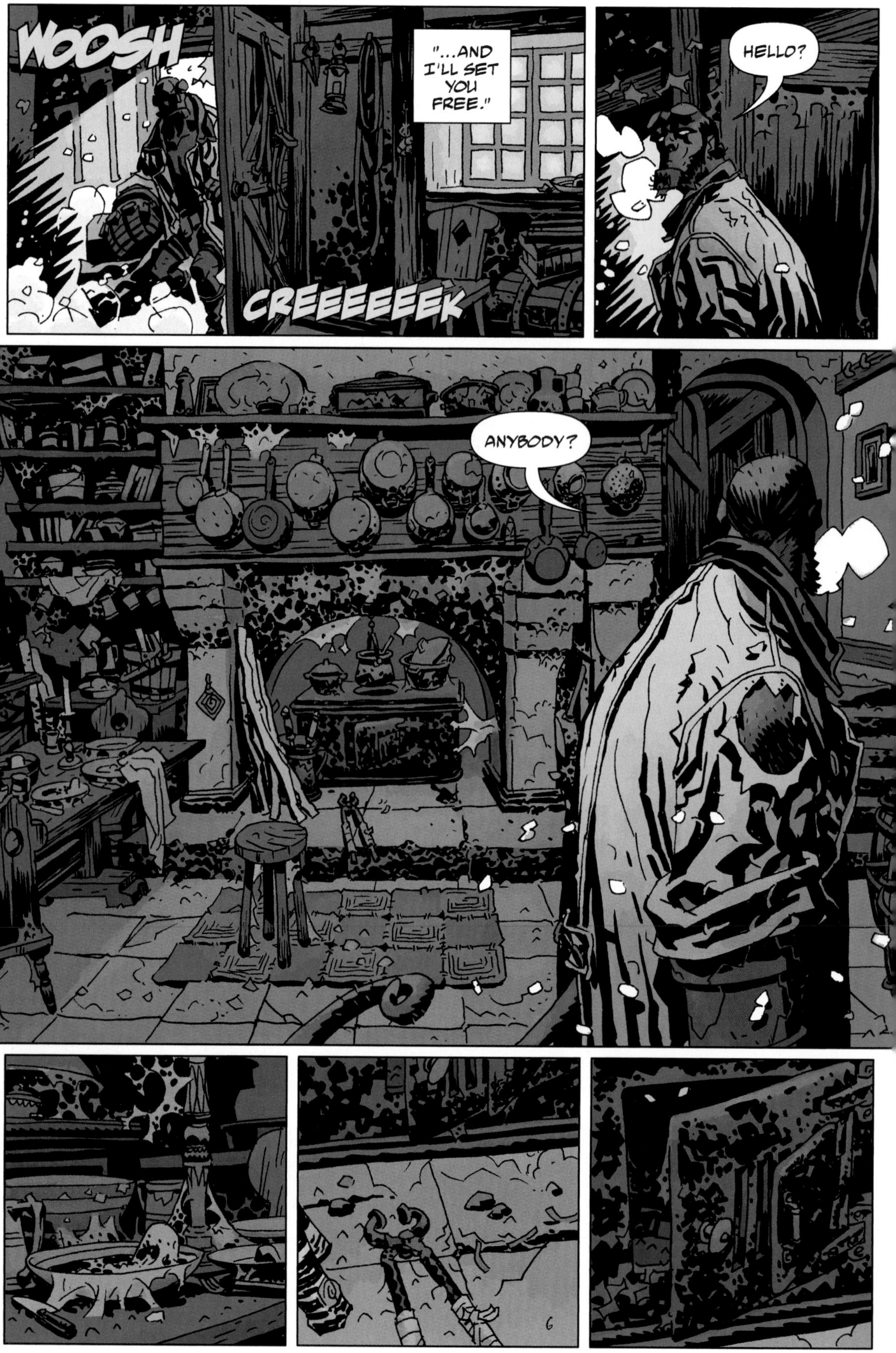
WOOSH
"...AND I'LL SET YOU FREE."
CREEEEEEEK
HELLO?
ANYBODY?

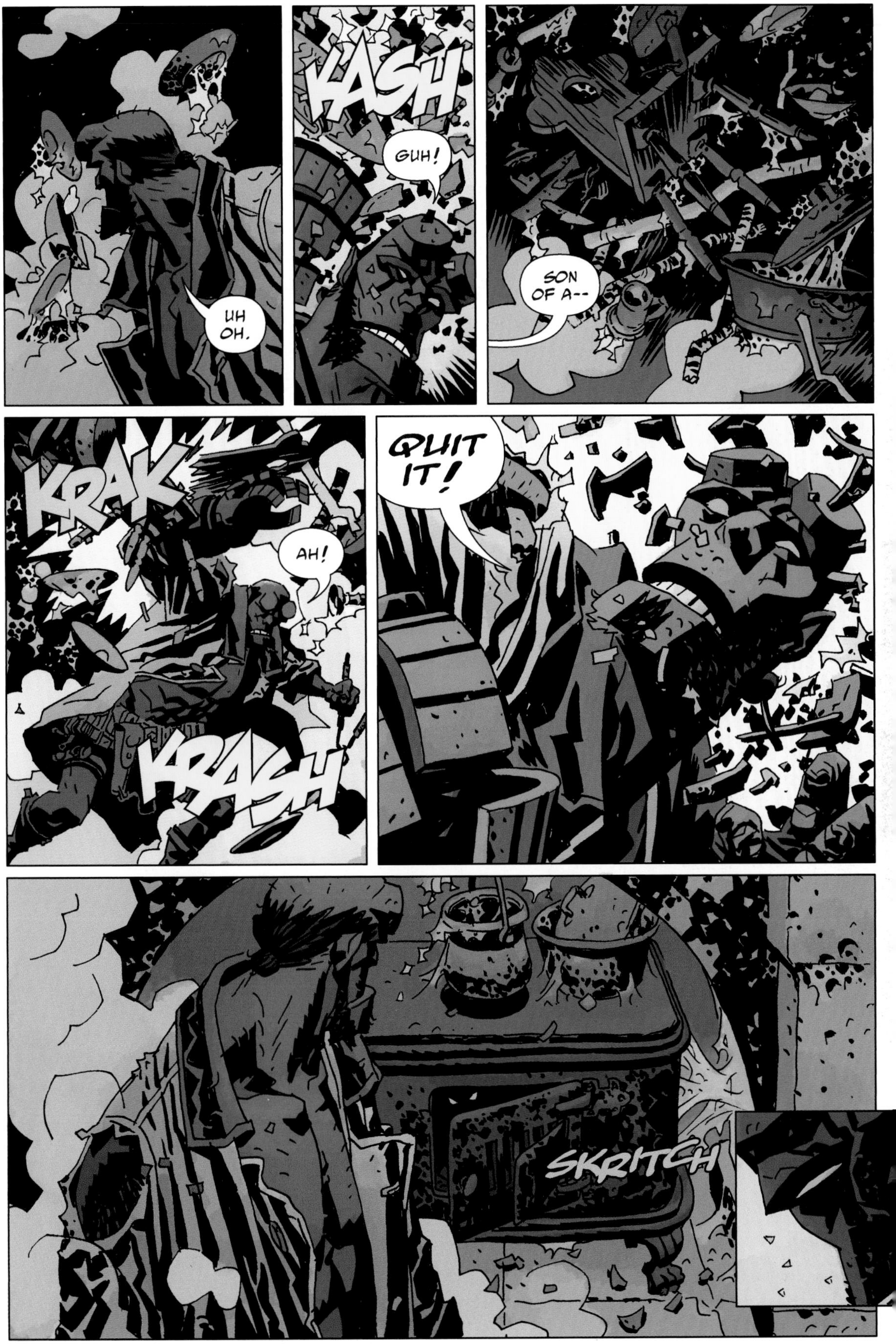
UH OH.
KASH
GUH!
SON OF A--
KRAK
AH!
KRASH
QUIT IT!
SKRITCH

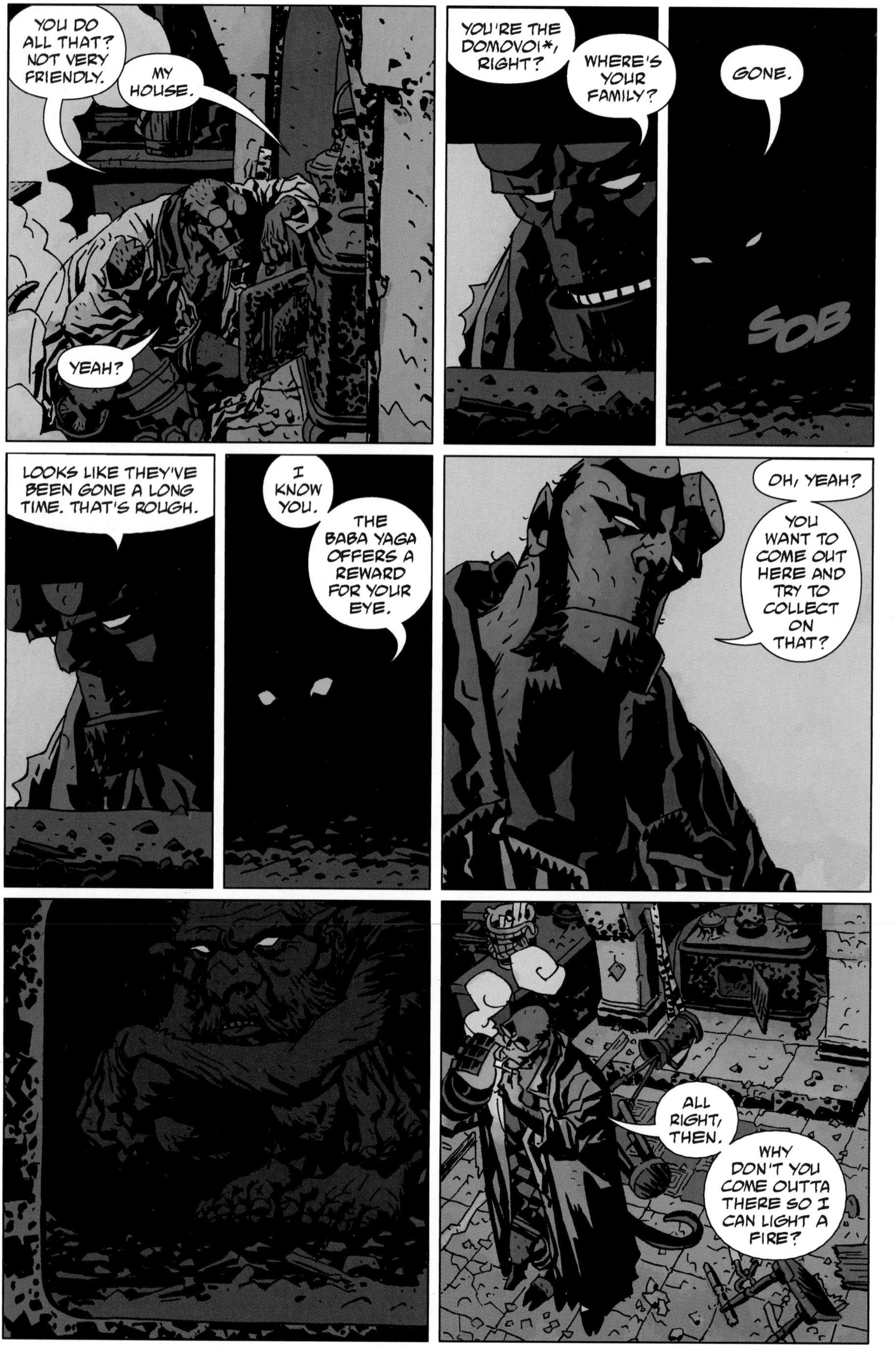
YOU DO ALL THAT? NOT VERY FRIENDLY.
MY HOUSE.
YEAH?
YOU'RE THE DOMOVOI*, RIGHT?
WHERE'S YOUR FAMILY?
GONE.
SOB
LOOKS LIKE THEY'VE BEEN GONE A LONG TIME. THAT'S ROUGH.
I KNOW YOU.
THE BABA YAGA OFFERS A REWARD FOR YOUR EYE.
OH, YEAH?
YOU WANT TO COME OUT HERE AND TRY TO COLLECT ON THAT?
ALL RIGHT, THEN.
WHY DON'T YOU COME OUTTA THERE SO I CAN LIGHT A FIRE?

*A RUSSIAN HOUSE SPIRIT--USUALLY THE SPIRIT OF AN ANCESTOR WHO LOOKS AFTER THE WELFARE OF THE FAMILY.

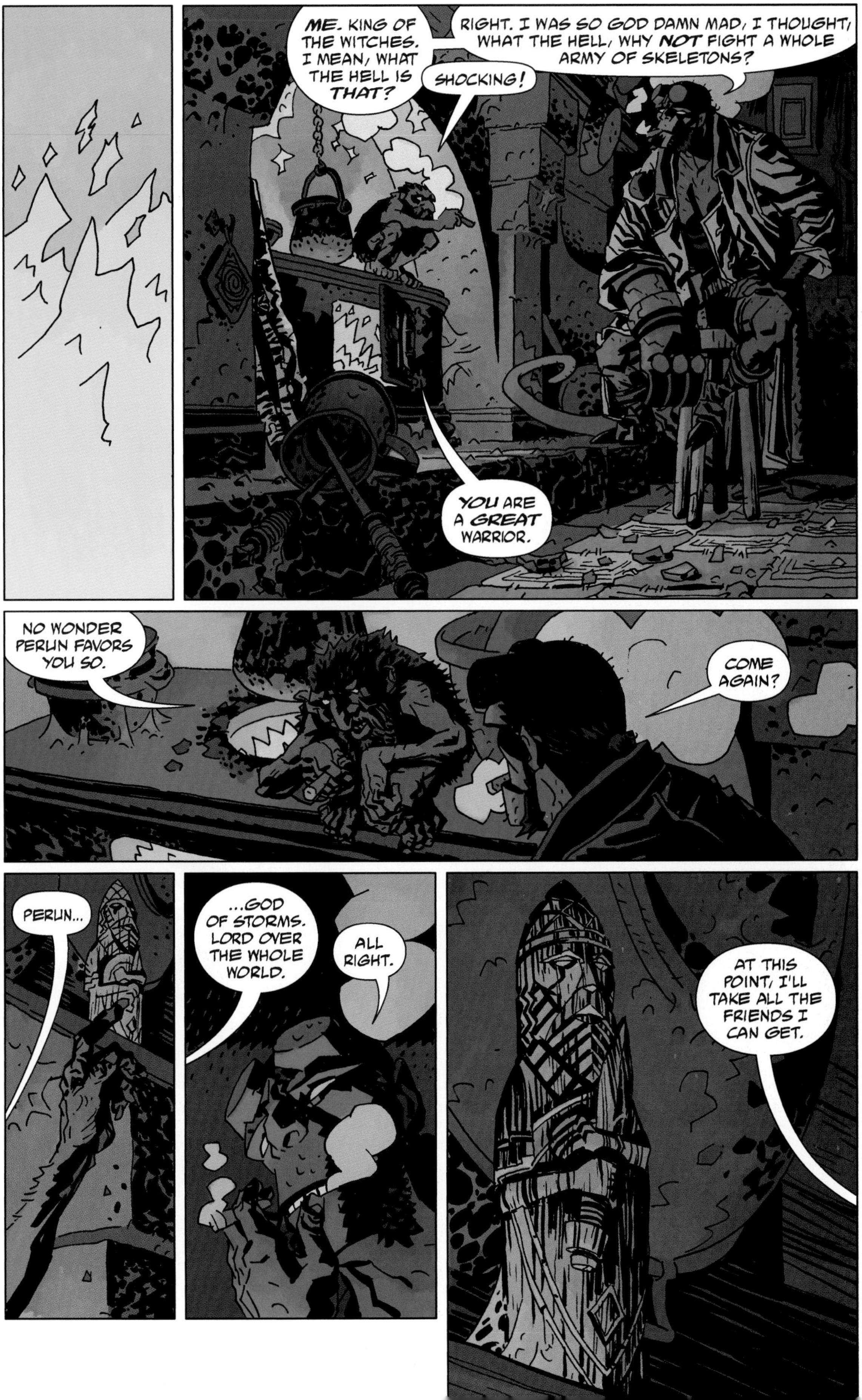
ME. KING OF THE WITCHES. I MEAN, WHAT THE HELL IS THAT?
RIGHT. I WAS SO GOD DAMN MAD, I THOUGHT, WHAT THE HELL, WHY NOT FIGHT A WHOLE ARMY OF SKELETONS?
SHOCKING!
YOU ARE A GREAT WARRIOR.
NO WONDER PERUN FAVORS YOU SO.
COME AGAIN?
PERUN...
...GOD OF STORMS. LORD OVER THE WHOLE WORLD.
ALL RIGHT.
AT THIS POINT, I'LL TAKE ALL THE FRIENDS I CAN GET.

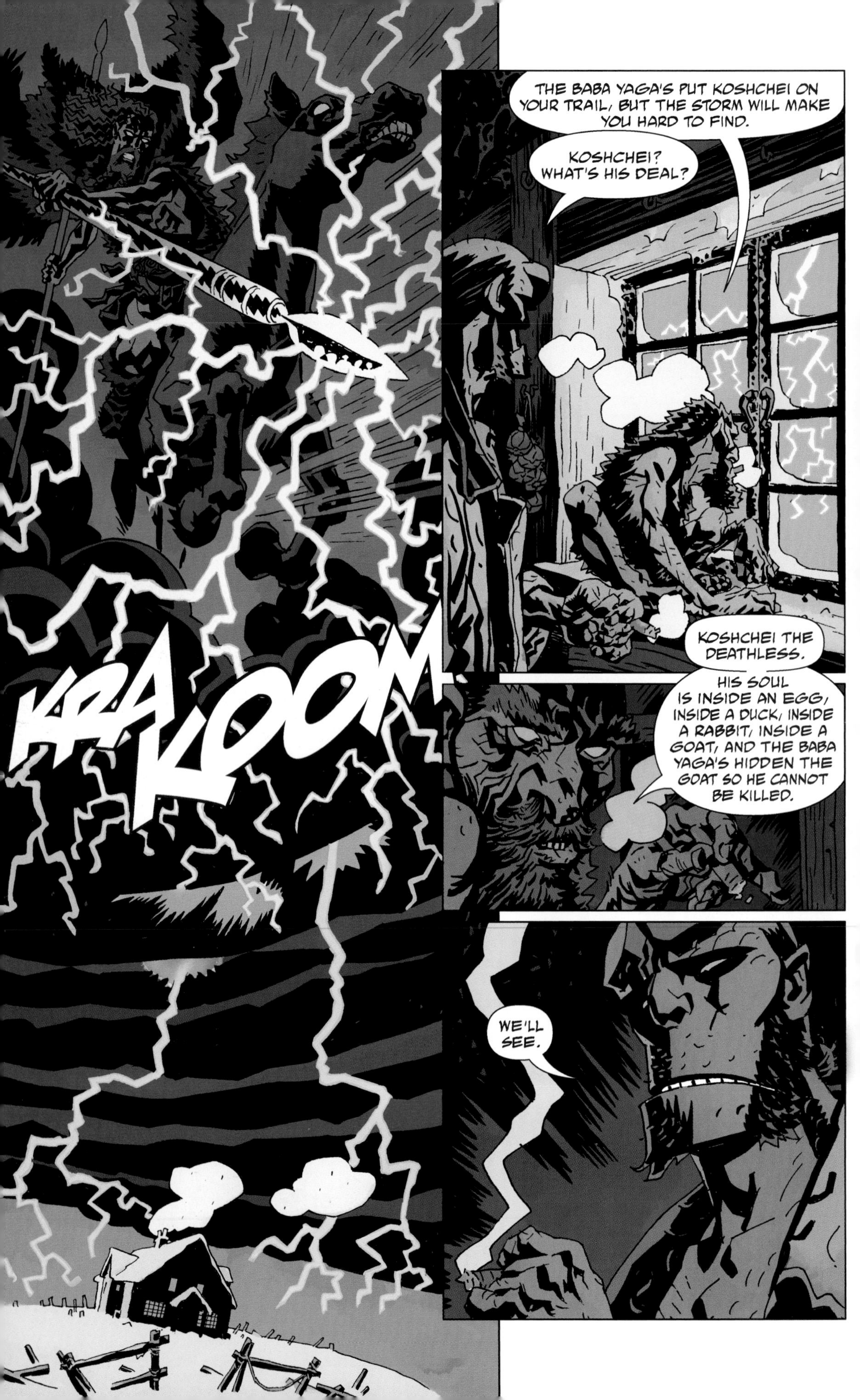
KRAKOOM
THE BABA YAGA'S PUT KOSHCHEI ON YOUR TRAIL, BUT THE STORM WILL MAKE YOU HARD TO FIND.
KOSHCHEI? WHAT'S HIS DEAL?
KOSHCHEI THE DEATHLESS.
HIS SOUL IS INSIDE AN EGG, INSIDE A DUCK, INSIDE A RABBIT, INSIDE A GOAT, AND THE BABA YAGA'S HIDDEN THE GOAT SO HE CANNOT BE KILLED.
WE'LL SEE.

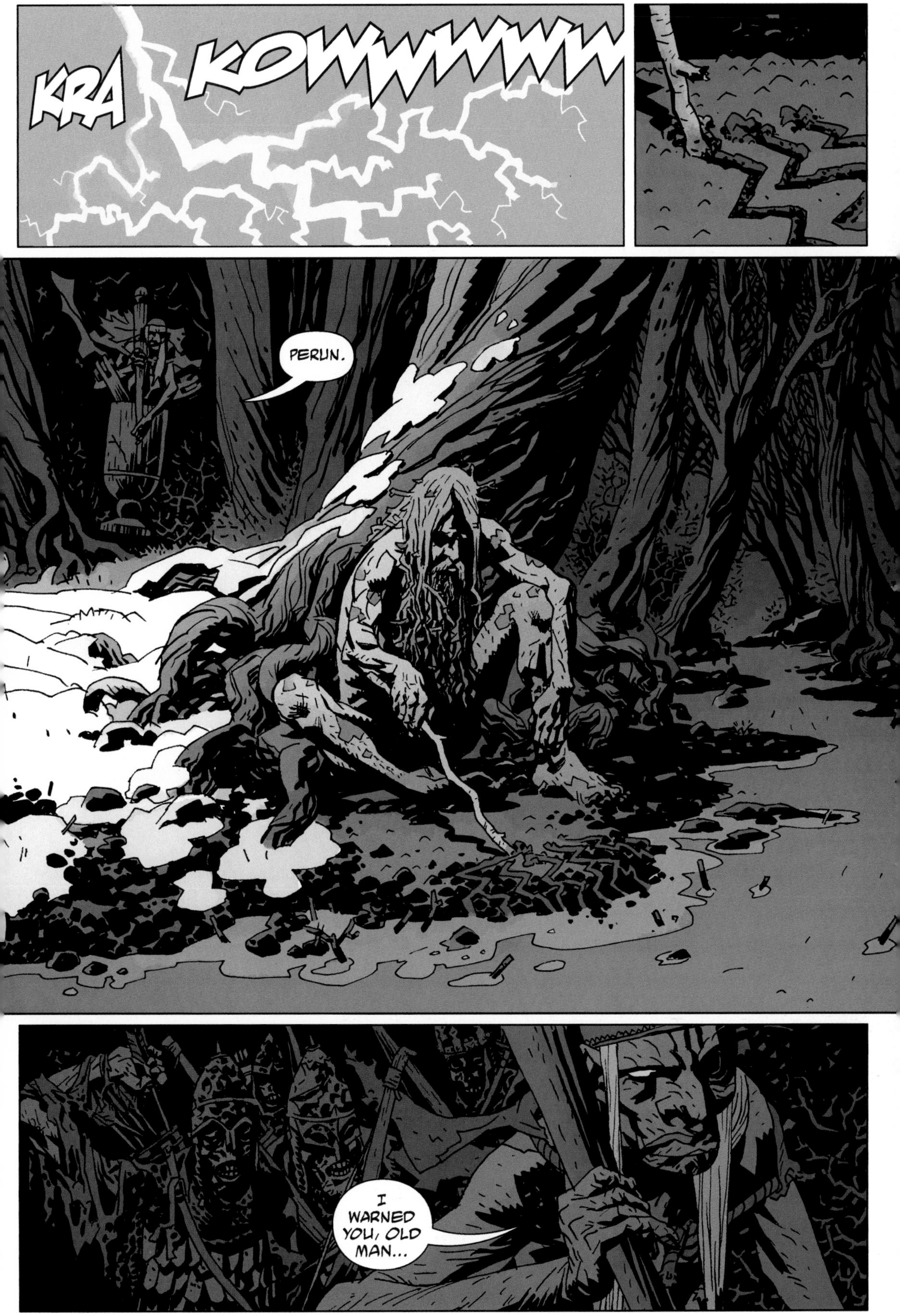
KRA KOWWWWW
PERUN.
I WARNED YOU, OLD MAN...

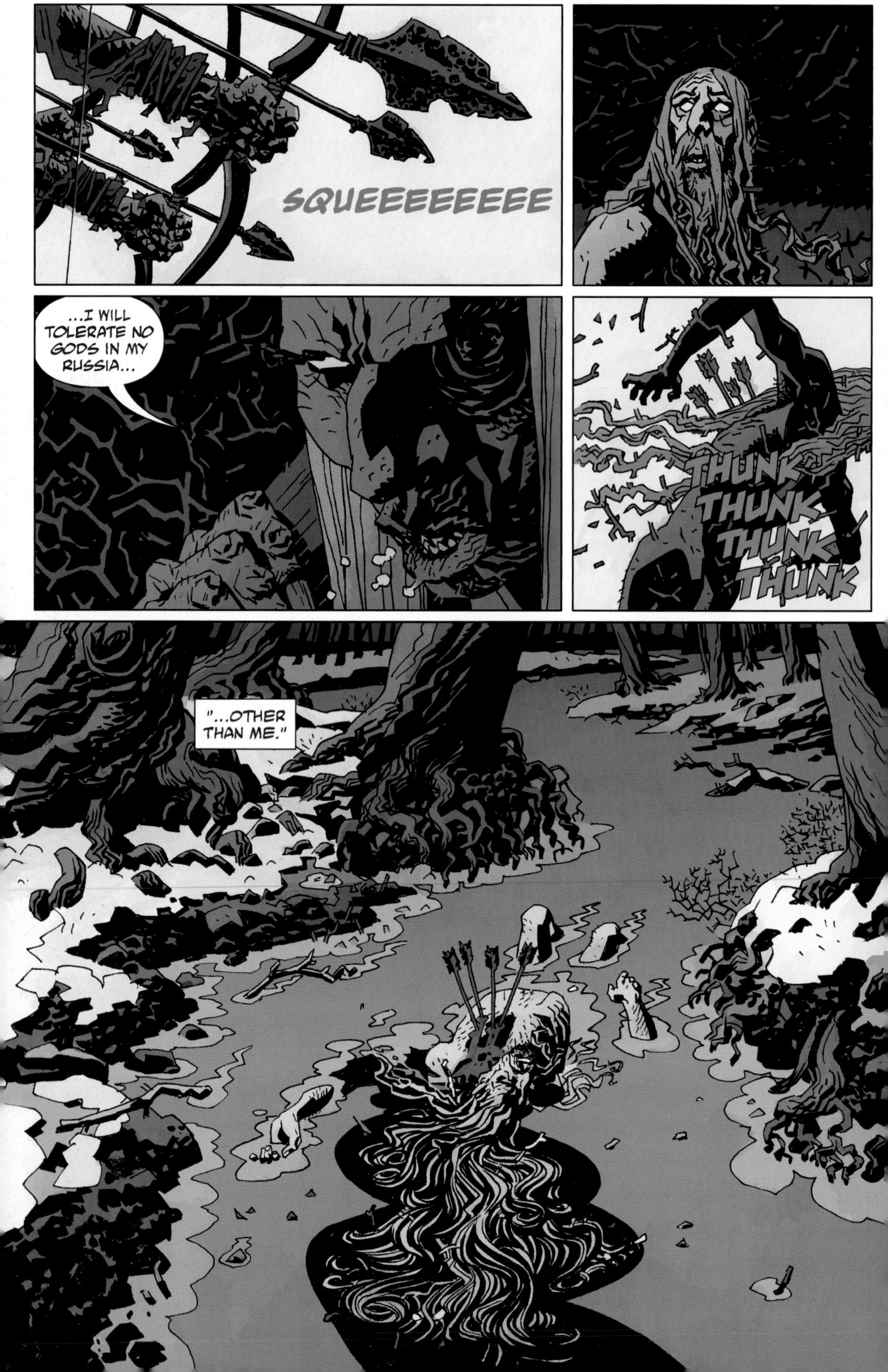
SQUEEEEEEEEE
...I WILL TOLERATE NO GODS IN MY RUSSIA...
THUNK
THUNK
THUNK
THUNK
"...OTHER THAN ME."

CHAPTER FOUR

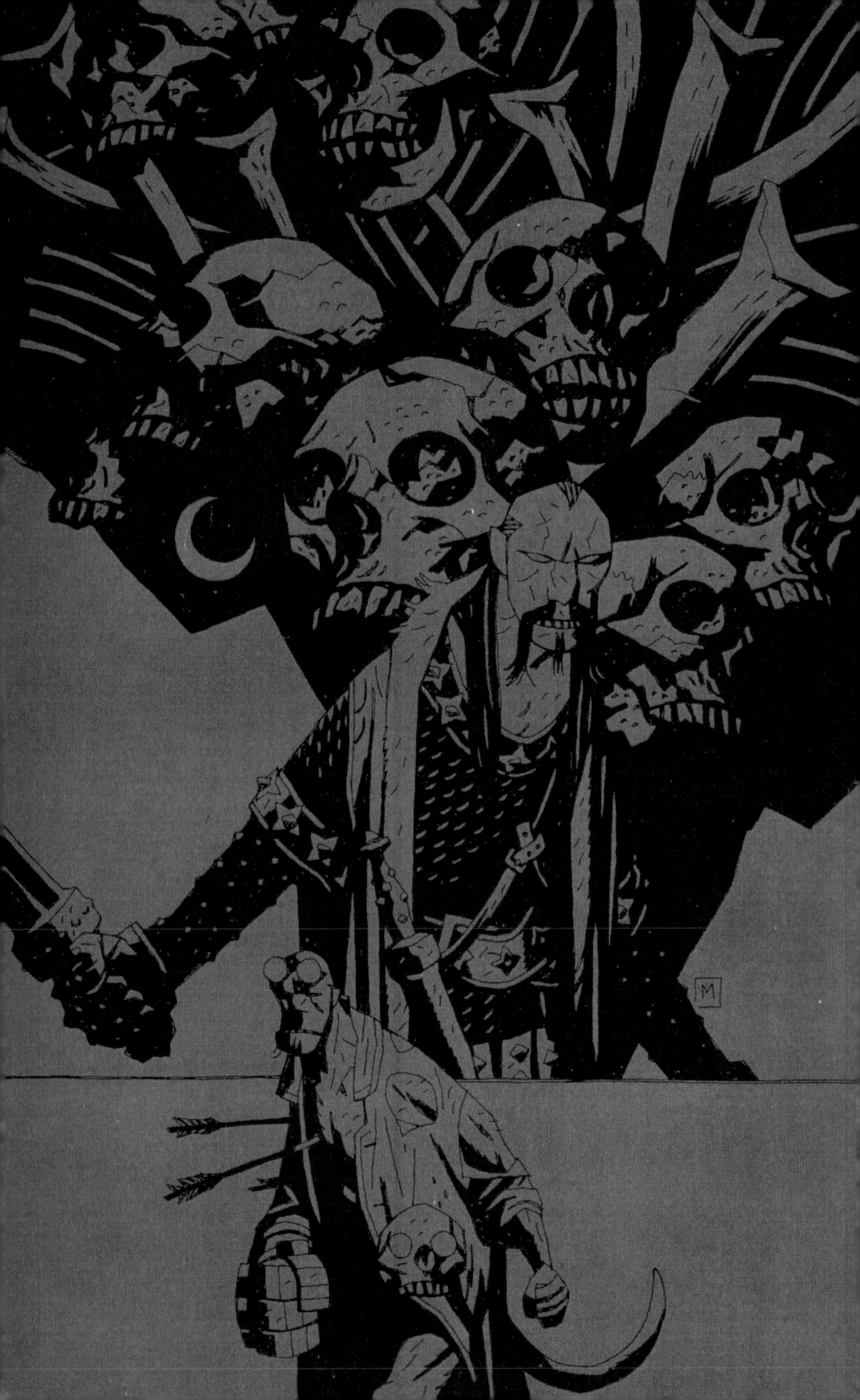

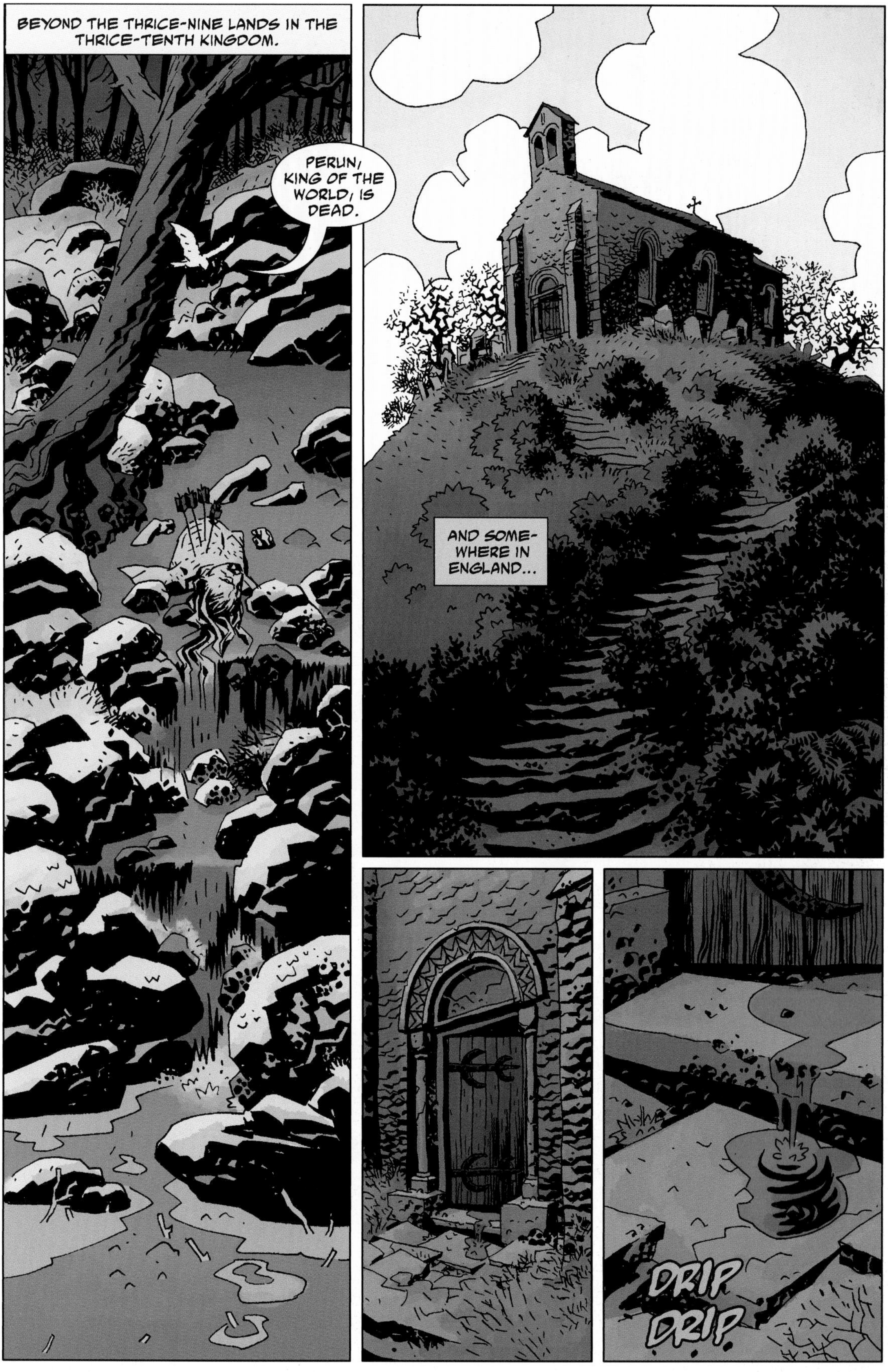
BEYOND THE THRICE-NINE LANDS IN THE THRICE-TENTH KINGDOM.
PERUN, KING OF THE WORLD, IS DEAD.
AND SOME-WHERE IN ENGLAND...
DRIP DRIP

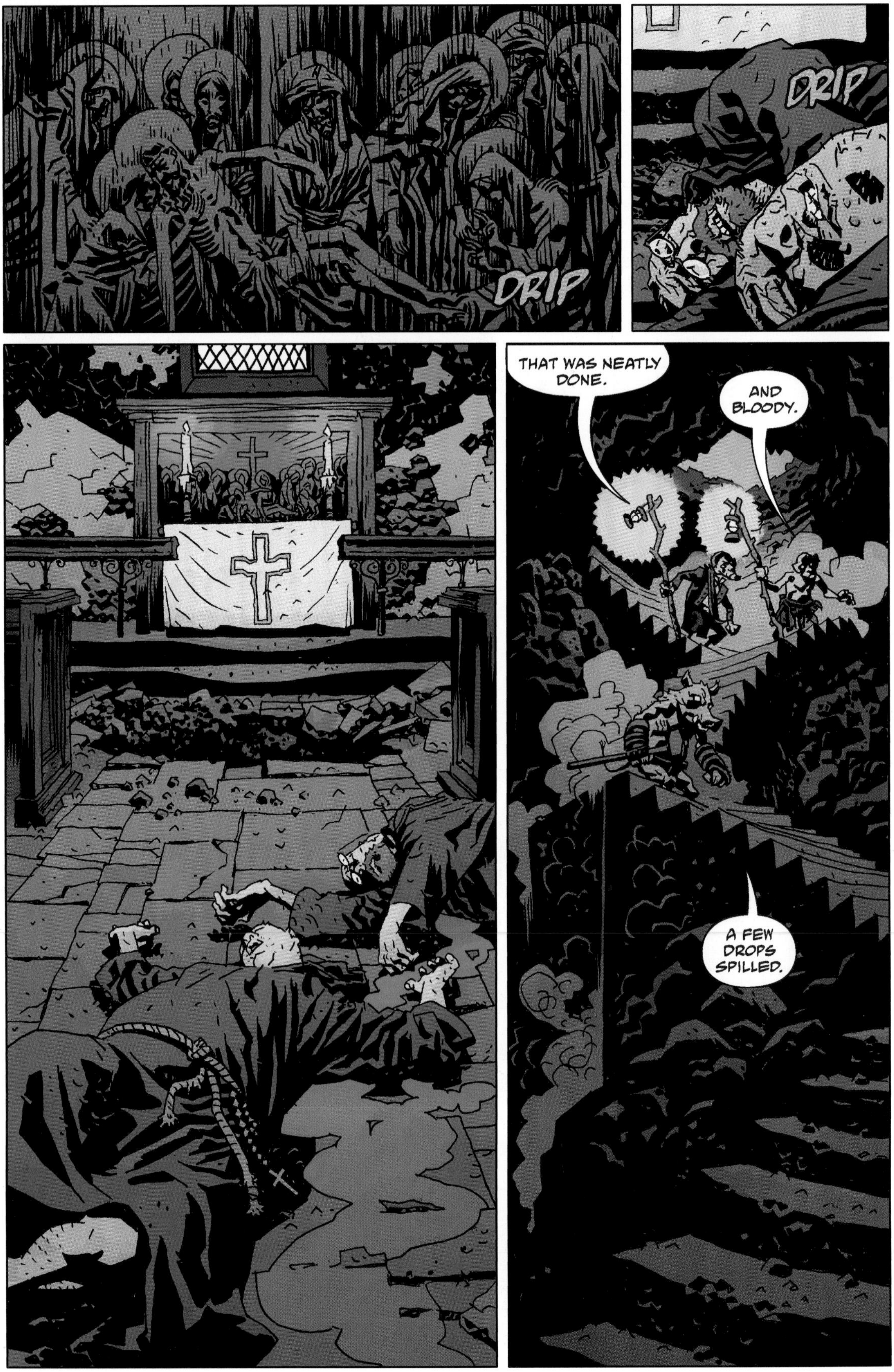
DRIP
DRIP
THAT WAS NEATLY DONE.
AND BLOODY.
A FEW DROPS SPILLED.

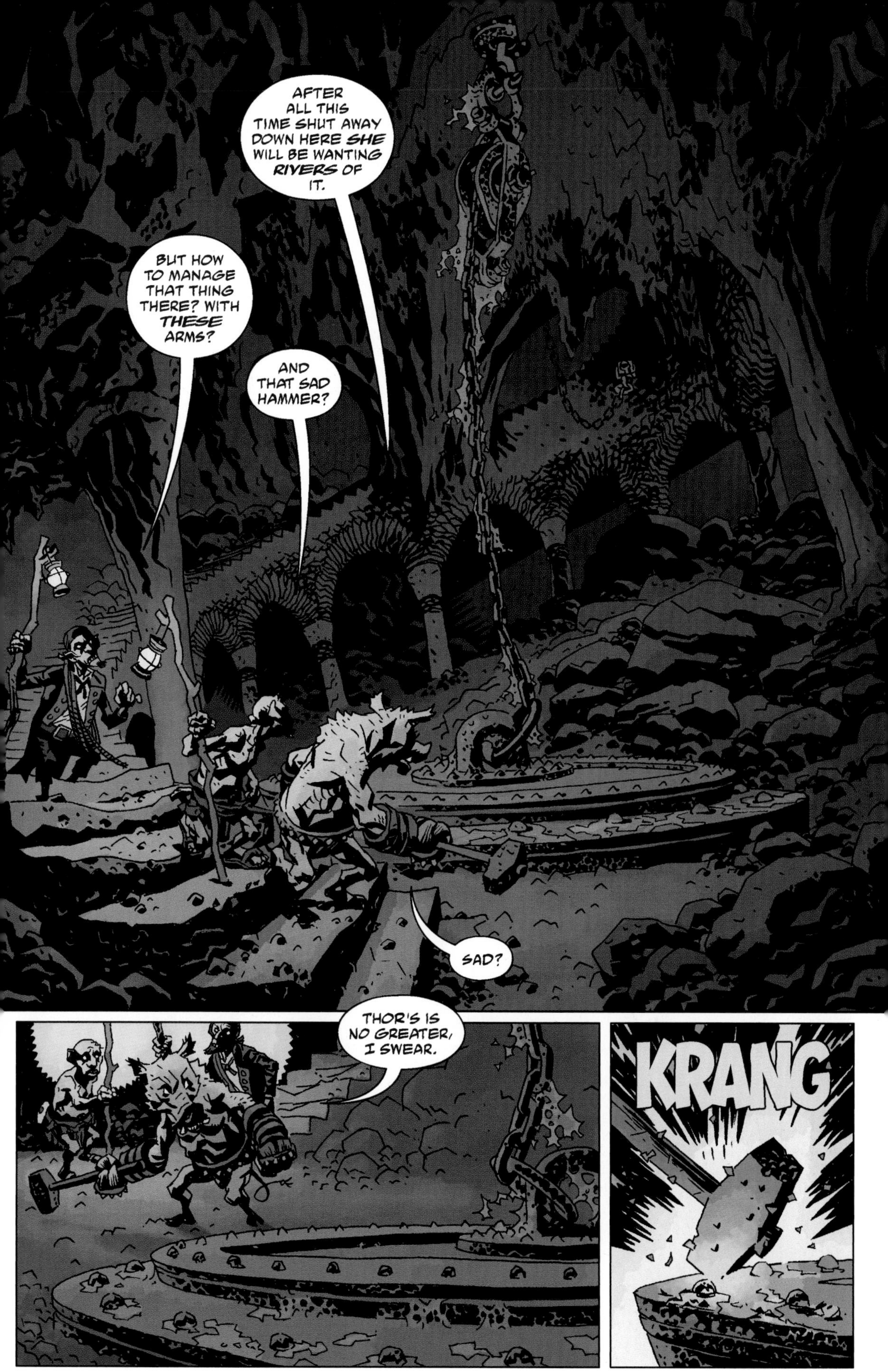

AFTER ALL THIS TIME SHUT AWAY DOWN HERE *SHE* WILL BE WANTING *RIVERS* OF IT.
BUT HOW TO MANAGE THAT THING THERE? WITH *THESE* ARMS?
AND THAT SAD HAMMER?
SAD?
THOR'S IS NO GREATER, I SWEAR.
KRANG

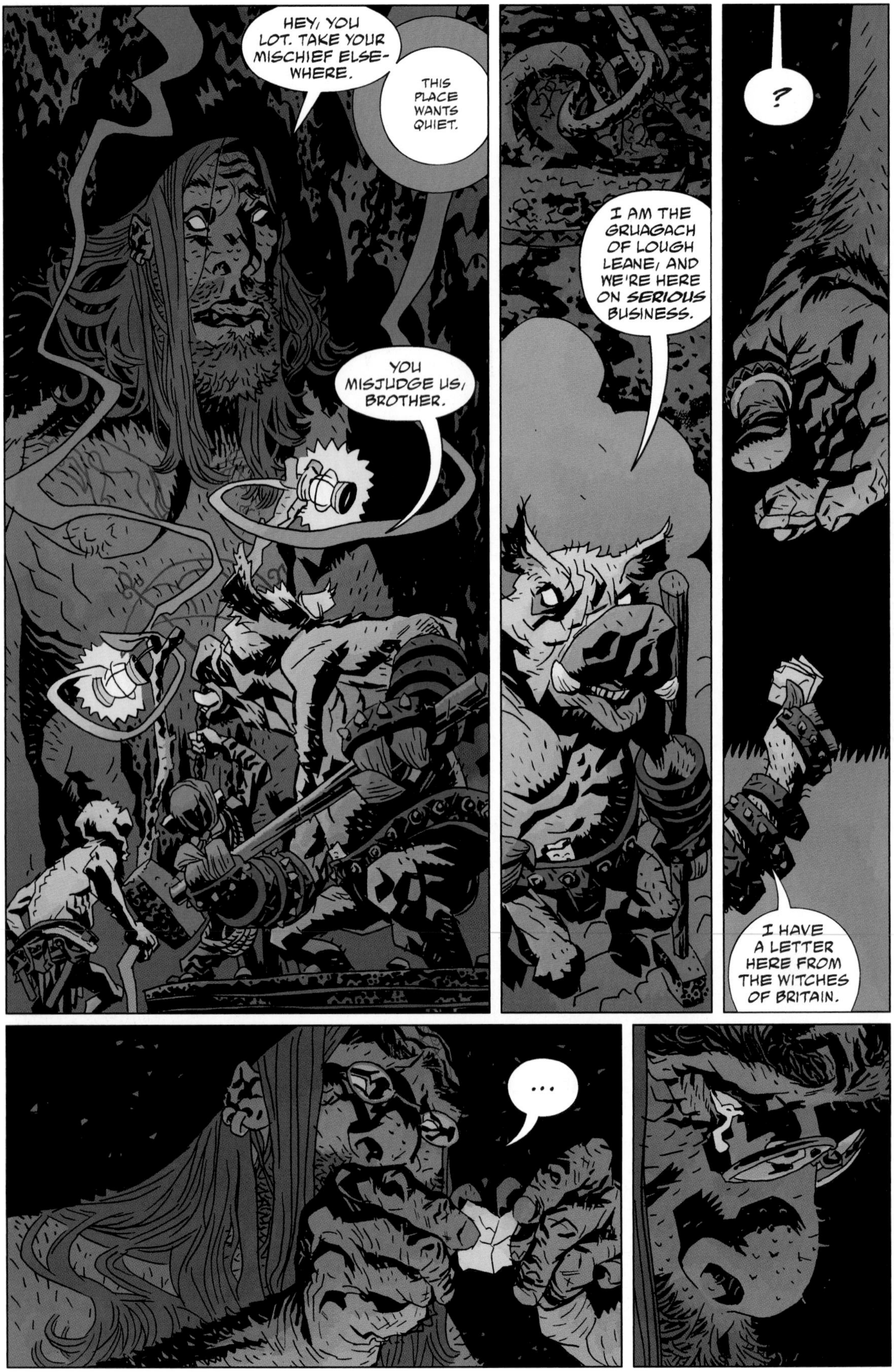

HEY, YOU LOT. TAKE YOUR MISCHIEF ELSE-WHERE.
THIS PLACE WANTS QUIET.
YOU MISJUDGE US, BROTHER.
I AM THE GRUAGACH OF LOUGH LEANE, AND WE'RE HERE ON *SERIOUS* BUSINESS.
?
I HAVE A LETTER HERE FROM THE WITCHES OF BRITAIN.
...

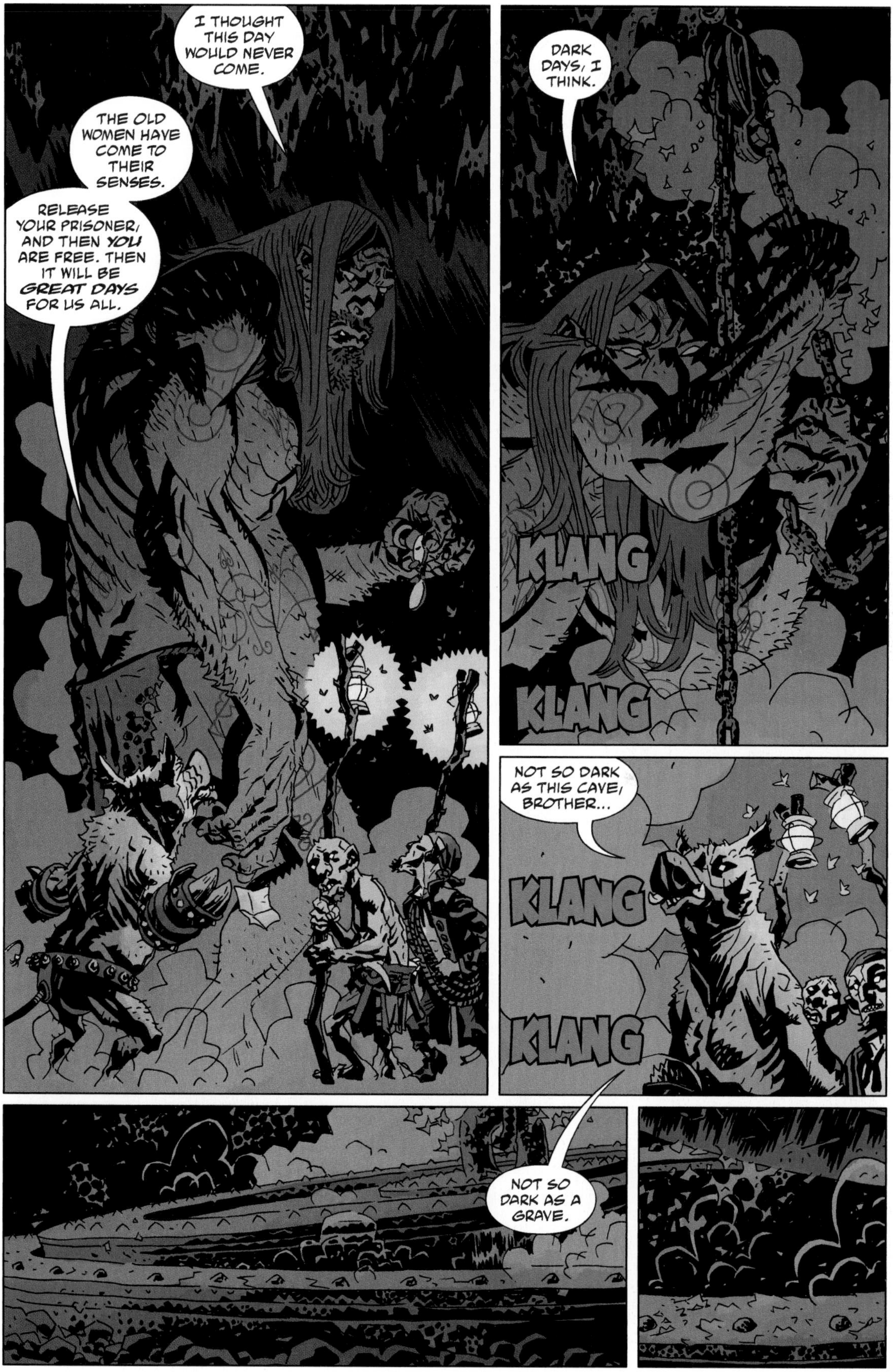

I THOUGHT THIS DAY WOULD NEVER COME.
THE OLD WOMEN HAVE COME TO THEIR SENSES.
RELEASE YOUR PRISONER, AND THEN YOU ARE FREE. THEN IT WILL BE GREAT DAYS FOR US ALL.
DARK DAYS, I THINK.
KLANG
KLANG
NOT SO DARK AS THIS CAVE, BROTHER...
KLANG
KLANG
NOT SO DARK AS A GRAVE.

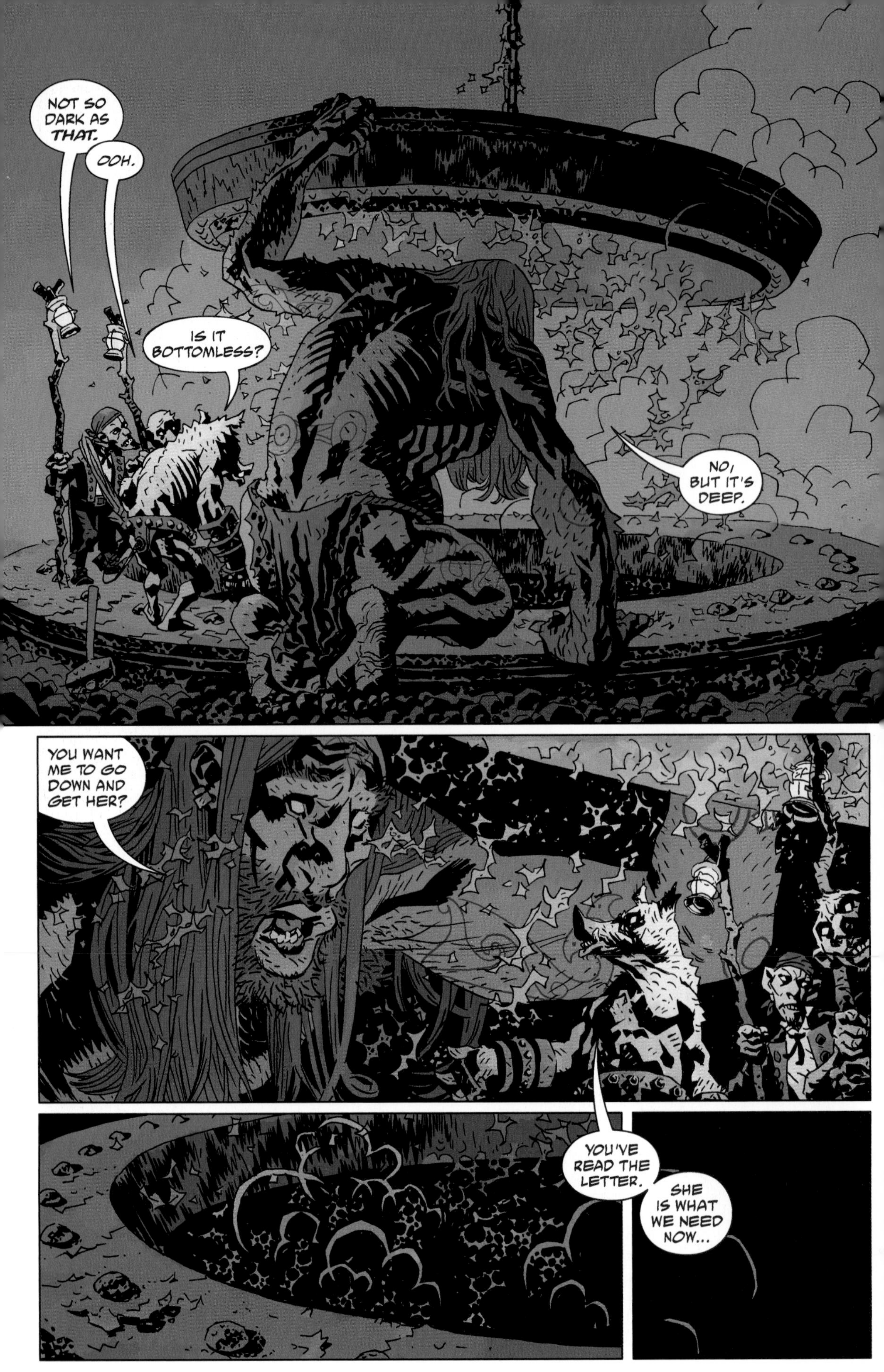
NOT SO DARK AS *THAT.*
OOH.
IS IT BOTTOMLESS?
NO, BUT IT'S DEEP.
YOU WANT ME TO GO DOWN AND GET HER?
YOU'VE READ THE LETTER.
SHE IS WHAT WE NEED NOW...

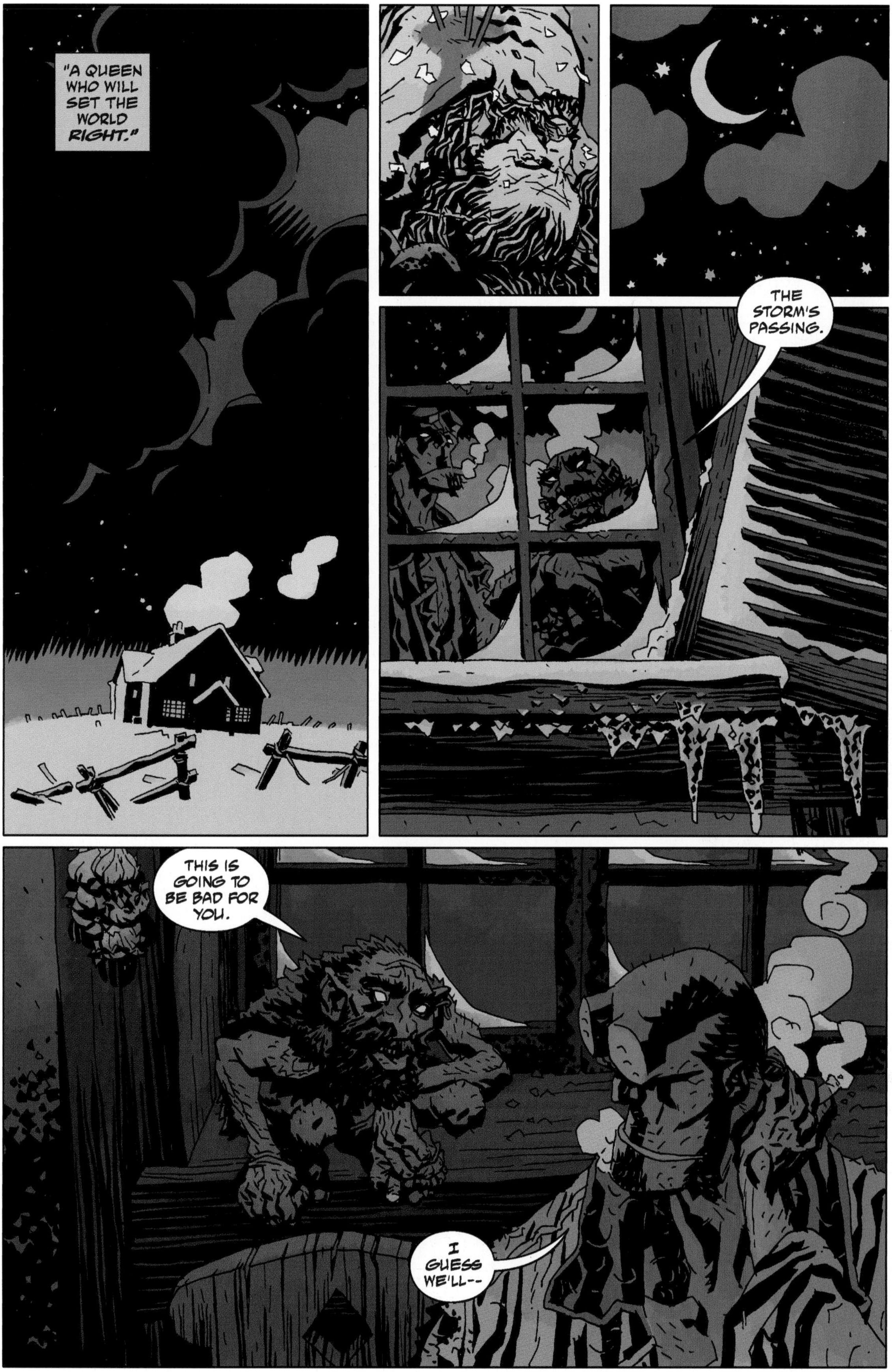
"A QUEEN WHO WILL SET THE WORLD *RIGHT.*"
THE STORM'S PASSING.
THIS IS GOING TO BE BAD FOR YOU.
I GUESS WE'LL--

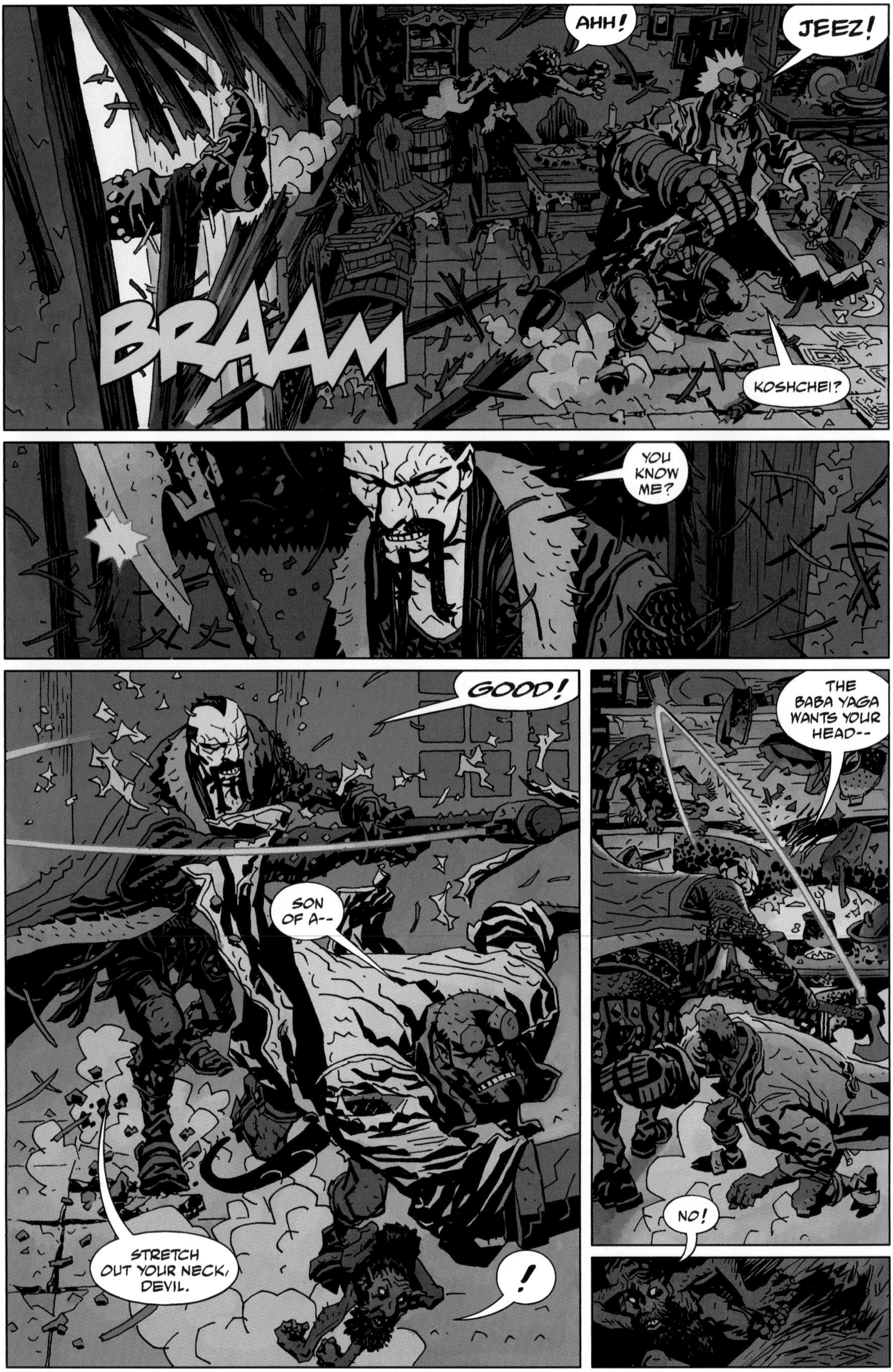
BRAAM
AHH!
JEEZ!
KOSHCHEI?
YOU KNOW ME?
GOOD!
SON OF A--
STRETCH OUT YOUR NECK, DEVIL.
!
THE BABA YAGA WANTS YOUR HEAD--
NO!

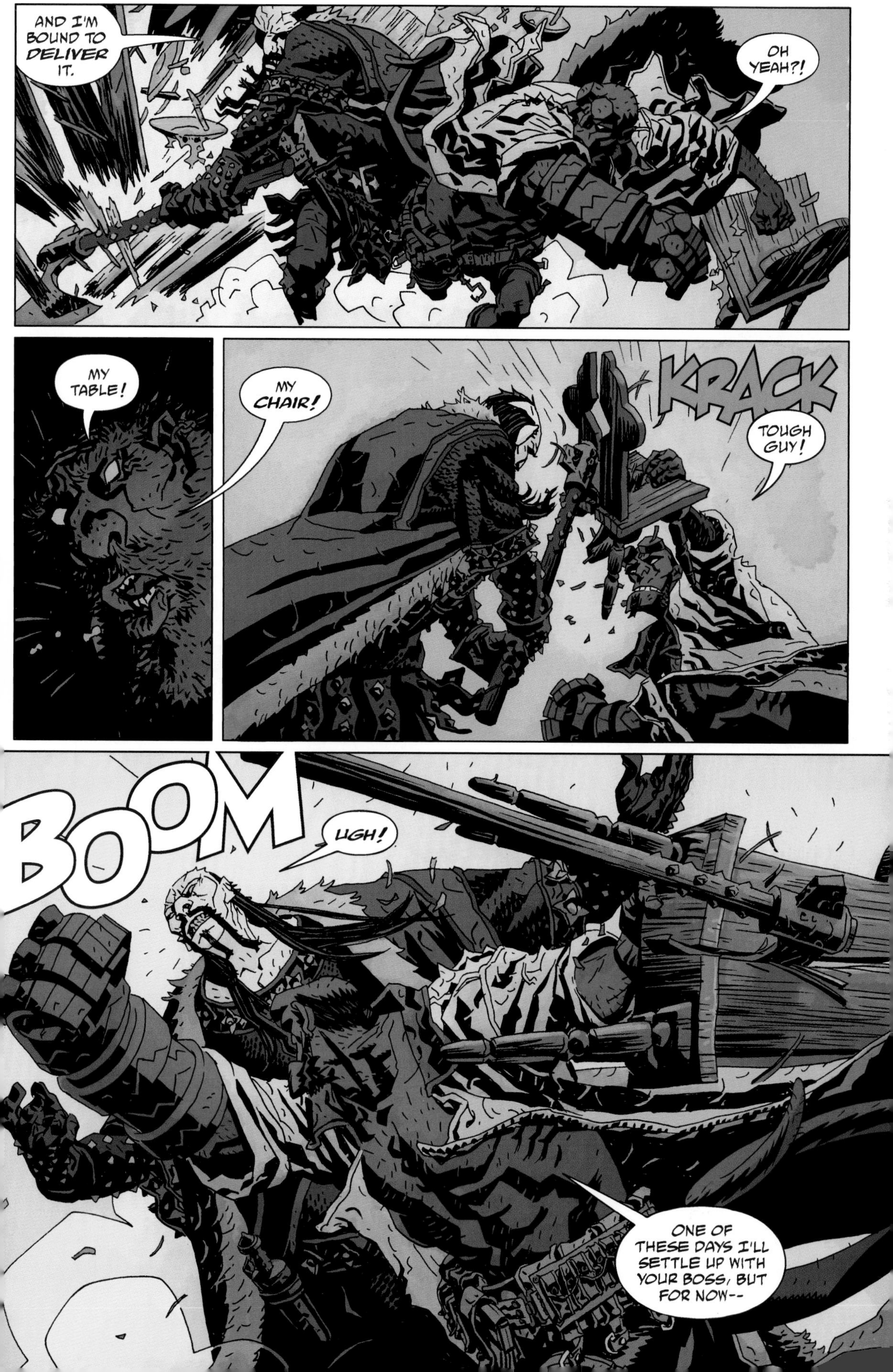
AND I'M BOUND TO DELIVER IT.
OH YEAH?!
MY TABLE!
MY CHAIR!
KRACK
TOUGH GUY!
BOOM
UGH!
ONE OF THESE DAYS I'LL SETTLE UP WITH YOUR BOSS, BUT FOR NOW--

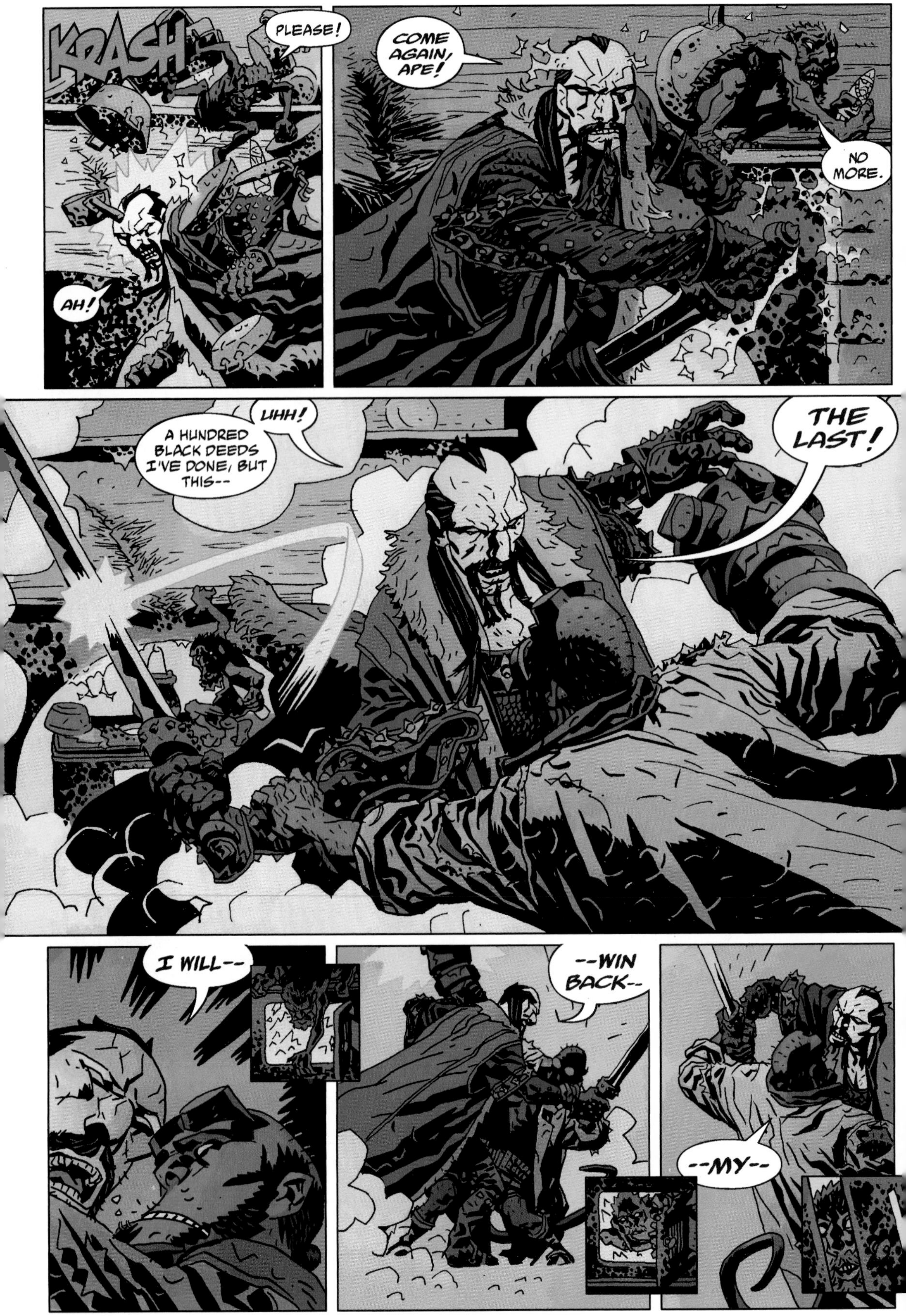
KRASH
PLEASE!
AH!
COME AGAIN, APE!
NO MORE.
UHH!
A HUNDRED BLACK DEEDS I'VE DONE, BUT THIS--
THE LAST!
I WILL--
--WIN BACK--
--MY--

--SOUL!
KLOK
THE WORD CAN MEAN NOTHING TO YOU, DEVIL, BUT I'LL HAVE IT...
KRANG
AND AT SMALL COST--
GIMME THAT!
!
MY TURN...

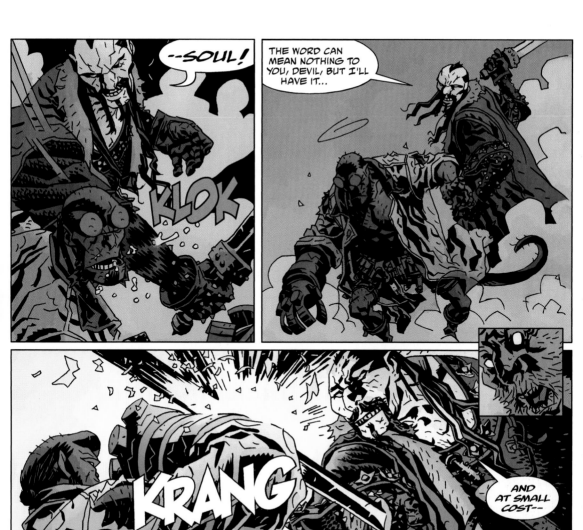

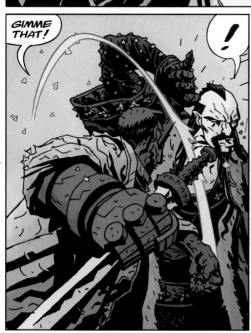

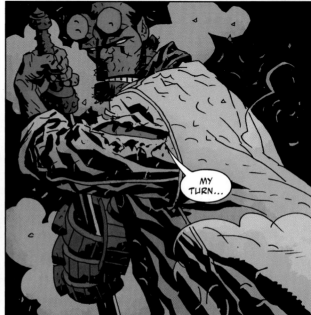

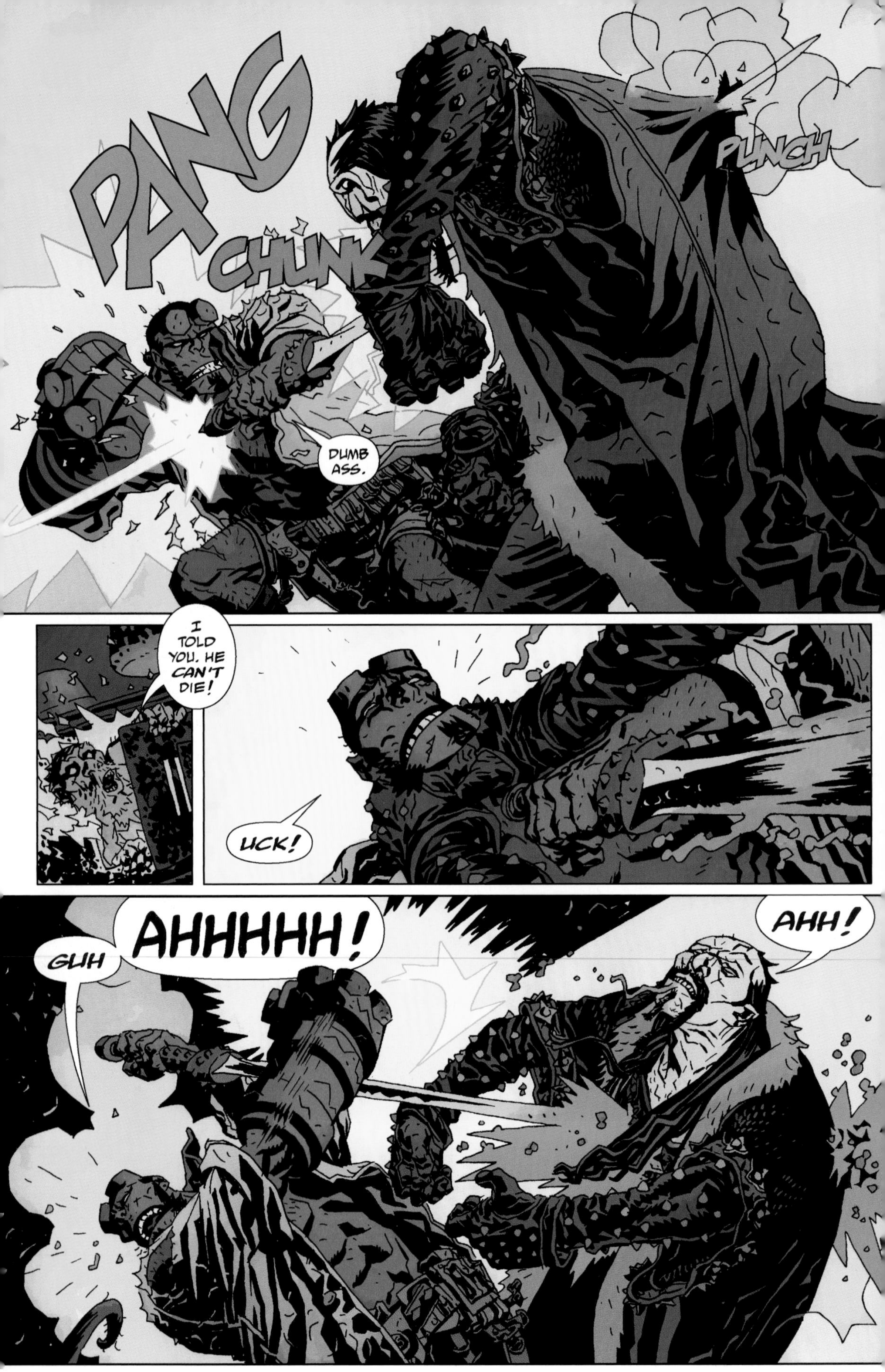
PANG
CHUNK
PUNCH
DUMB ASS.
I TOLD YOU. HE CAN'T DIE!
UCK!
GUH
AHHHHH!
AHH!

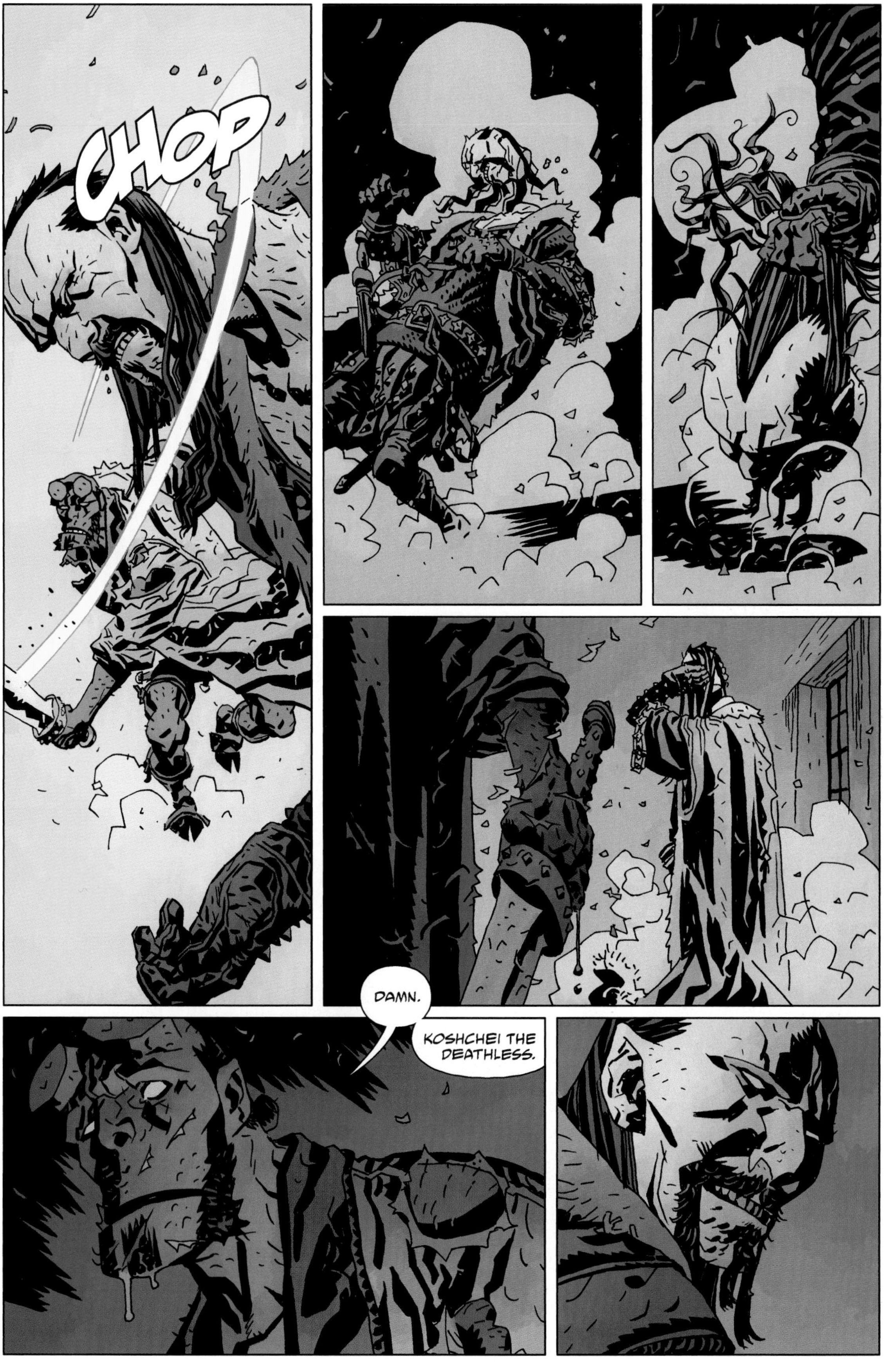
CHOP
DAMN.
KOSHCHEI THE DEATHLESS.

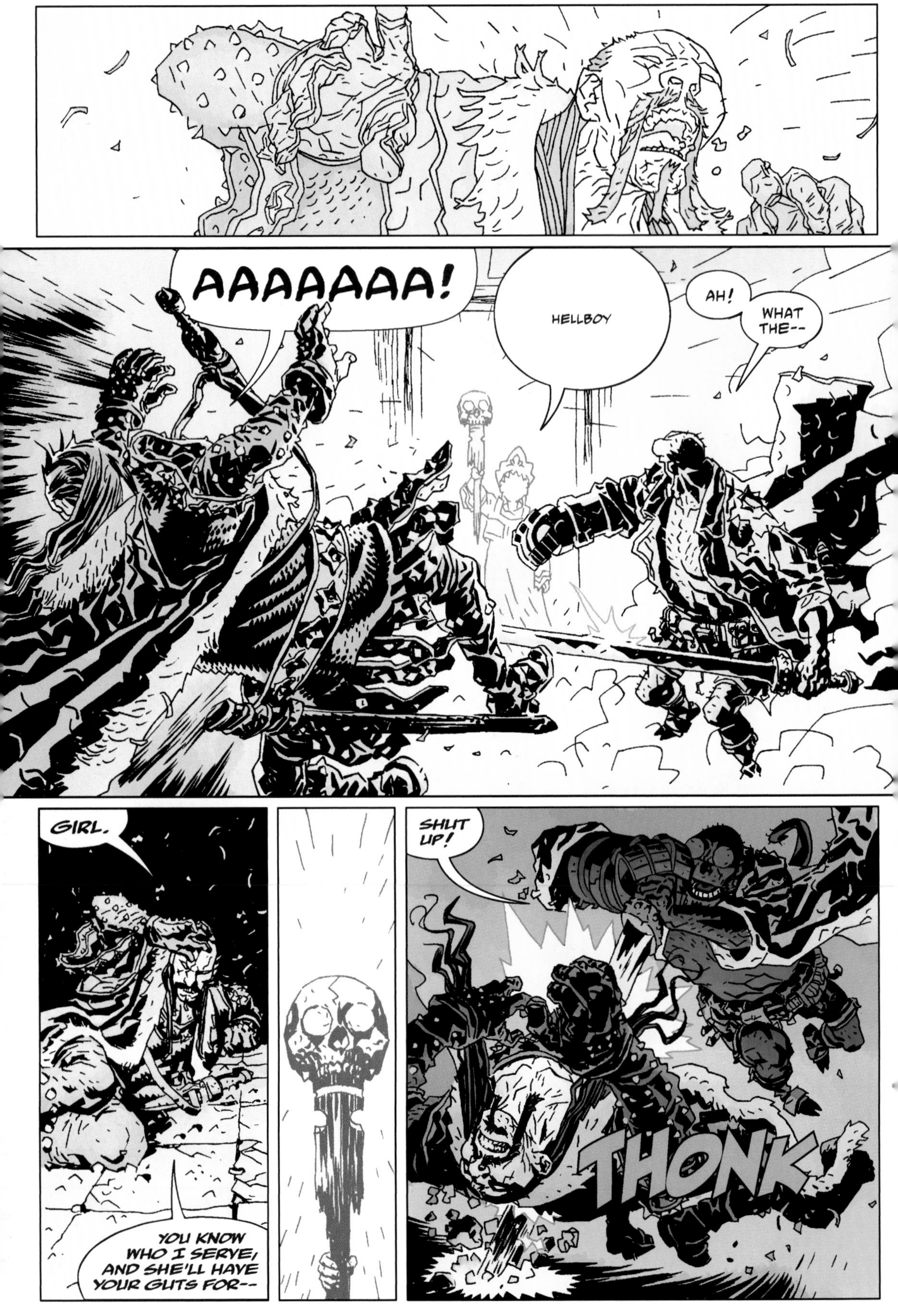
AAAAAAA!
HELLBOY
AH!
WHAT THE--
GIRL.
YOU KNOW WHO I SERVE, AND SHE'LL HAVE YOUR GUTS FOR--
SHUT UP!
THONK

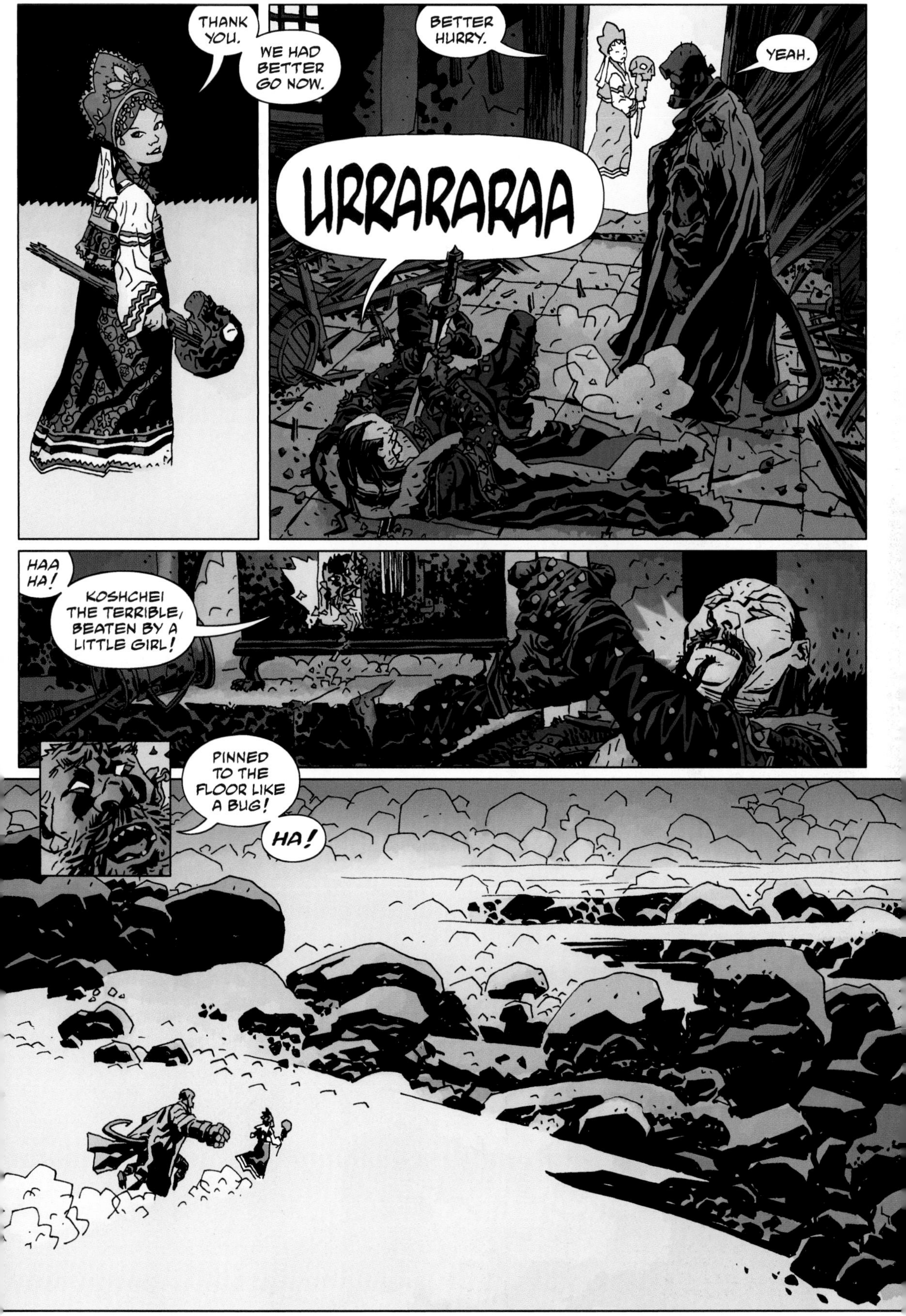
THANK YOU.
WE HAD BETTER GO NOW.
BETTER HURRY.
YEAH.
URRARARAA
HAA HA!
KOSHCHEI THE TERRIBLE, BEATEN BY A LITTLE GIRL!
PINNED TO THE FLOOR LIKE A BUG!
HA!

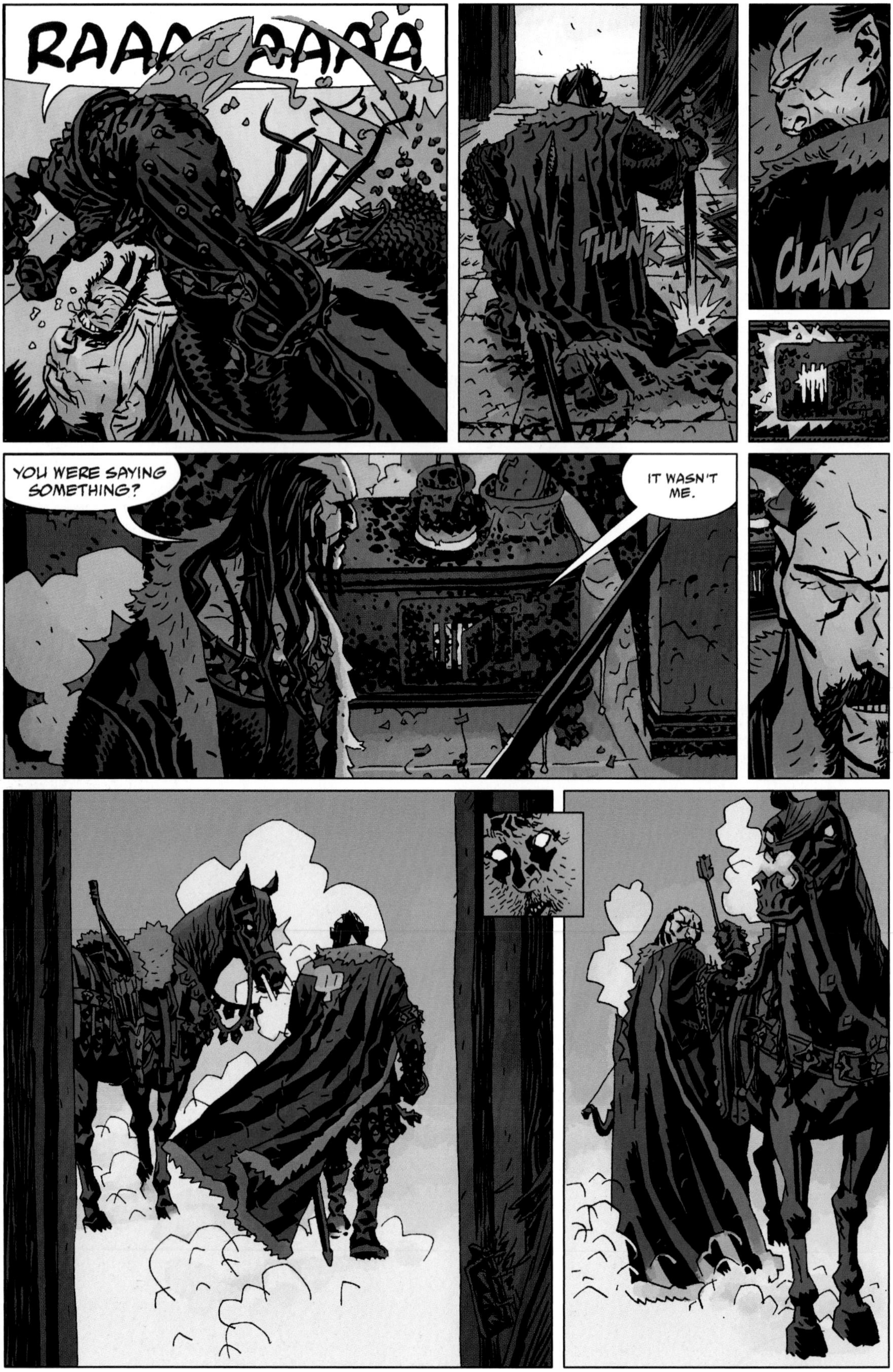
RAAAAAAAA
THUNK
CLANG
YOU WERE SAYING SOMETHING?
IT WASN'T ME.

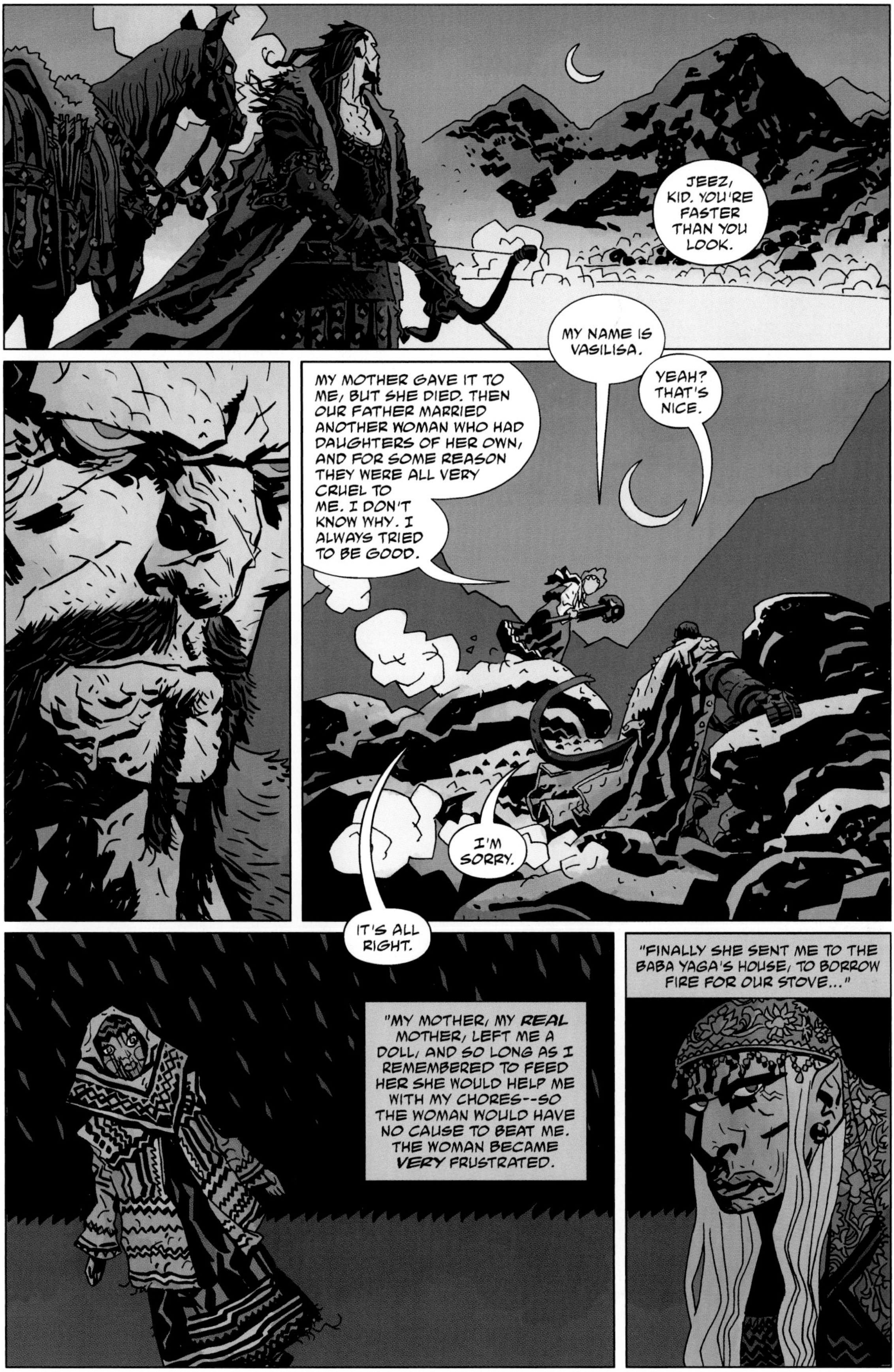
JEEZ, KID. YOU'RE FASTER THAN YOU LOOK.
MY NAME IS VASILISA.
YEAH? THAT'S NICE.
MY MOTHER GAVE IT TO ME, BUT SHE DIED. THEN OUR FATHER MARRIED ANOTHER WOMAN WHO HAD DAUGHTERS OF HER OWN, AND FOR SOME REASON THEY WERE ALL VERY CRUEL TO ME. I DON'T KNOW WHY. I ALWAYS TRIED TO BE GOOD.
I'M SORRY.
IT'S ALL RIGHT.
"MY MOTHER, MY REAL MOTHER, LEFT ME A DOLL, AND SO LONG AS I REMEMBERED TO FEED HER SHE WOULD HELP ME WITH MY CHORES--SO THE WOMAN WOULD HAVE NO CAUSE TO BEAT ME. THE WOMAN BECAME VERY FRUSTRATED.
"FINALLY SHE SENT ME TO THE BABA YAGA'S HOUSE, TO BORROW FIRE FOR OUR STOVE..."

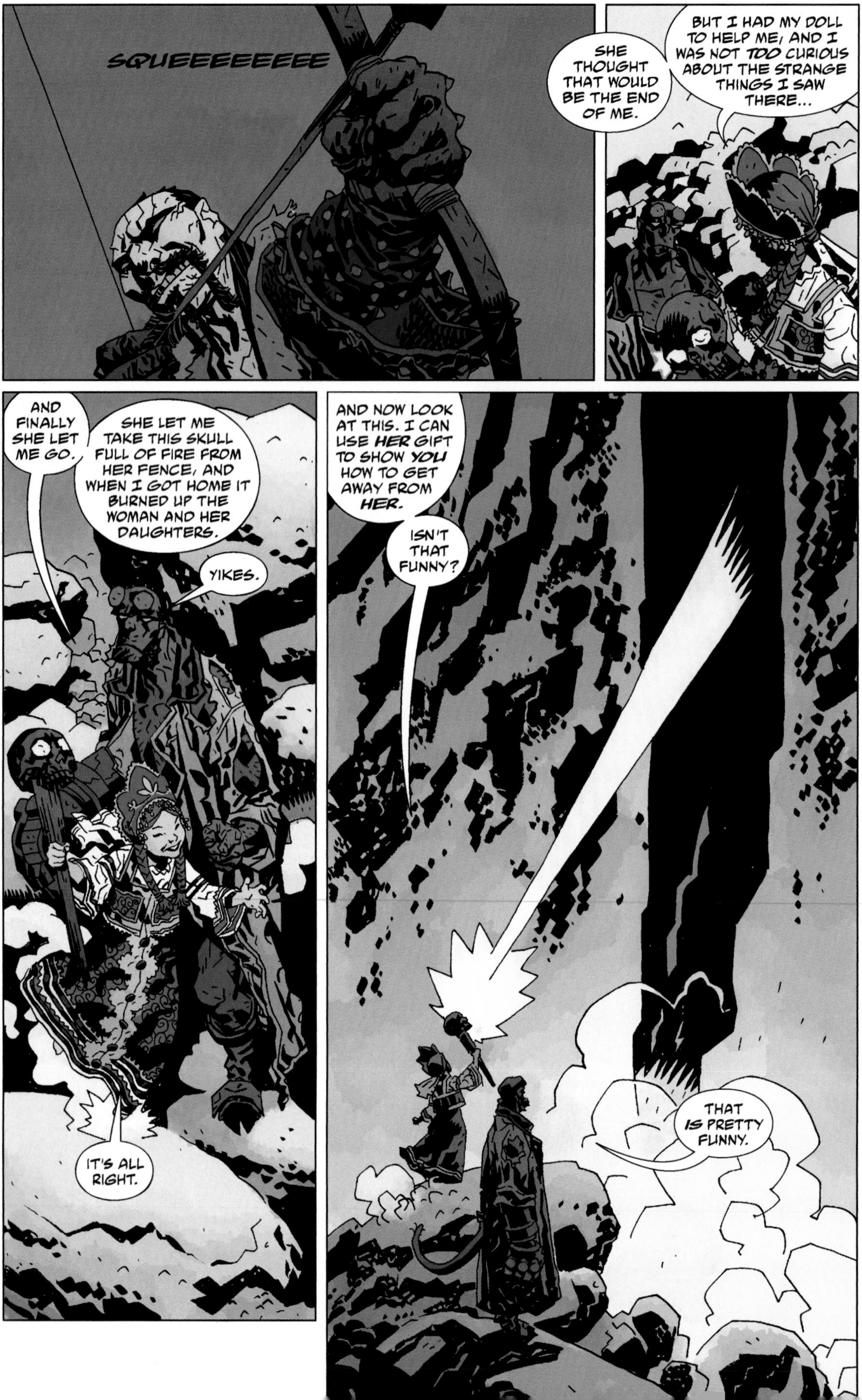
SQUEEEEEEEEE
SHE THOUGHT THAT WOULD BE THE END OF ME.
BUT I HAD MY DOLL TO HELP ME, AND I WAS NOT TOO CURIOUS ABOUT THE STRANGE THINGS I SAW THERE...
AND FINALLY SHE LET ME GO.
SHE LET ME TAKE THIS SKULL FULL OF FIRE FROM HER FENCE, AND WHEN I GOT HOME IT BURNED UP THE WOMAN AND HER DAUGHTERS.
YIKES.
IT'S ALL RIGHT.
AND NOW LOOK AT THIS. I CAN USE HER GIFT TO SHOW YOU HOW TO GET AWAY FROM HER.
ISN'T THAT FUNNY?
THAT IS PRETTY FUNNY.

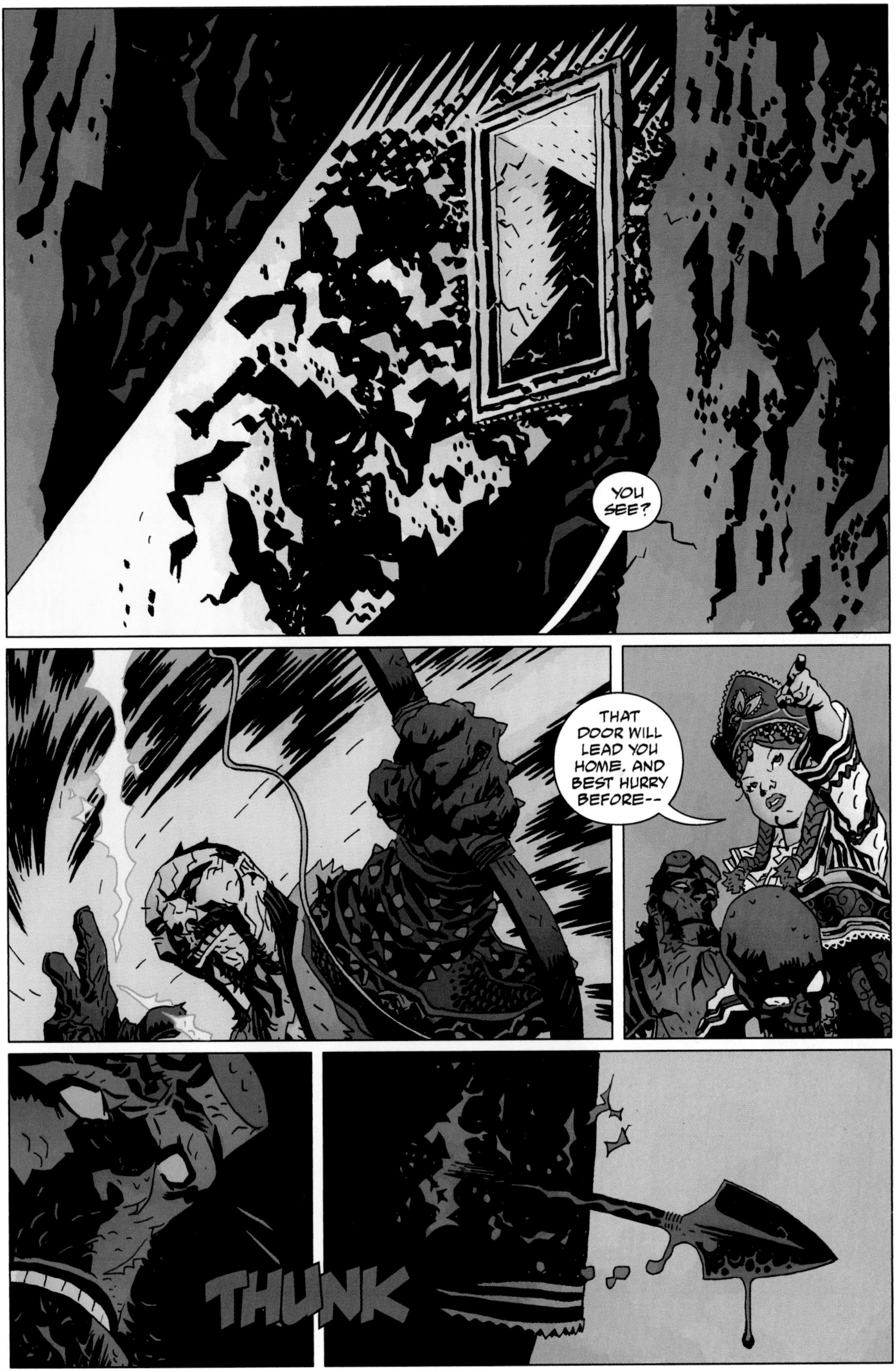
YOU SEE?
THAT DOOR WILL LEAD YOU HOME. AND BEST HURRY BEFORE--
THUNK

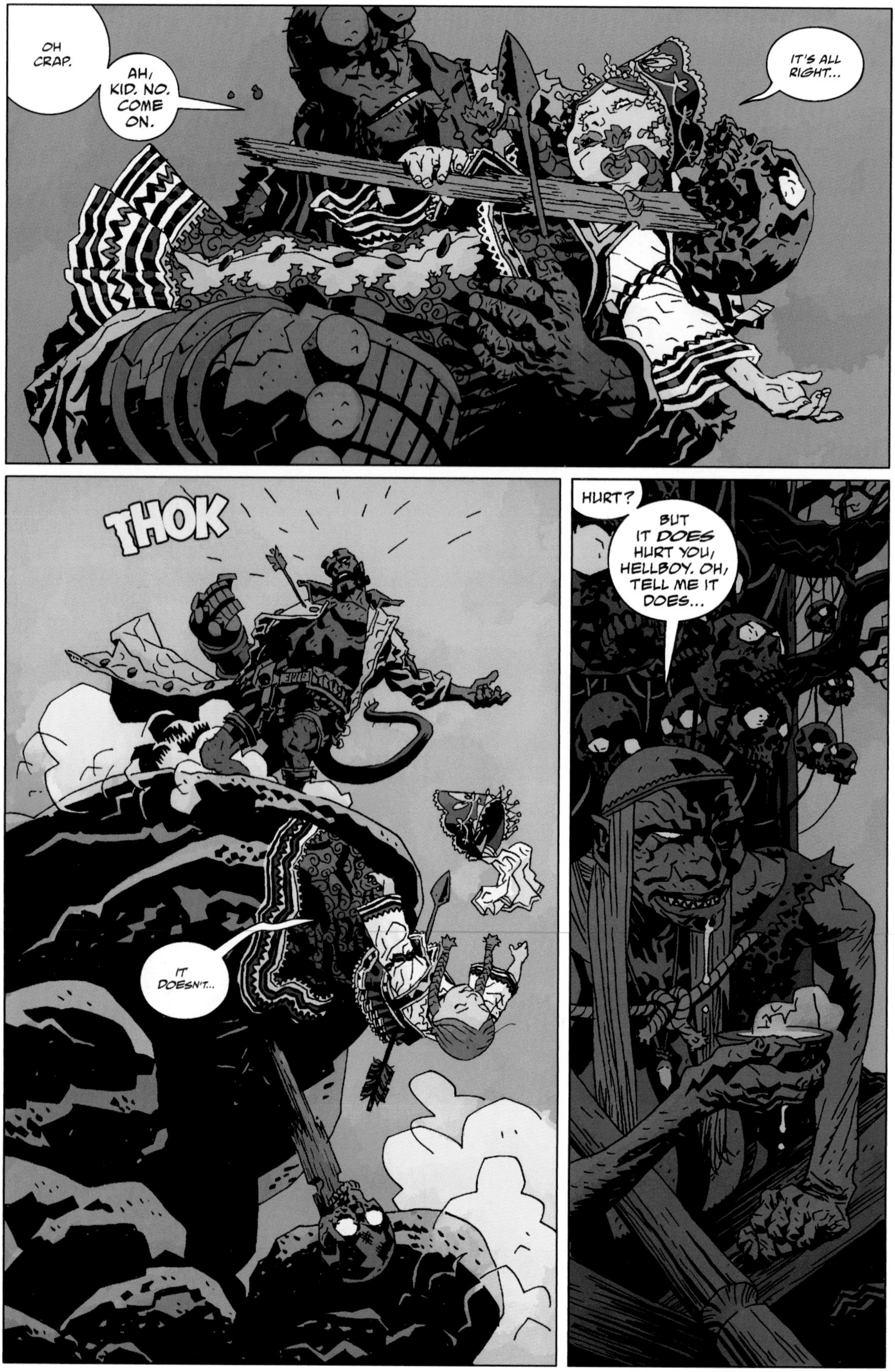
OH CRAP.
AH, KID. NO. COME ON.
IT'S ALL RIGHT...
THOK
IT DOESN'T...
HURT?
BUT IT DOES HURT YOU, HELLBOY. OH, TELL ME IT DOES...

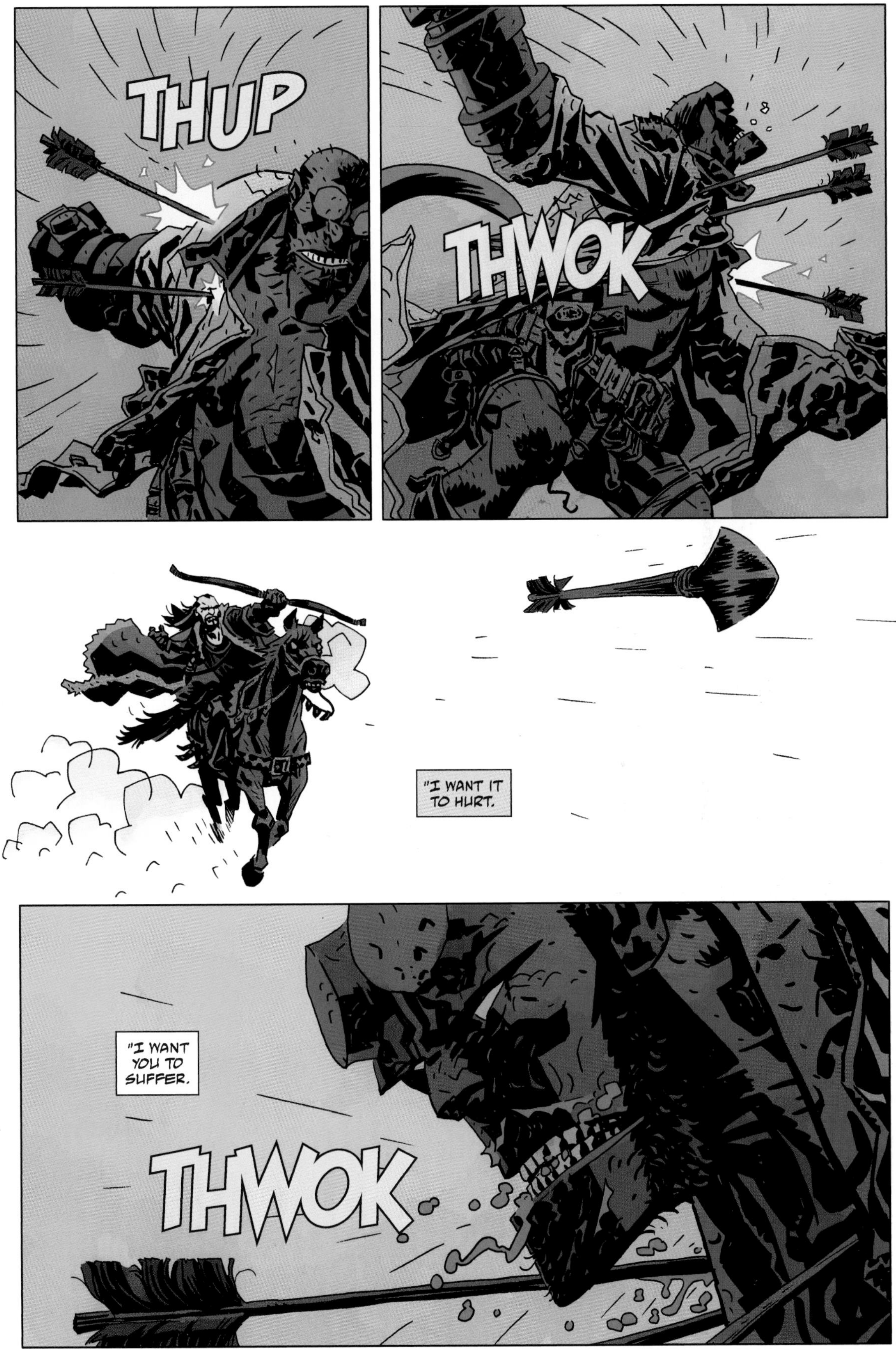
THUP
THWOK
"I WANT IT TO HURT.
"I WANT YOU TO SUFFER.
THWOK

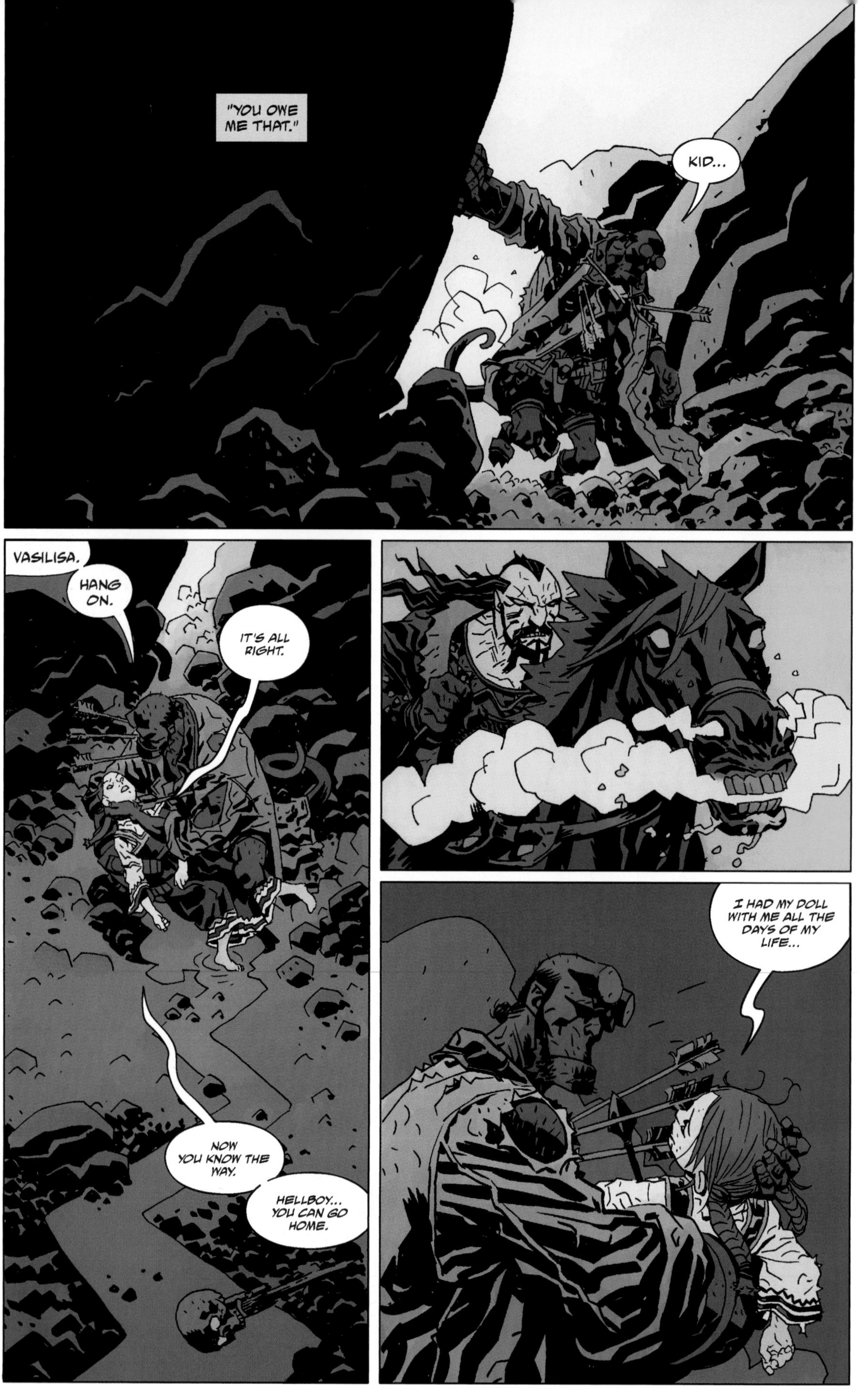
"YOU OWE ME THAT."
KID...
VASILISA.
HANG ON.
IT'S ALL RIGHT.
NOW YOU KNOW THE WAY.
HELLBOY... YOU CAN GO HOME.
I HAD MY DOLL WITH ME ALL THE DAYS OF MY LIFE...

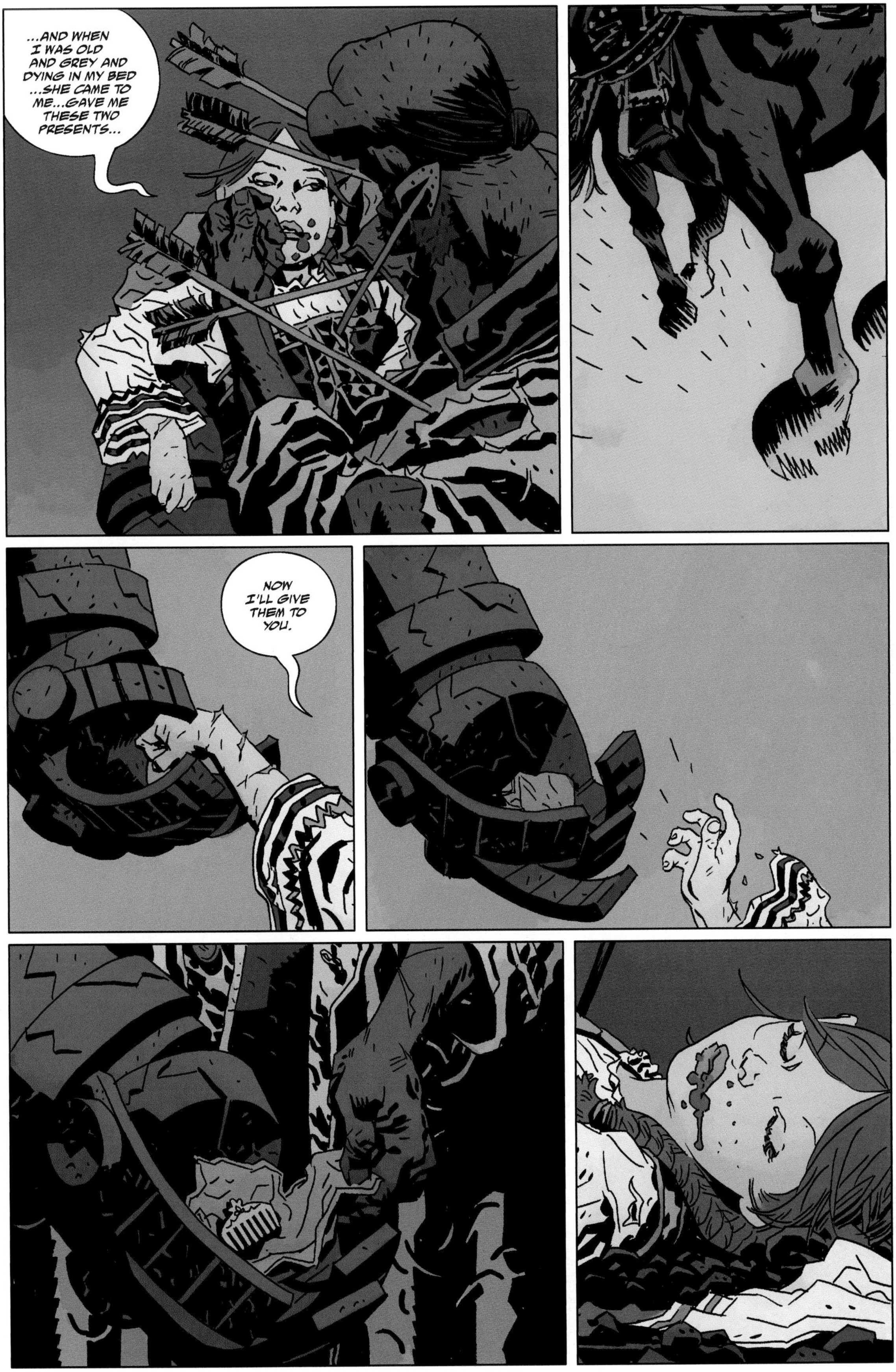
...AND WHEN I WAS OLD AND GREY AND DYING IN MY BED ...SHE CAME TO ME...GAVE ME THESE TWO PRESENTS...
NOW I'LL GIVE THEM TO YOU.

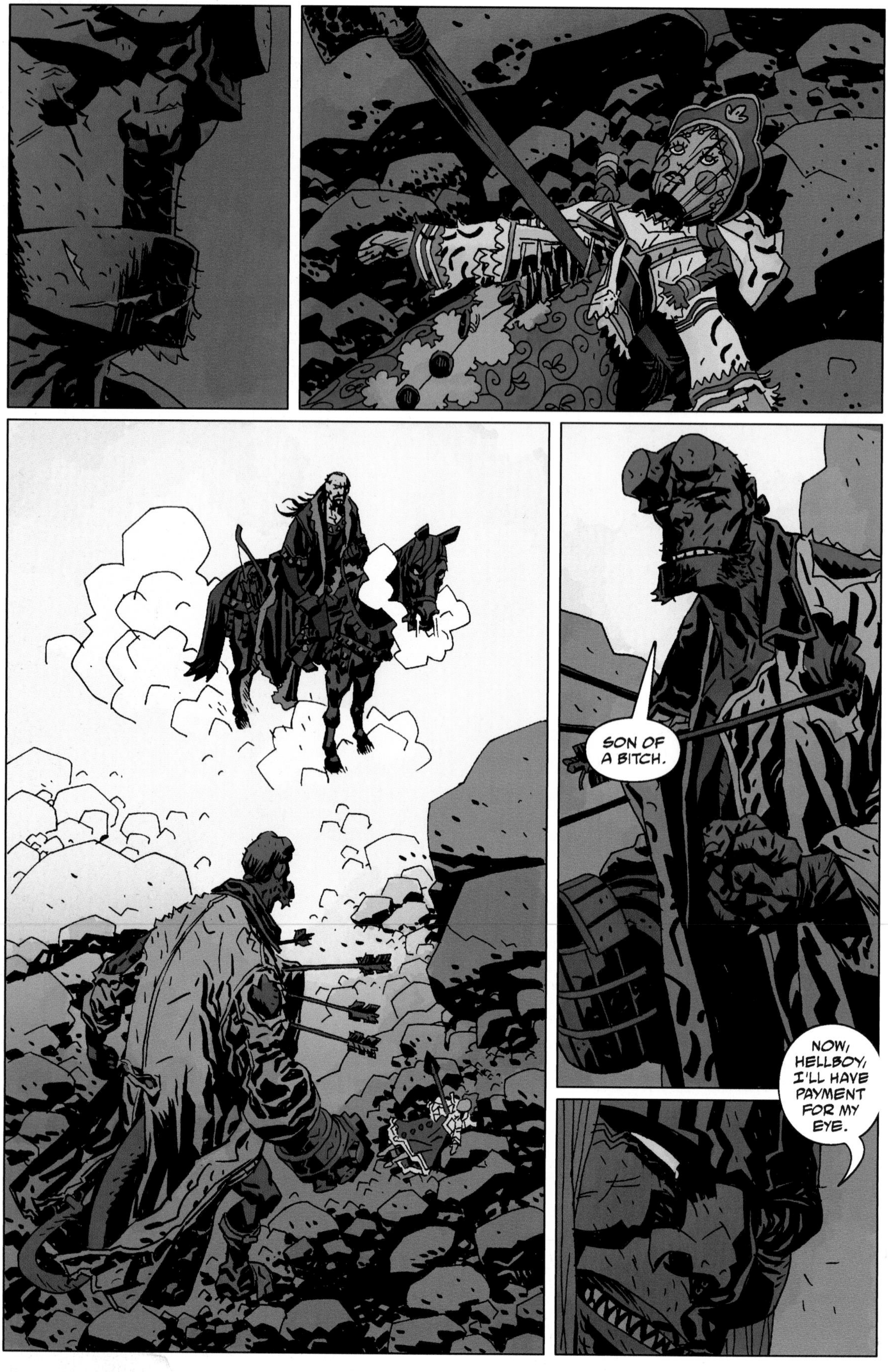
SON OF A BITCH.
NOW, HELLBOY, I'LL HAVE PAYMENT FOR MY EYE.

CHAPTER FIVE

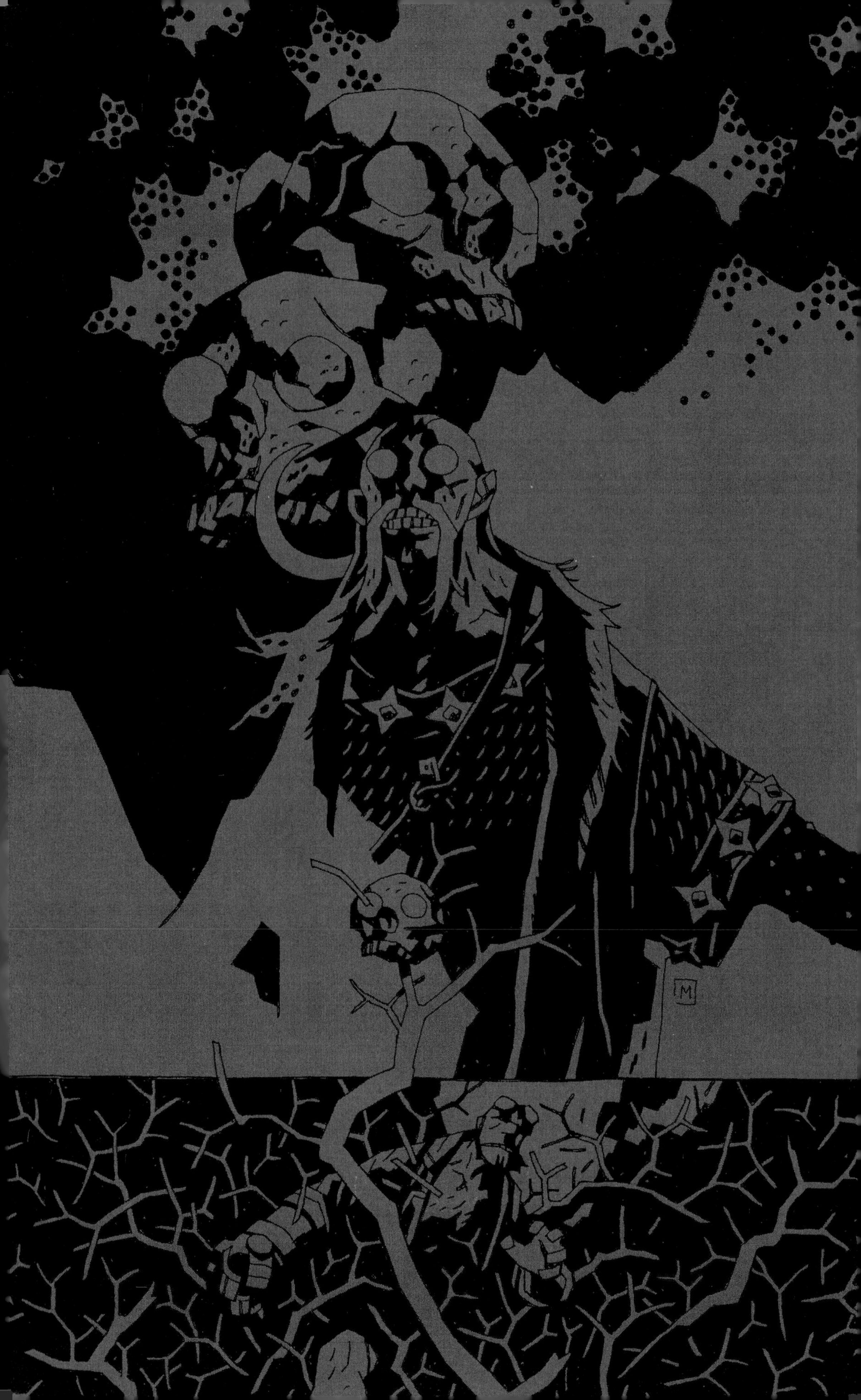

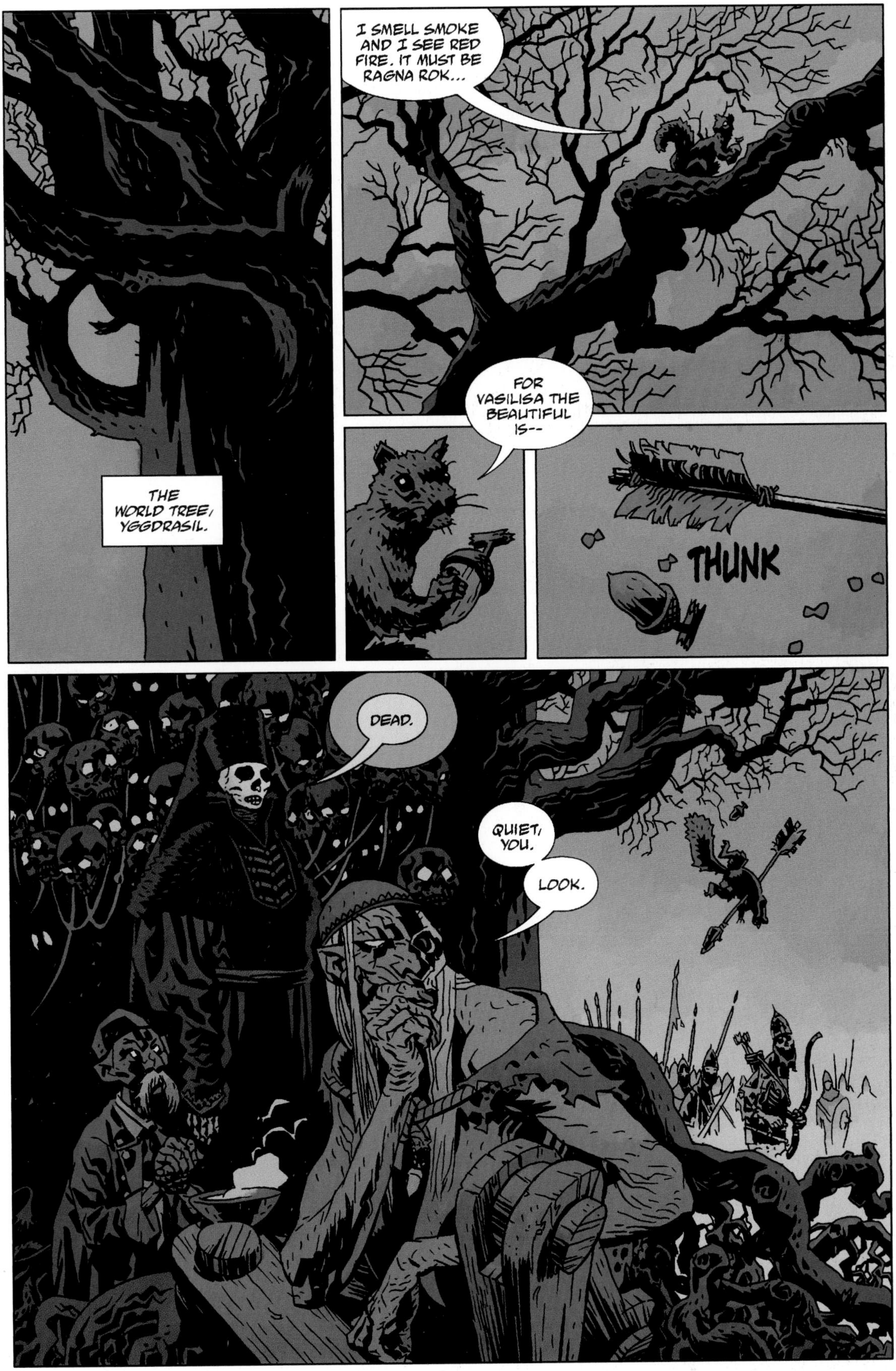
THE WORLD TREE, YGGDRASIL.
I SMELL SMOKE AND I SEE RED FIRE. IT MUST BE RAGNA ROK...
FOR VASILISA THE BEAUTIFUL IS--
THUNK
DEAD.
QUIET, YOU.
LOOK.

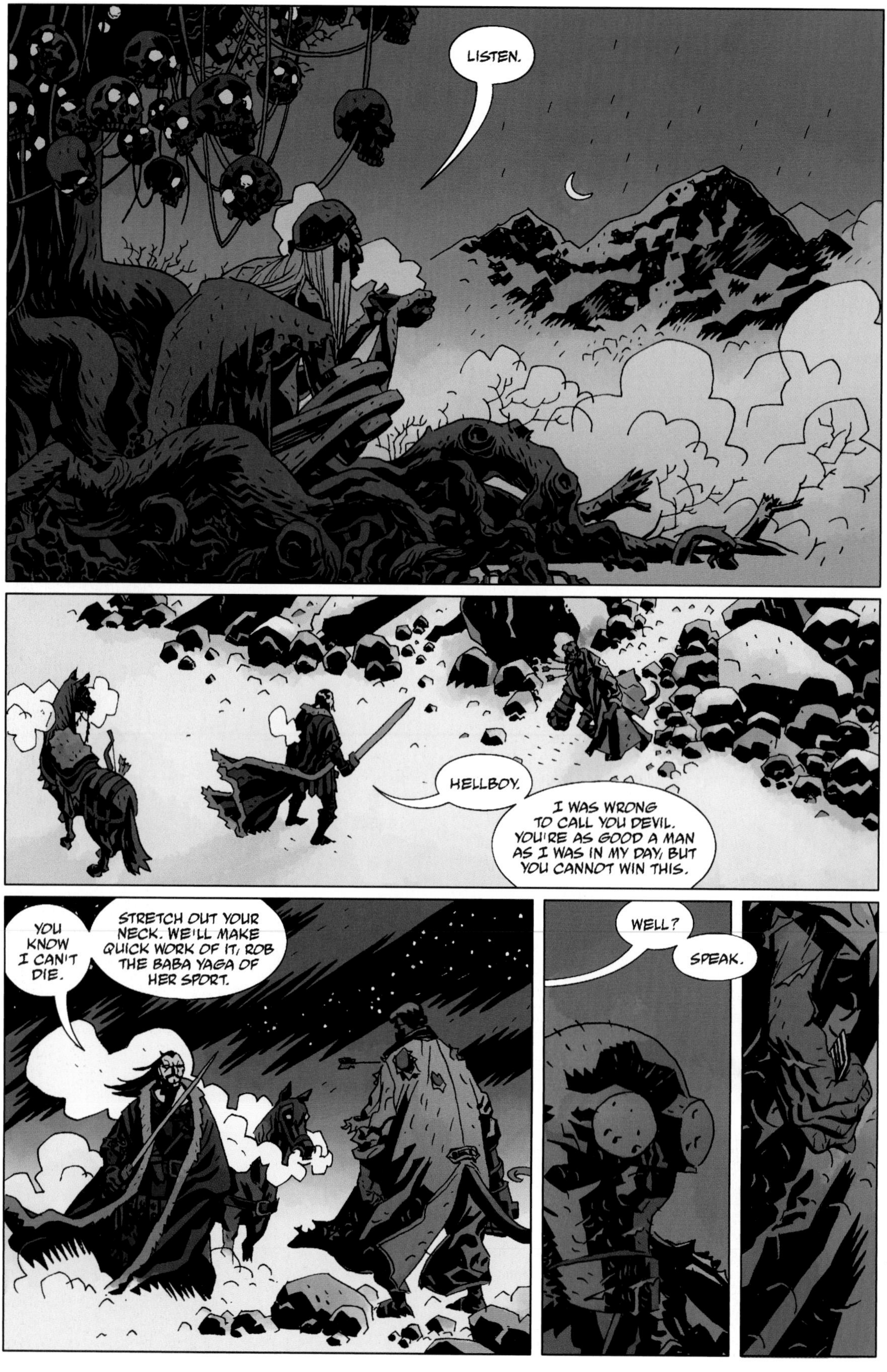

LISTEN.
HELLBOY.
I WAS WRONG TO CALL YOU DEVIL. YOU'RE AS GOOD A MAN AS I WAS IN MY DAY, BUT YOU CANNOT WIN THIS.
STRETCH OUT YOUR NECK. WE'LL MAKE QUICK WORK OF IT, ROB THE BABA YAGA OF HER SPORT.
YOU KNOW I CAN'T DIE.
WELL?
SPEAK.

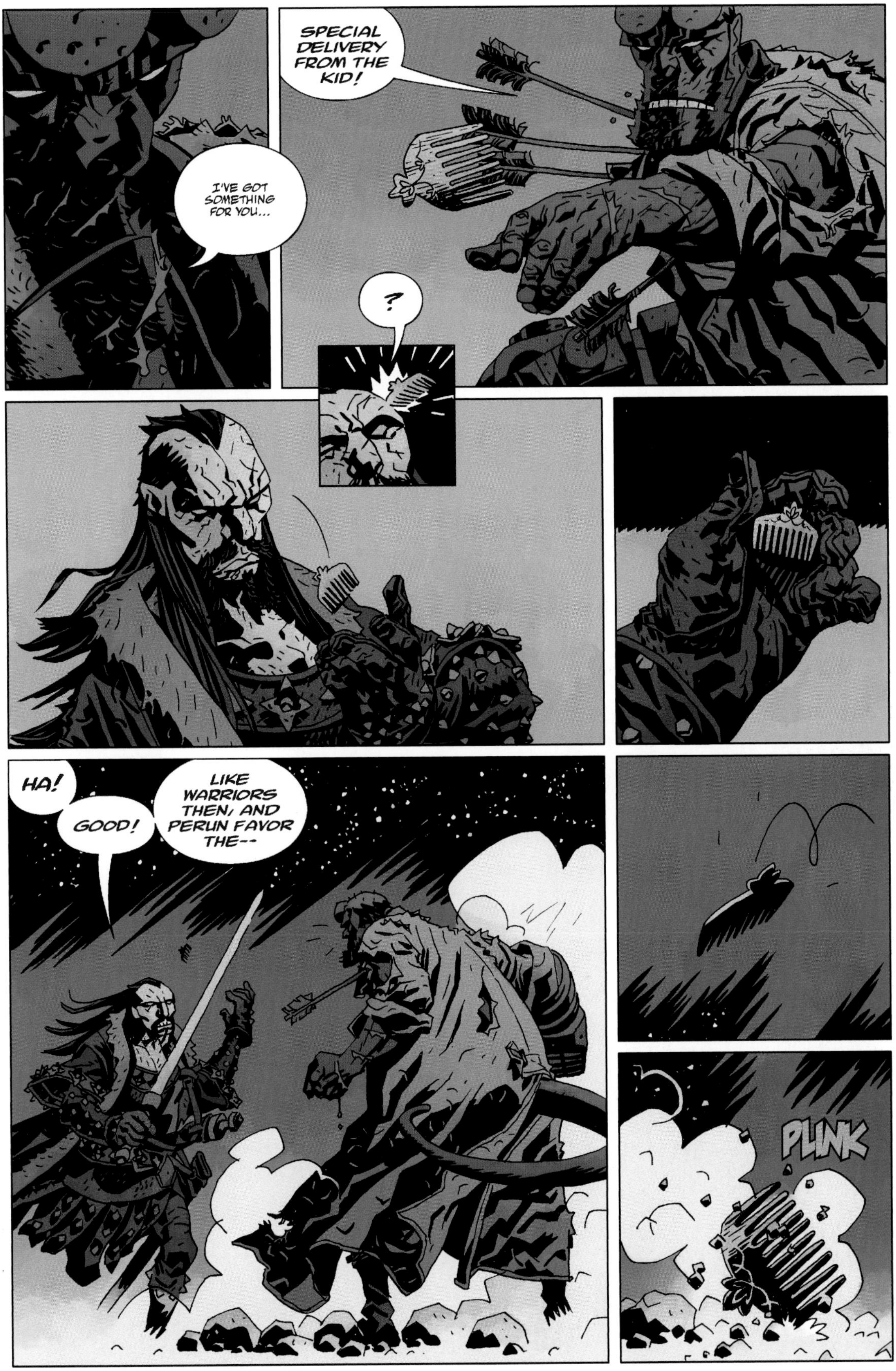

I'VE GOT SOMETHING FOR YOU...
SPECIAL DELIVERY FROM THE KID!
?
HA!
GOOD!
LIKE WARRIORS THEN, AND PERUN FAVOR THE--
PLINK

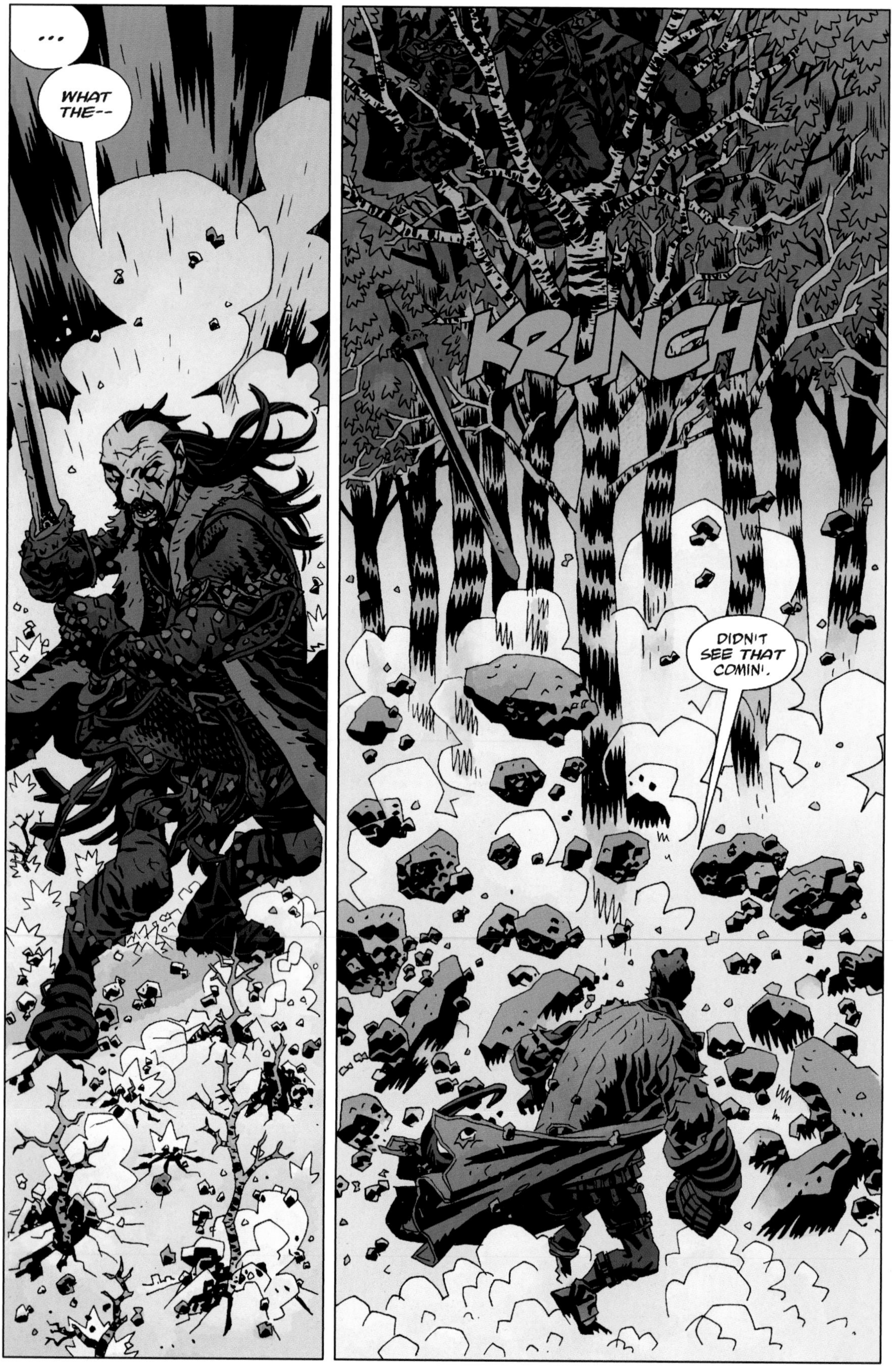
...
WHAT THE--
KRUNCH
DIDN'T SEE THAT COMIN'.

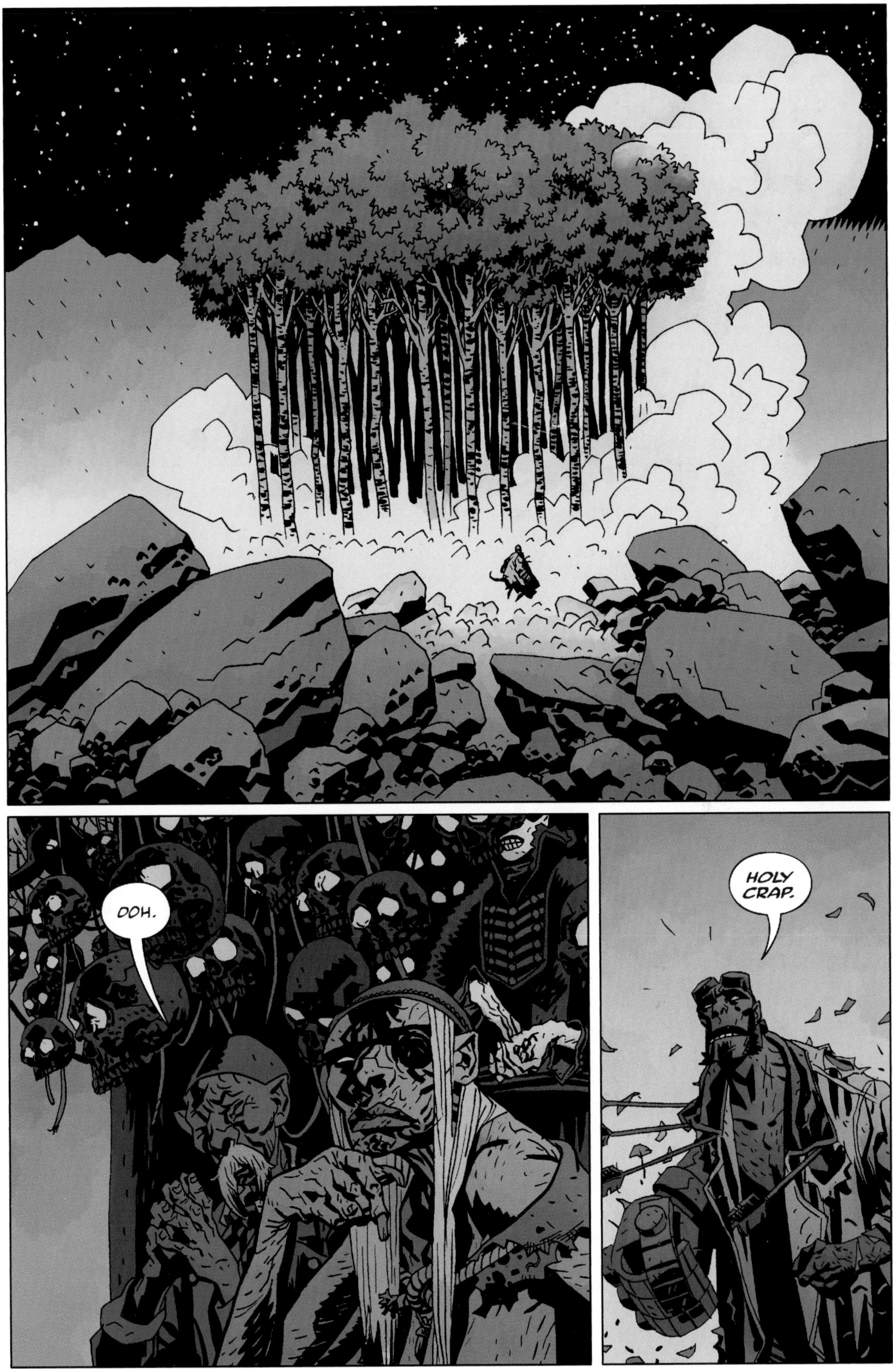
OOH.
HOLY CRAP.

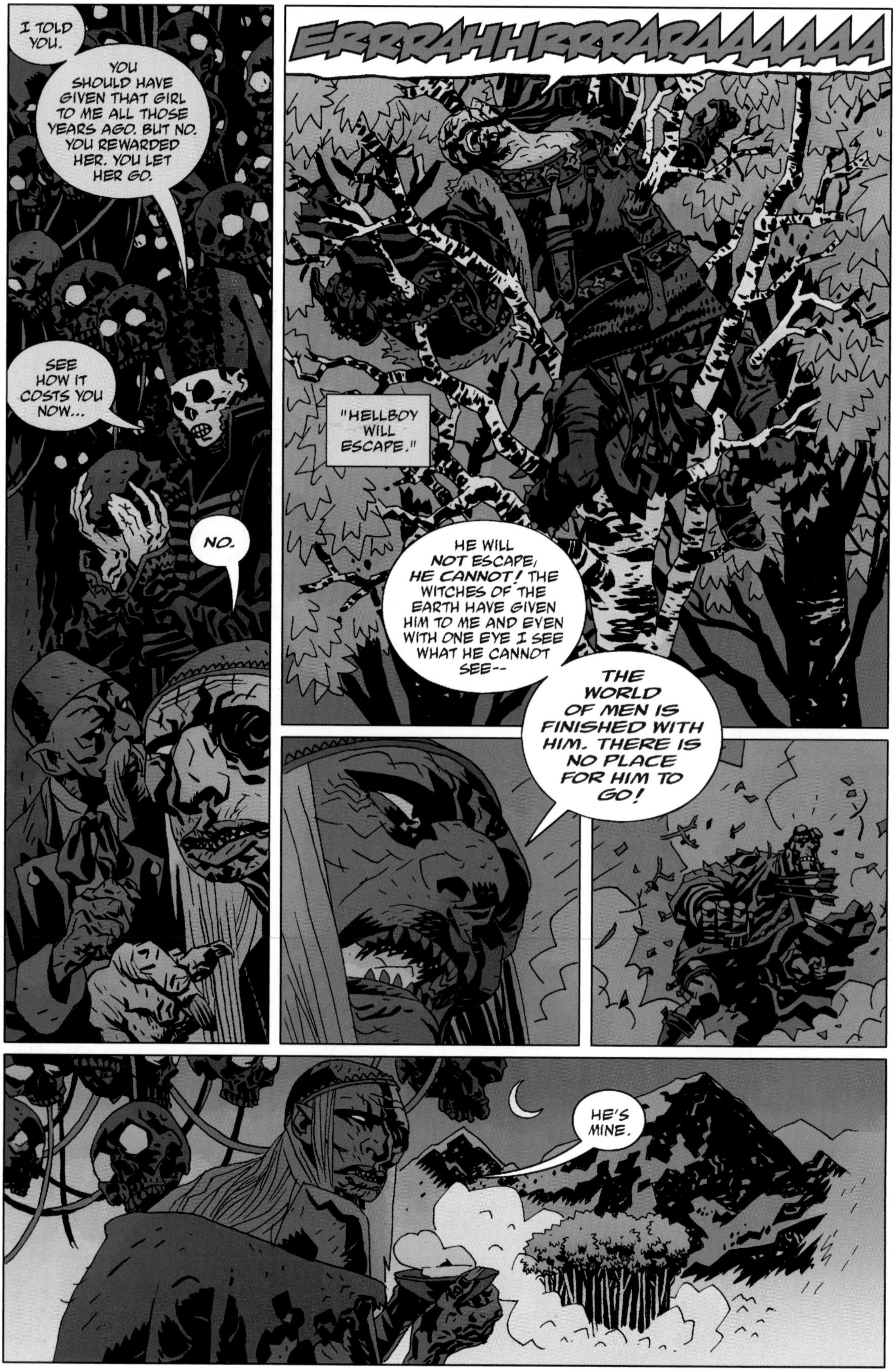
I TOLD YOU.
YOU SHOULD HAVE GIVEN THAT GIRL TO ME ALL THOSE YEARS AGO. BUT NO. YOU REWARDED HER. YOU LET HER GO.
SEE HOW IT COSTS YOU NOW...
NO.
ERRRAHHRRRARAAAAAA
"HELLBOY WILL ESCAPE."
HE WILL NOT ESCAPE, HE CANNOT! THE WITCHES OF THE EARTH HAVE GIVEN HIM TO ME AND EVEN WITH ONE EYE I SEE WHAT HE CANNOT SEE--
THE WORLD OF MEN IS FINISHED WITH HIM. THERE IS NO PLACE FOR HIM TO GO!
HE'S MINE.

ENGLAND.

WELL, BROTHER?

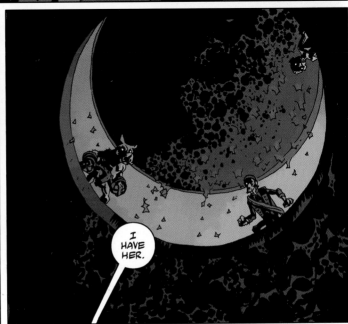

I HAVE HER.

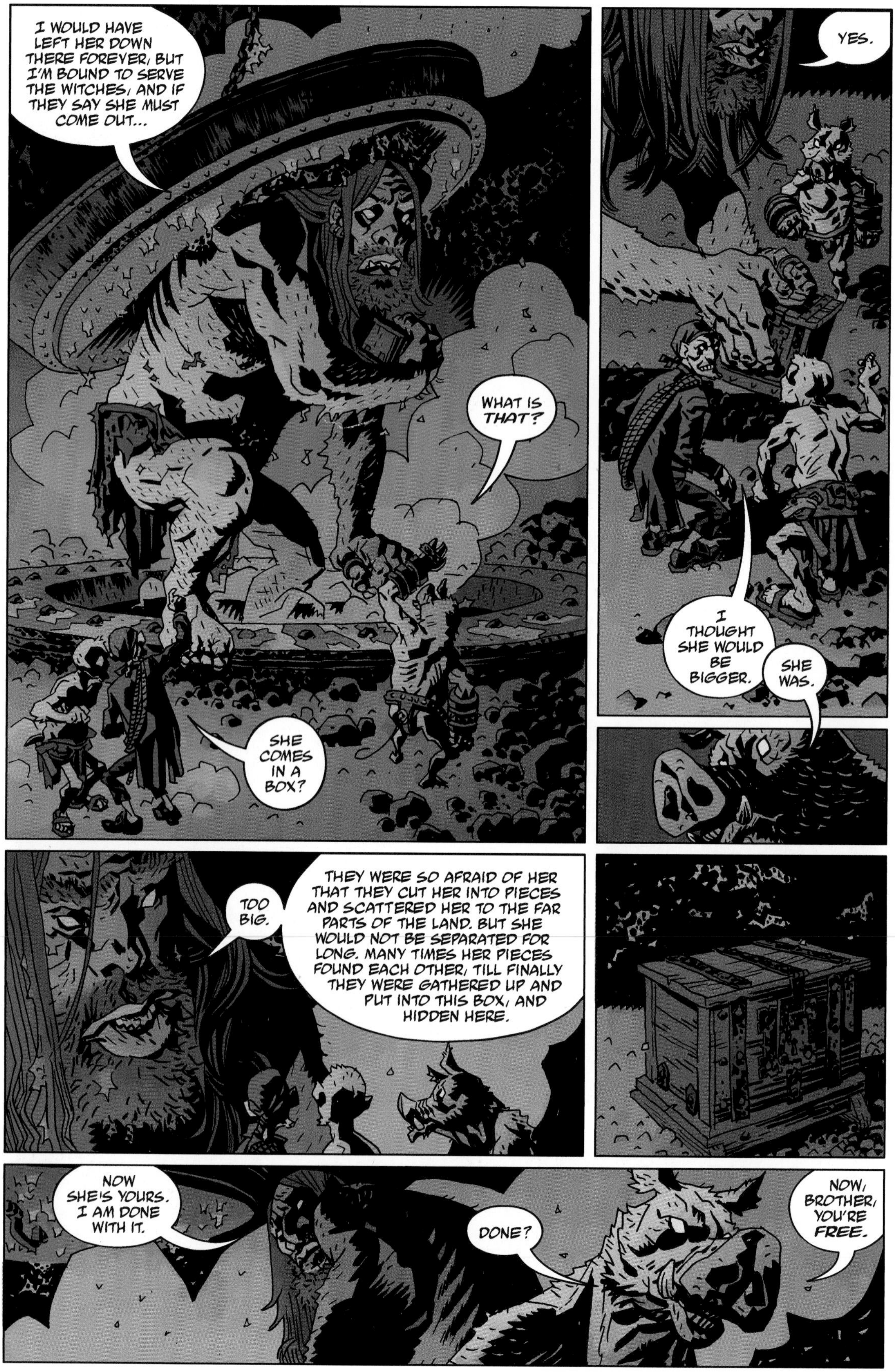
I WOULD HAVE LEFT HER DOWN THERE FOREVER, BUT I'M BOUND TO SERVE THE WITCHES, AND IF THEY SAY SHE MUST COME OUT...
WHAT IS *THAT?*
SHE COMES IN A BOX?
YES.
I THOUGHT SHE WOULD BE BIGGER.
SHE WAS.
TOO BIG.
THEY WERE SO AFRAID OF HER THAT THEY CUT HER INTO PIECES AND SCATTERED HER TO THE FAR PARTS OF THE LAND. BUT SHE WOULD NOT BE SEPARATED FOR LONG. MANY TIMES HER PIECES FOUND EACH OTHER, TILL FINALLY THEY WERE GATHERED UP AND PUT INTO THIS BOX, AND HIDDEN HERE.
NOW SHE'S YOURS. I AM DONE WITH IT.
DONE?
NOW, BROTHER, YOU'RE FREE.

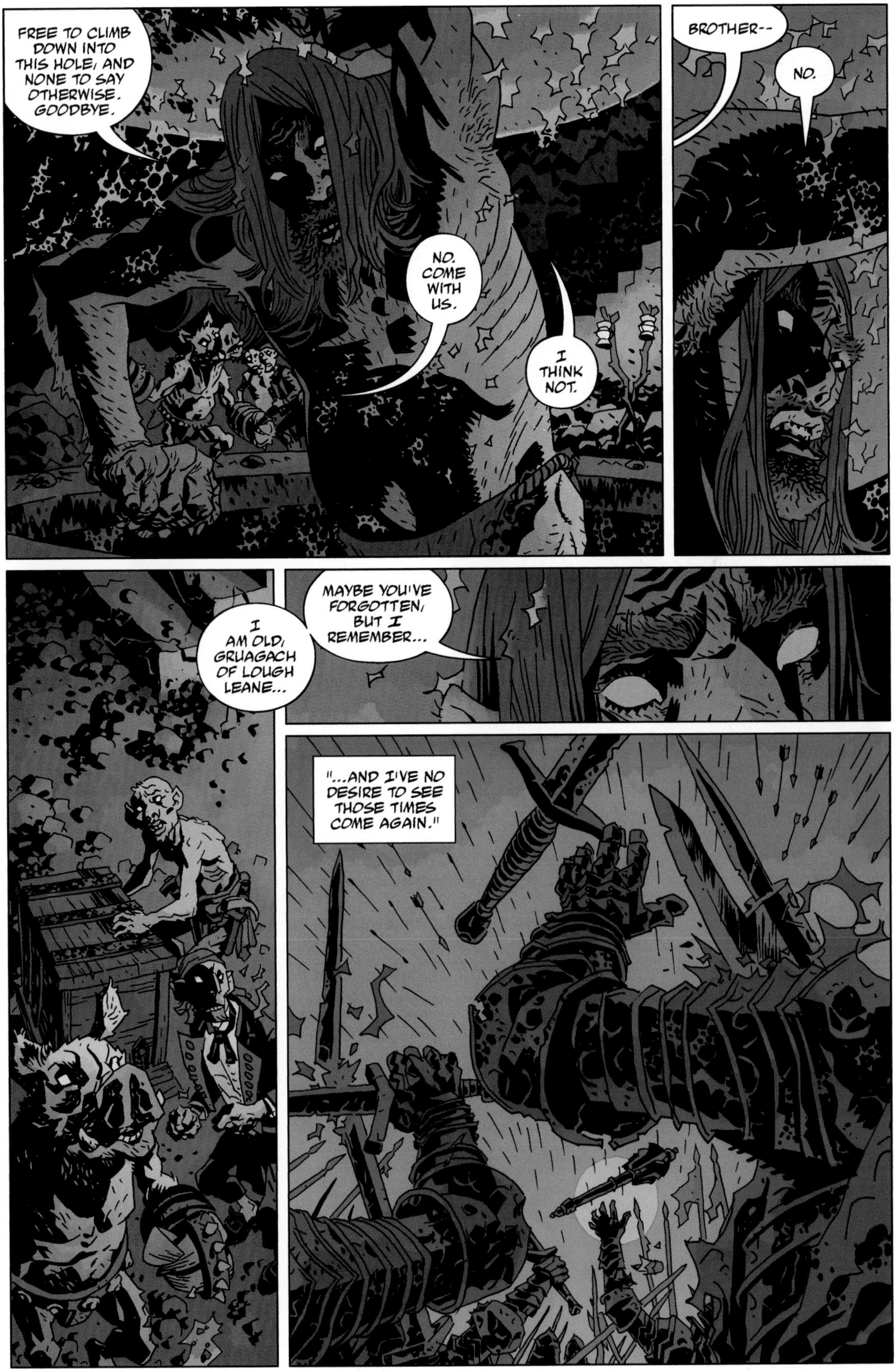
FREE TO CLIMB DOWN INTO THIS HOLE, AND NONE TO SAY OTHERWISE. GOODBYE.
NO. COME WITH US.
I THINK NOT.
BROTHER--
NO.
I AM OLD, GRUAGACH OF LOUGH LEANE...
MAYBE YOU'VE FORGOTTEN, BUT I REMEMBER...
"...AND I'VE NO DESIRE TO SEE THOSE TIMES COME AGAIN."

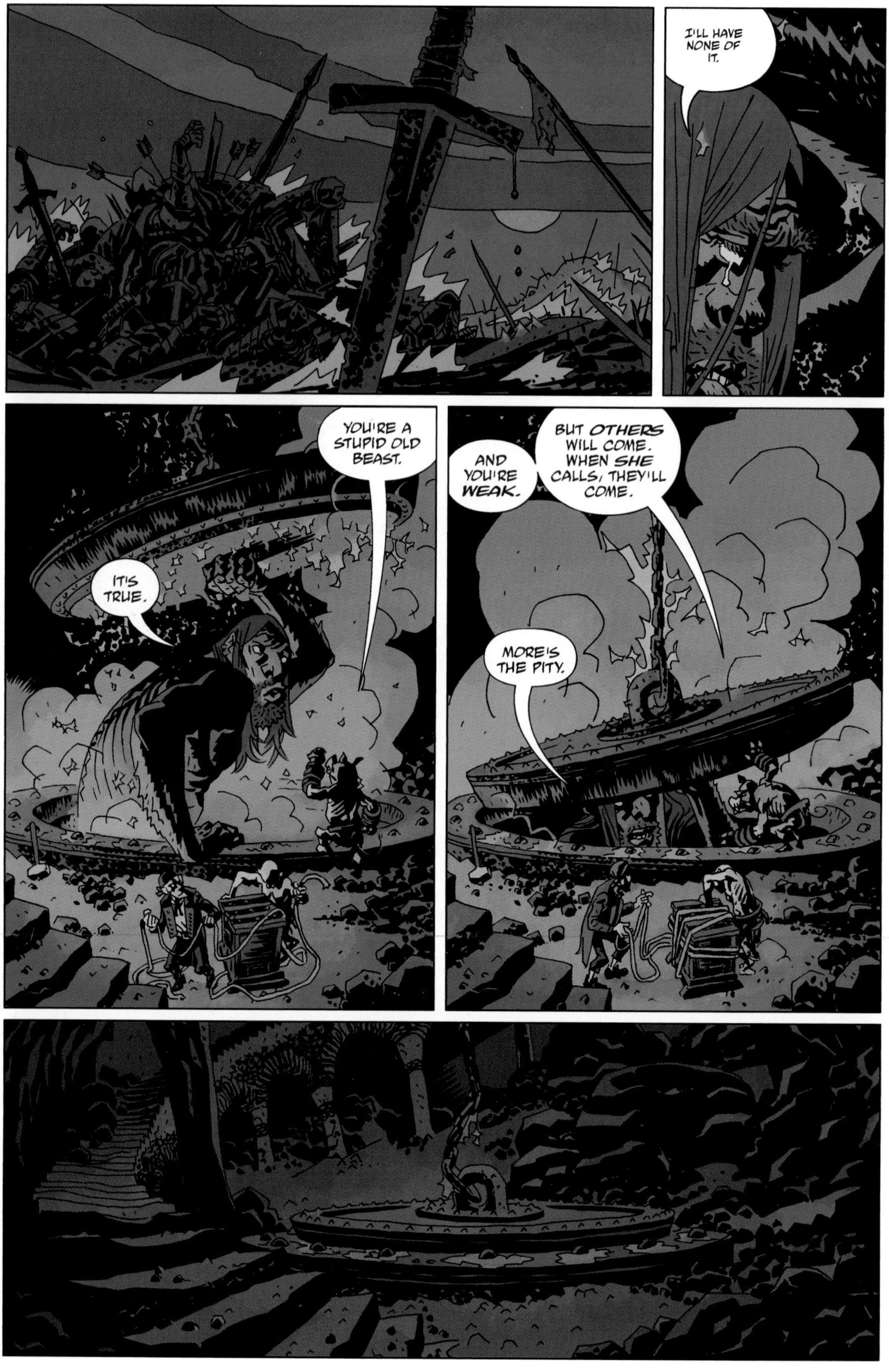
I'LL HAVE NONE OF IT.
IT'S TRUE.
YOU'RE A STUPID OLD BEAST.
AND YOU'RE WEAK.
BUT OTHERS WILL COME. WHEN SHE CALLS, THEY'LL COME.
MORE'S THE PITY.

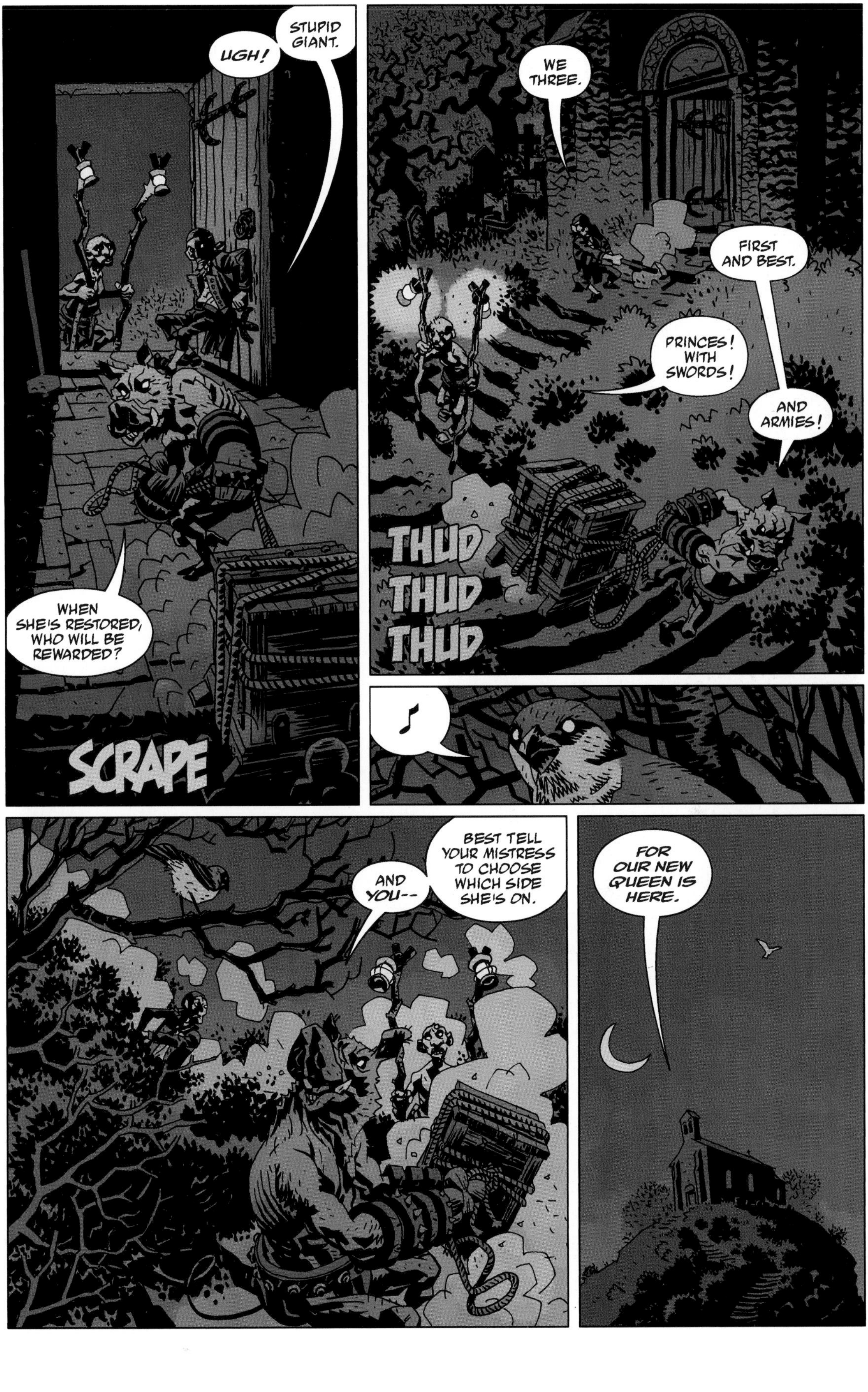

UGH!
STUPID GIANT.
WHEN SHE'S RESTORED, WHO WILL BE REWARDED?
SCRAPE
WE THREE.
FIRST AND BEST.
PRINCES! WITH SWORDS!
AND ARMIES!
THUD THUD THUD
♪
AND YOU--
BEST TELL YOUR MISTRESS TO CHOOSE WHICH SIDE SHE'S ON.
FOR OUR NEW QUEEN IS HERE.

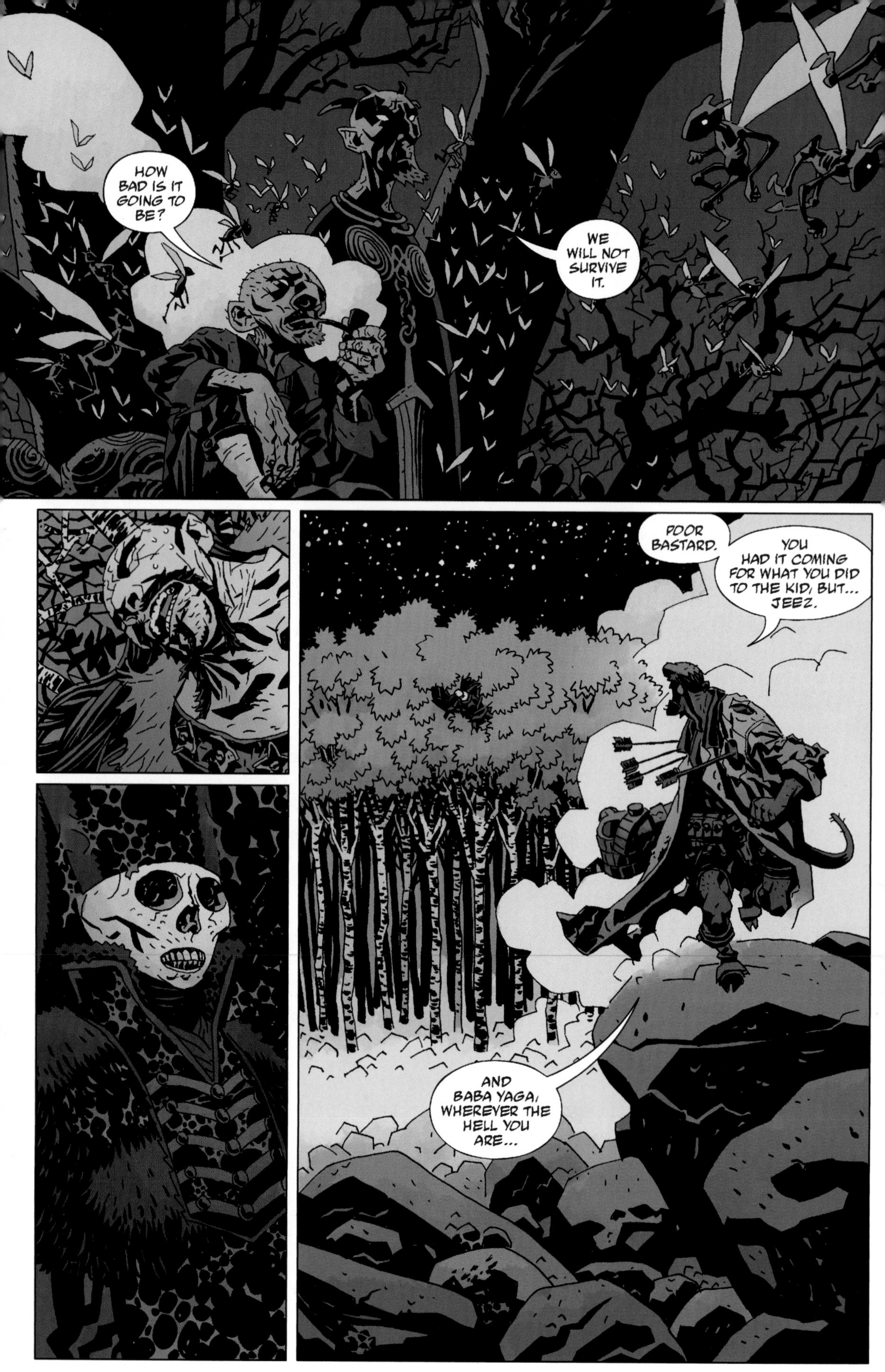
HOW BAD IS IT GOING TO BE?
WE WILL NOT SURVIVE IT.
POOR BASTARD.
YOU HAD IT COMING FOR WHAT YOU DID TO THE KID, BUT... JEEZ.
AND BABA YAGA, WHEREVER THE HELL YOU ARE...

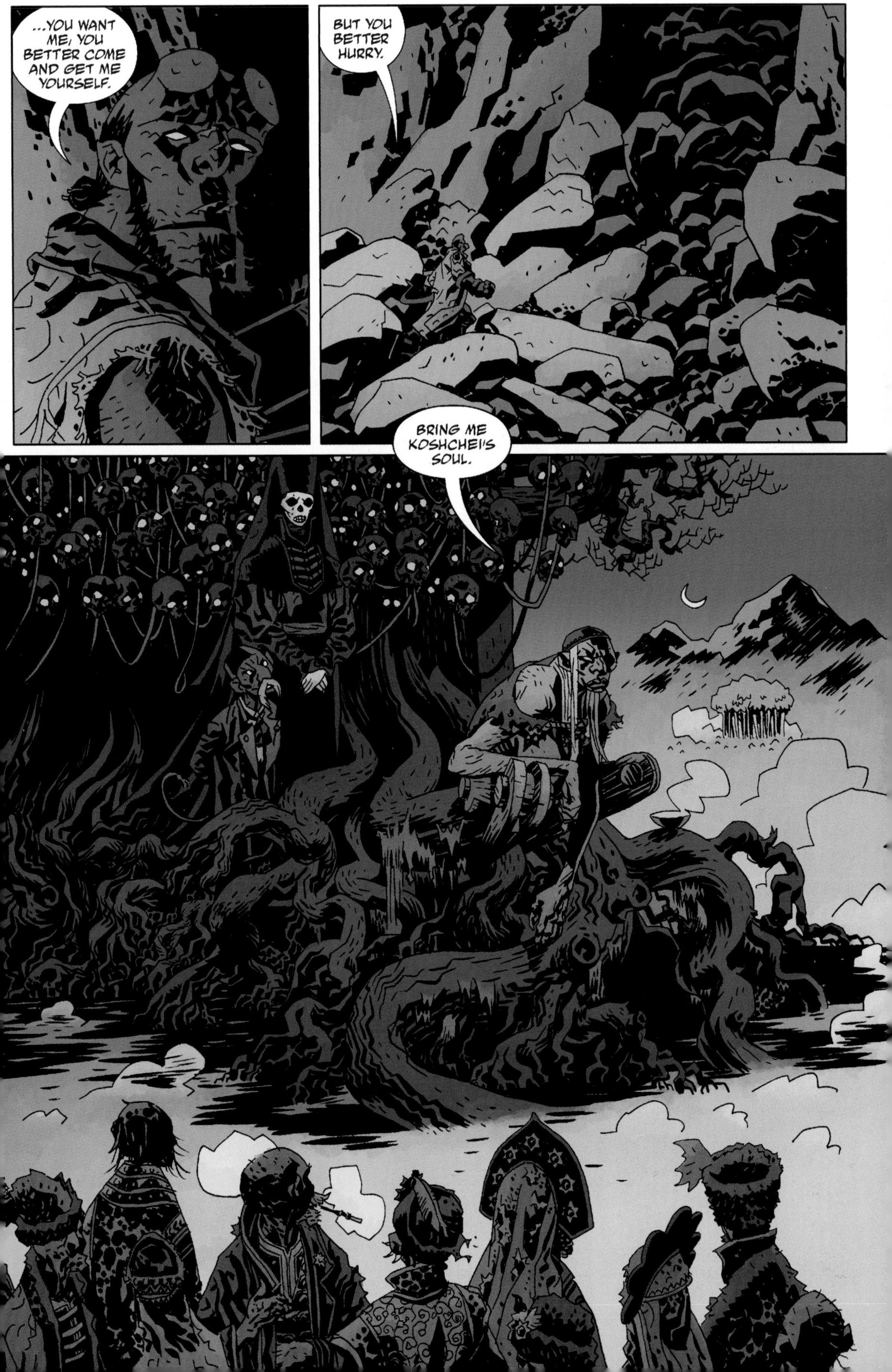
...YOU WANT ME, YOU BETTER COME AND GET ME YOURSELF.
BUT YOU BETTER HURRY.
BRING ME KOSHCHEI'S SOUL.

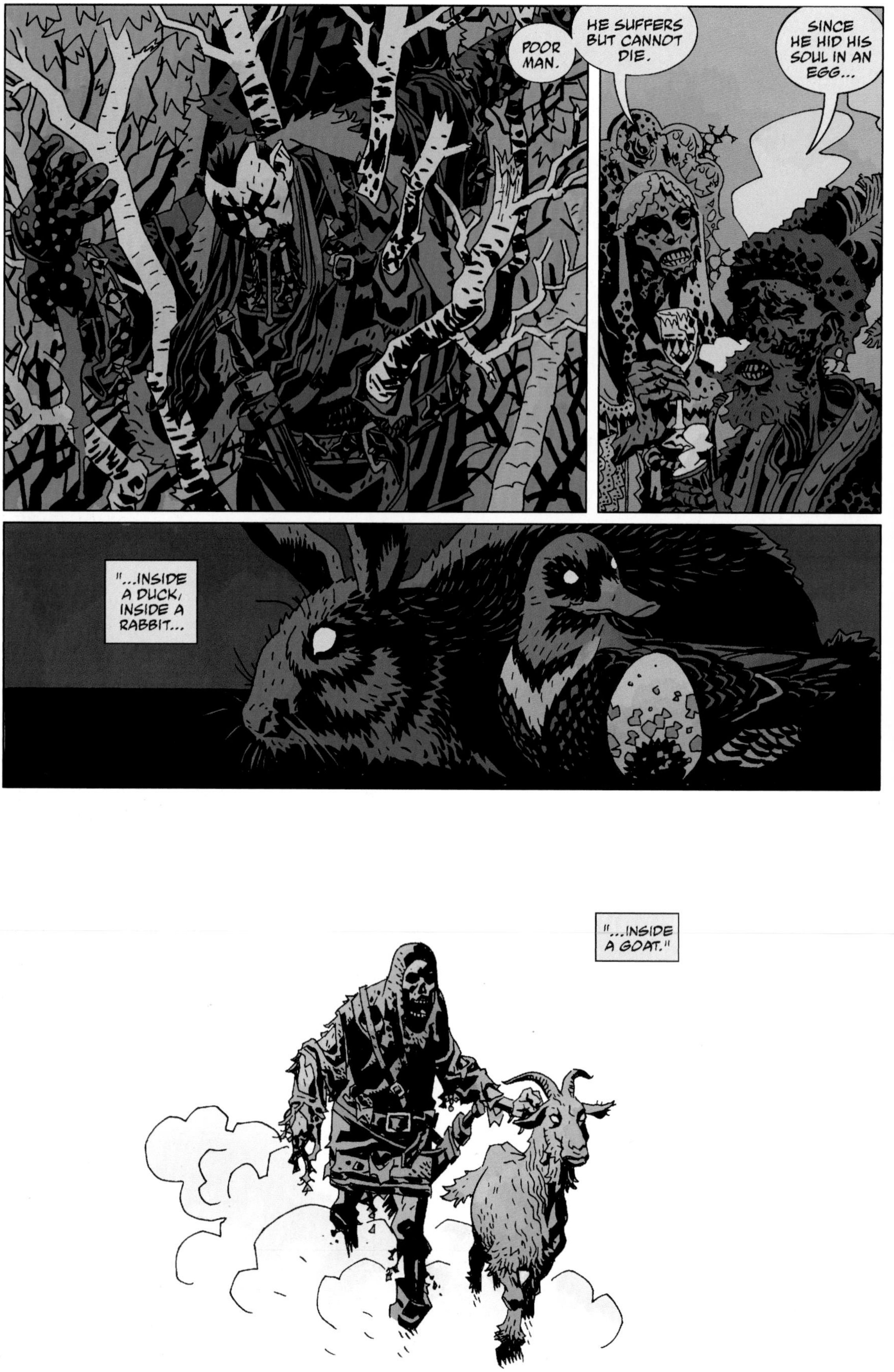
POOR MAN.
HE SUFFERS BUT CANNOT DIE.
SINCE HE HID HIS SOUL IN AN EGG...
"...INSIDE A DUCK, INSIDE A RABBIT...
"...INSIDE A GOAT."

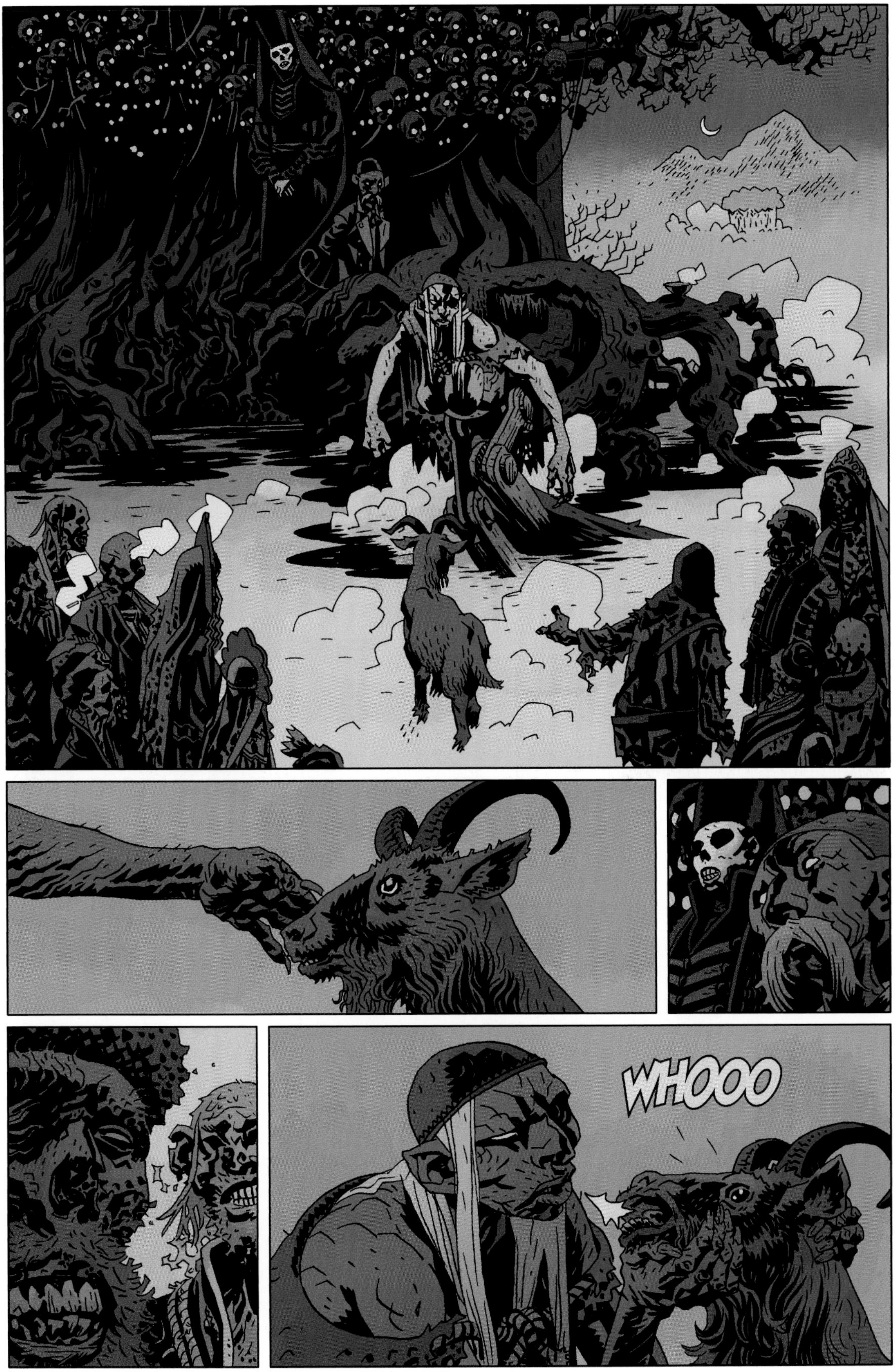
WHOOO

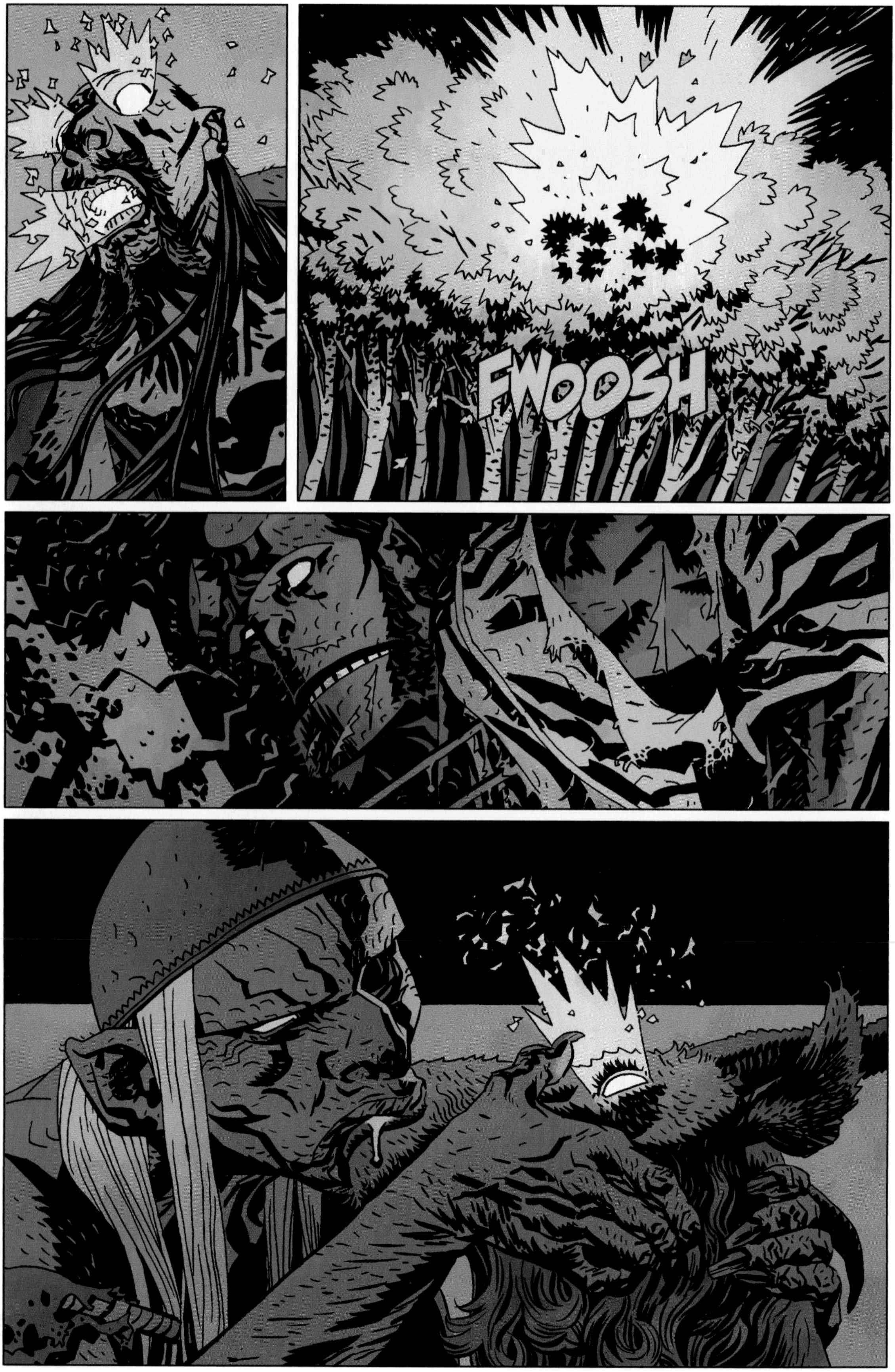
FWOOSH

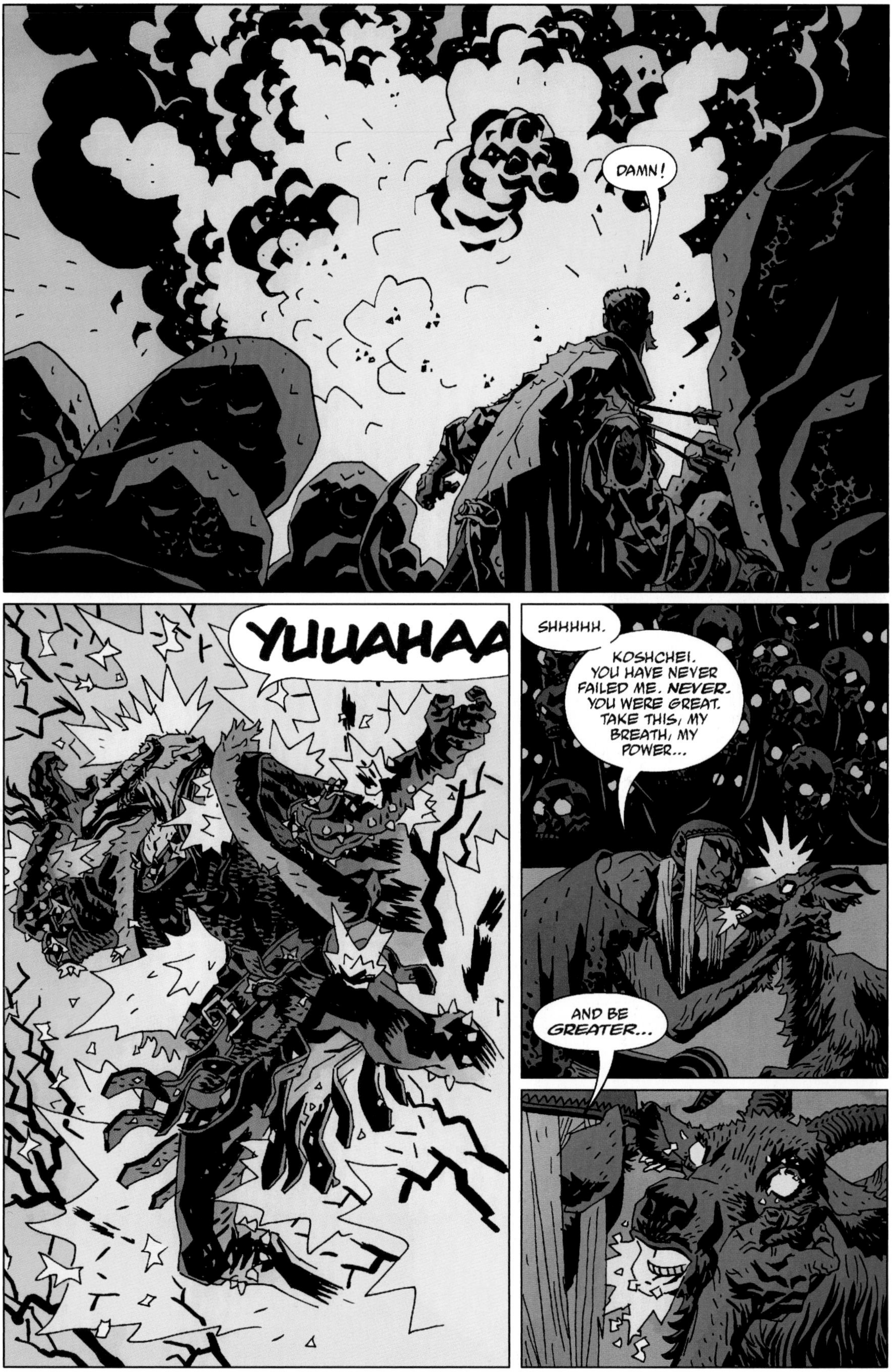
DAMN!
YUUAHAA
SHHHHH.
KOSHCHEI. YOU HAVE NEVER FAILED ME. NEVER. YOU WERE GREAT. TAKE THIS, MY BREATH, MY POWER...
AND BE GREATER...

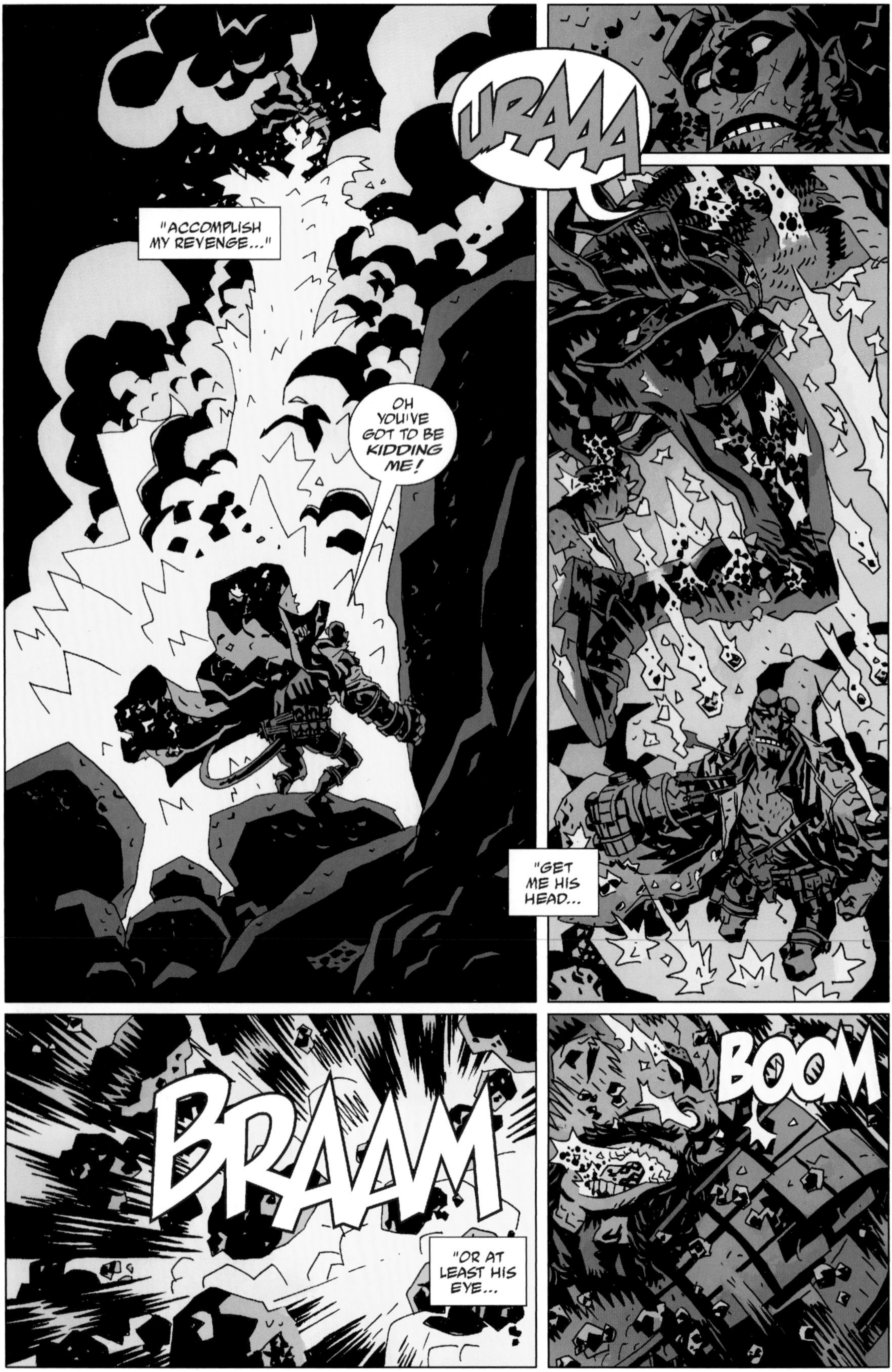
"ACCOMPLISH MY REVENGE..."
OH YOU'VE GOT TO BE KIDDING ME!
URAAA
"GET ME HIS HEAD...
BRAAM
"OR AT LEAST HIS EYE...
BOOM

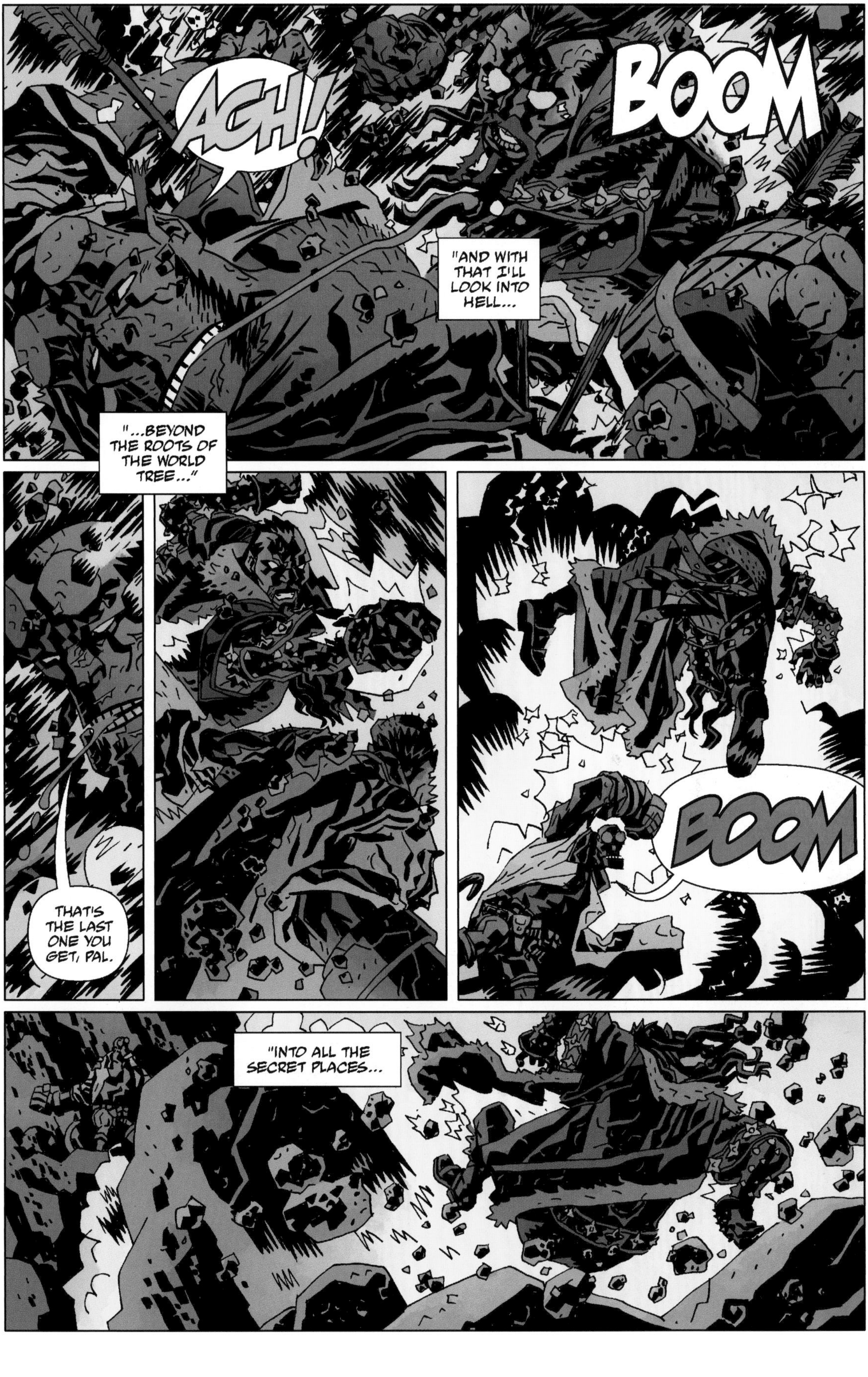
AGH!!
BOOM
"AND WITH THAT I'LL LOOK INTO HELL...
"...BEYOND THE ROOTS OF THE WORLD TREE..."
THAT'S THE LAST ONE YOU GET, PAL.
BOOM
"INTO ALL THE SECRET PLACES...

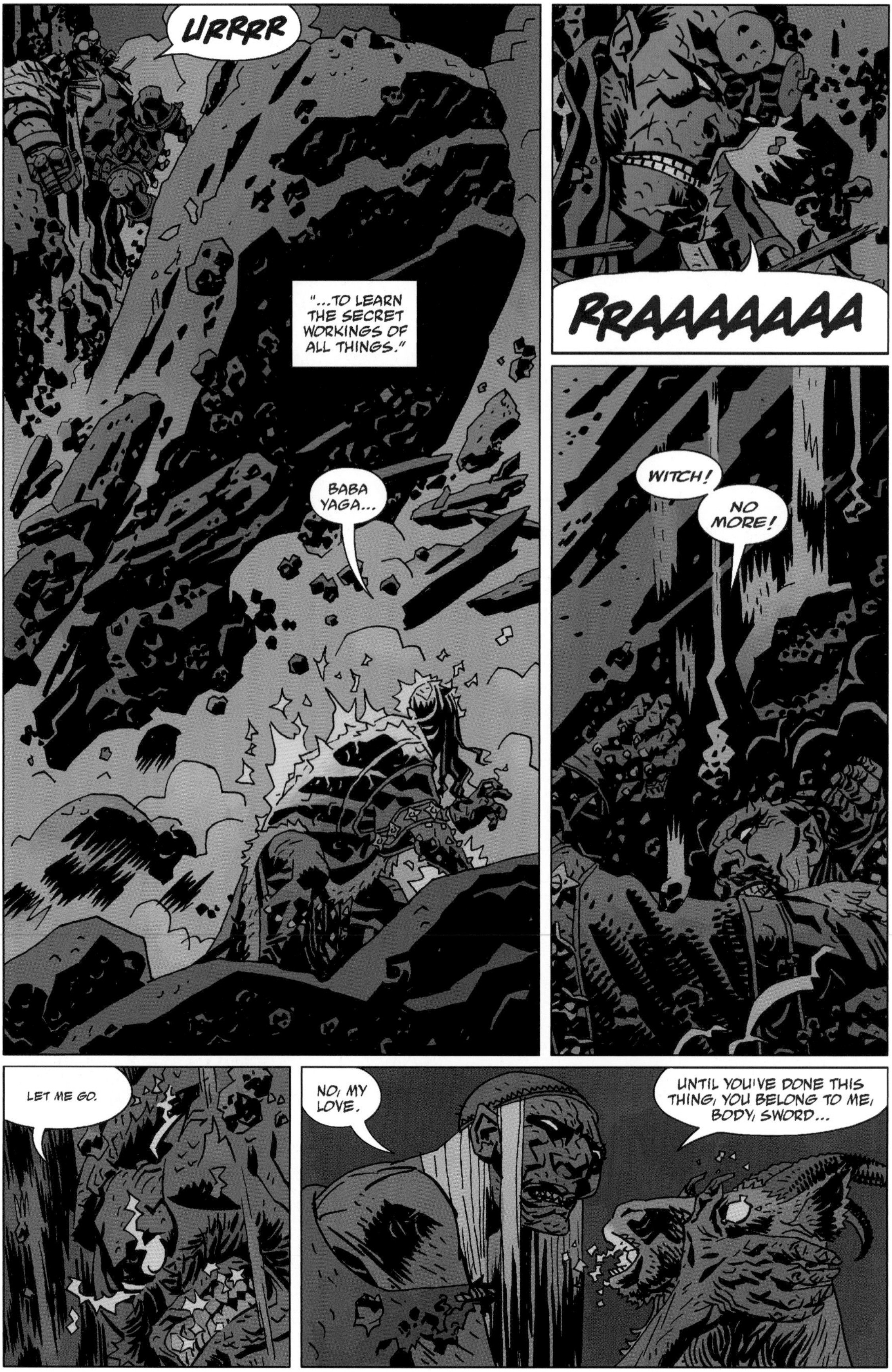
URRRR
"...TO LEARN THE SECRET WORKINGS OF ALL THINGS."
BABA YAGA...
RRAAAAAAAA
WITCH!
NO MORE!
LET ME GO.
NO, MY LOVE.
UNTIL YOU'VE DONE THIS THING, YOU BELONG TO ME, BODY, SWORD...

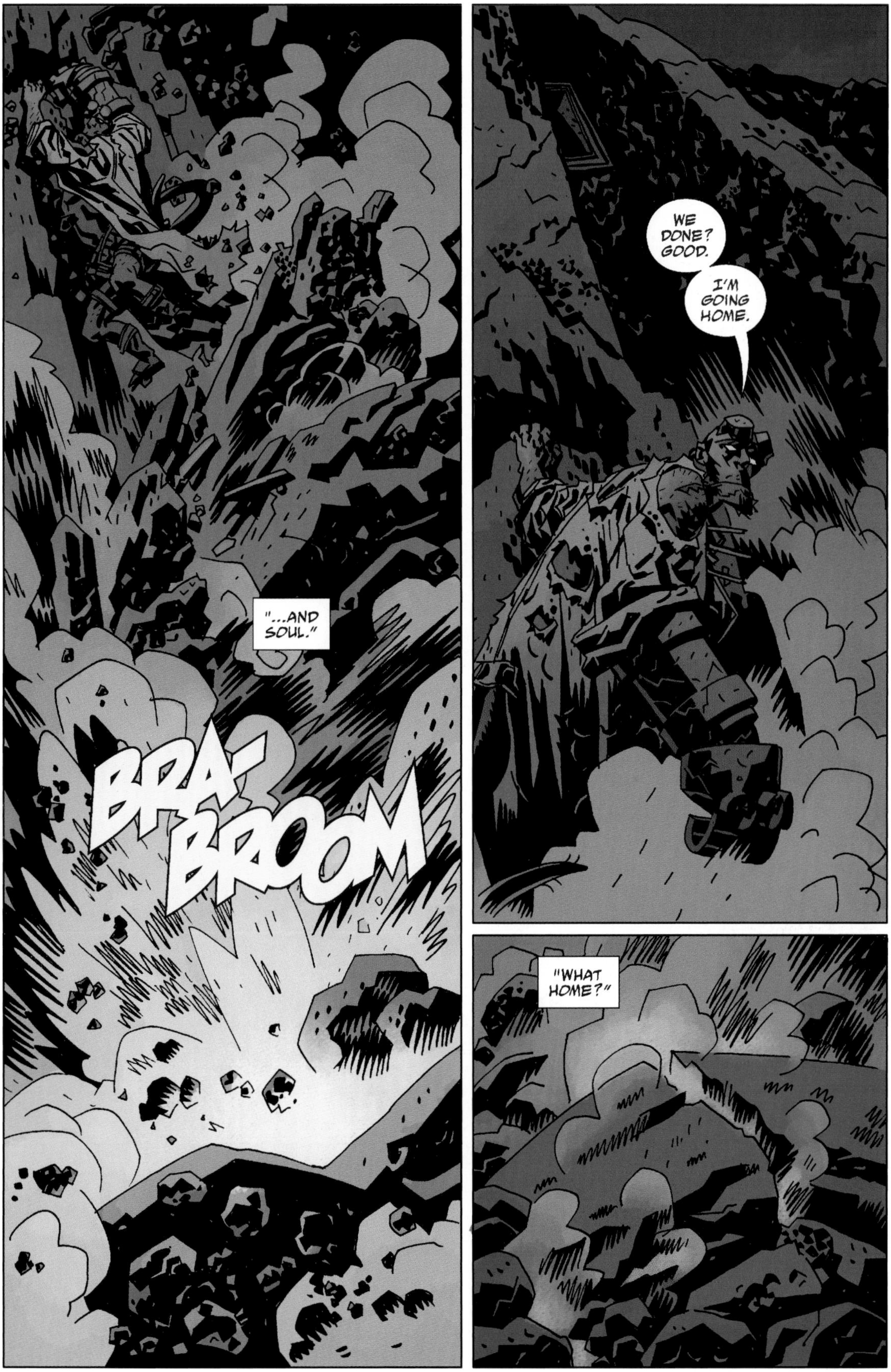
"...AND SOUL."
BRA-BROOM
WE DONE? GOOD.
I'M GOING HOME.
"WHAT HOME?"

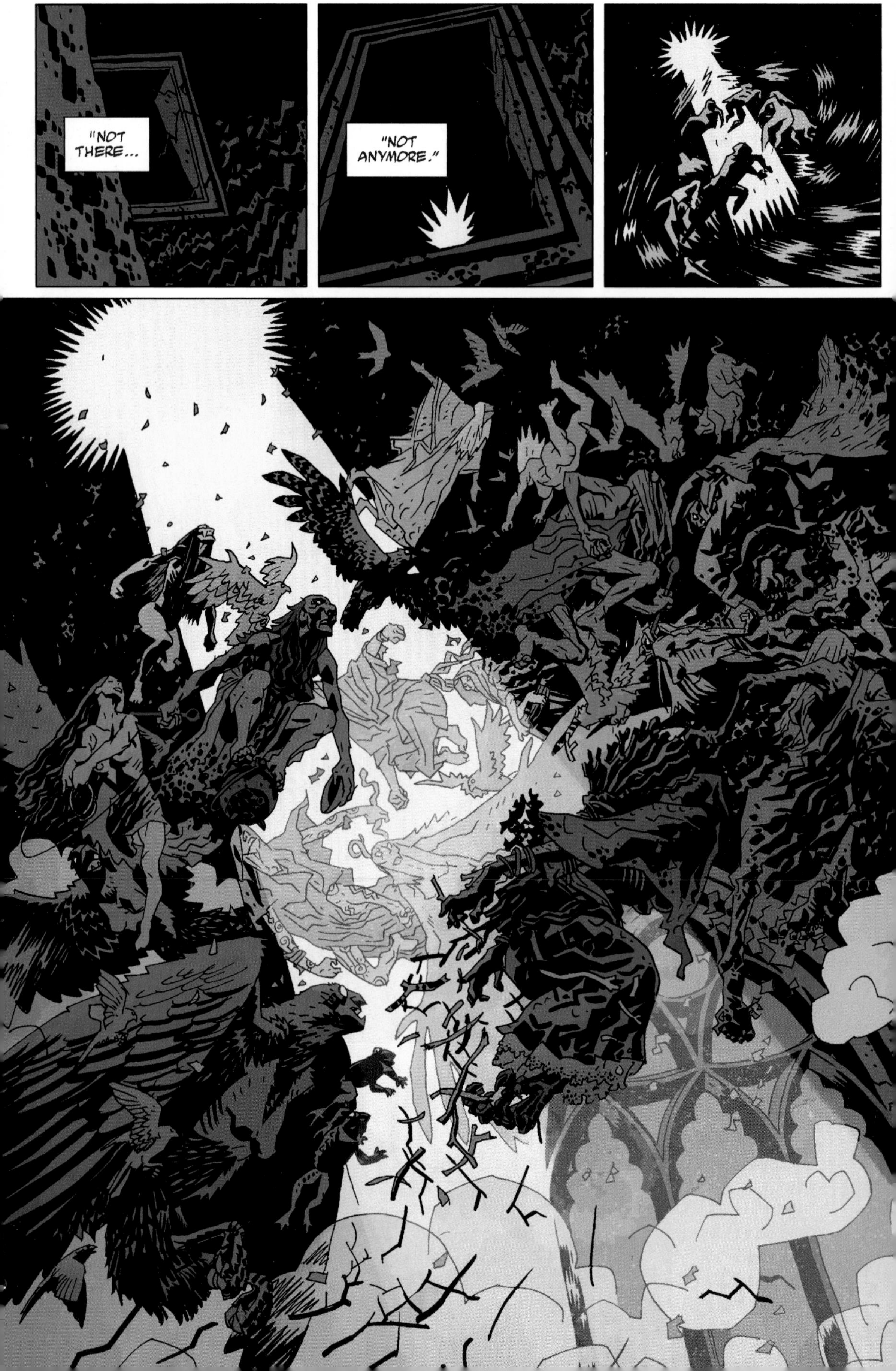
"NOT THERE...
"NOT ANYMORE."

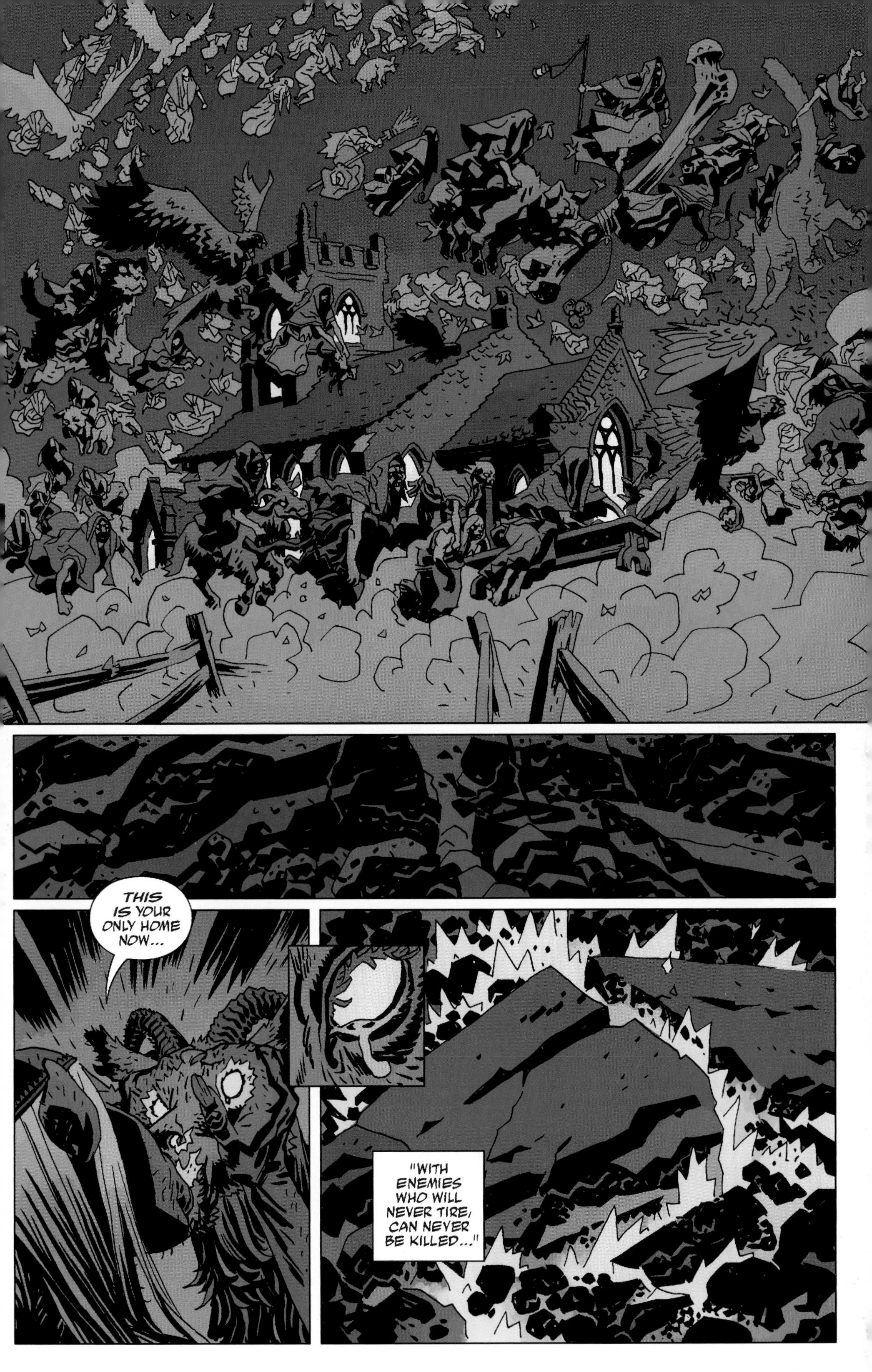
THIS IS YOUR ONLY HOME NOW...
"WITH ENEMIES WHO WILL NEVER TIRE, CAN NEVER BE KILLED..."

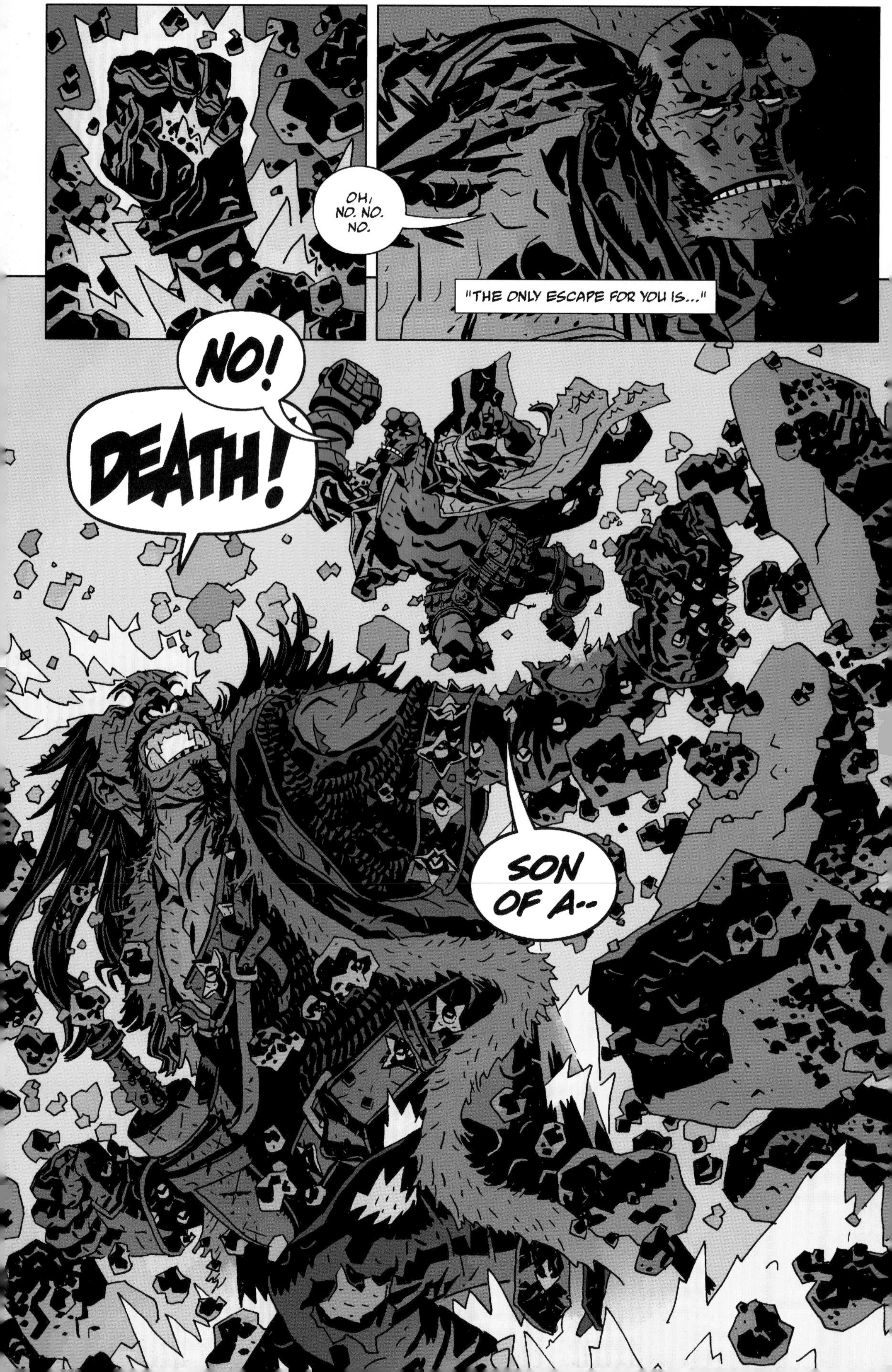
OH, NO. NO. NO.
"THE ONLY ESCAPE FOR YOU IS..."
NO!
DEATH!
SON OF A--

CHAPTER SIX

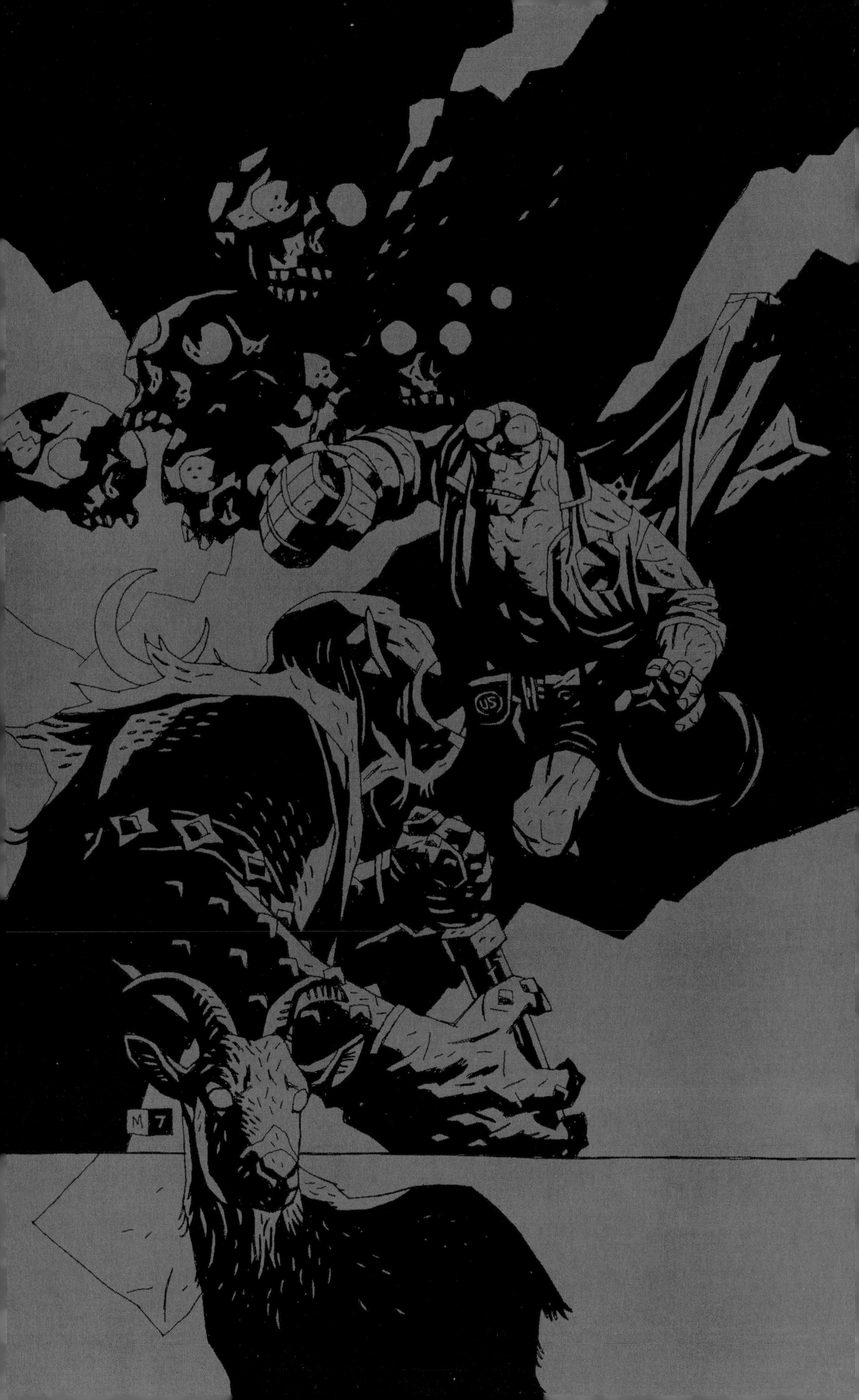
US

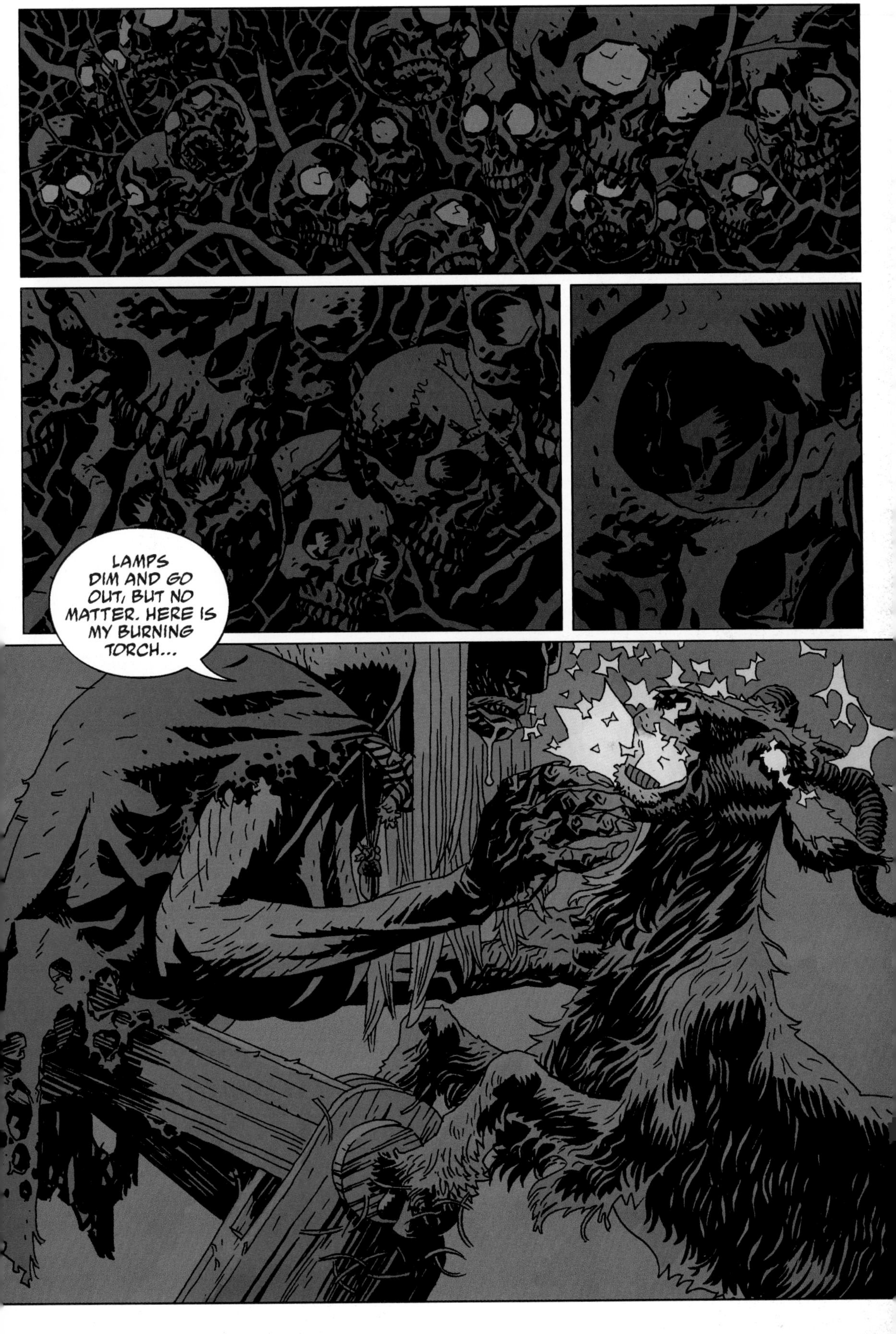
LAMPS DIM AND GO OUT, BUT NO MATTER. HERE IS MY BURNING TORCH...

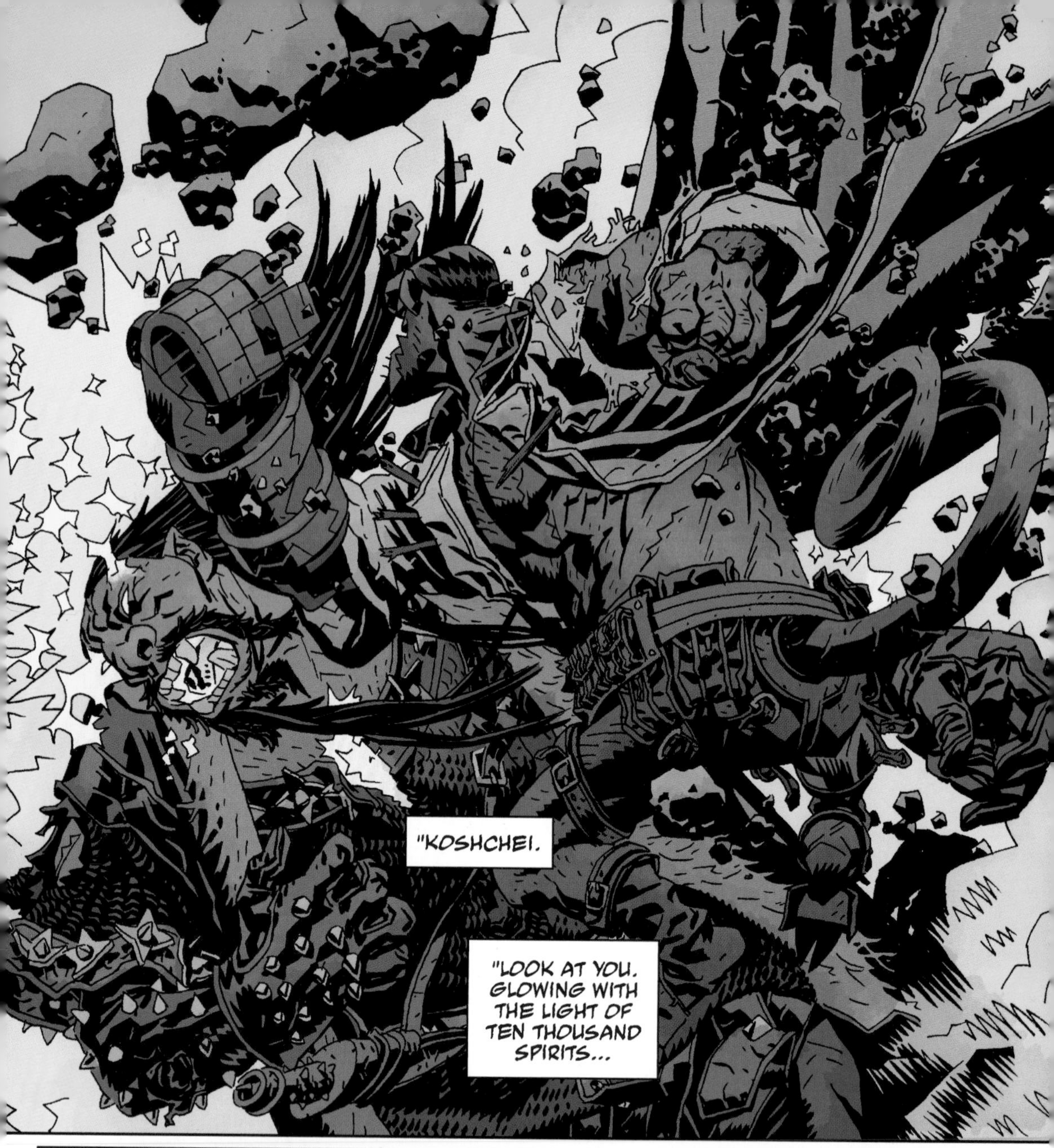
"KOSHCHEI.
"LOOK AT YOU. GLOWING WITH THE LIGHT OF TEN THOUSAND SPIRITS...

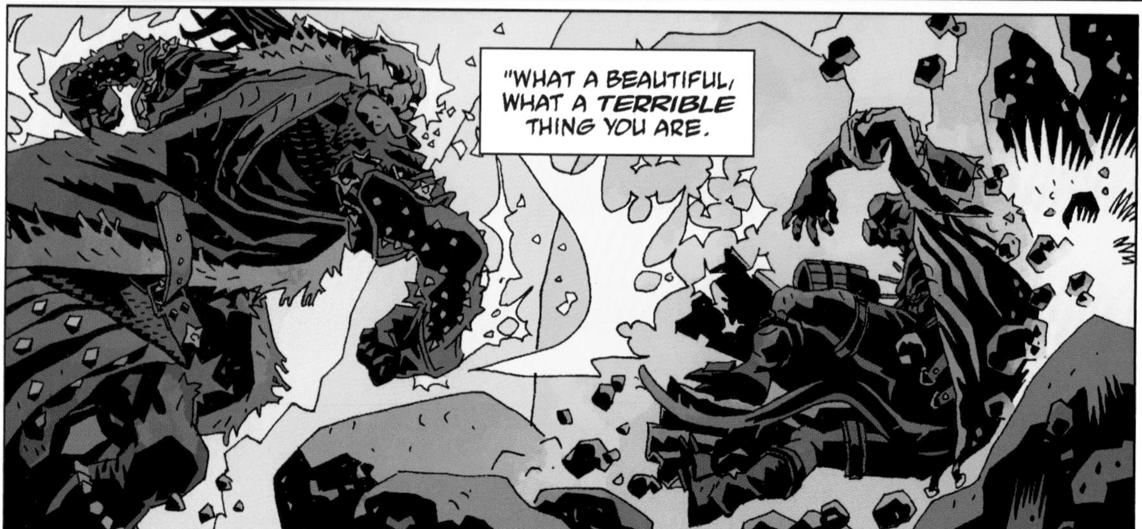
"WHAT A BEAUTIFUL, WHAT A *TERRIBLE* THING YOU ARE.

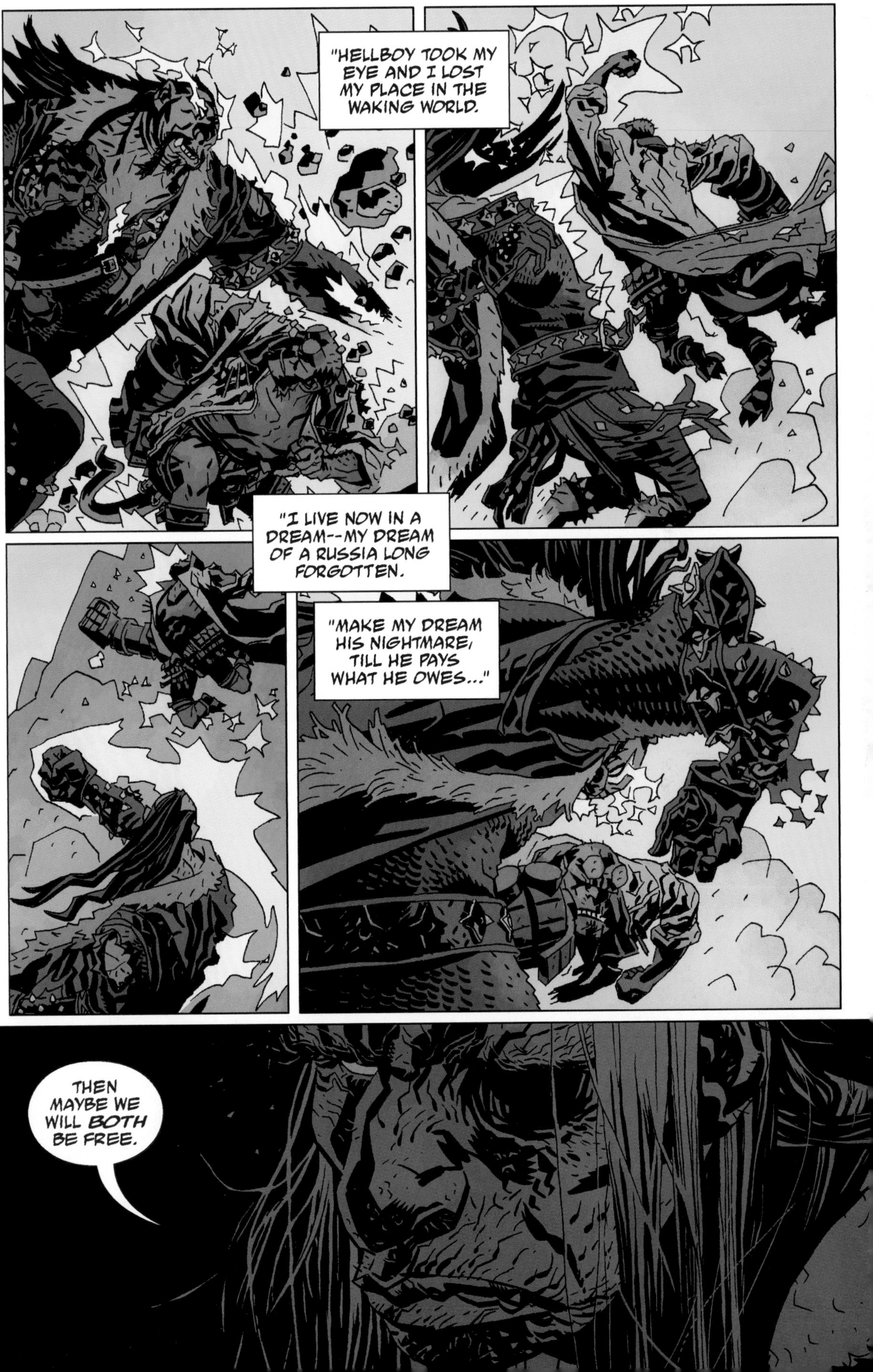
"HELLBOY TOOK MY EYE AND I LOST MY PLACE IN THE WAKING WORLD.
"I LIVE NOW IN A DREAM--MY DREAM OF A RUSSIA LONG FORGOTTEN.
"MAKE MY DREAM HIS NIGHTMARE, TILL HE PAYS WHAT HE OWES..."
THEN MAYBE WE WILL BOTH BE FREE.

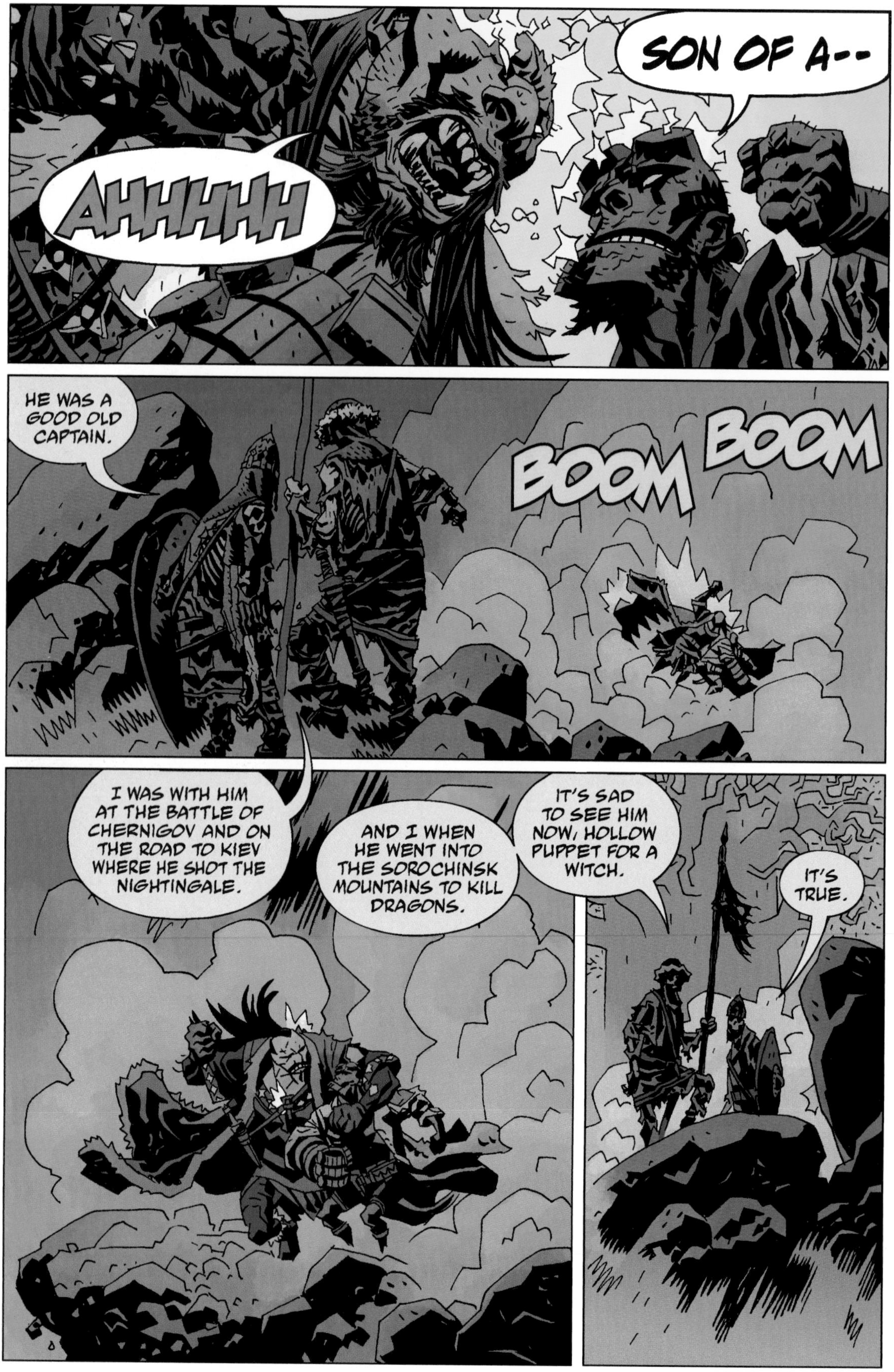
SON OF A--
AHHHHH
HE WAS A GOOD OLD CAPTAIN.
BOOM BOOM
I WAS WITH HIM AT THE BATTLE OF CHERNIGOV AND ON THE ROAD TO KIEV WHERE HE SHOT THE NIGHTINGALE.
AND I WHEN HE WENT INTO THE SOROCHINSK MOUNTAINS TO KILL DRAGONS.
IT'S SAD TO SEE HIM NOW, HOLLOW PUPPET FOR A WITCH.
IT'S TRUE.

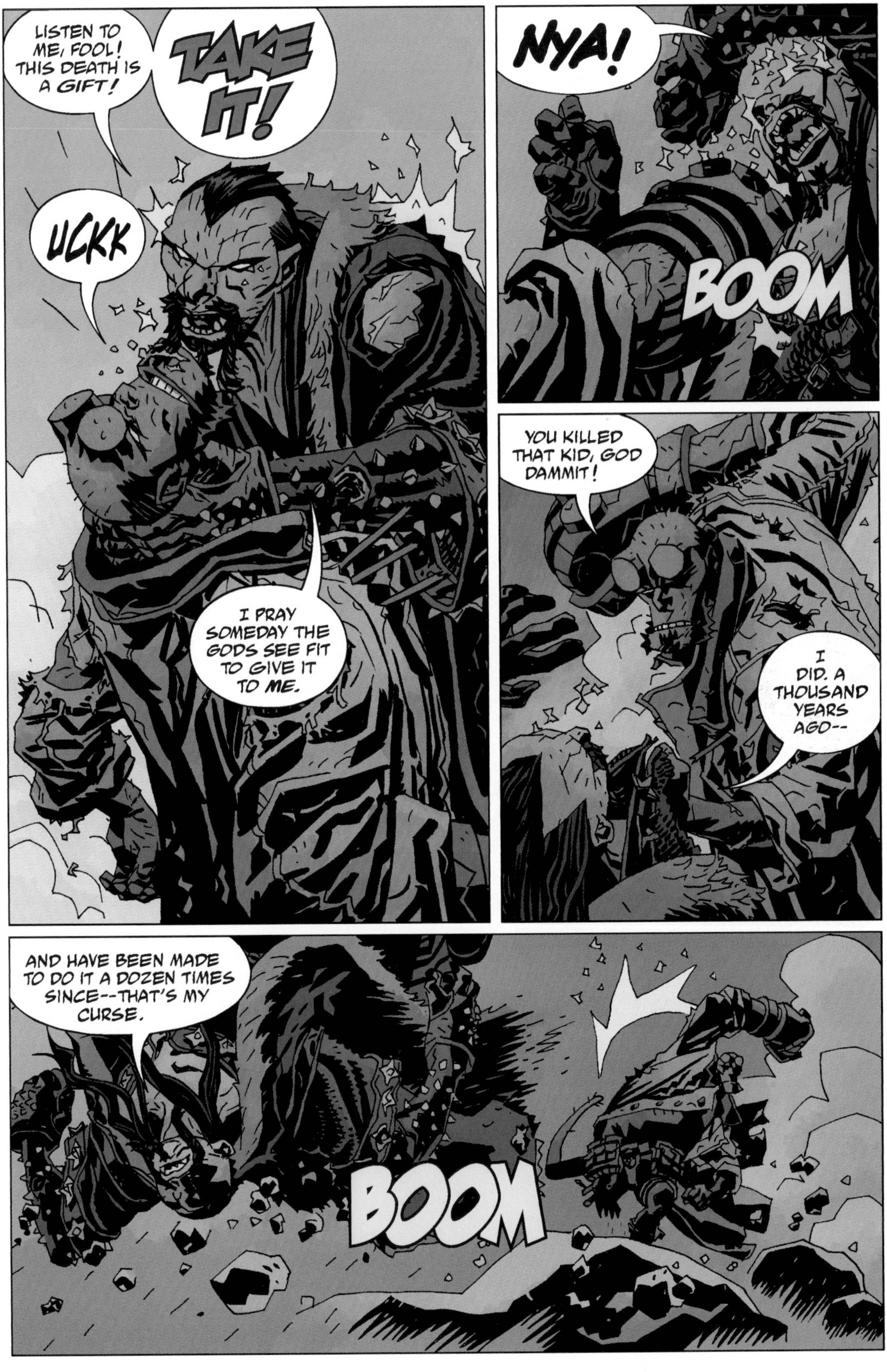
LISTEN TO ME, FOOL! THIS DEATH IS A GIFT!
TAKE IT!
UCKK
I PRAY SOMEDAY THE GODS SEE FIT TO GIVE IT TO ME.
NYA!
BOOM
YOU KILLED THAT KID, GOD DAMMIT!
I DID. A THOUSAND YEARS AGO--
AND HAVE BEEN MADE TO DO IT A DOZEN TIMES SINCE--THAT'S MY CURSE.
BOOM

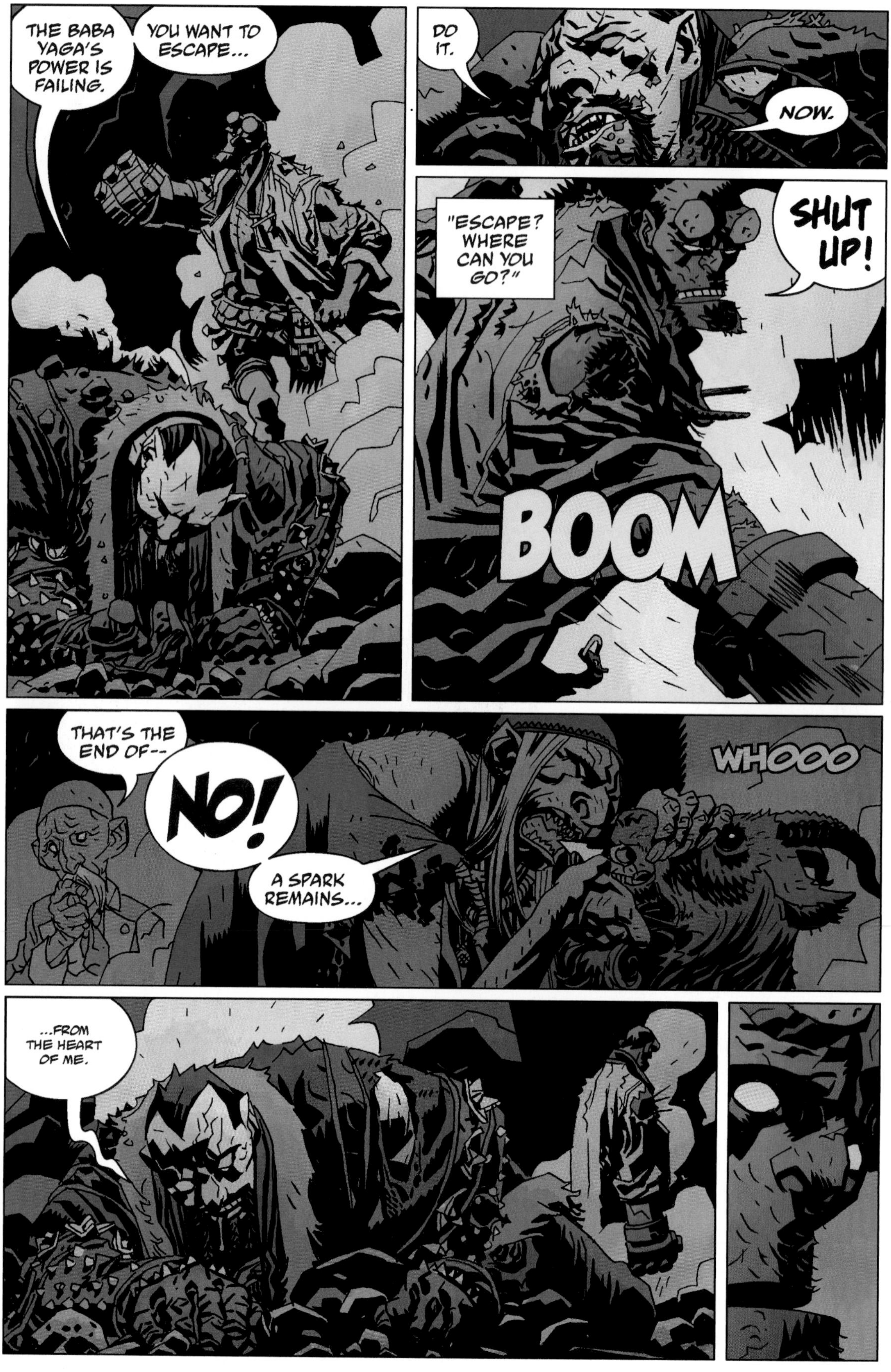
THE BABA YAGA'S POWER IS FAILING.
YOU WANT TO ESCAPE...
DO IT.
NOW.
"ESCAPE? WHERE CAN YOU GO?"
SHUT UP!
BOOM
THAT'S THE END OF--
NO!
WHOOO
A SPARK REMAINS...
...FROM THE HEART OF ME.

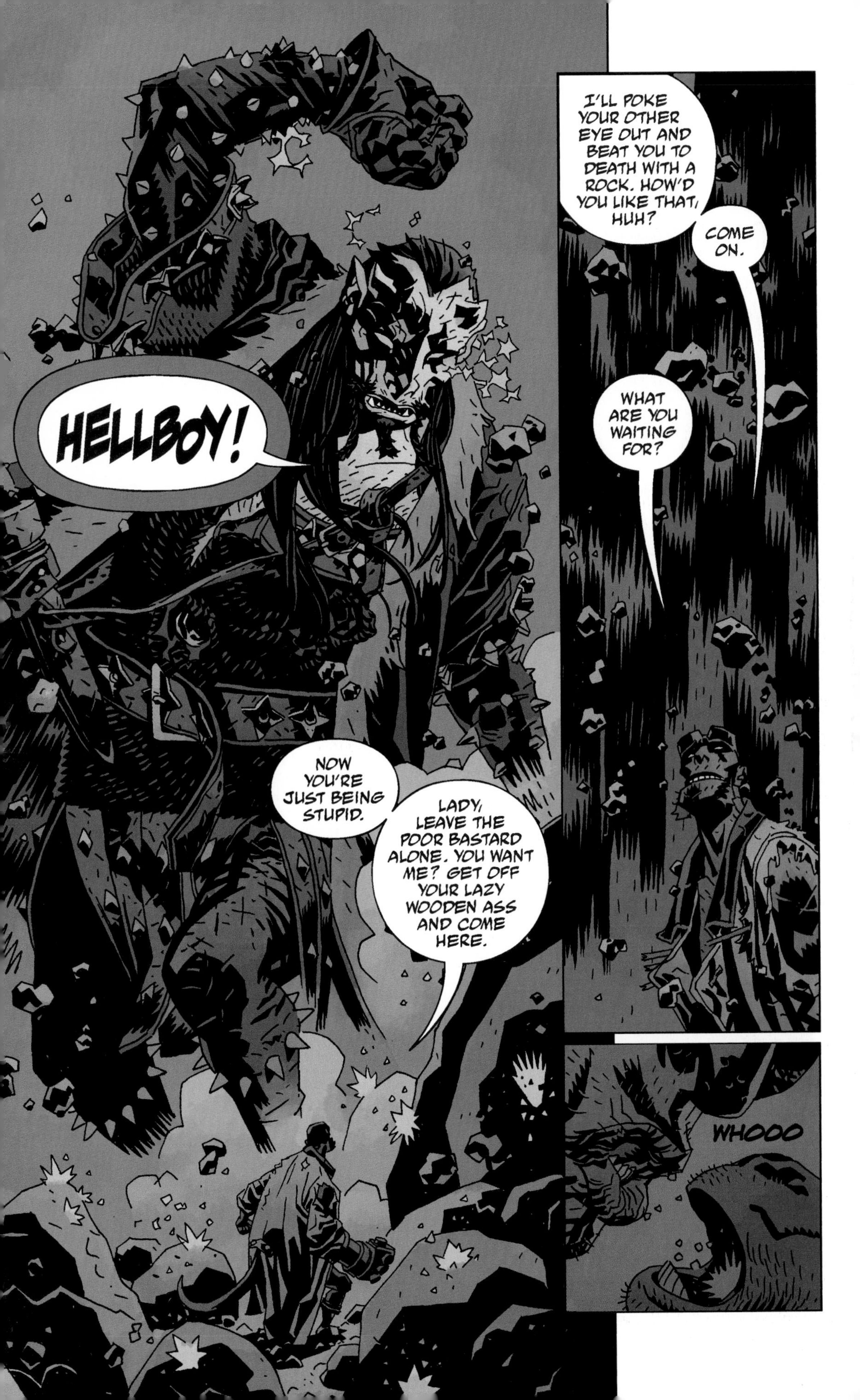
HELLBOY!
NOW YOU'RE JUST BEING STUPID.
LADY, LEAVE THE POOR BASTARD ALONE. YOU WANT ME? GET OFF YOUR LAZY WOODEN ASS AND COME HERE.
I'LL POKE YOUR OTHER EYE OUT AND BEAT YOU TO DEATH WITH A ROCK. HOW'D YOU LIKE THAT, HUH?
COME ON.
WHAT ARE YOU WAITING FOR?
WHOOO

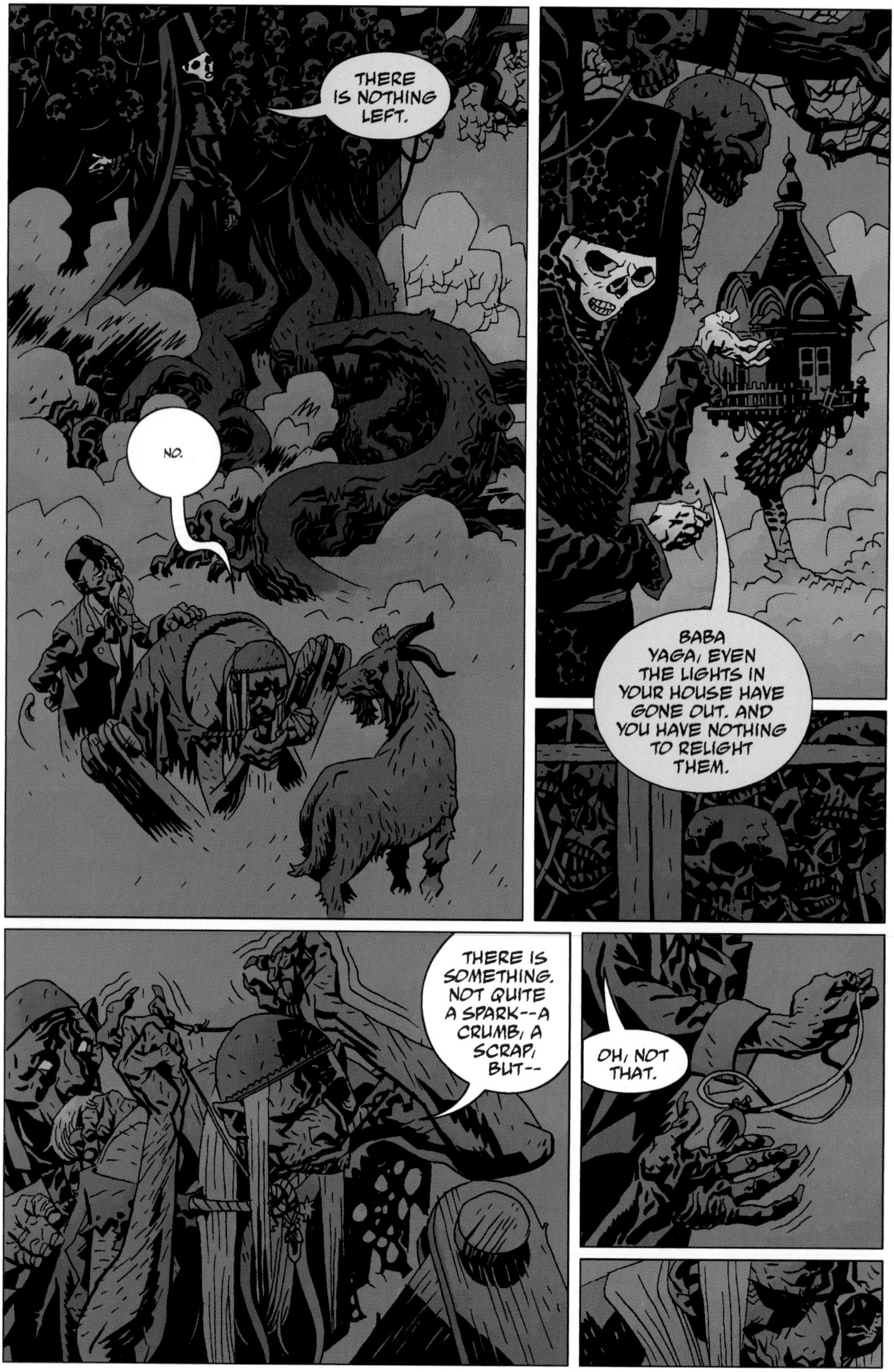
THERE IS NOTHING LEFT.
NO.
BABA YAGA, EVEN THE LIGHTS IN YOUR HOUSE HAVE GONE OUT. AND YOU HAVE NOTHING TO RELIGHT THEM.
THERE IS SOMETHING. NOT QUITE A SPARK--A CRUMB, A SCRAP, BUT--
OH, NOT THAT.

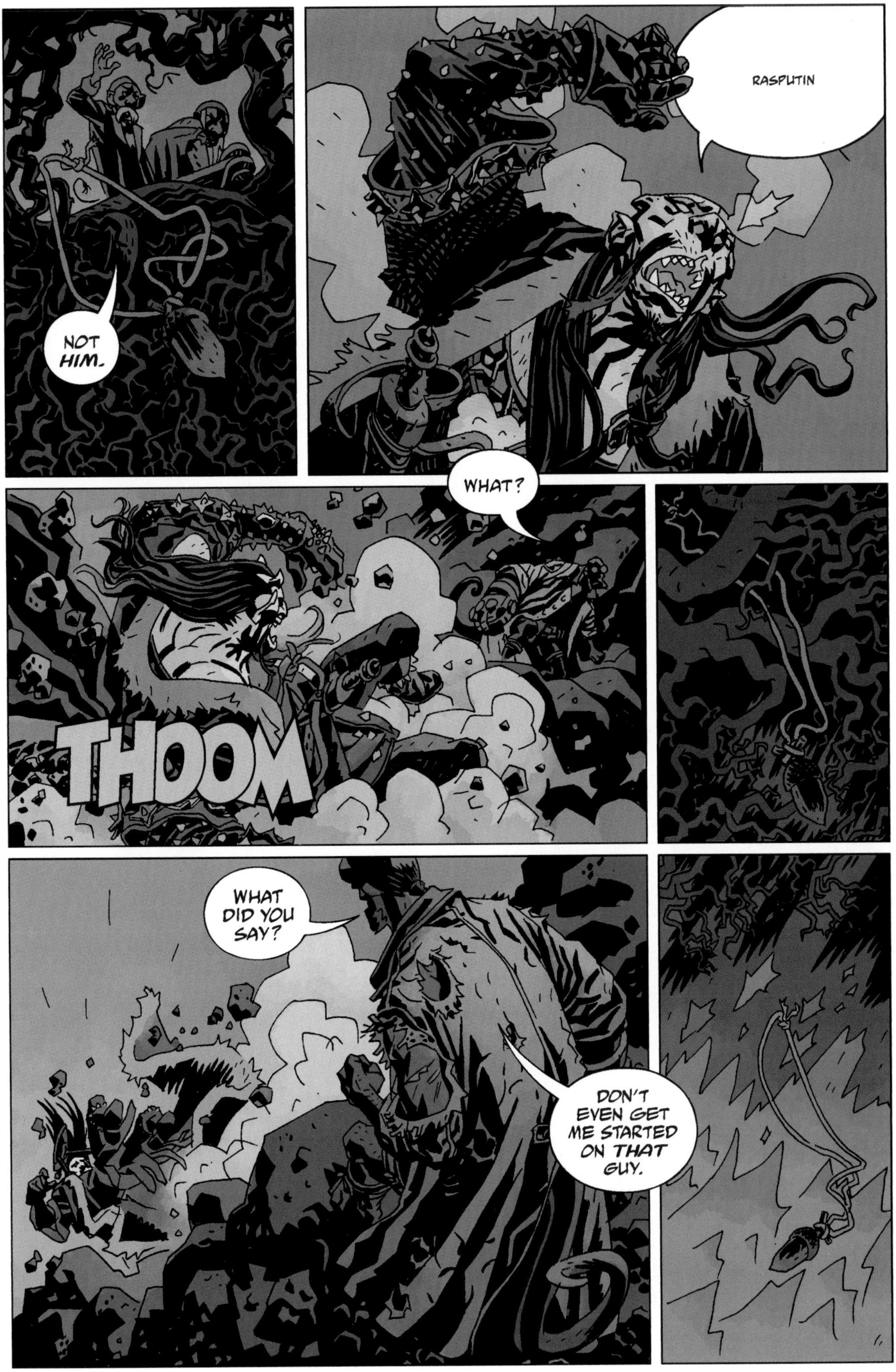
NOT HIM.
RASPUTIN
WHAT?
THOOM
WHAT DID YOU SAY?
DON'T EVEN GET ME STARTED ON *THAT* GUY.

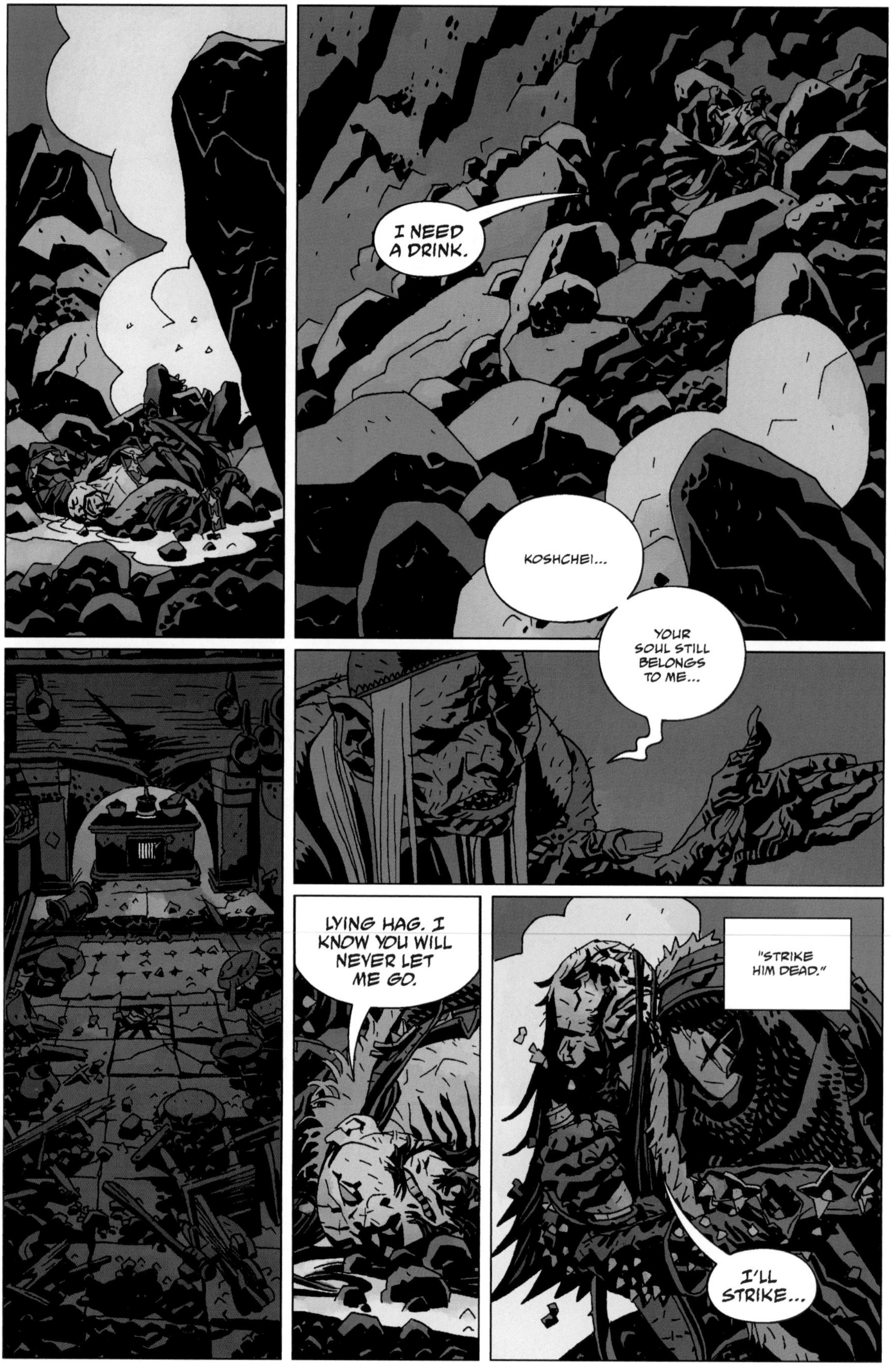
I NEED A DRINK.
KOSHCHEI...
YOUR SOUL STILL BELONGS TO ME...
LYING HAG. I KNOW YOU WILL NEVER LET ME GO.
"STRIKE HIM DEAD."
I'LL STRIKE...

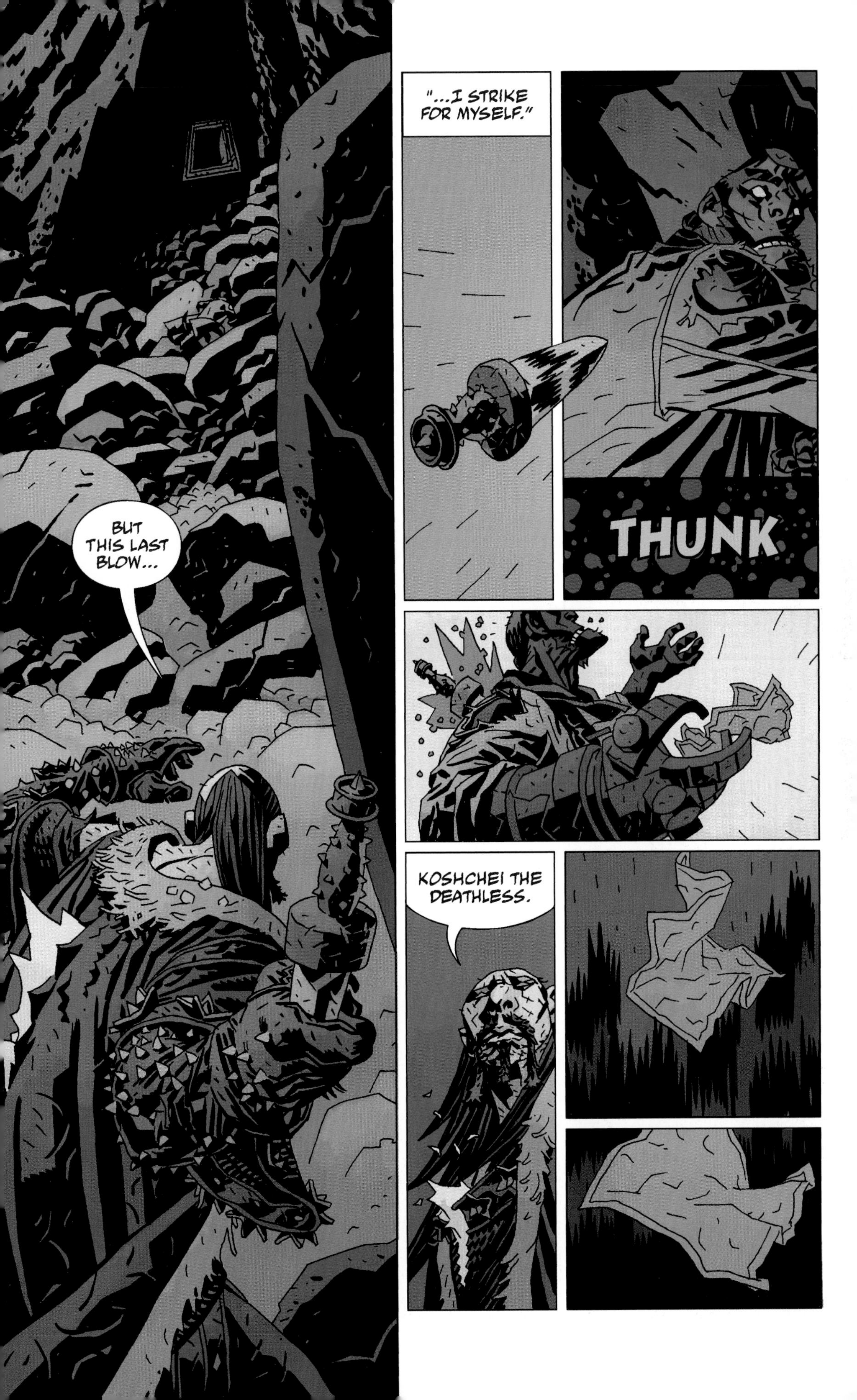
BUT THIS LAST BLOW...
"...I STRIKE FOR MYSELF."
THUNK
KOSHCHEI THE DEATHLESS.

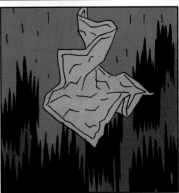

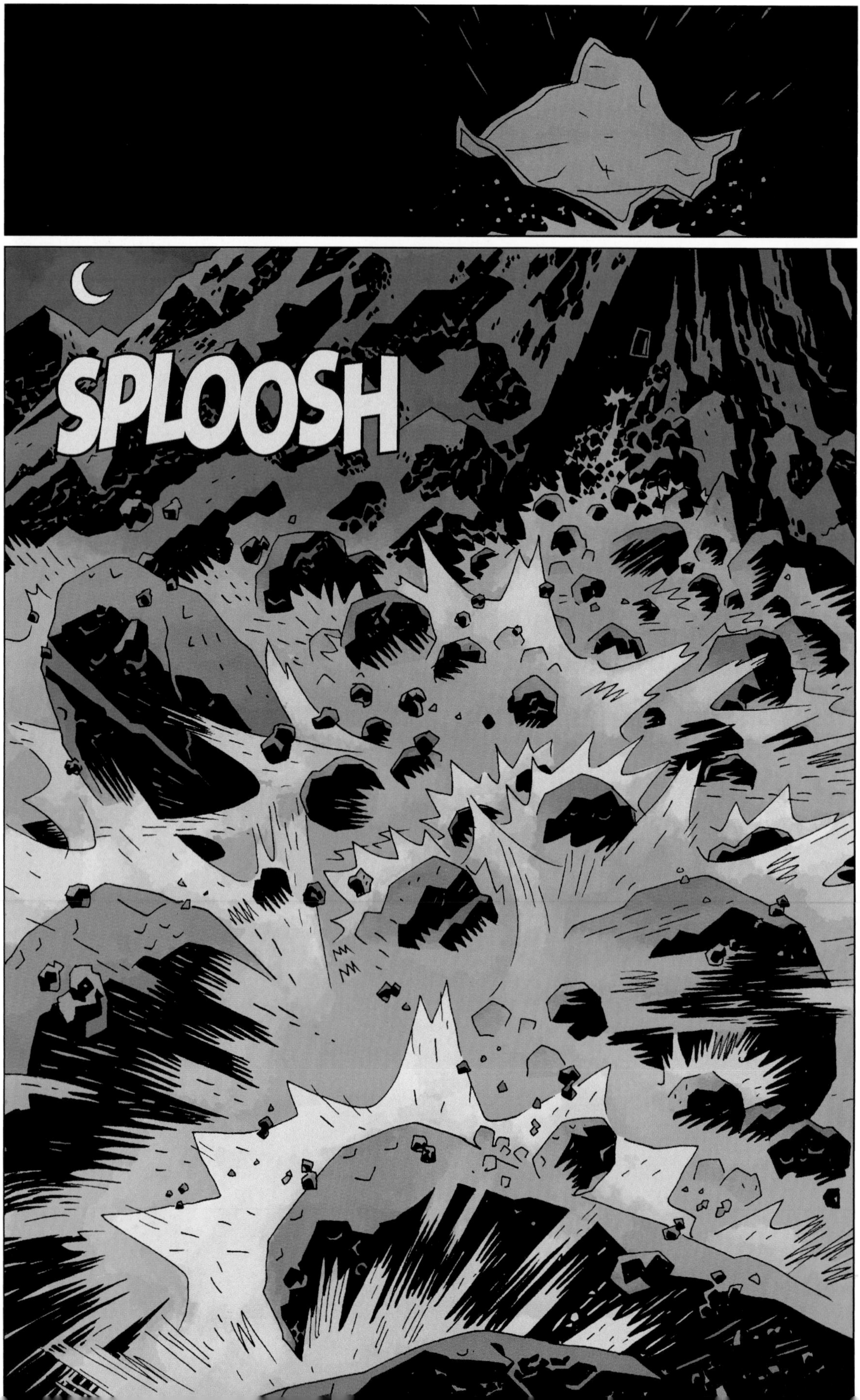
SPLOOSH

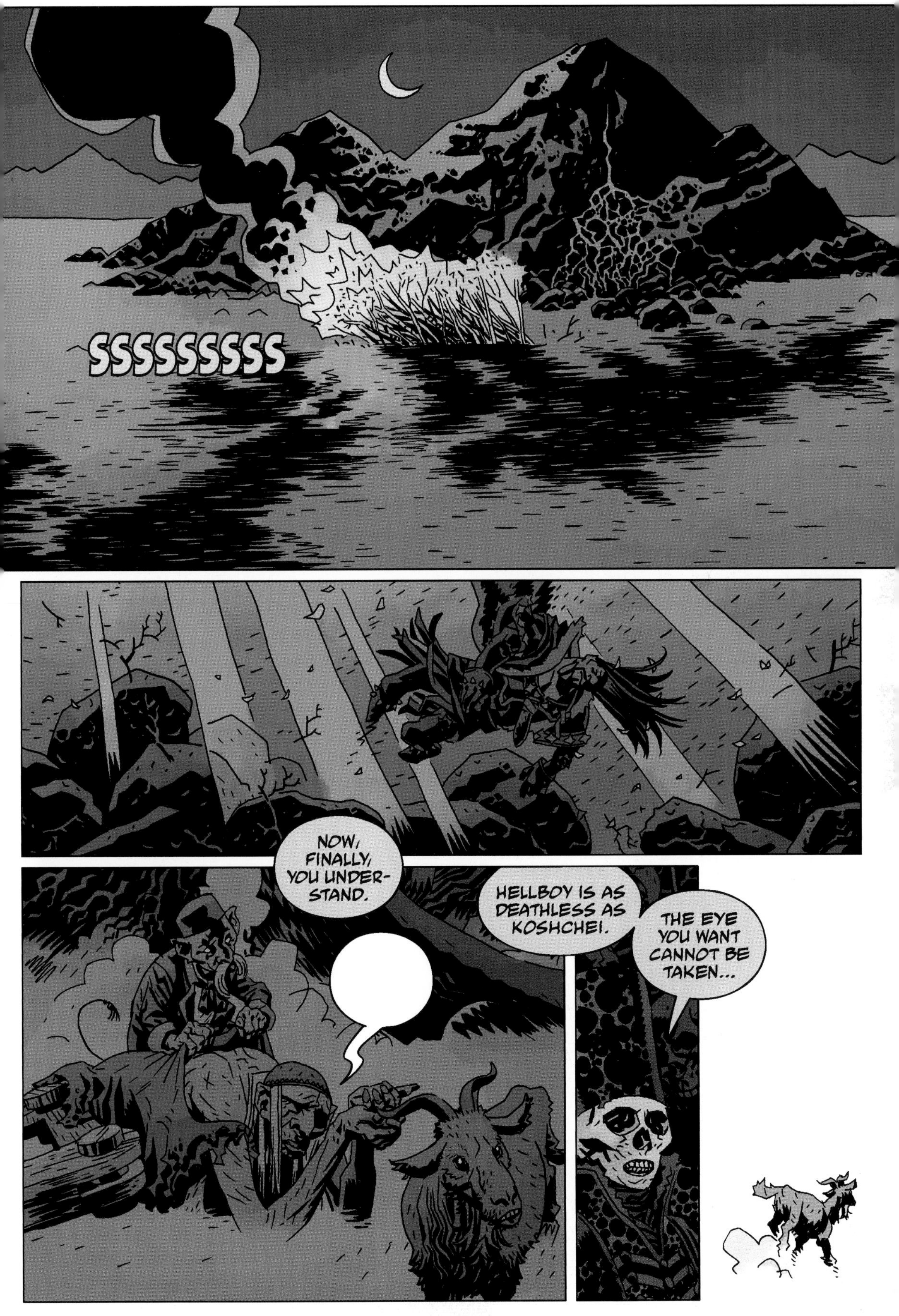
SSSSSSSSS
NOW, FINALLY, YOU UNDER-STAND.
HELLBOY IS AS DEATHLESS AS KOSHCHEI.
THE EYE YOU WANT CANNOT BE TAKEN...

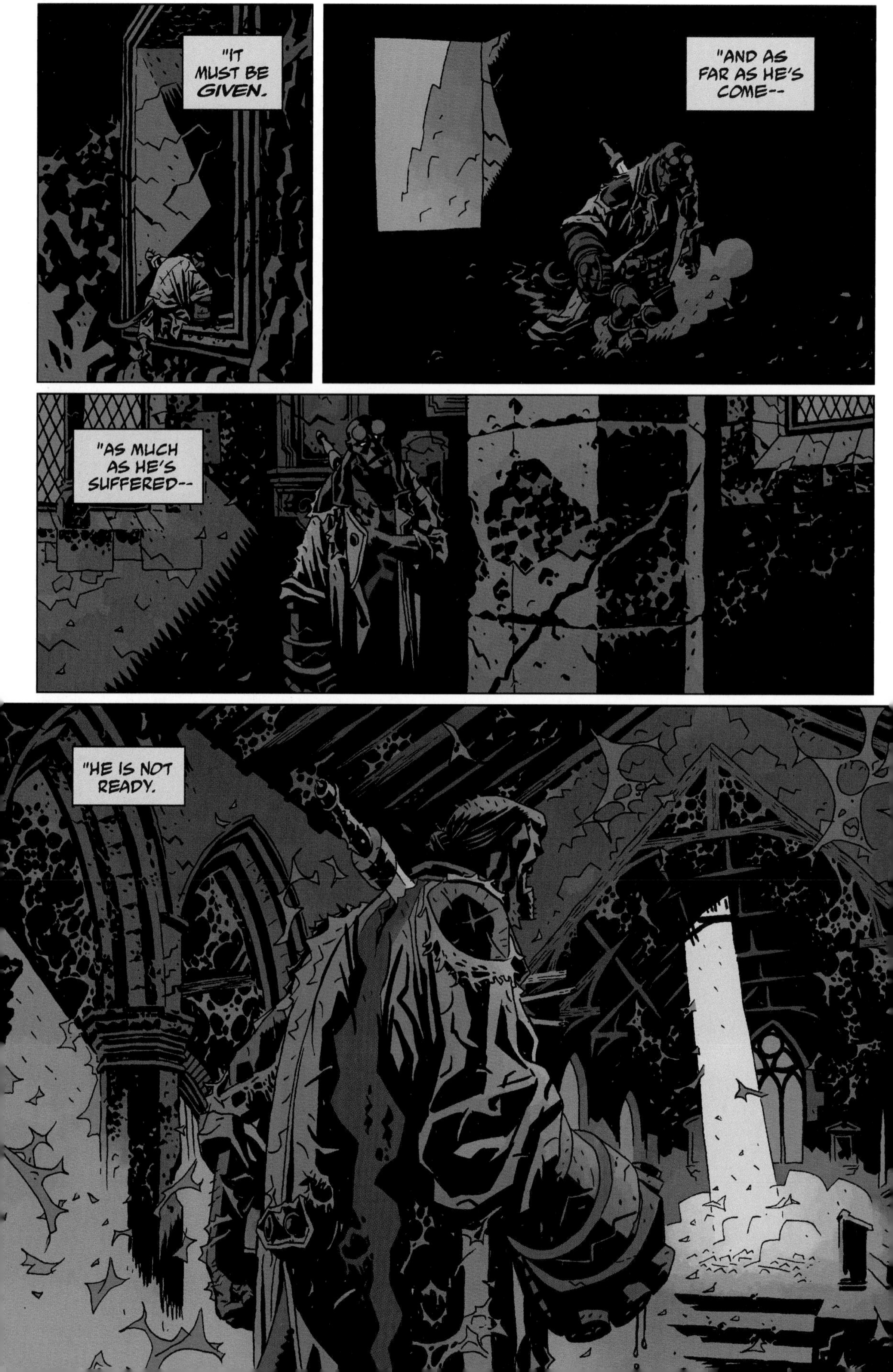
"IT MUST BE GIVEN.
"AND AS FAR AS HE'S COME--
"AS MUCH AS HE'S SUFFERED--
"HE IS NOT READY.

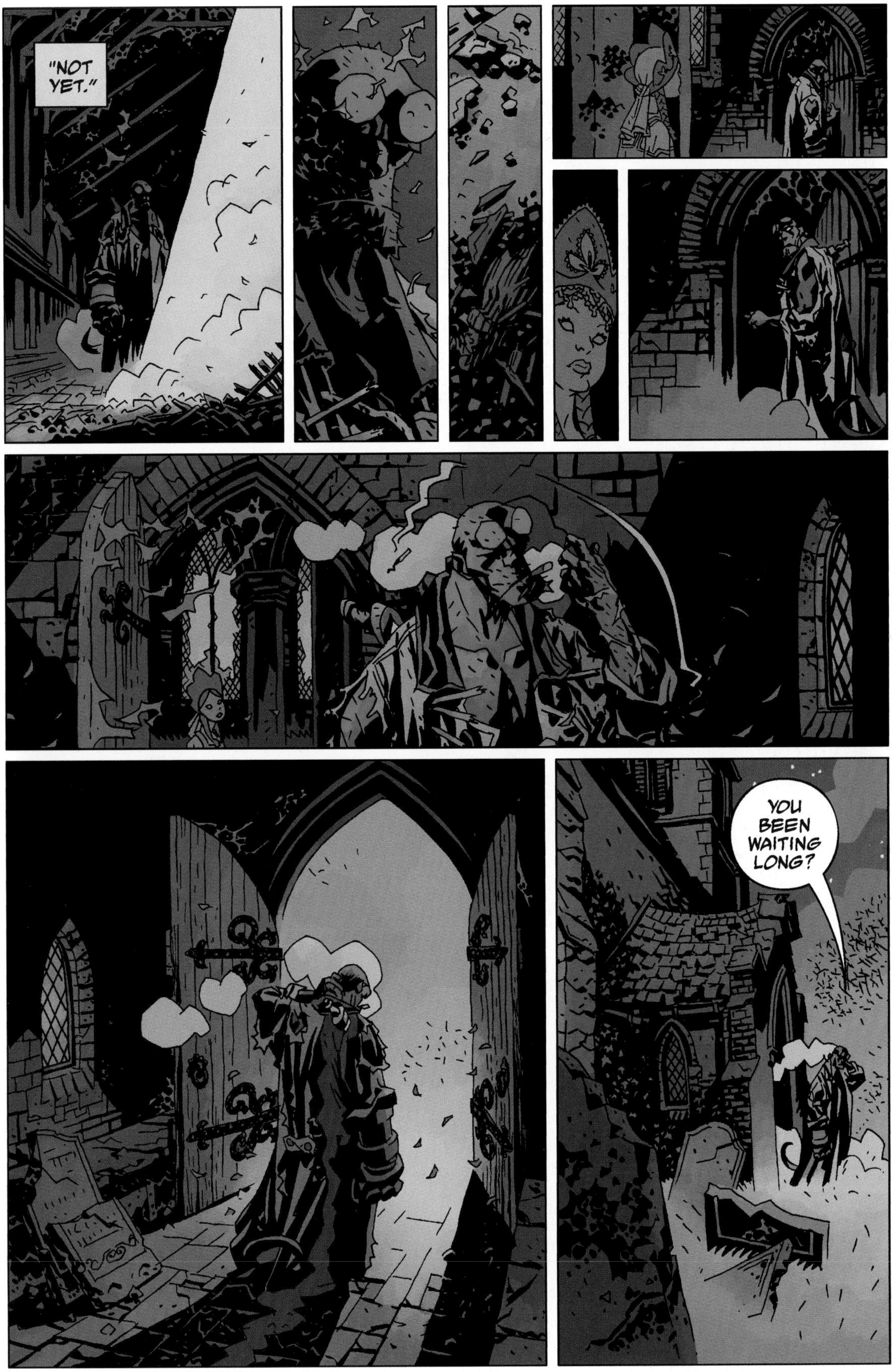
"NOT YET."
YOU BEEN WAITING LONG?

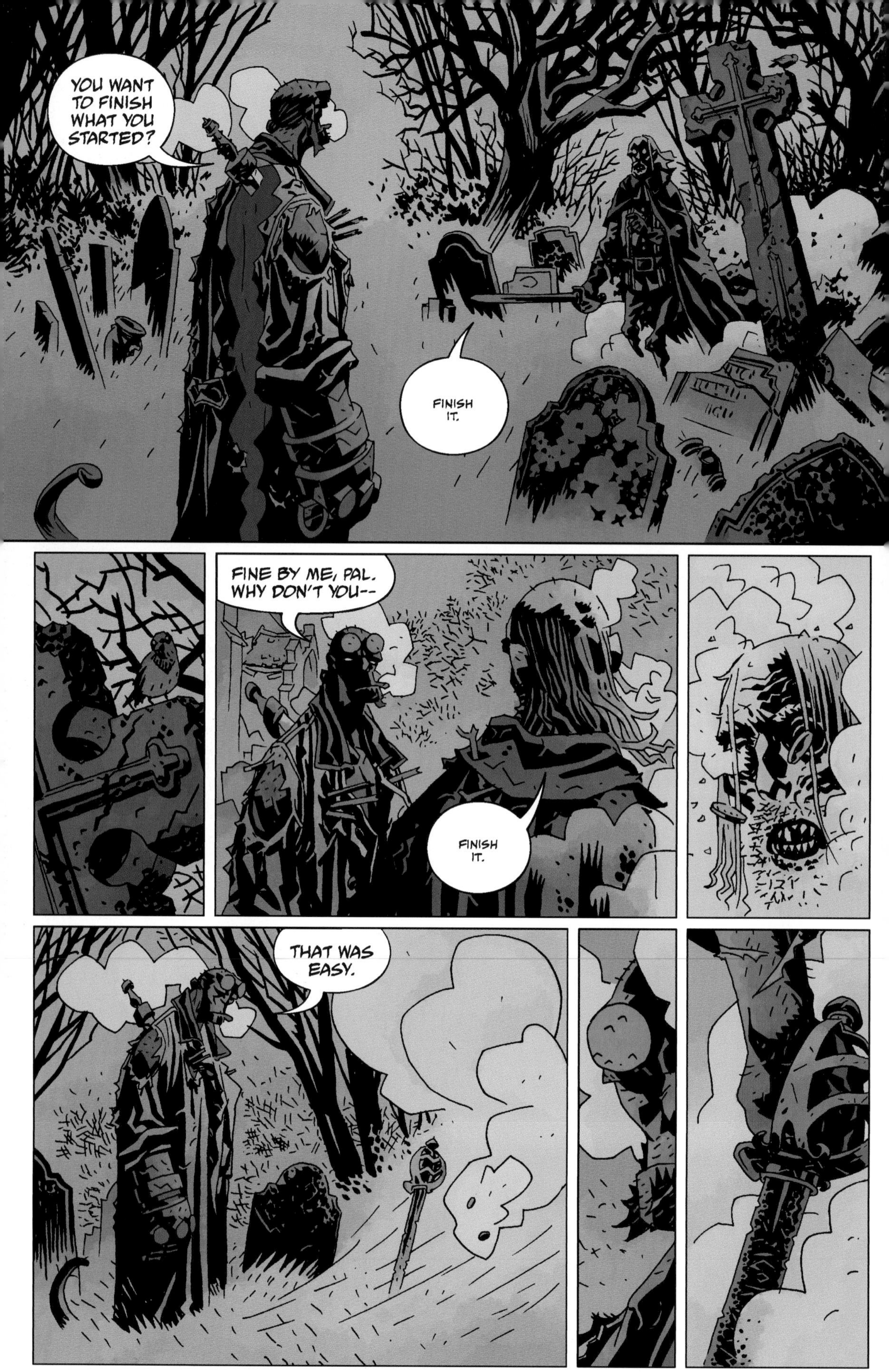
YOU WANT TO FINISH WHAT YOU STARTED?
FINISH IT.
FINE BY ME, PAL. WHY DON'T YOU--
FINISH IT.
THAT WAS EASY.

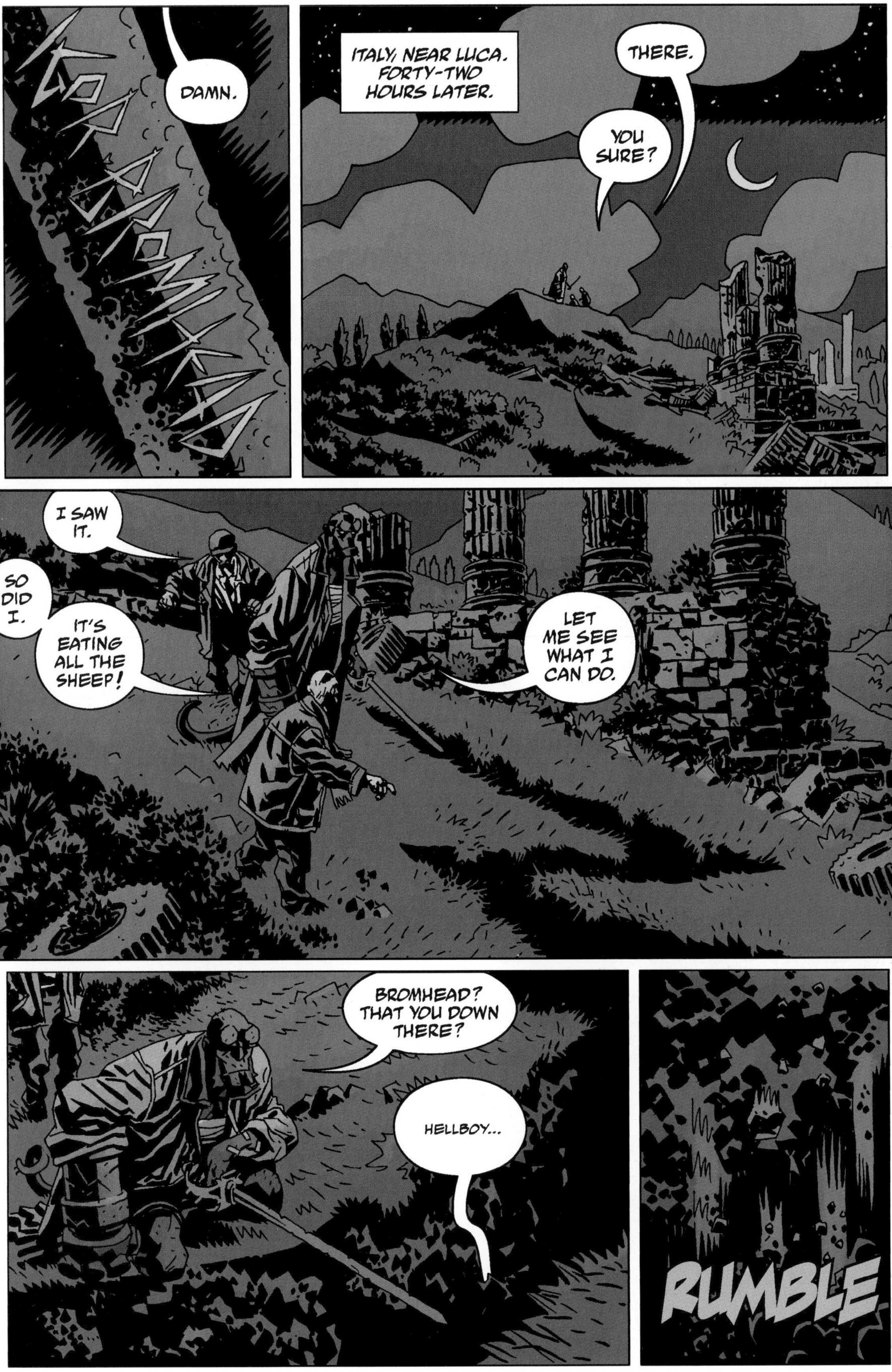
DAMN.
ITALY, NEAR LUCA. FORTY-TWO HOURS LATER.
THERE.
YOU SURE?
I SAW IT.
SO DID I.
IT'S EATING ALL THE SHEEP!
LET ME SEE WHAT I CAN DO.
BROMHEAD? THAT YOU DOWN THERE?
HELLBOY...
RUMBLE

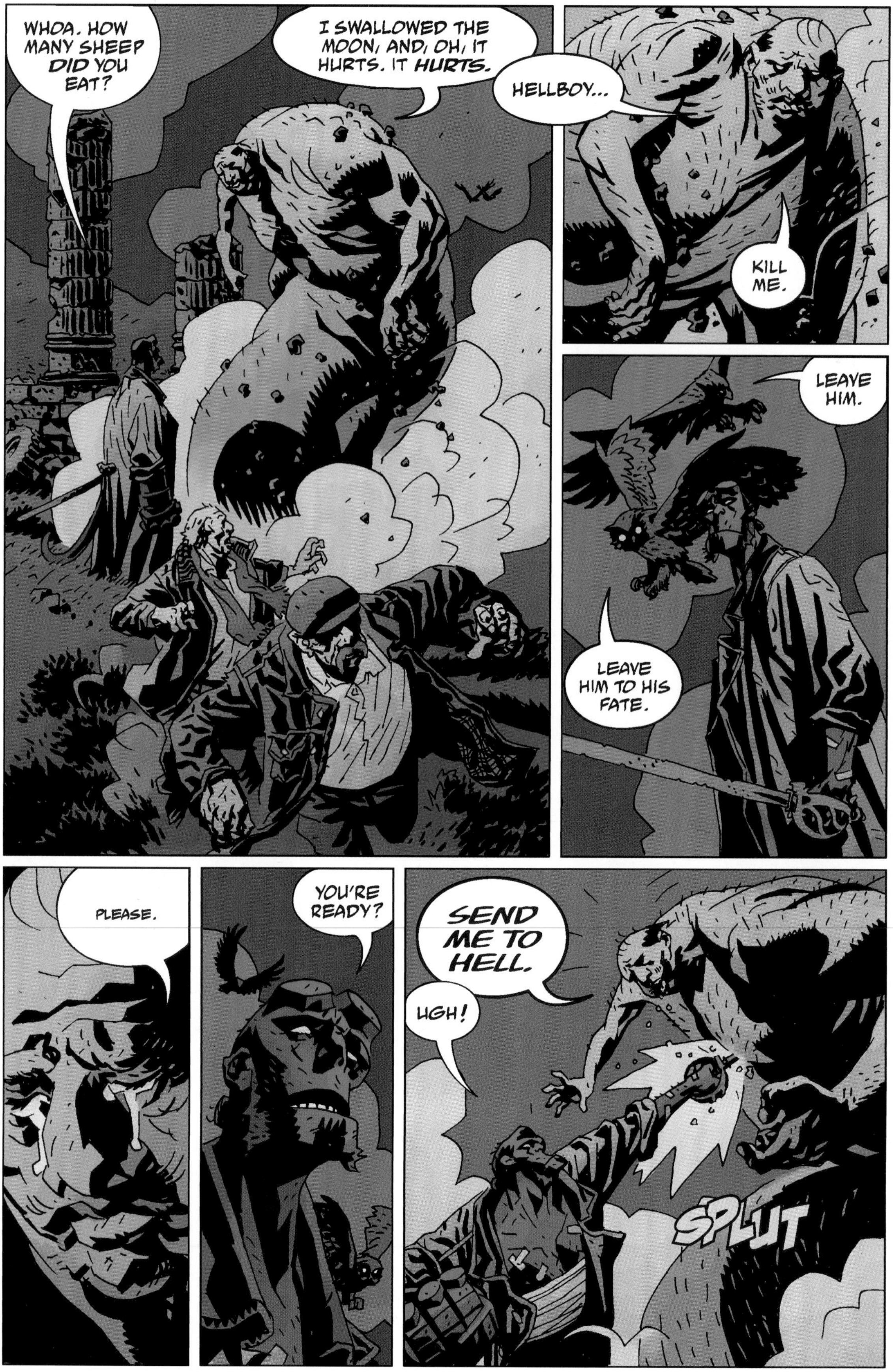
WHOA. HOW MANY SHEEP DID YOU EAT?
I SWALLOWED THE MOON, AND, OH, IT HURTS. IT HURTS.
HELLBOY...
KILL ME.
LEAVE HIM.
LEAVE HIM TO HIS FATE.
PLEASE.
YOU'RE READY?
SEND ME TO HELL.
UGH!
SPLUT

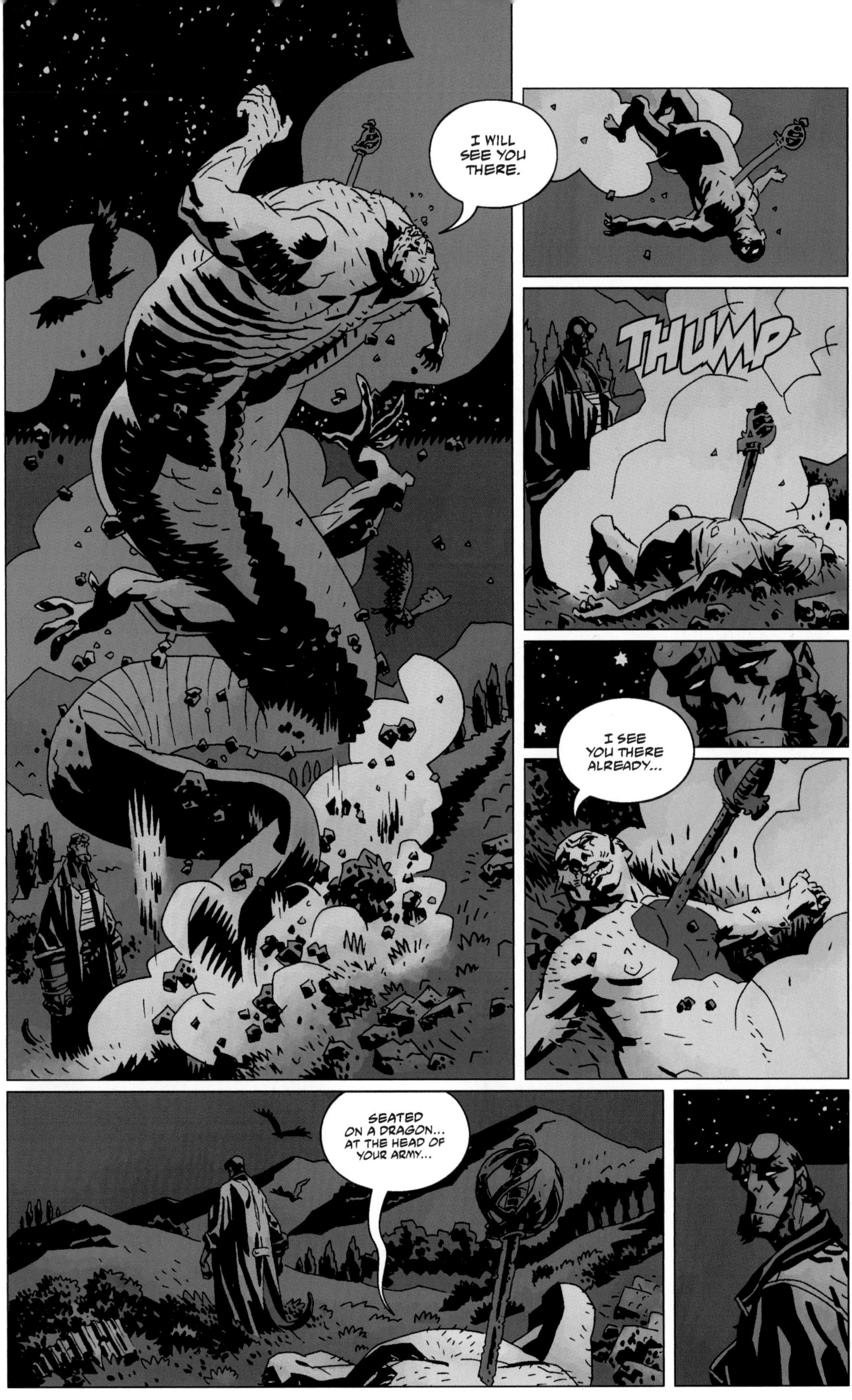
I WILL SEE YOU THERE.
THUMP
I SEE YOU THERE ALREADY...
SEATED ON A DRAGON... AT THE HEAD OF YOUR ARMY...

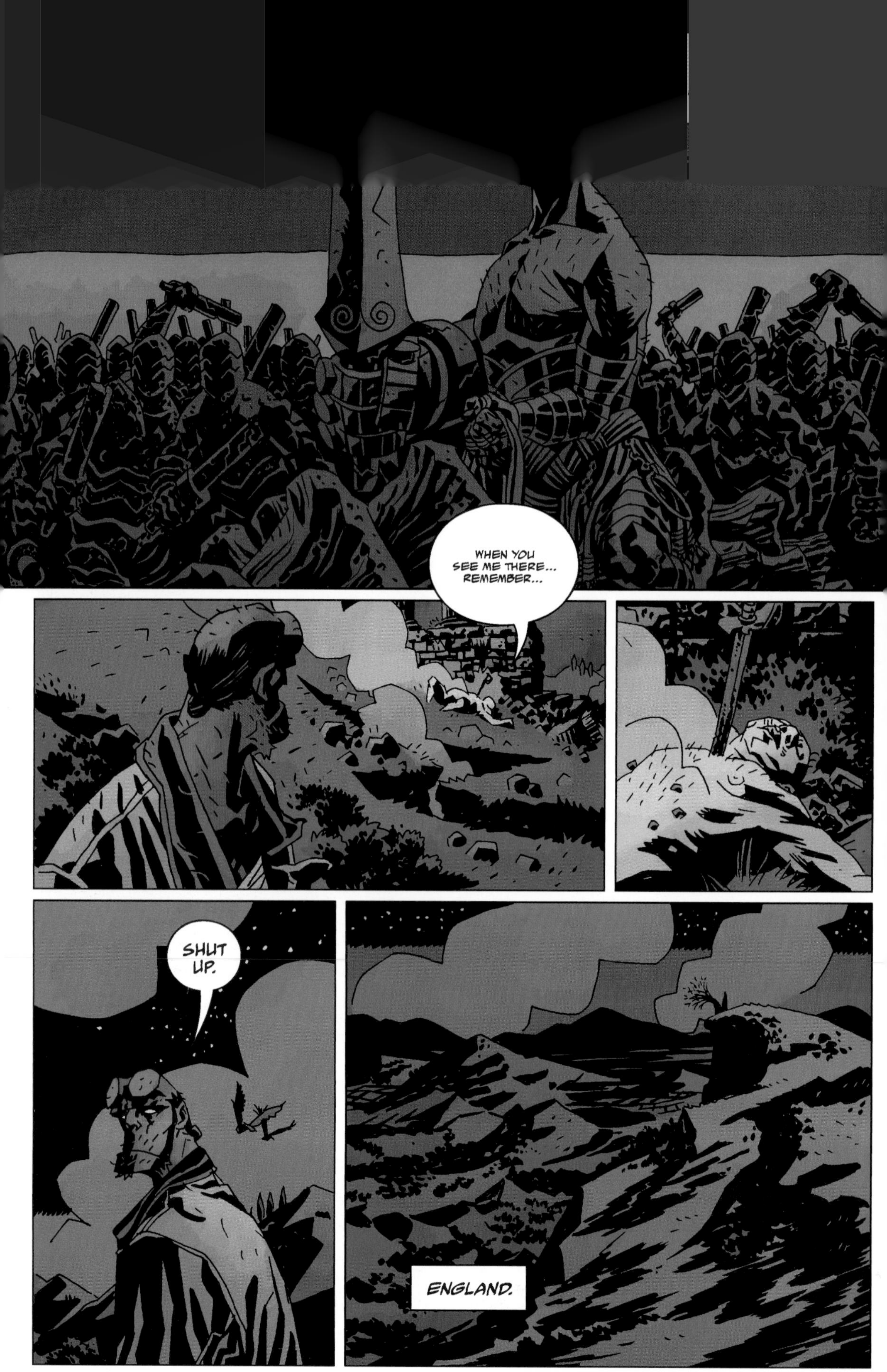
WHEN YOU SEE ME THERE... REMEMBER...
SHUT UP.
ENGLAND.

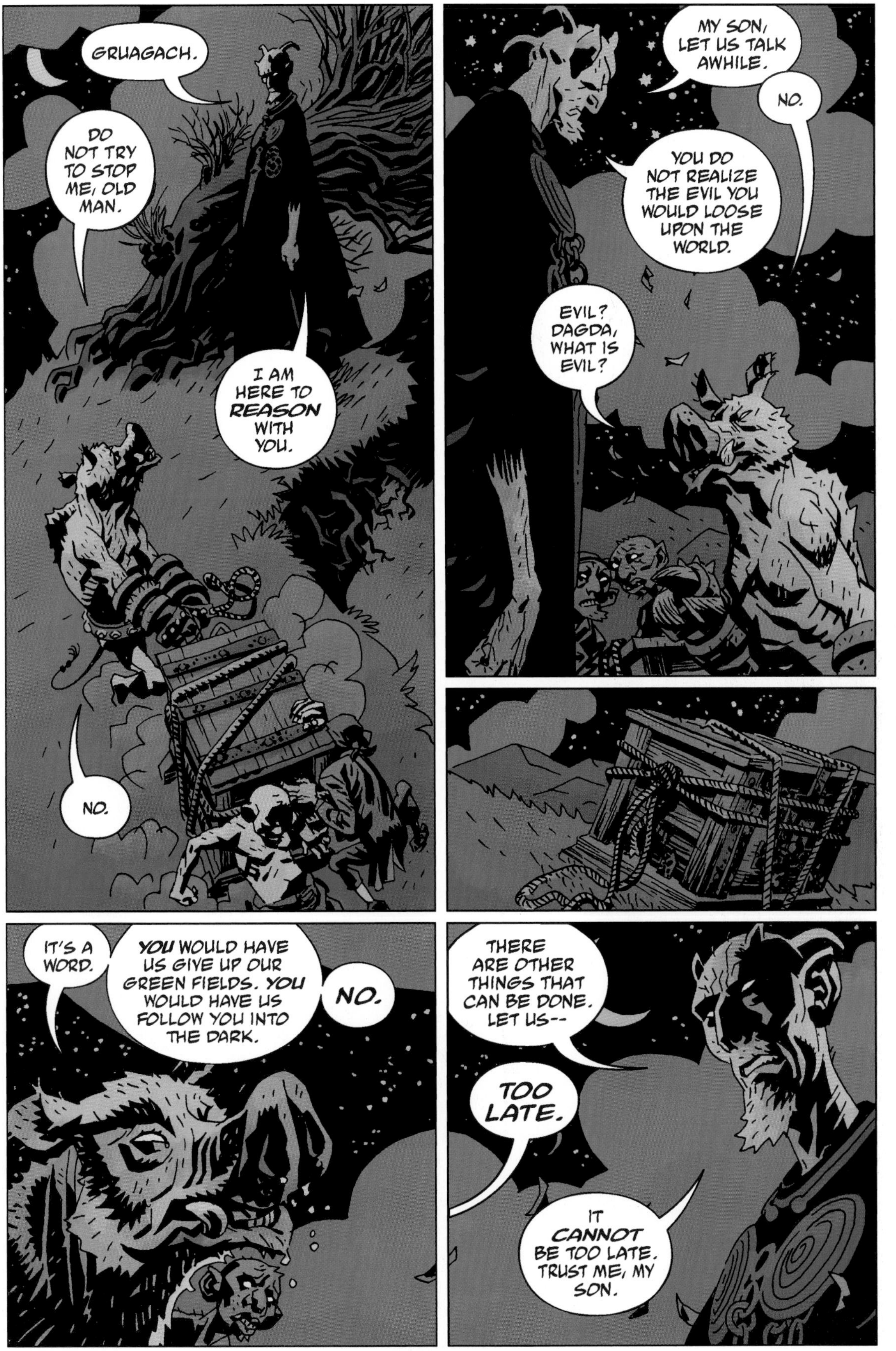
GRUAGACH.
DO NOT TRY TO STOP ME, OLD MAN.
I AM HERE TO REASON WITH YOU.
NO.
MY SON, LET US TALK AWHILE.
NO.
YOU DO NOT REALIZE THE EVIL YOU WOULD LOOSE UPON THE WORLD.
EVIL? DAGDA, WHAT IS EVIL?
IT'S A WORD.
YOU WOULD HAVE US GIVE UP OUR GREEN FIELDS. YOU WOULD HAVE US FOLLOW YOU INTO THE DARK.
NO.
THERE ARE OTHER THINGS THAT CAN BE DONE. LET US--
TOO LATE.
IT CANNOT BE TOO LATE. TRUST ME, MY SON.

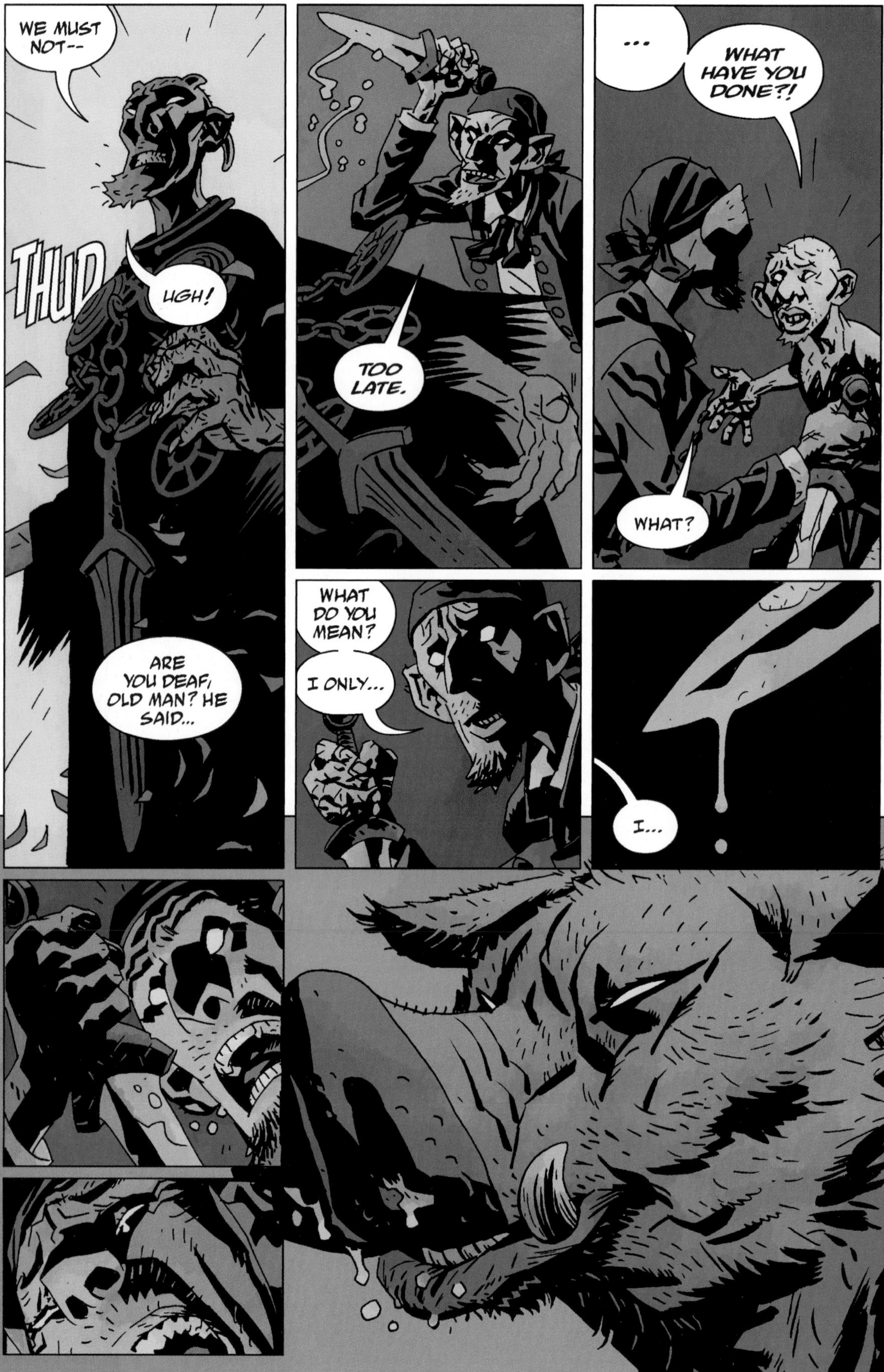

WE MUST NOT--
THUD
UGH!
ARE YOU DEAF, OLD MAN? HE SAID...
TOO LATE.
...
WHAT HAVE YOU DONE?!
WHAT?
WHAT DO YOU MEAN?
I ONLY...
I...

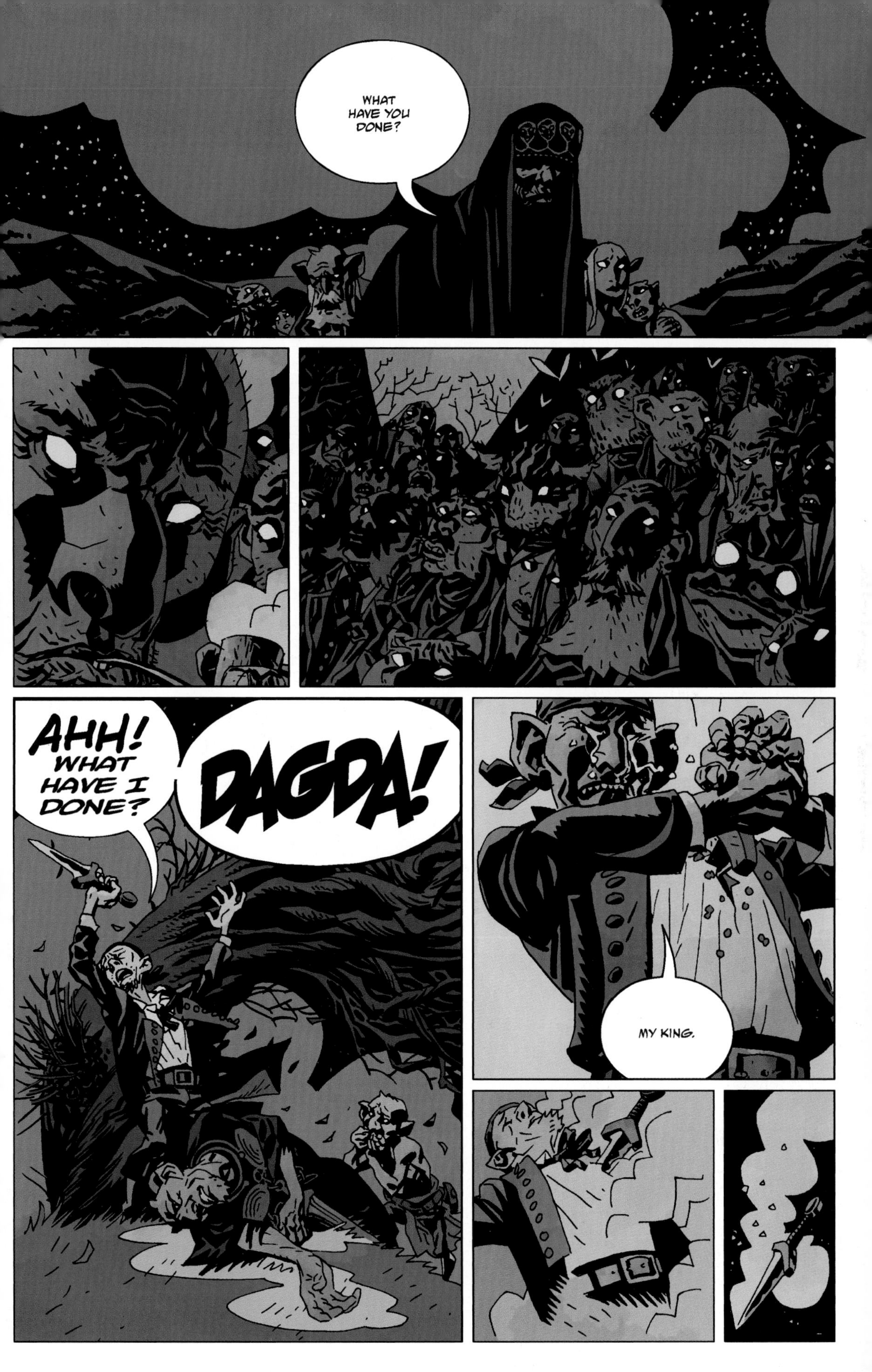
WHAT HAVE YOU DONE?
AHH! WHAT HAVE I DONE?
DAGDA!
MY KING.

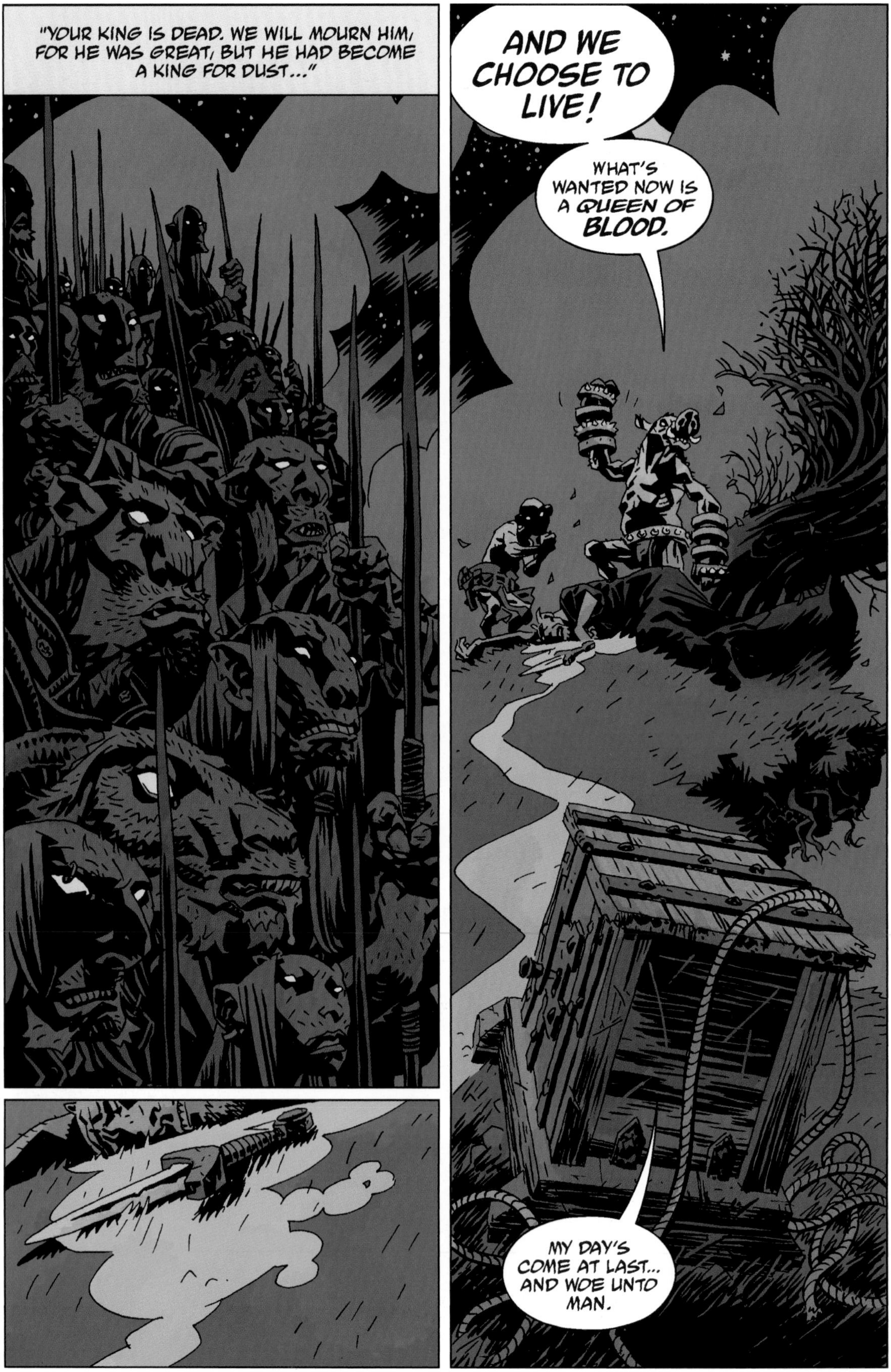
"YOUR KING IS DEAD. WE WILL MOURN HIM, FOR HE WAS GREAT, BUT HE HAD BECOME A KING FOR DUST..."
AND WE CHOOSE TO LIVE!
WHAT'S WANTED NOW IS A QUEEN OF BLOOD.
MY DAY'S COME AT LAST... AND WOE UNTO MAN.

THE END

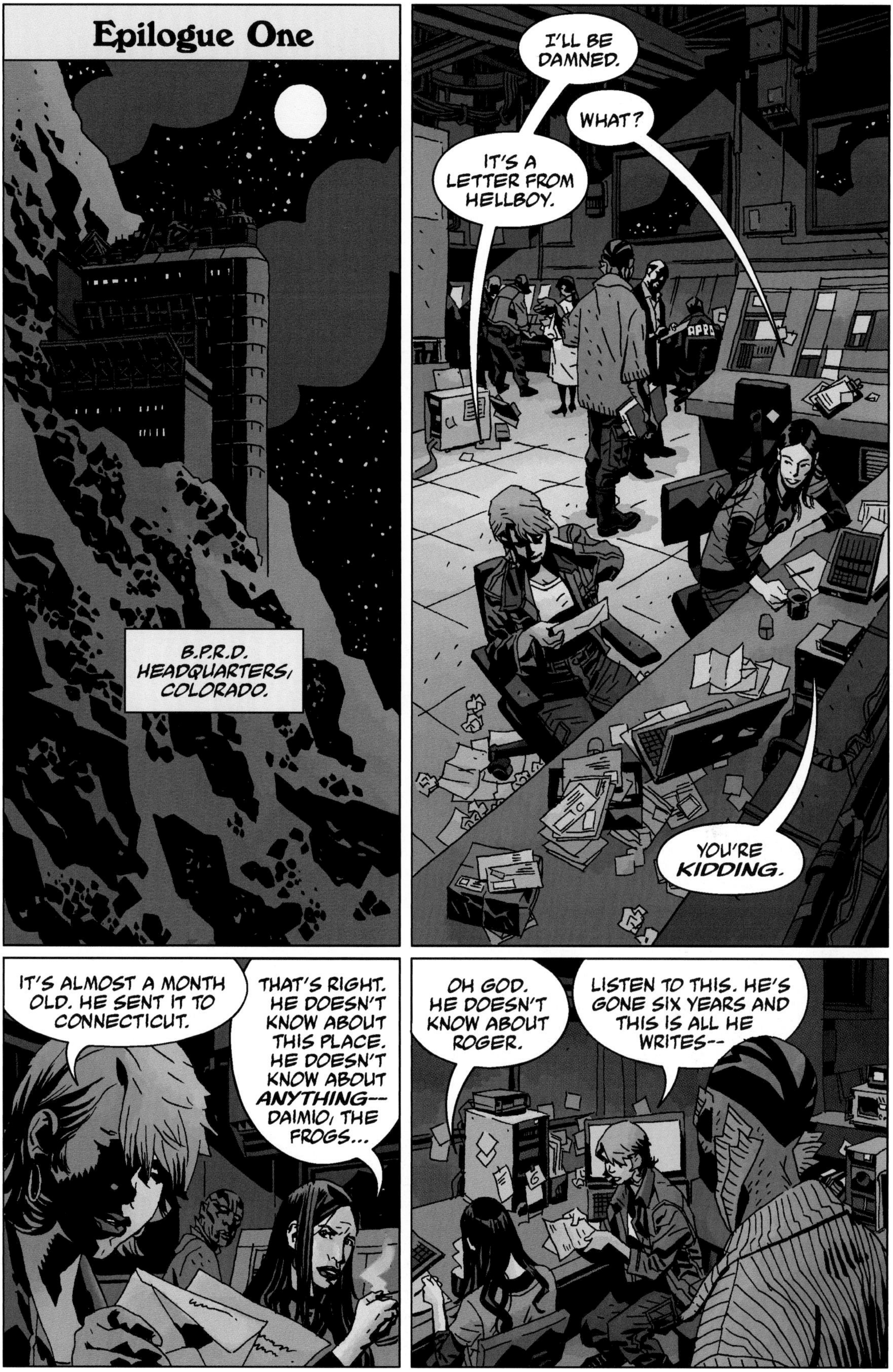
Epilogue One
B.P.R.D. HEADQUARTERS, COLORADO.
I'LL BE DAMNED.
WHAT?
IT'S A LETTER FROM HELLBOY.
YOU'RE KIDDING.
IT'S ALMOST A MONTH OLD. HE SENT IT TO CONNECTICUT.
THAT'S RIGHT. HE DOESN'T KNOW ABOUT THIS PLACE. HE DOESN'T KNOW ABOUT ANYTHING-- DAIMIO, THE FROGS...
OH GOD. HE DOESN'T KNOW ABOUT ROGER.
LISTEN TO THIS. HE'S GONE SIX YEARS AND THIS IS ALL HE WRITES--

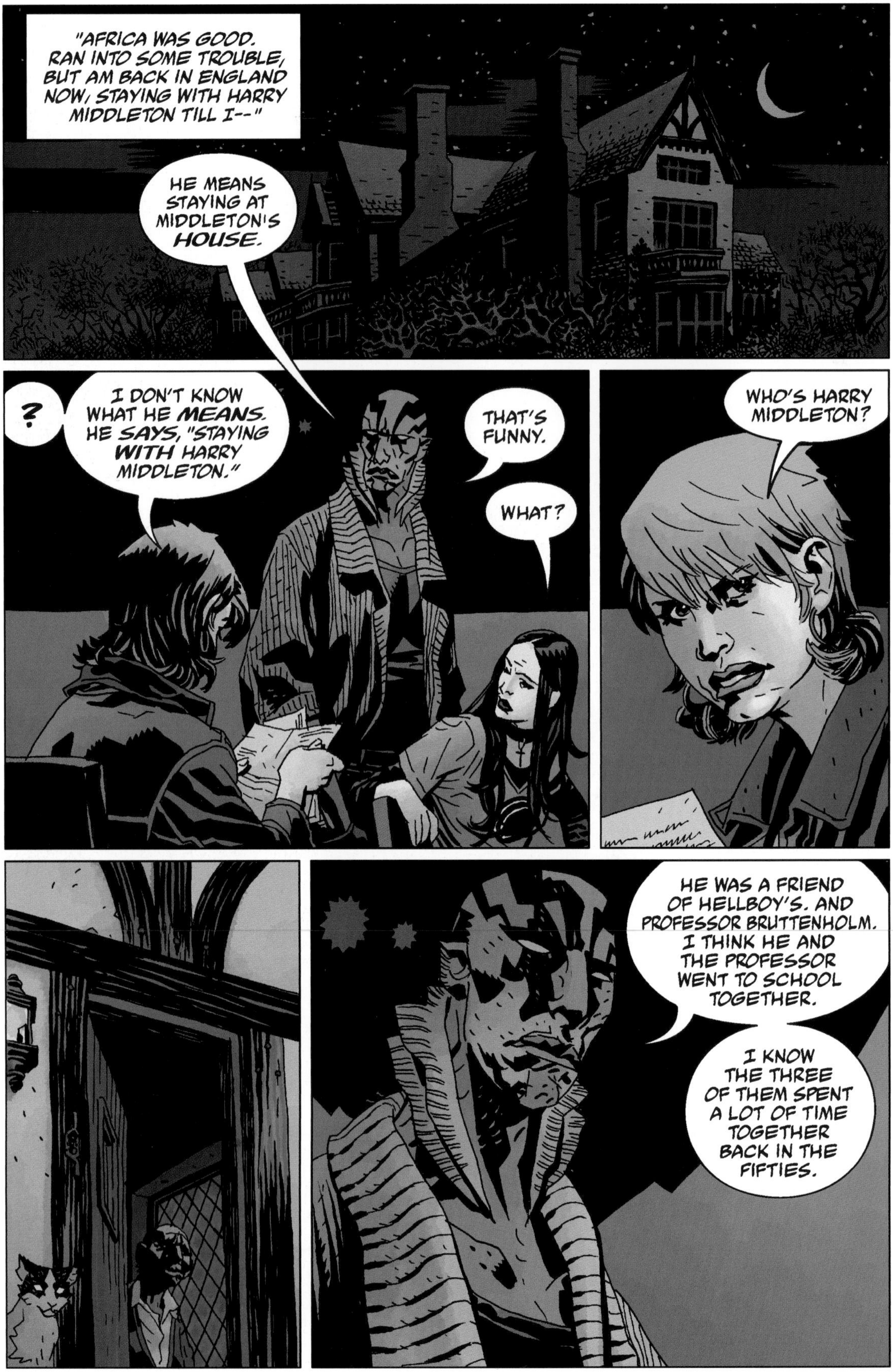
"AFRICA WAS GOOD. RAN INTO SOME TROUBLE, BUT AM BACK IN ENGLAND NOW, STAYING WITH HARRY MIDDLETON TILL I--"
HE MEANS STAYING AT MIDDLETON'S HOUSE.
?
I DON'T KNOW WHAT HE MEANS. HE SAYS, "STAYING WITH HARRY MIDDLETON."
THAT'S FUNNY.
WHAT?
WHO'S HARRY MIDDLETON?
HE WAS A FRIEND OF HELLBOY'S. AND PROFESSOR BRUTTENHOLM. I THINK HE AND THE PROFESSOR WENT TO SCHOOL TOGETHER.
I KNOW THE THREE OF THEM SPENT A LOT OF TIME TOGETHER BACK IN THE FIFTIES.

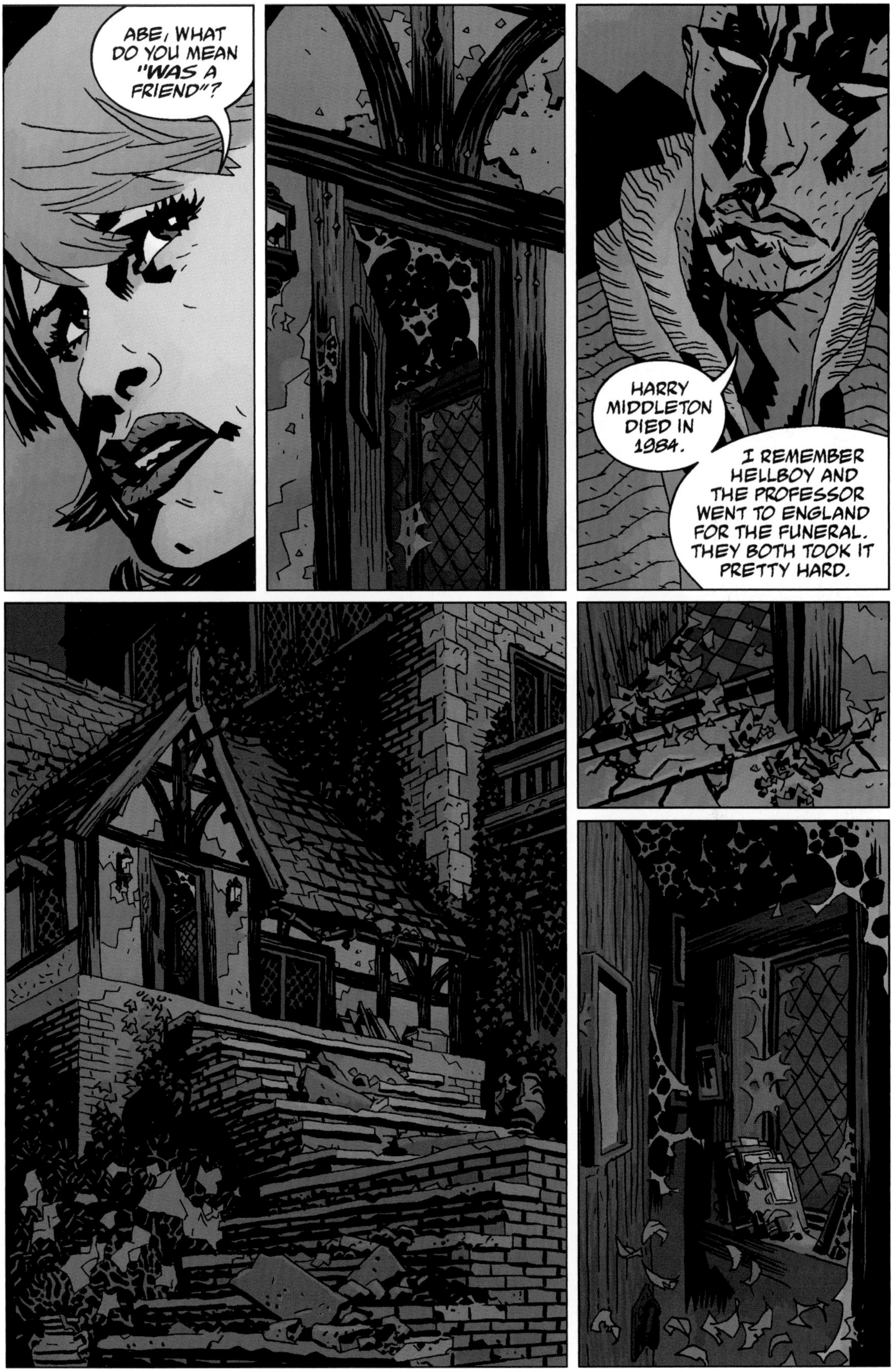
ABE, WHAT DO YOU MEAN "WAS A FRIEND"?
HARRY MIDDLETON DIED IN 1984.
I REMEMBER HELLBOY AND THE PROFESSOR WENT TO ENGLAND FOR THE FUNERAL. THEY BOTH TOOK IT PRETTY HARD.

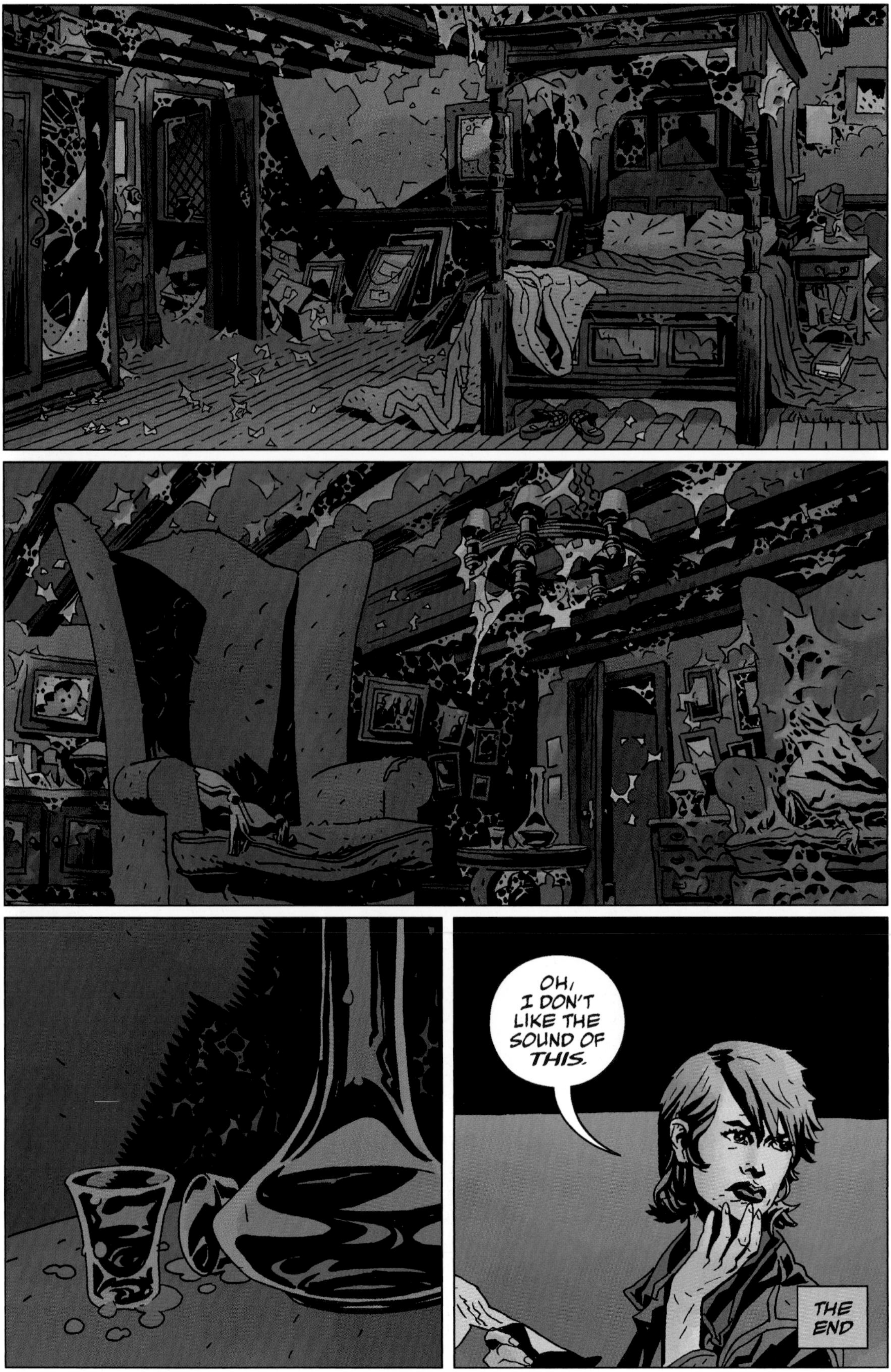
OH, I DON'T LIKE THE SOUND OF THIS.
THE END

Epilogue Two

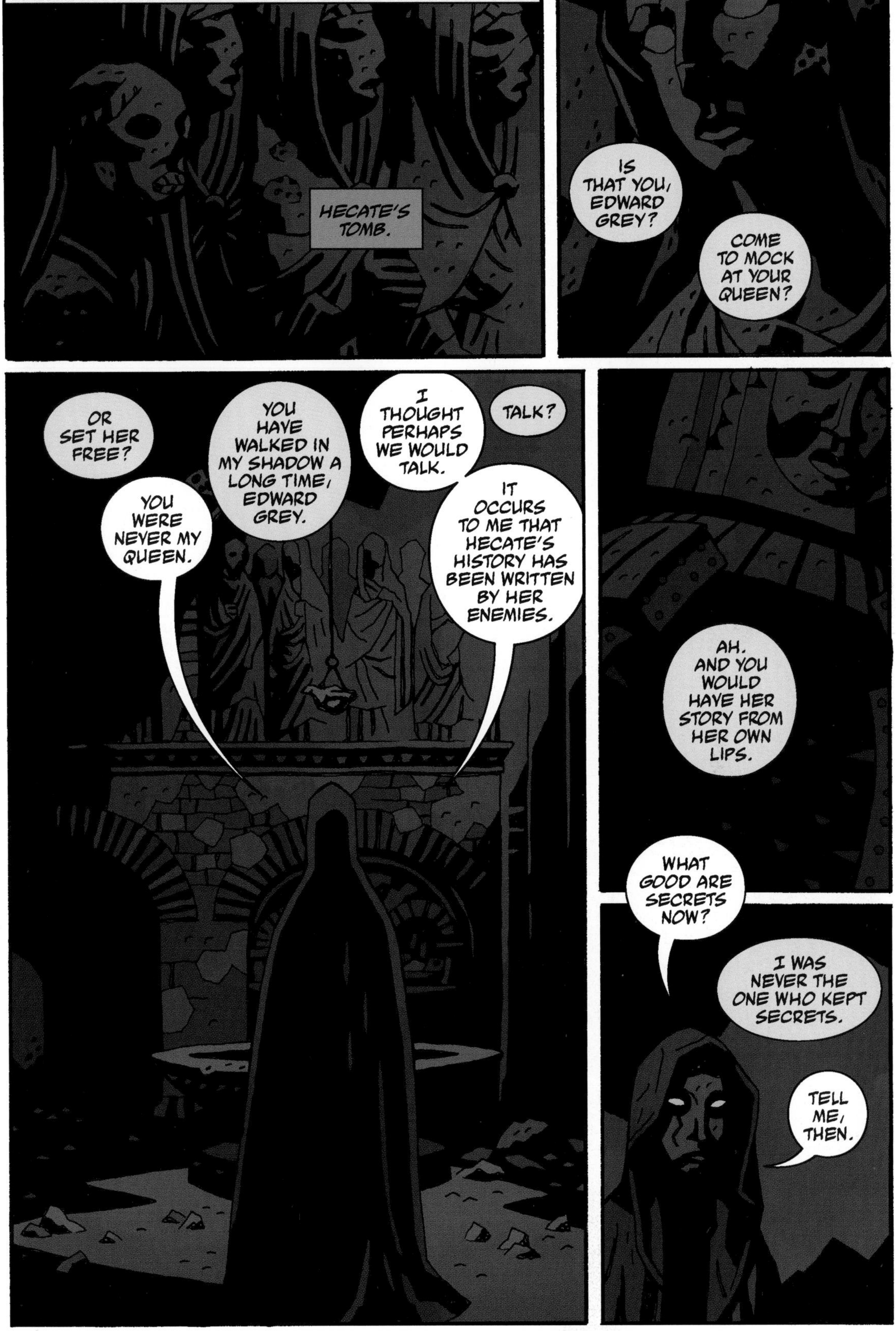
HECATE'S TOMB.
IS THAT YOU, EDWARD GREY?
COME TO MOCK AT YOUR QUEEN?
OR SET HER FREE?
YOU WERE NEVER MY QUEEN.
YOU HAVE WALKED IN MY SHADOW A LONG TIME, EDWARD GREY.
I THOUGHT PERHAPS WE WOULD TALK.
TALK?
IT OCCURS TO ME THAT HECATE'S HISTORY HAS BEEN WRITTEN BY HER ENEMIES.
AH. AND YOU WOULD HAVE HER STORY FROM HER OWN LIPS.
WHAT GOOD ARE SECRETS NOW?
I WAS NEVER THE ONE WHO KEPT SECRETS.
TELL ME, THEN.

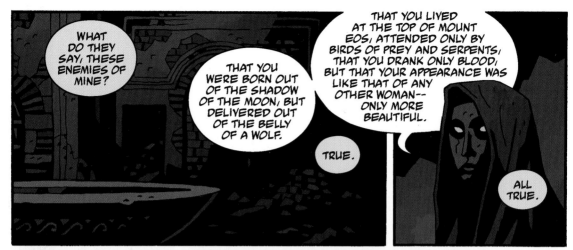

WHAT DO THEY SAY, THESE ENEMIES OF MINE?

THAT YOU WERE BORN OUT OF THE SHADOW OF THE MOON, BUT DELIVERED OUT OF THE BELLY OF A WOLF.

THAT YOU LIVED AT THE TOP OF MOUNT EOS, ATTENDED ONLY BY BIRDS OF PREY AND SERPENTS, THAT YOU DRANK ONLY BLOOD, BUT THAT YOUR APPEARANCE WAS LIKE THAT OF ANY OTHER WOMAN-- ONLY MORE BEAUTIFUL.

TRUE.

ALL TRUE.

"AND THAT ONE DAY YOU WENT TO GORINIUM, CAPITAL CITY OF HYPERBOREA--

"WHERE YOU SEDUCED ITS KING, DESTROYED HIM, AND BROUGHT THAT GREAT EMPIRE TO RUIN."

THEY SAY THAT?

AND WHAT DO THEY SAY OF THAT KING? THOTH. DO THEY REMEMBER HIM AT ALL? DO THEY TELL THAT HE HAD A SECRET GARDEN AND WHAT HE KEPT THERE...?

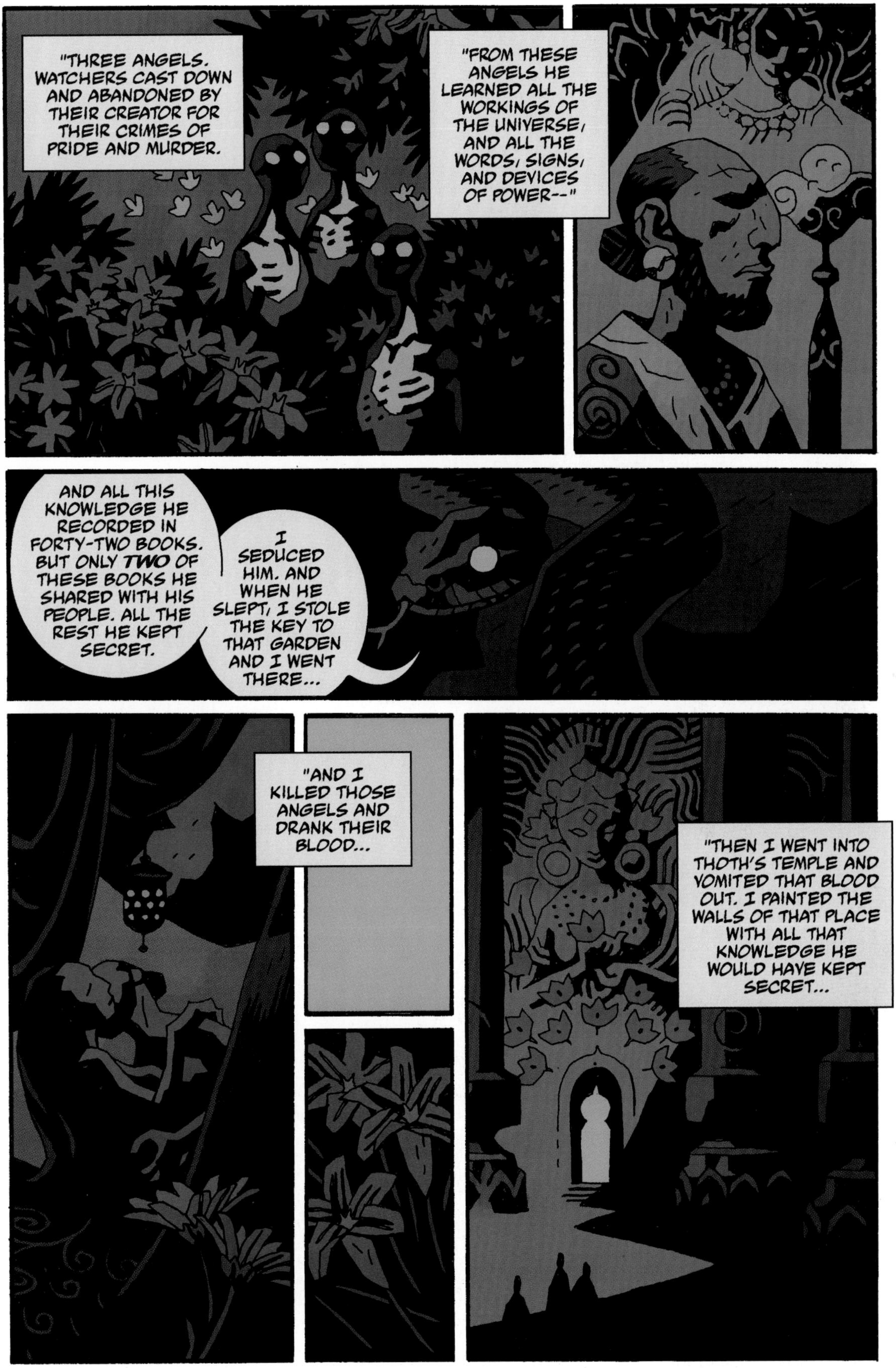
"THREE ANGELS. WATCHERS CAST DOWN AND ABANDONED BY THEIR CREATOR FOR THEIR CRIMES OF PRIDE AND MURDER.
"FROM THESE ANGELS HE LEARNED ALL THE WORKINGS OF THE UNIVERSE, AND ALL THE WORDS, SIGNS, AND DEVICES OF POWER--"
AND ALL THIS KNOWLEDGE HE RECORDED IN FORTY-TWO BOOKS. BUT ONLY *TWO* OF THESE BOOKS HE SHARED WITH HIS PEOPLE. ALL THE REST HE KEPT SECRET.
I SEDUCED HIM. AND WHEN HE SLEPT, I STOLE THE KEY TO THAT GARDEN AND I WENT THERE...
"AND I KILLED THOSE ANGELS AND DRANK THEIR BLOOD...
"THEN I WENT INTO THOTH'S TEMPLE AND VOMITED THAT BLOOD OUT. I PAINTED THE WALLS OF THAT PLACE WITH ALL THAT KNOWLEDGE HE WOULD HAVE KEPT SECRET...

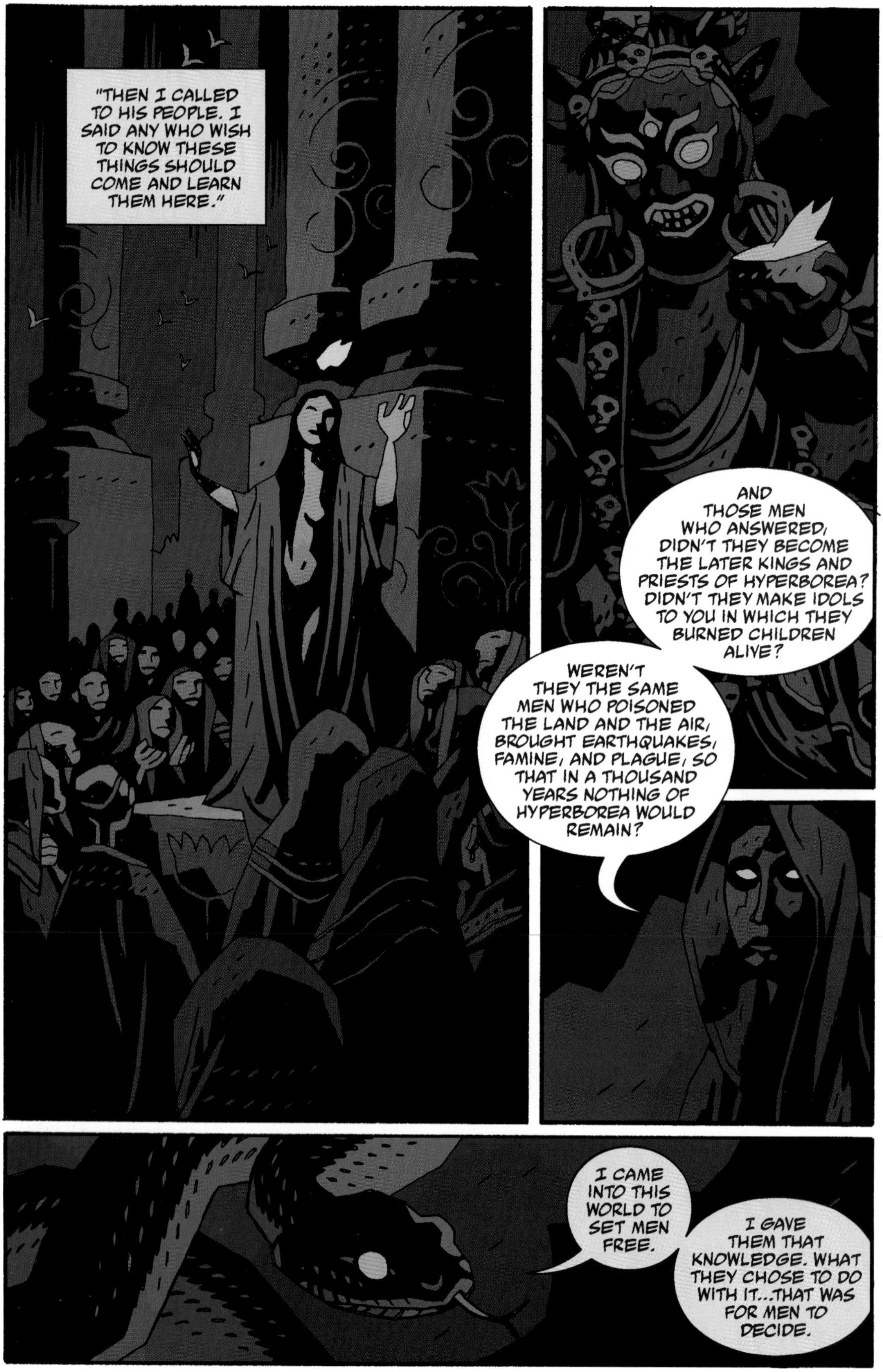
"THEN I CALLED TO HIS PEOPLE. I SAID ANY WHO WISH TO KNOW THESE THINGS SHOULD COME AND LEARN THEM HERE."
AND THOSE MEN WHO ANSWERED, DIDN'T THEY BECOME THE LATER KINGS AND PRIESTS OF HYPERBOREA? DIDN'T THEY MAKE IDOLS TO YOU IN WHICH THEY BURNED CHILDREN ALIVE?
WEREN'T THEY THE SAME MEN WHO POISONED THE LAND AND THE AIR, BROUGHT EARTHQUAKES, FAMINE, AND PLAGUE, SO THAT IN A THOUSAND YEARS NOTHING OF HYPERBOREA WOULD REMAIN?
I CAME INTO THIS WORLD TO SET MEN FREE.
I GAVE THEM THAT KNOWLEDGE. WHAT THEY CHOSE TO DO WITH IT...THAT WAS FOR MEN TO DECIDE.

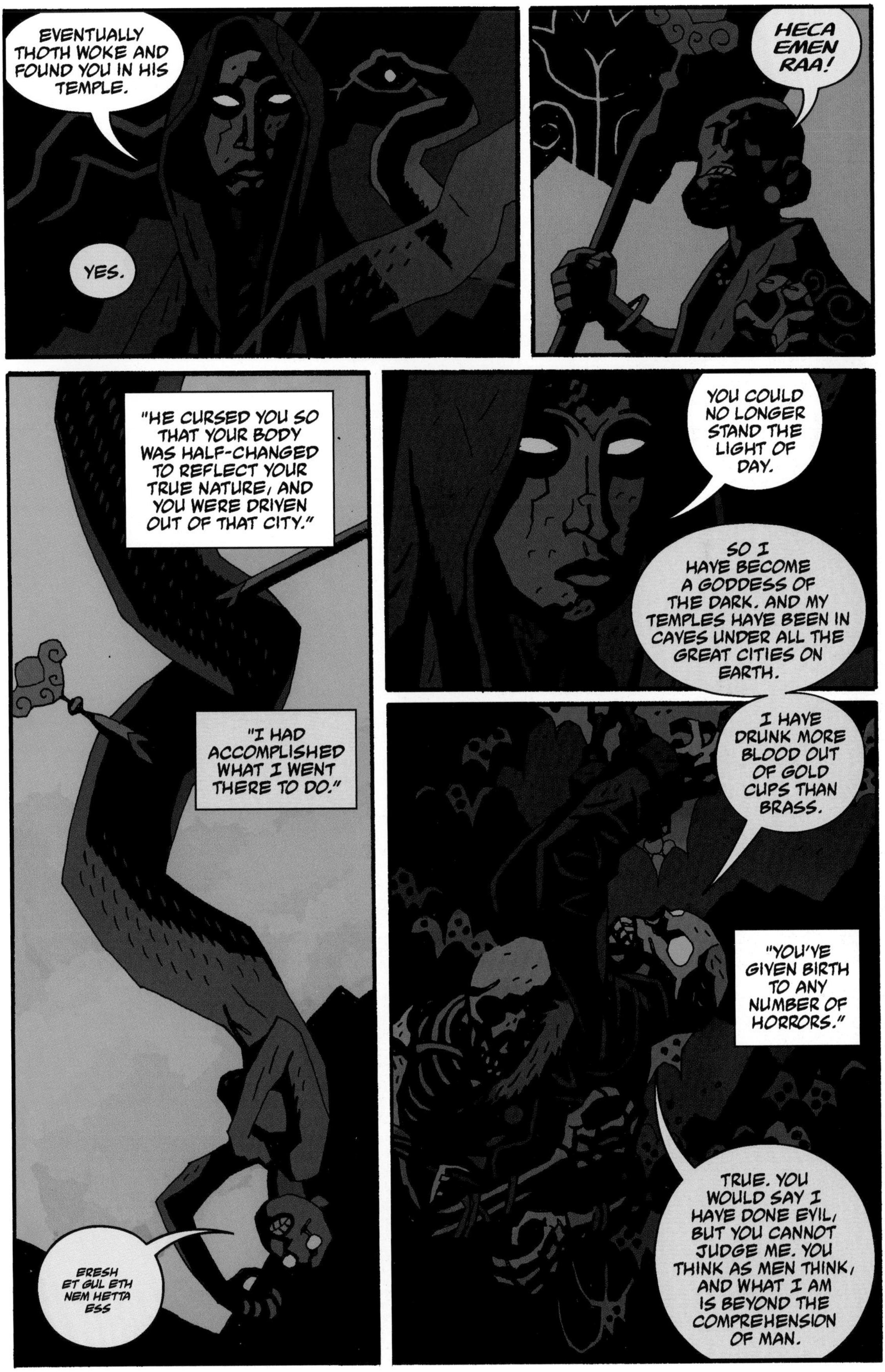
EVENTUALLY THOTH WOKE AND FOUND YOU IN HIS TEMPLE.
YES.
HECA EMEN RAA!
"HE CURSED YOU SO THAT YOUR BODY WAS HALF-CHANGED TO REFLECT YOUR TRUE NATURE, AND YOU WERE DRIVEN OUT OF THAT CITY."
"I HAD ACCOMPLISHED WHAT I WENT THERE TO DO."
ERESH ET GUL ETH NEM HETTA ESS
YOU COULD NO LONGER STAND THE LIGHT OF DAY.
SO I HAVE BECOME A GODDESS OF THE DARK. AND MY TEMPLES HAVE BEEN IN CAVES UNDER ALL THE GREAT CITIES ON EARTH.
I HAVE DRUNK MORE BLOOD OUT OF GOLD CUPS THAN BRASS.
"YOU'VE GIVEN BIRTH TO ANY NUMBER OF HORRORS."
TRUE. YOU WOULD SAY I HAVE DONE EVIL, BUT YOU CANNOT JUDGE ME. YOU THINK AS MEN THINK, AND WHAT I AM IS BEYOND THE COMPREHENSION OF MAN.

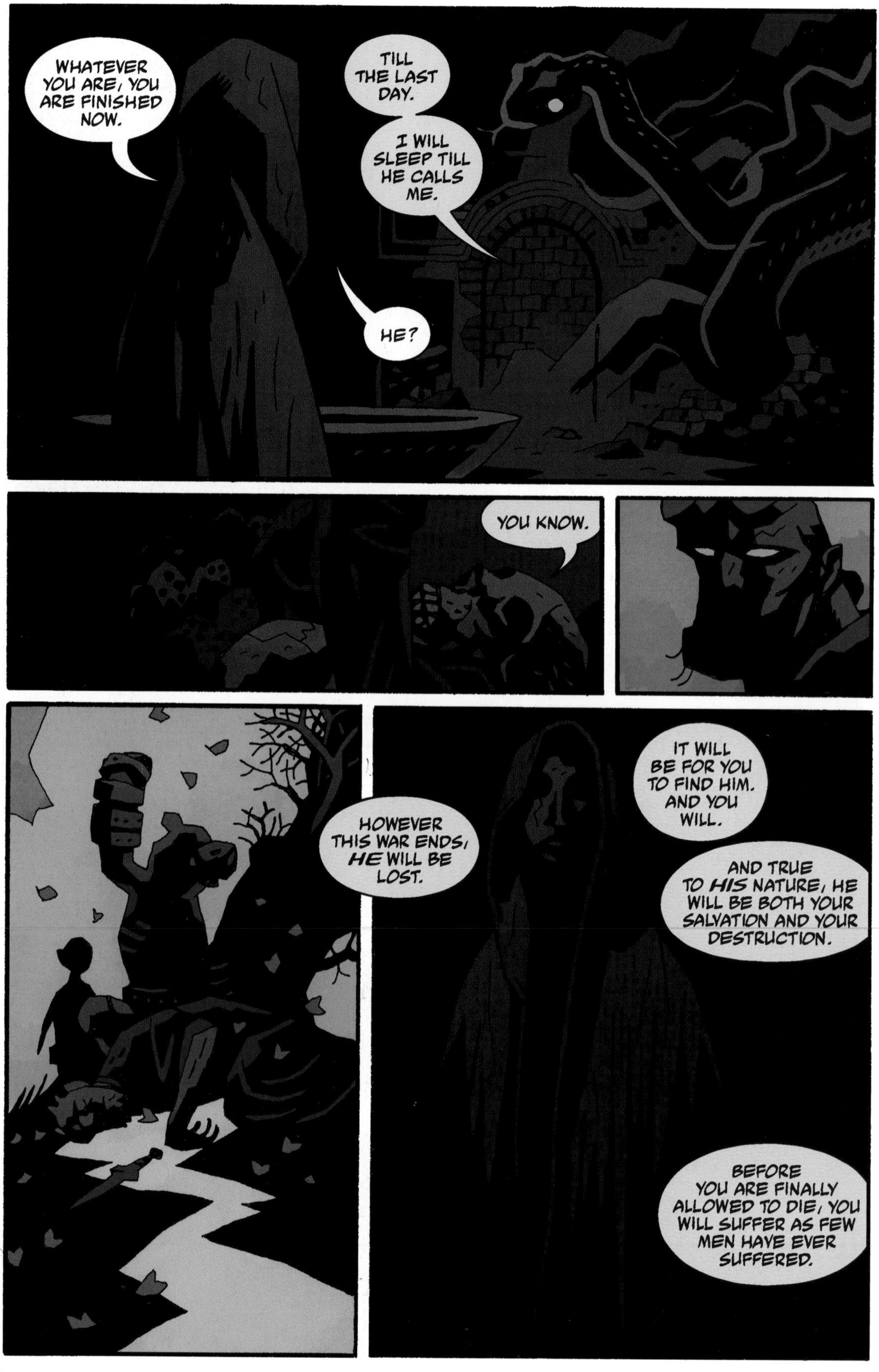

WHATEVER YOU ARE, YOU ARE FINISHED NOW.
TILL THE LAST DAY.
I WILL SLEEP TILL HE CALLS ME.
HE?
YOU KNOW.
HOWEVER THIS WAR ENDS, HE WILL BE LOST.
IT WILL BE FOR YOU TO FIND HIM. AND YOU WILL.
AND TRUE TO HIS NATURE, HE WILL BE BOTH YOUR SALVATION AND YOUR DESTRUCTION.
BEFORE YOU ARE FINALLY ALLOWED TO DIE, YOU WILL SUFFER AS FEW MEN HAVE EVER SUFFERED.

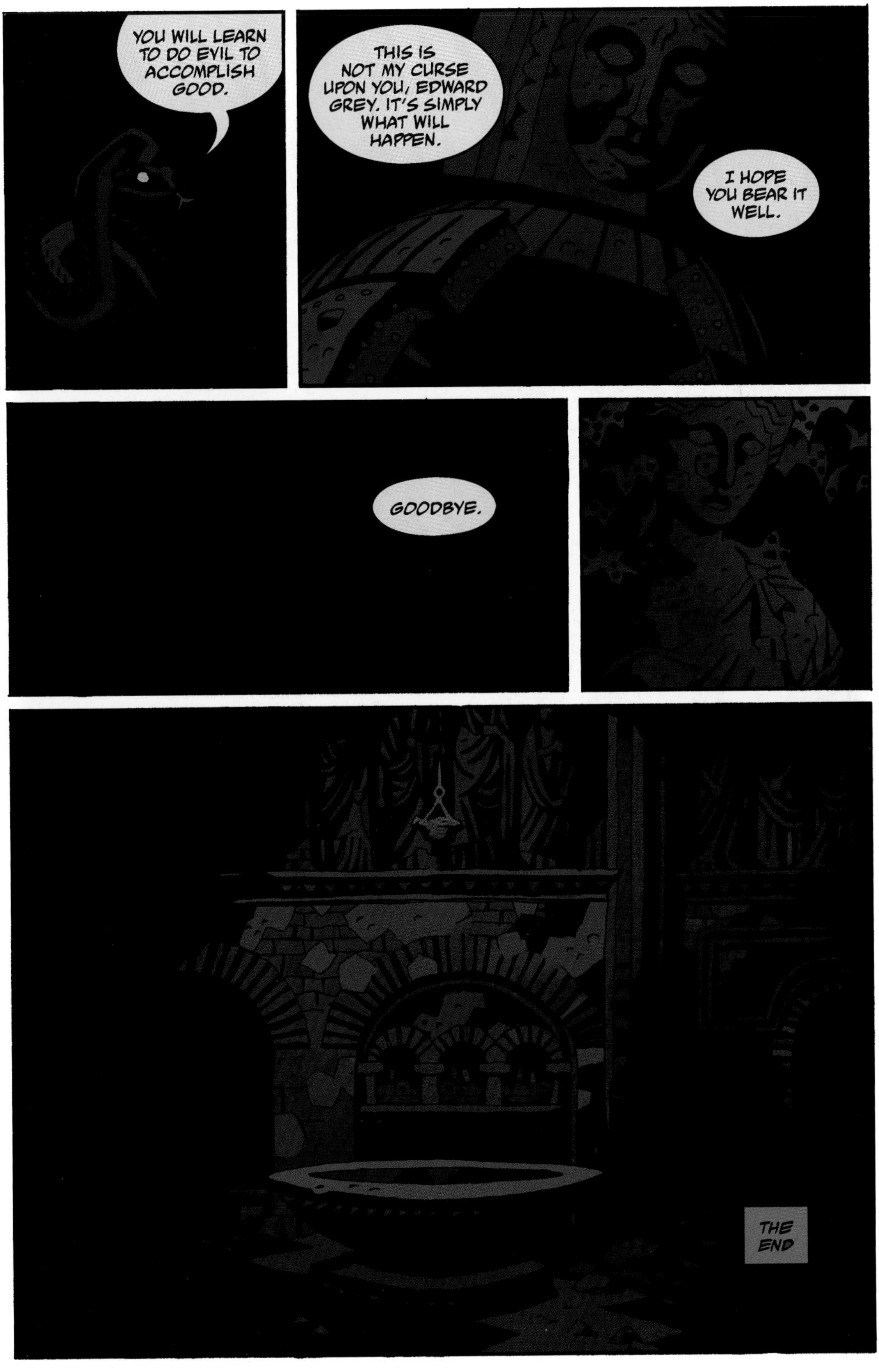
YOU WILL LEARN TO DO EVIL TO ACCOMPLISH GOOD.
THIS IS NOT MY CURSE UPON YOU, EDWARD GREY. IT'S SIMPLY WHAT WILL HAPPEN.
I HOPE YOU BEAR IT WELL.
GOODBYE.
THE END

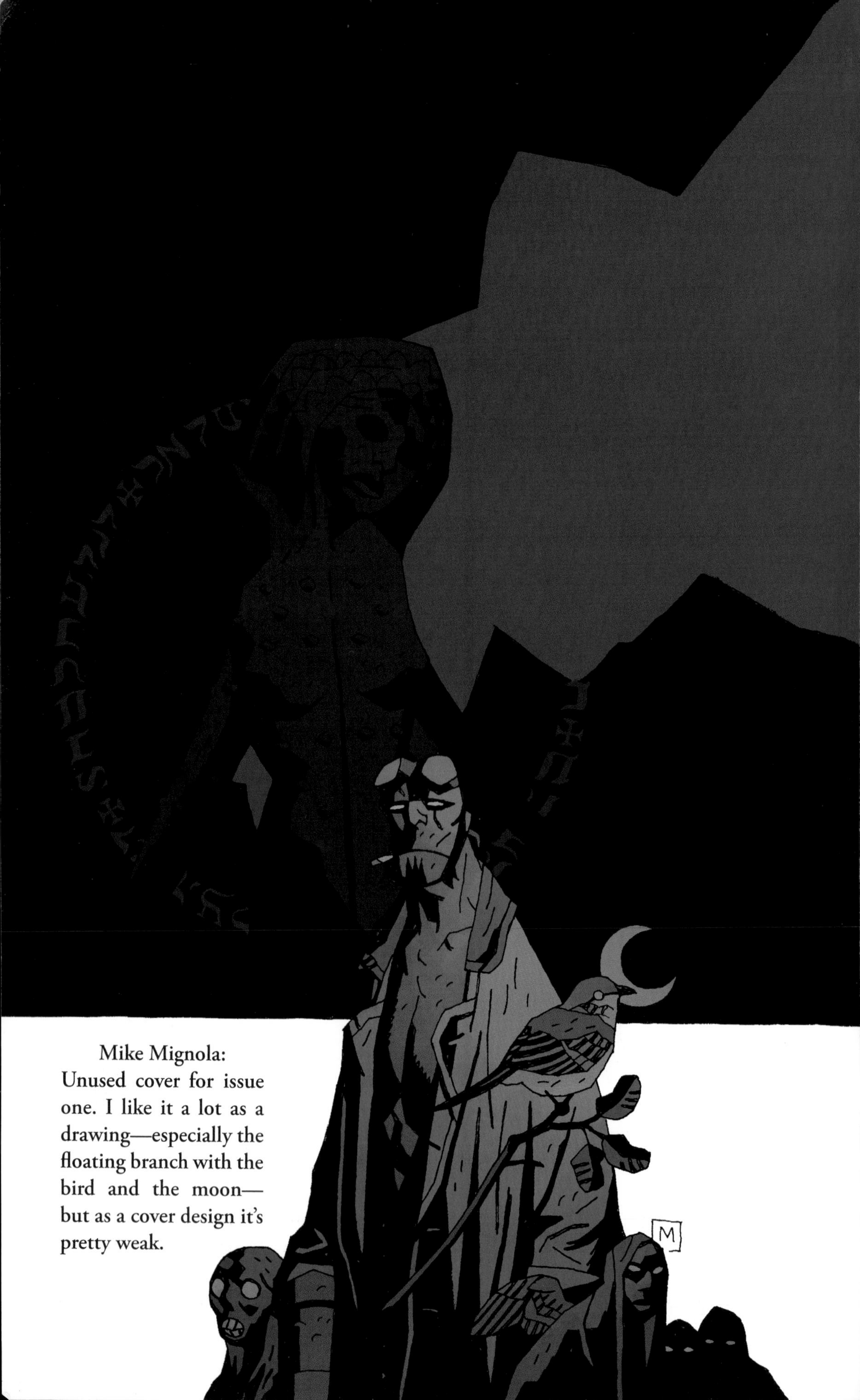

Mike Mignola: Unused cover for issue one. I like it a lot as a drawing—especially the floating branch with the bird and the moon—but as a cover design it's pretty weak.

HELLBOY™

SKETCHBOOK

With notes from the artists

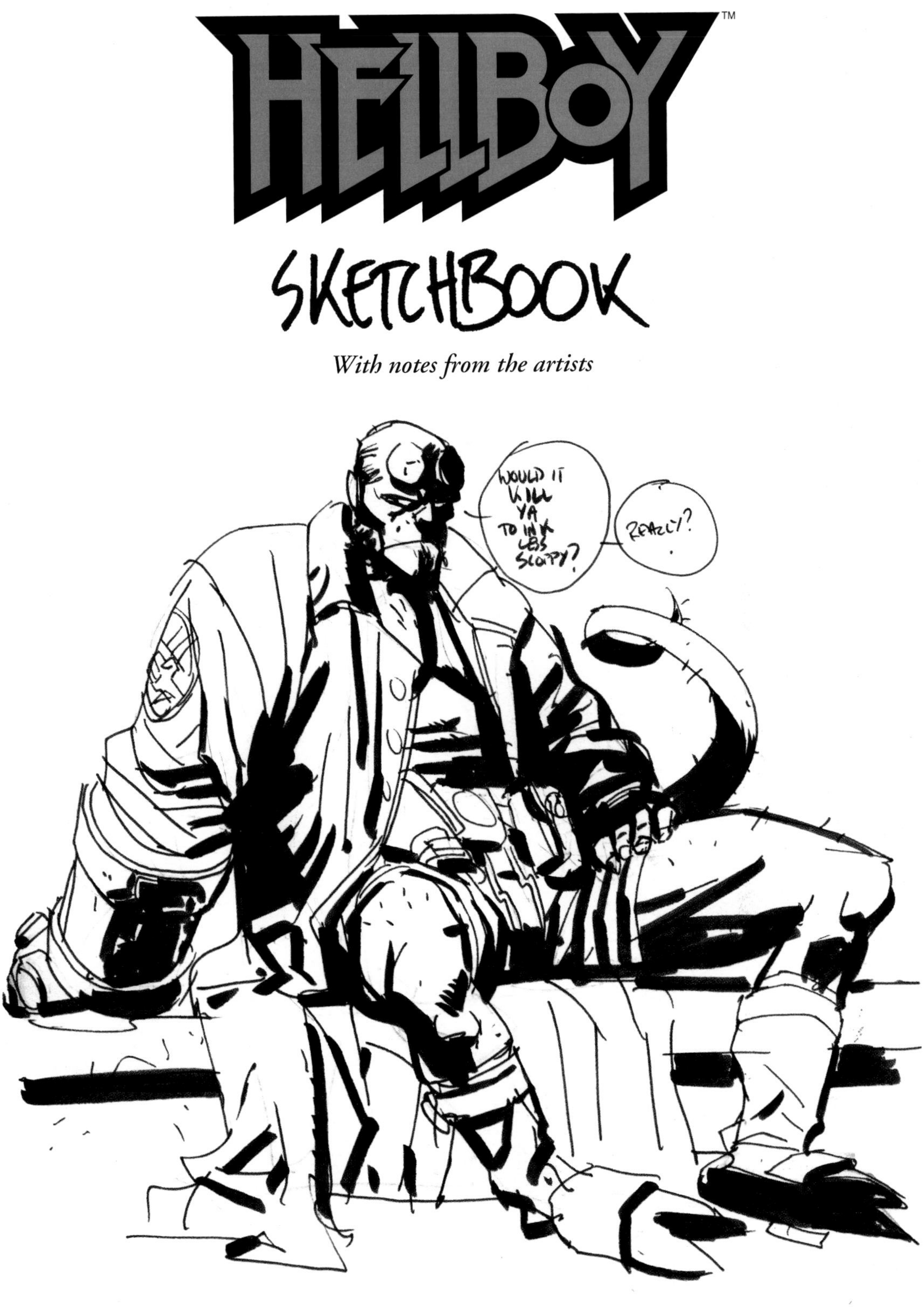
WOULD IT KILL YA TO INK LESS SLOPPY?
REALLY?

Duncan Fegredo: Well, it's a start … this was drawn just after I came onboard *Hellboy*. I wanted to try a quick sketch to prove to Mike and Scott they hadn't made a huge mistake. What the heck was I thinking—it's unbelievably crude! It also reminds me of the gallery piece I drew so long ago for *The Chained Coffin* trade. Funny how things come around.

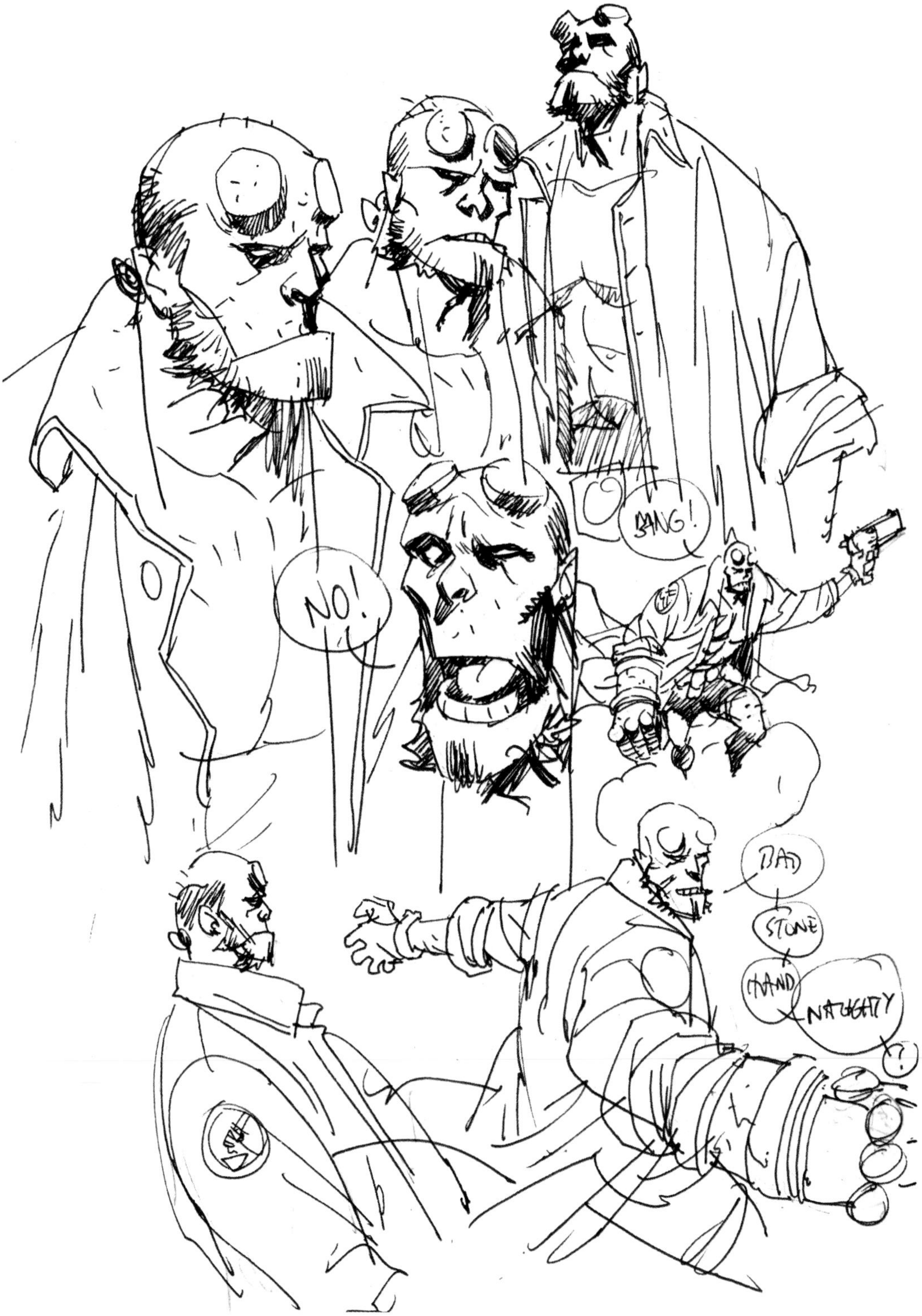
BANG!
NO!
BAD
STONE
HAND
NAUGHTY
?

DF: Still early days, I was trying to get a feel for the character, what works, and, in the case of the central face here, what doesn't. It's fun to push Hellboy's expressions the way I would a human character, but it's really off model.

Speaking of humans, that's another thing I learned early on: you can't just slap a pair of horn stumps and a big jaw onto a human skull and hope for instant Hellboy—doesn't work!

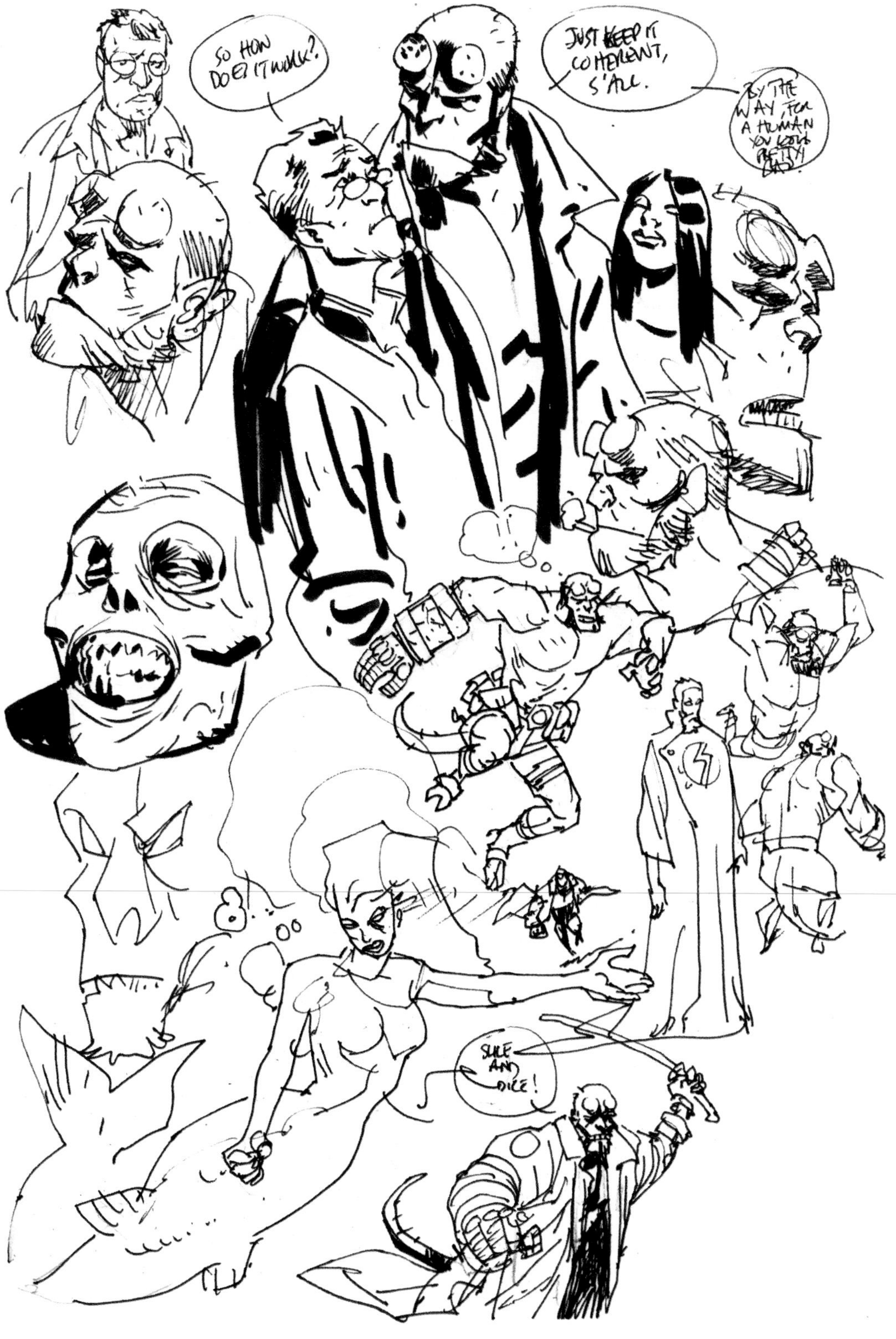
SO HOW DOES IT WORK?
JUST KEEP IT COHERENT, S'ALL.
SLICE AND DICE!

DF: I prefer to sketch purely in line, and, in fact, before Hellboy dropped on me, I'd been considering open line and tone as the direction I wanted to develop ... oh well. So here you can see I was playing with a combo of open line and really poorly considered blacks. Hey, it's a sketchbook, I didn't know you were going to see it!

Mummified heads, check; mermaids, check ... well, it is *Hellboy* after all.

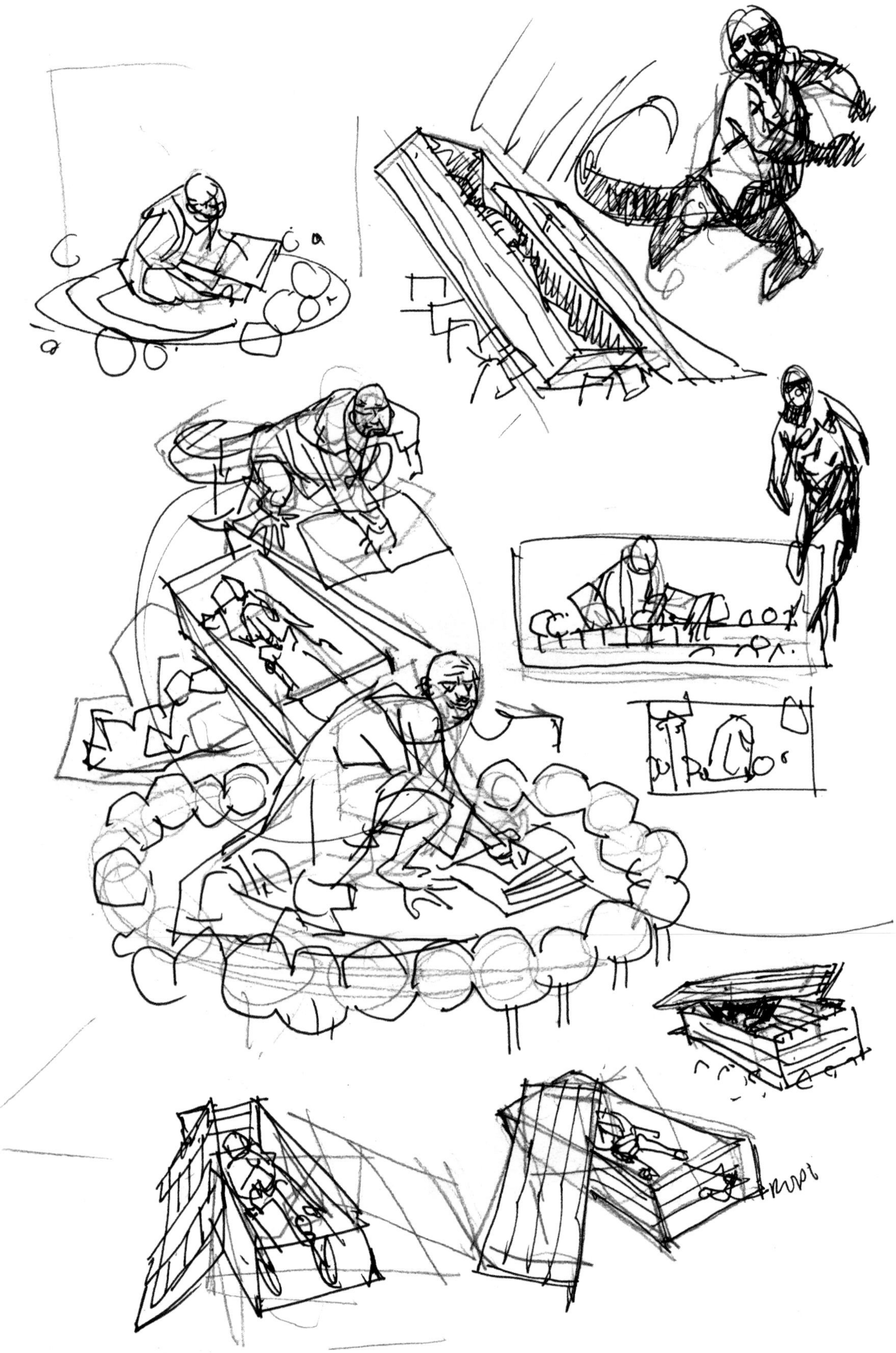

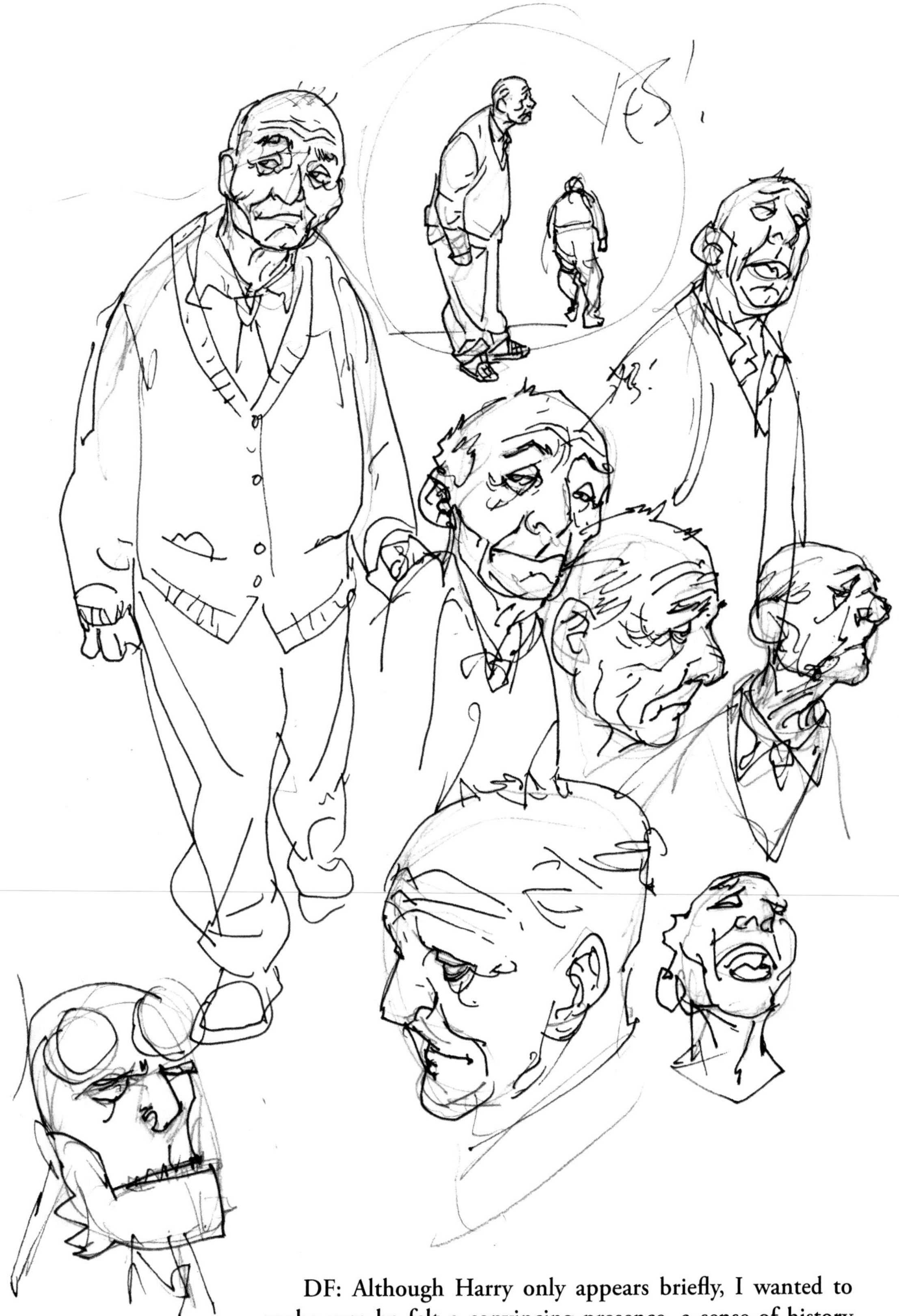
YES!

DF: Although Harry only appears briefly, I wanted to make sure he felt a convincing presence, a sense of history with Hellboy.

Opposite
Working out Bromhead's misdeeds. How many ways can you draw a skeleton in an open crate?

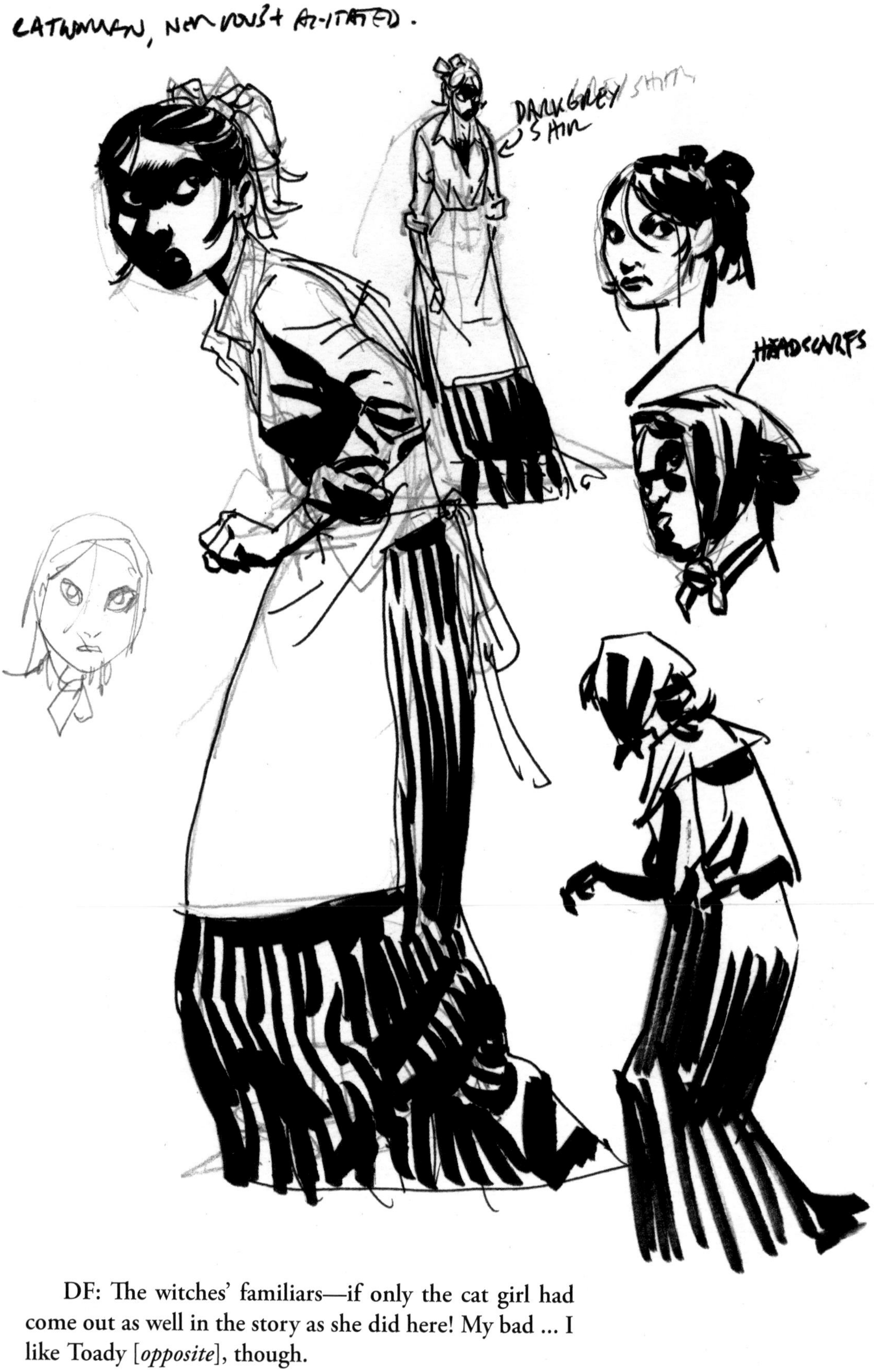
CATWOMAN, NERVOUS + AGITATED.
DARKGREY
HEADSCARFS

DF: The witches' familiars—if only the cat girl had come out as well in the story as she did here! My bad ... I like Toady [*opposite*], though.

3 FAMILIARS - A TOAD } MEN } RESEMBLANCE TO THEIR ANIMALS.
A CROW }
A CAT — WOMAN }

IN BLACK & SLIGHTLY SHABBY WORN CLOTHES. COUNTRY CLOTHES.

BEAKY MANNERISM?

3 LENGTH COAT THINK THIN LEATHER - BLACK ON BLACK

'BOUCLÉ'

TOO MUCH BAD!

HEAVY SHADOW OVER EYES?

MM: I've been a huge fan of Duncan's work for years, and was thrilled (and more than a little amazed) when he agreed to draw this series. For *Hellboy*, I felt I needed an artist with a similar graphic storytelling sensibility to my own, but I *didn't* want an imitator. Duncan was the perfect choice, and I hope he'll stick around for a very long time.

DF: The Witchfinder was based on Vincent Price's character in *The Witchfinder General*; he even had the hat in one of my sketches, but I think Mike thought he looked a little silly. He was not wrong!

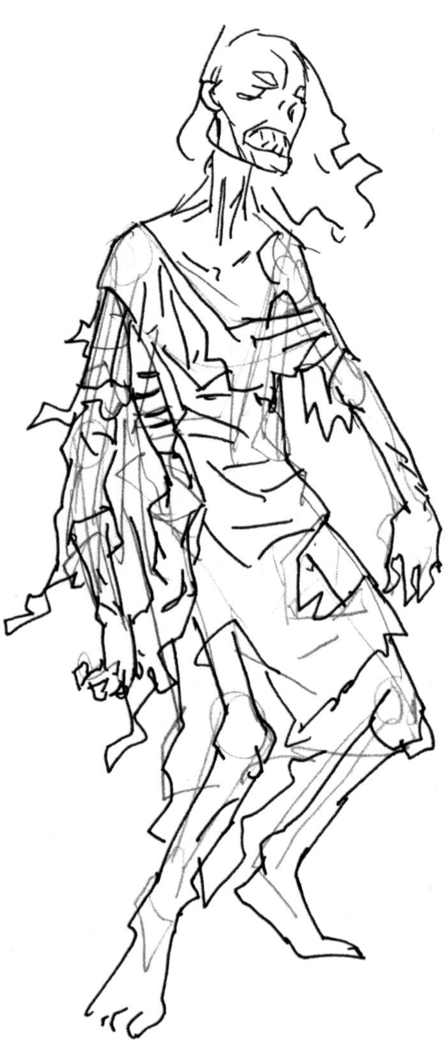

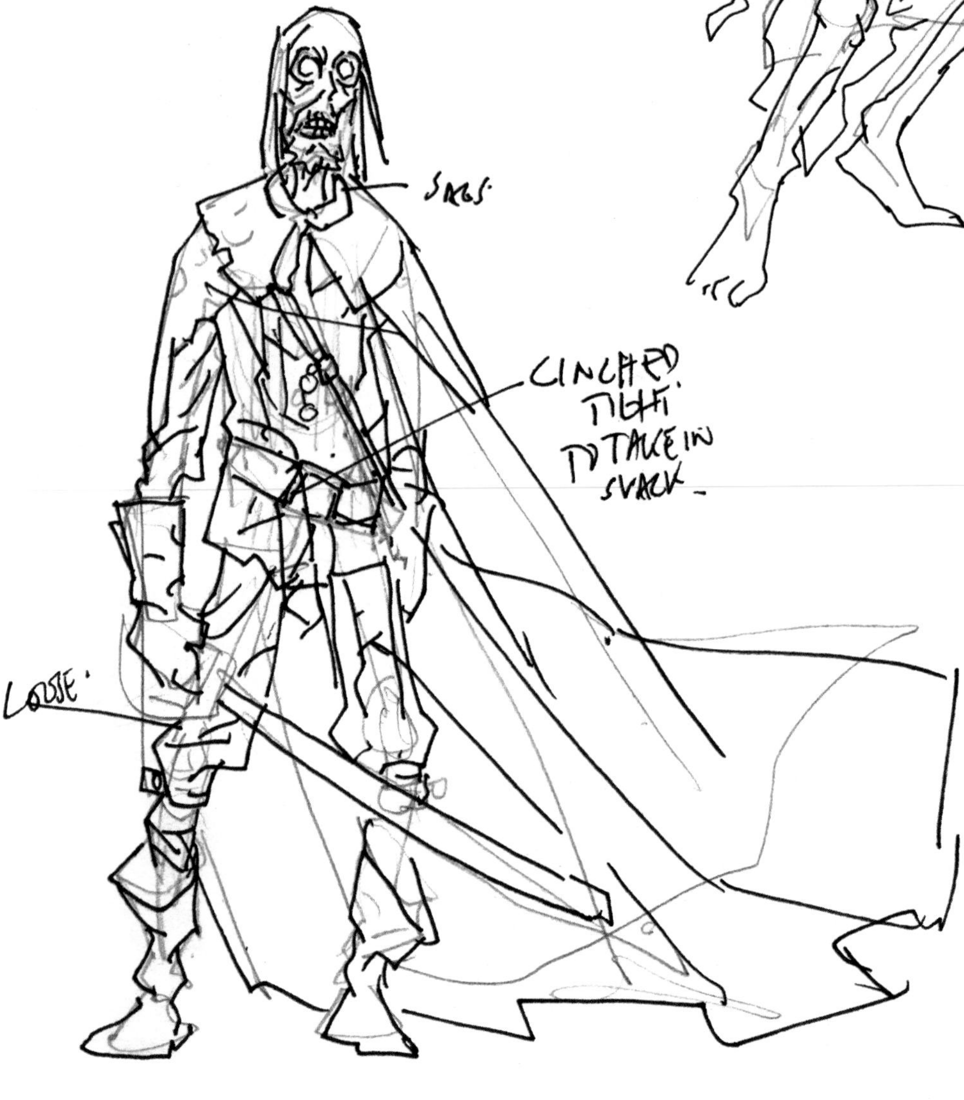
SAGS.
CINCHED TIGHT TO TAKE IN SLACK.
LOOSE.

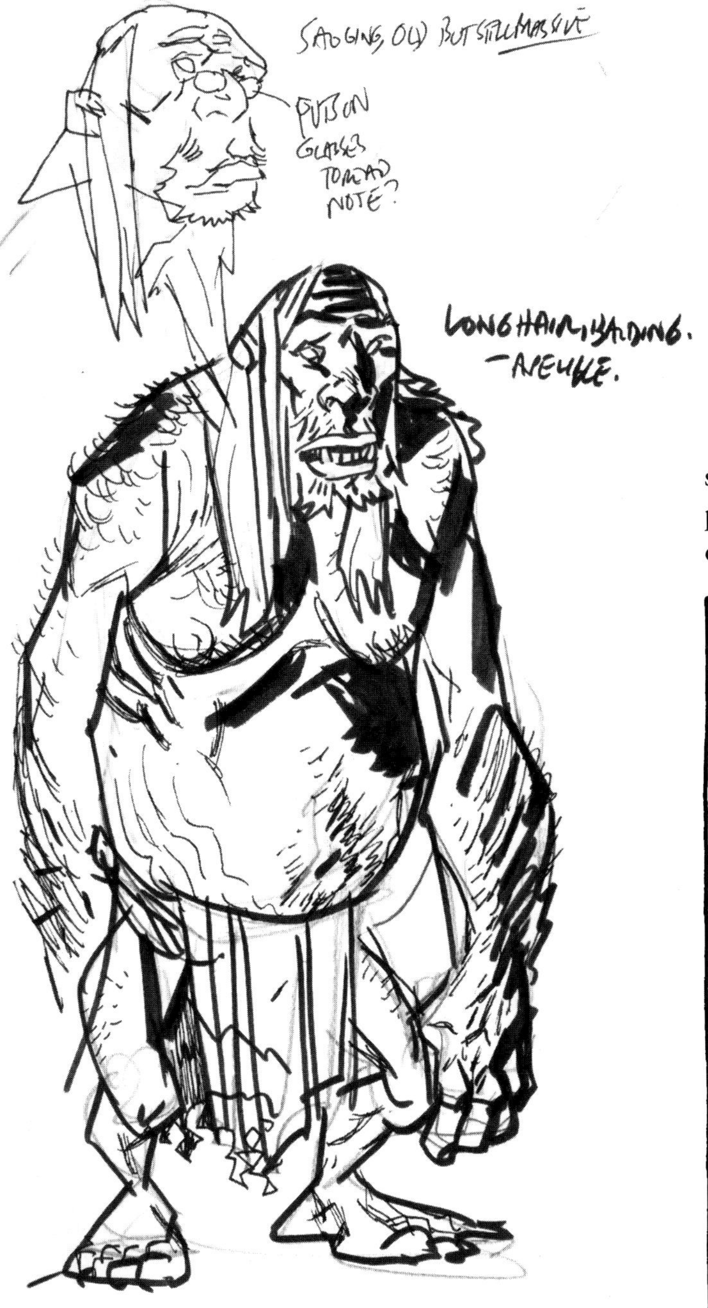
SAGGING, OLD BUT STILL MASSIVE
PUT ON GLASSES TO READ NOTE?
LONG HAIR, BALDING. —APELIKE.

MM: The little wooden statue of Perun, chief god of pagan Russia—meant to be cute, not awe inspiring.

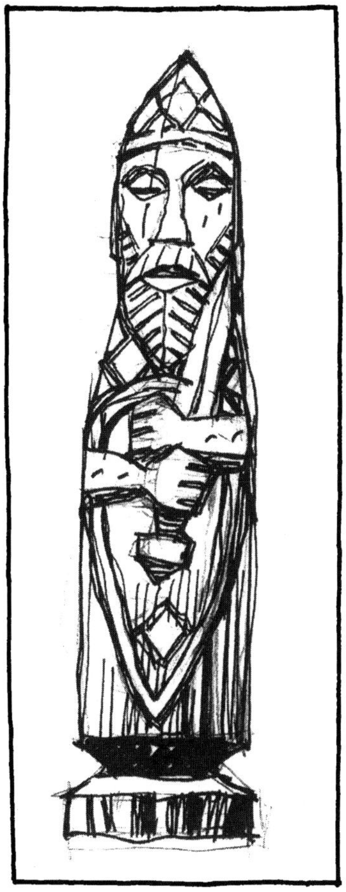

DF: I think Mike had originally envisioned the giant to be wearing ancient, rusting armor, although he neglected to mention that to me. Consequently I gave the big guy a dirty loincloth and a relaxed attitude to body hair. We compromised and I added the Pictish tattoos, although I dropped them in his later appearance, as I felt it made my already cluttered art even more muddled. Sorry about that. I did at least add the spectacles, though, in order to raise his apparent IQ.

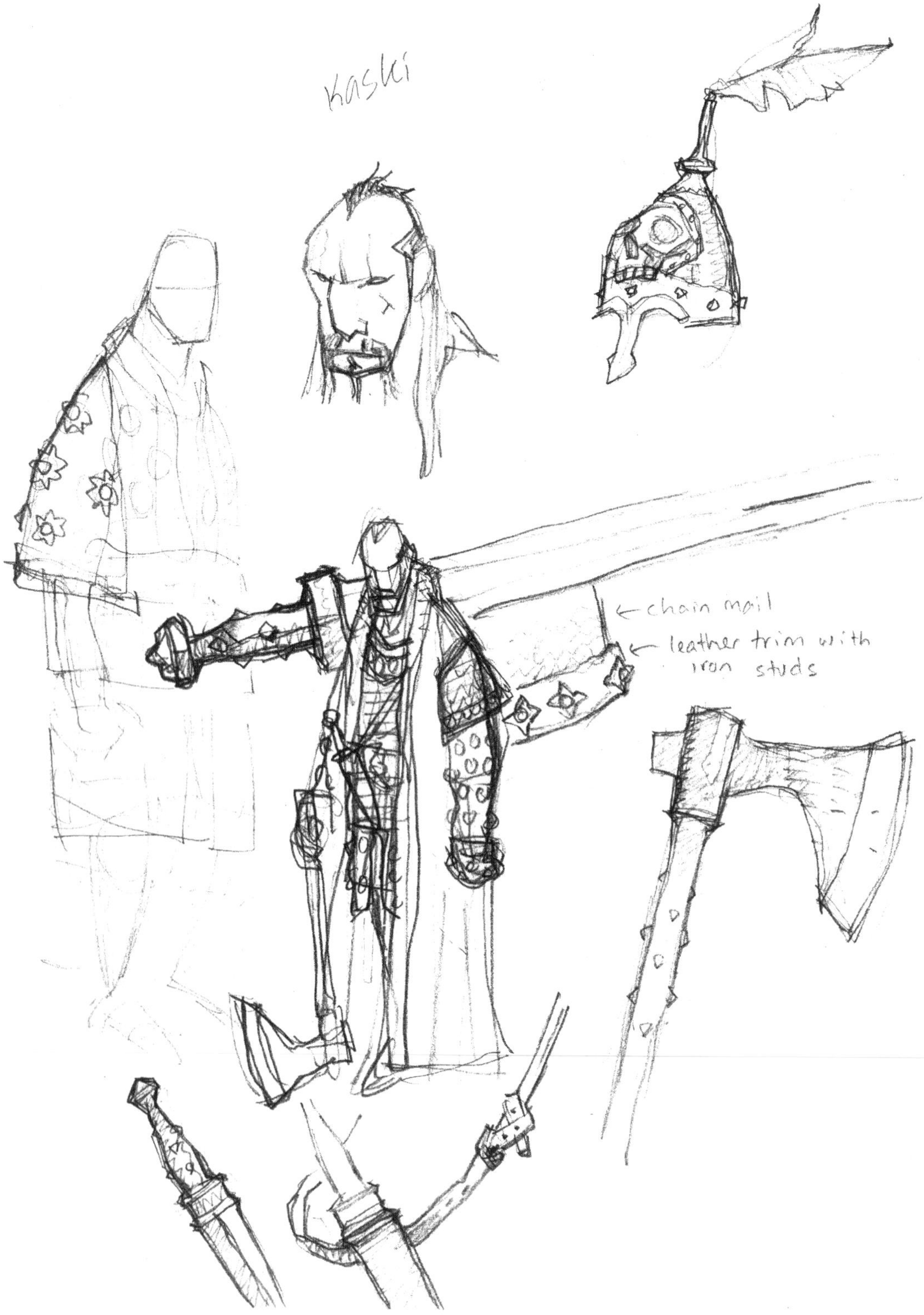
Kaski
← chain mail
← leather trim with iron studs

MM: The first sketchbook drawing of Koshchei the Deathless, done at least a year before I conceived this story. Now that I think of it, this page of drawings probably set the whole thing in motion. At the time I just thought I was fooling around.

DF: If I could go back I'd stick a little closer to Mike's original sketches here. I love the way Koshchei's leather gauntlets are the same size as his skull.

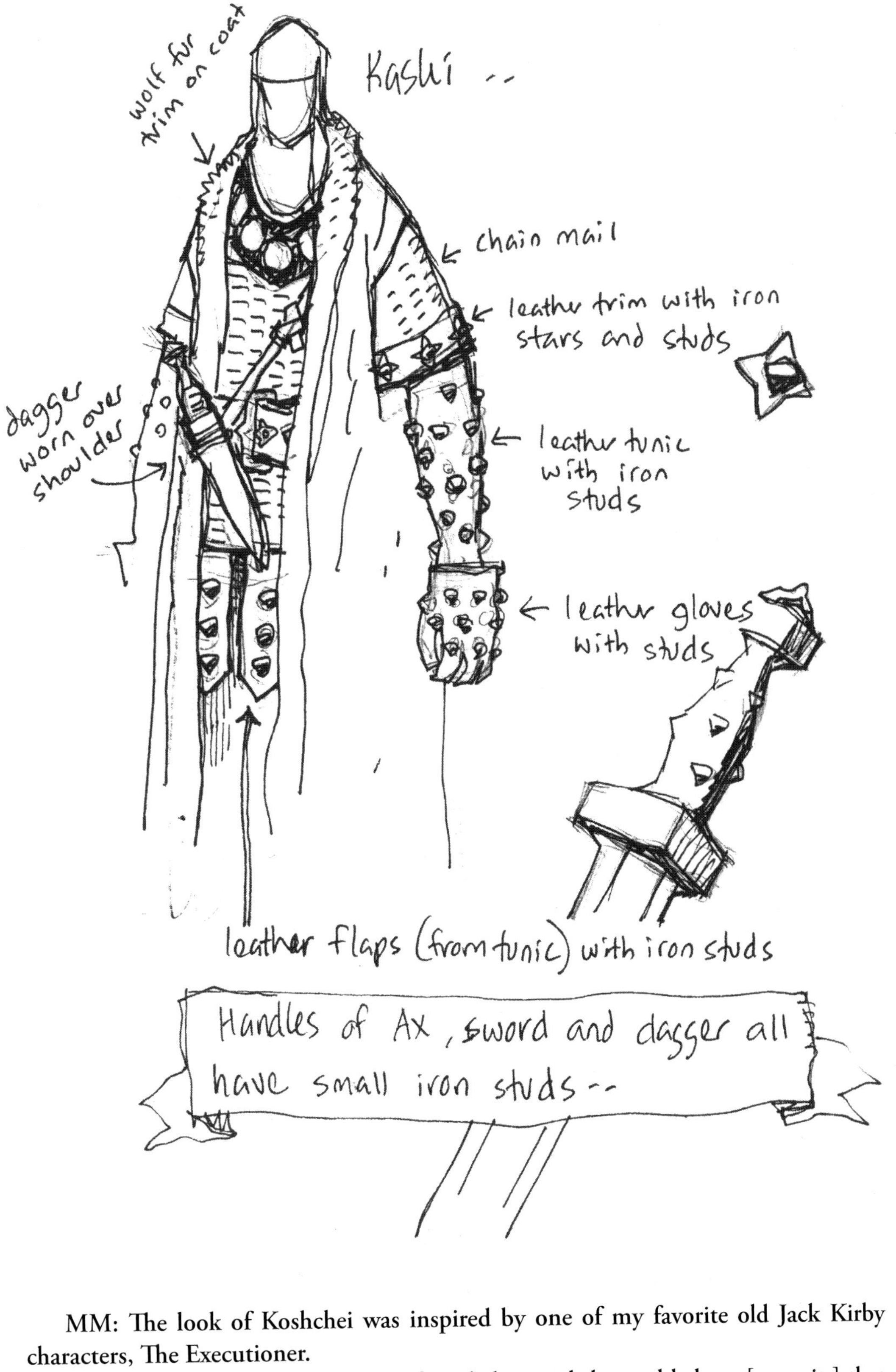
Kashi --
wolf fur trim on coat
chain mail
leather trim with iron stars and studs
dagger worn over shoulder
leather tunic with iron studs
leather gloves with studs
leather flaps (from tunic) with iron studs
Handles of Ax, sword and dagger all have small iron studs --

MM: The look of Koshchei was inspired by one of my favorite old Jack Kirby characters, The Executioner.

Note the not-even-close spelling of Koshchei, and the cool helmet [*opposite*] that both Duncan and I forgot about.

DF: Although I did some research on the costumes, Mike's designs were invaluable, as they perfectly distilled everything I needed. Look closely at that undead swarm bearing down on Hellboy in chapter two and you'll find that every one of them is a variant of Mike's little guys.

Baba Yaga's undead army --

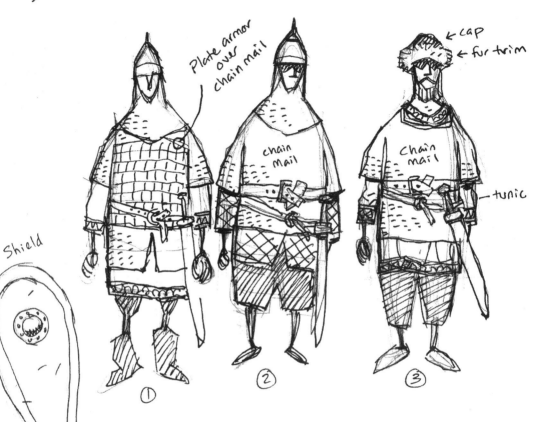

Plate armor over chain mail

chain mail

chain mail

← cap
← fur trim

— tunic

Shield

① ② ③

The army is made up of the common soldiers. They are dead - armor should be battered - shields and Helmets dented and ~~gashed~~ gashed. Many would have no head covering at all. Mix and match different pants types, shoes, boots, etc.

Helmets
--

All helmets are tall and have that point on the top.

MM: After thirteen years of drawing Hellboy myself, I went into this series as a near psychotic control freak. As soon as Duncan began to turn in pages, however, I was able to relax a little, and, eventually, let Duncan take over almost all the character designs.

When you've been doing something for this long it's a little hard to let go—even when you're turning it over to someone as great as Duncan.

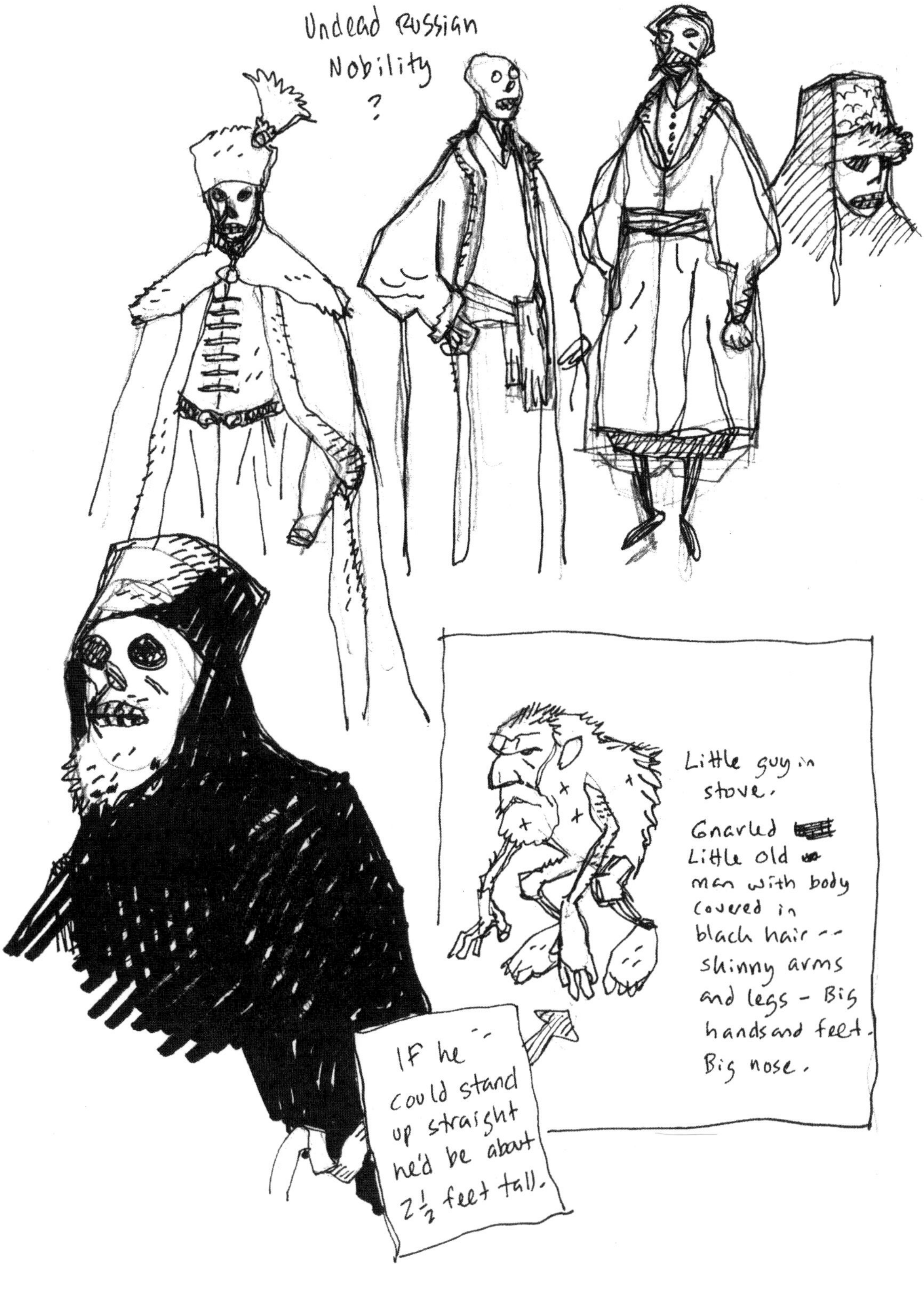
Undead Russian
Nobility
?
Little guy in
stove.
Gnarled
Little old
man with body
covered in
black hair --
skinny arms
and legs - Big
hands and feet.
Big nose.
If he
could stand
up straight
he'd be about
2½ feet tall.

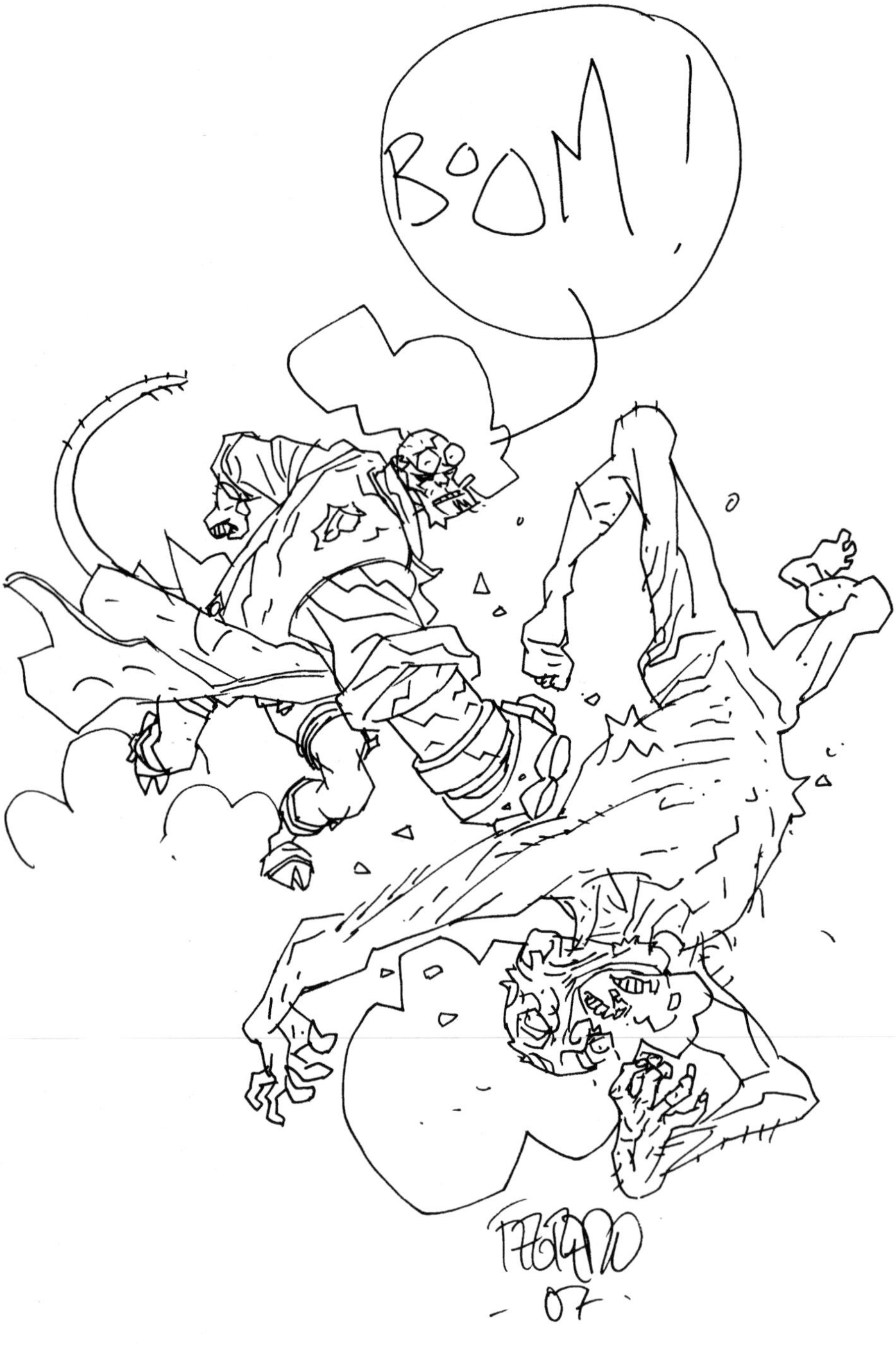
BOOM!

DF: It's a drawing of Hellboy hitting a zombie, what do you want?

Opposite
A drawing for a San Diego sketchbook.

HELLBOY - SANDIEGO 2007

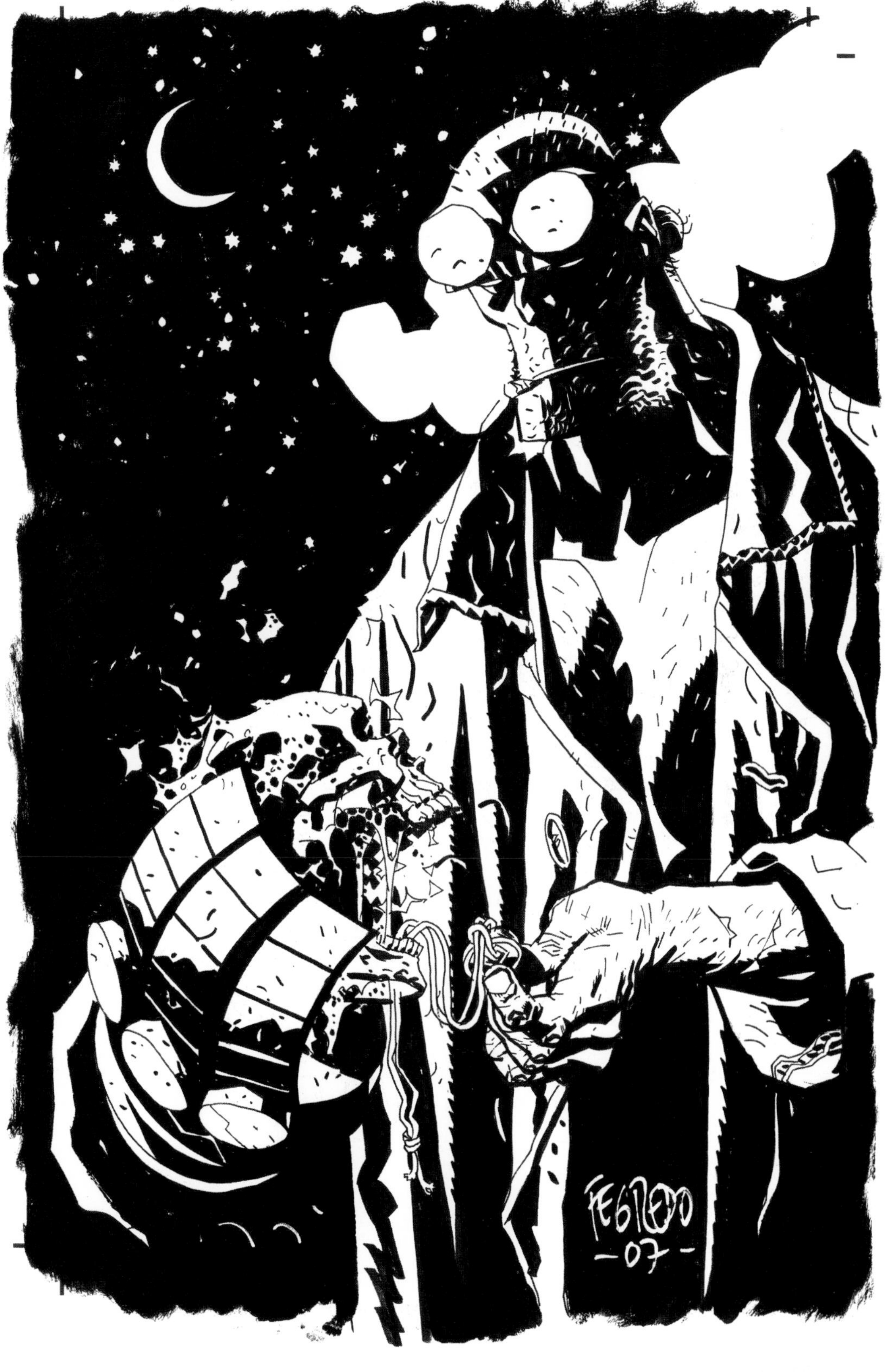
FEGREDO
-07-

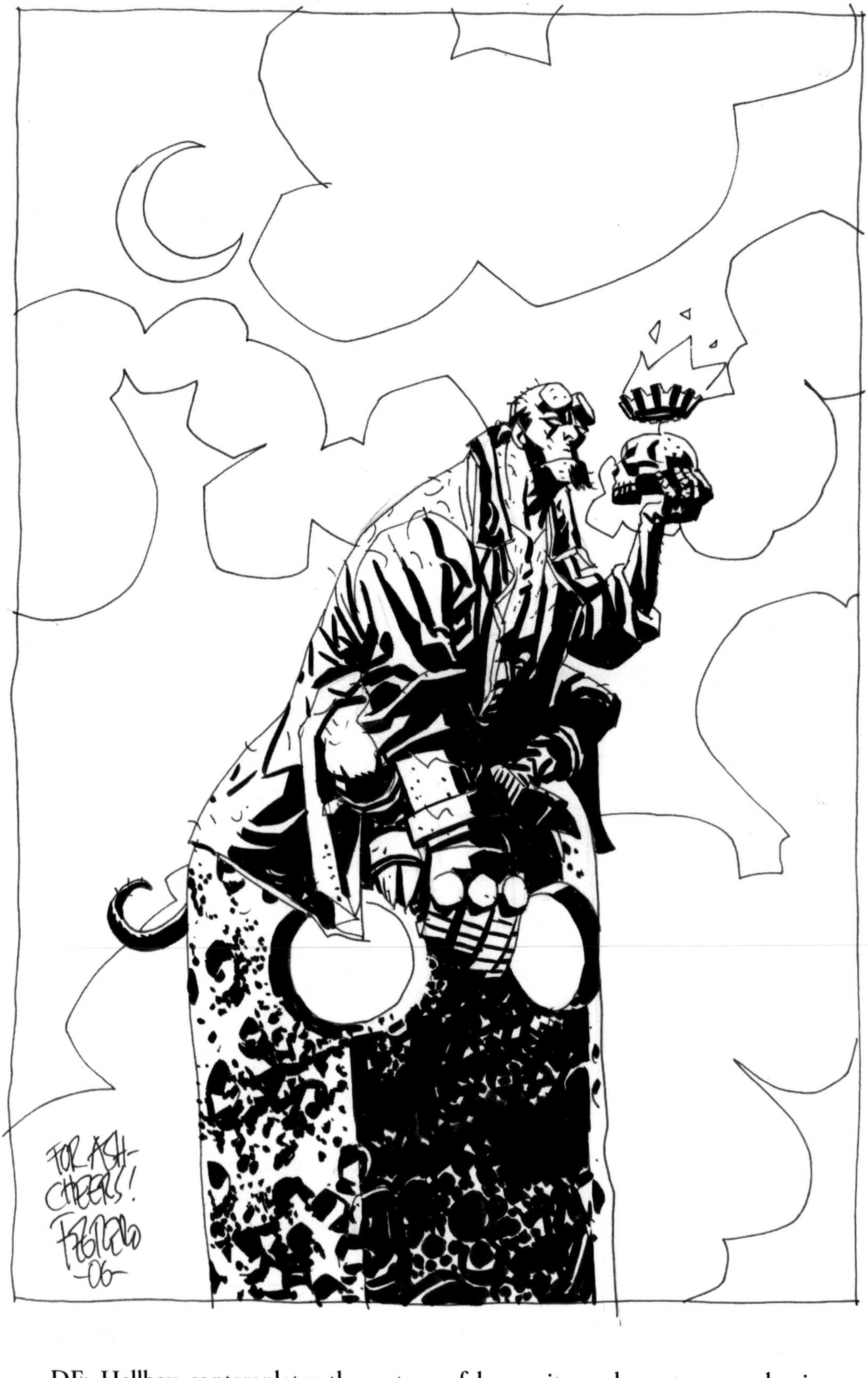
FOR ASH-
CHEERS!
-06-

DF: Hellboy contemplates the nature of humanity and amateur mechanics ... drawn for *Popbot* creator Ashley Wood.

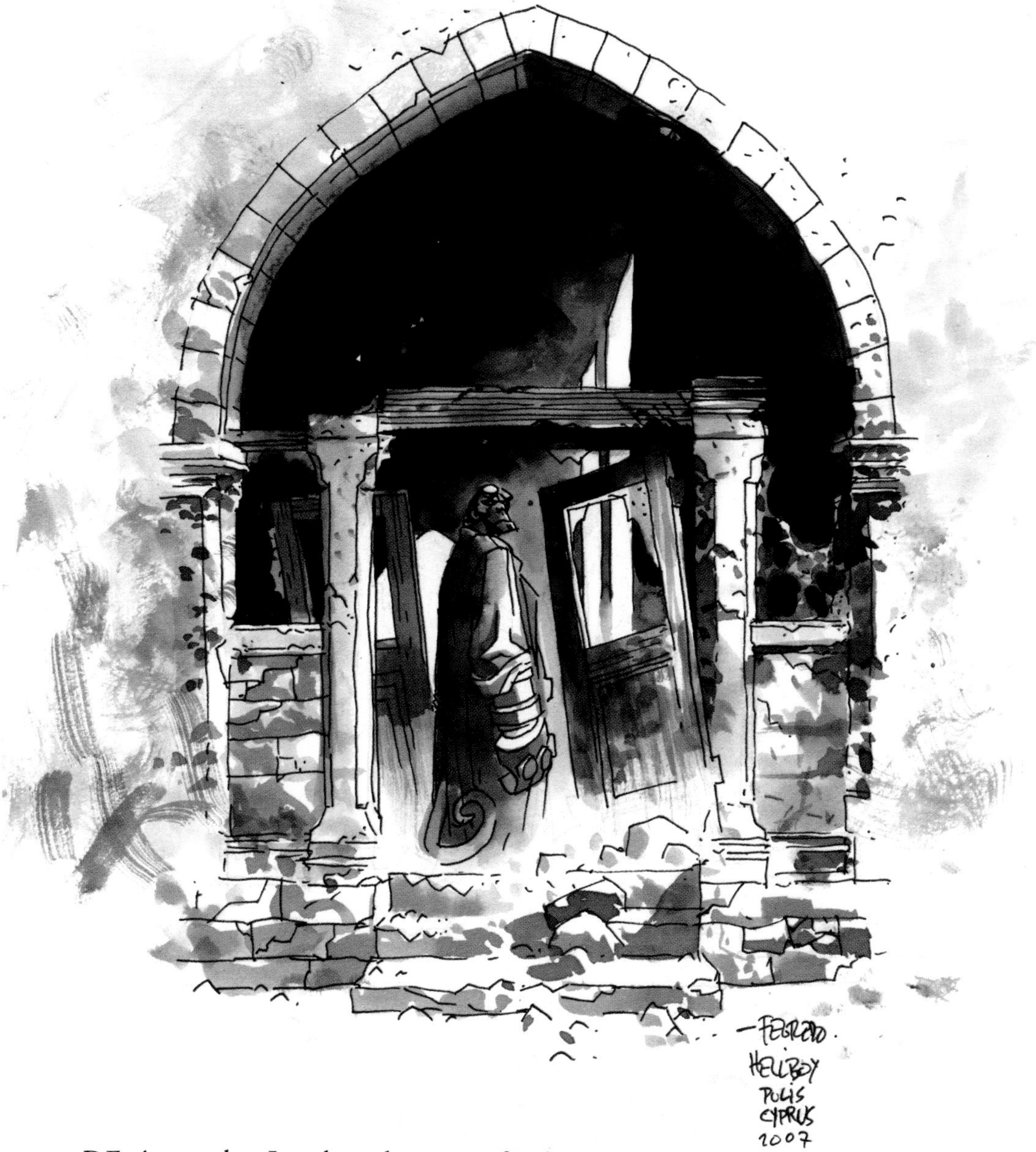
—FEGREDO.
HELLBOY
POLIS
CYPRUS
2007

DF: A snapshot I took in the town of Polis, Cyprus.

A few thanks: to my wife Diana; my family and friends for bearing with me during my transition into Hellboy's world; to Scott and Rachel for coping with my alternative definition of "deadline"; to Glen Murakami for suggesting "that Fegredo bloke might do"; to Dave Stewart for saving my ass repeatedly; and of course to Mike Mignola for giving me this amazing opportunity ... hey, I get to draw my favorite comic!

FEGREDO

England
Late 2007

HELLBOY™

by MIKE MIGNOLA

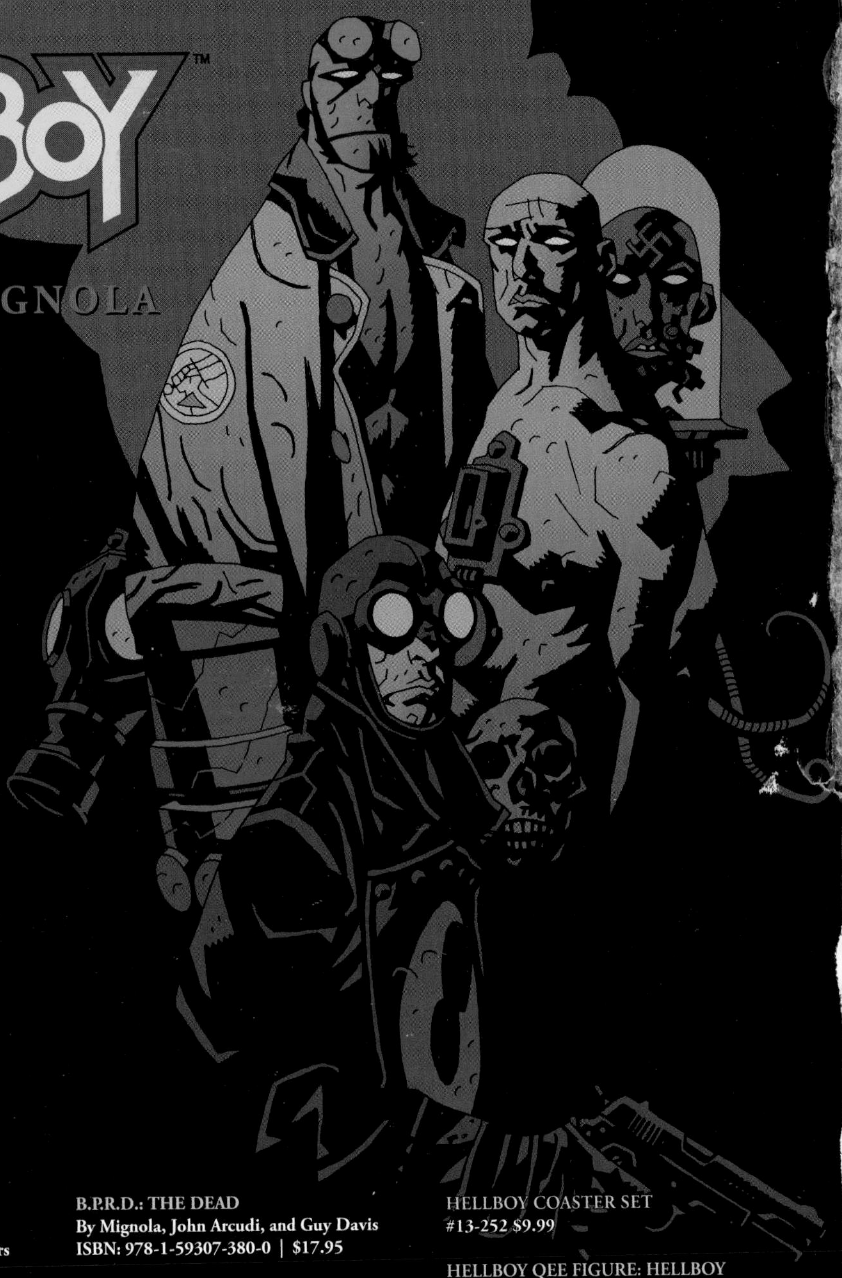

SEED OF DESTRUCTION
with John Byrne
ISBN: 978-1-59307-094-6 | $17.95

WAKE THE DEVIL
ISBN: 978-1-59307-095-3 | $17.95

THE CHAINED COFFIN
AND OTHERS
ISBN: 978-1-59307-091-5 | $17.95

THE RIGHT HAND OF DOOM
ISBN: 978-1-59307-093-9 | $17.95

CONQUEROR WORM
ISBN: 978-1-59307-092-2 | $17.95

STRANGE PLACES
ISBN: 978-1-59307-475-3 | $17.95

THE TROLL WITCH AND OTHERS
By Mignola, Corben, and Russell
ISBN: 978-1-59307-860-7 | $17.95

THE ART OF HELLBOY
ISBN: 978-1-59307-089-2 | $29.95

HELLBOY WEIRD TALES
Volume 1
ISBN: 978-1-56971-622-9 | $17.95

Volume 2
ISBN: 978-1-56971-953-4 | $17.95

ODD JOBS
Short stories by Mignola,
Poppy Z. Brite, Chris Golden, and others
Illustrations by Mignola
ISBN: 978-1-56971-440-9 | $14.95

ODDER JOBS
Short stories by Frank Darabont,
Guillermo del Toro, and others
Illustrations by Mignola
ISBN: 978-1-59307-226-1 | $14.95

B.P.R.D.: HOLLOW EARTH
By Mignola, Chris Golden,
Ryan Sook, and others
ISBN: 978-1-56971-862-9 | $17.95

B.P.R.D.: THE SOUL OF VENICE
By Mignola, Mike Oeming, Guy Davis,
Scott Kolins, Geoff Johns, and others
ISBN: 978-1-59307-132-5 | $17.95

B.P.R.D.: PLAGUE OF FROGS
By Mignola and Guy Davis
ISBN: 978-1-59307-288-9 | $17.95

B.P.R.D.: THE DEAD
By Mignola, John Arcudi, and Guy Davis
ISBN: 978-1-59307-380-0 | $17.95

B.P.R.D.: THE BLACK FLAME
By Mignola, Arcudi, and Davis
ISBN: 978-1-59307-550-7 | $17.95

B.P.R.D.: THE UNIVERSAL MACHINE
By Mignola, Arcudi, and Davis
ISBN: 978-1-59307-710-5 | $17.95

B.P.R.D.: GARDEN OF SOULS
By Mignola, Arcudi, and Davis
ISBN: 978-1-59307-882-9 | $17.95

HELLBOY ZIPPO LIGHTER
#17-101 $29.95

HELLBOY TALKING BOARD
#10-248 $24.99

HELLBOY DELUXE TALKING BOARD
#10-380 $99.99

HELLBOY COASTER SET
#13-252 $9.99

HELLBOY QEE FIGURE: HELLBOY
#13-821 $7.99

HELLBOY QEE FIGURE: ABE SAPIEN
#13-822 $7.99

To find a comics shop in your area,
call 1-888-266-4226
For more information or to order direct:
• On the web: darkhorse.com
• E-mail: mailorder@darkhorse.com
• Phone: 1-800-862-0052
Mon.–Fri. 9 AM to 5 PM Pacific Time

DARK HORSE COMICS™ drawing on your nightmares™
darkhorse.com